DATE DUE

| | | | |
|---|---|---|---|
| | | | |
| | | | |
| | | | |
| | | | |
| | | | |
| | | | |
| | | | |
| | | | |
| | | | |
| | | | |
| | | | |
| | | | |
| | | | |
| GAYLORD 234 | | | PRINTED IN U. S. A. |

WITHDRAWN

# HERBERT HOOVER

Volume One

Herbert Hoover, 1935 (*Associated Press photo*)

# HERBERT HOOVER

## The Postpresidential Years
## 1933–1964

### Volume One: 1933–1945

## GARY DEAN BEST

HOOVER INSTITUTION PRESS
Stanford University, Stanford, California

Hoover Press Publication 274

Library of Congress Cataloging in Publication Data

Best, Gary Dean.
  Herbert Hoover, the postpresidential years, 1933–1964.

  (Hoover Press publication; 274)
  Includes bibliographical references and index.
  Contents: v. 1. 1933–1945—v. 2. 1946–1964.
  1. Hoover, Herbert, 1874–1964.
  2. Presidents—United States—Biography.   I.  Title.
E802.B46 1983        973.91′6′0924 [B]        82-23212
ISBN 0-8179-7761-9 (set)
ISBN 0-8179-7741-4 (v. 1)
ISBN 0-8179-7751-1 (v. 2)

Manufactured in the United States of America

*Design by P. Kelley Baker*

For my mother,
MAXINE BASSETT ULLENSVANG

# Contents

# Preface

pon reading an early draft of this book, a fellow historian was surprised to find a Herbert Hoover so much at variance with the image that has been formed from published works dealing with the three decades of 1933–1964. "But nobody wants to read a book about Hoover," he warned, "so it's important that you write an introduction that will get historians to read it." This remark, by one of the leading historians of the period dealt with in this work, indicates a recognition of the hold that a half century of misinformed and distorted writing still exerts on the historical profession.

In 1949 Eugene Lyons published *Our Unknown Ex-President*, in which he observed: "A fantastic Hoover myth, factually false and humanly unjust has been industriously promoted during many years by hordes of official and volunteer propagandists and is still very much in circulation."[1] Lyons found hopeful signs that the myth was disintegrating and that a new understanding and appreciation of the former president was gaining currency in the second half of the twentieth century; but he underestimated the power of the myth, and he confused the deference being shown to an aging American statesman with an appreciation of the man and his contribution to American life. In 1963, the year before Hoover's death, historian Carl N. Degler wrote that there were two Hoovers. The first was the visible Hoover who had "unstintingly and very capably served Democratic and Republican Administrations alike," who was the object of "nation-wide birthday celebrations, or rhapsodic editorials, of admiring Republican national conventions." This Hoover bore almost no relation to the other, the Hoover of history books, which presented a very negative picture of the former president.[2] A decade later, historian William Appleman Williams felt obliged to justify his favorable assessment of Hoover by writing in a footnote: "Hoover offers a classic example of the necessity for historians to break out of their own frame of reference if they are to understand the past. More than any other 20th–century American's, Hoover's reputation is the product of misinformation and distortion."[3]

The misinformation and distortion persists, but gradually it is being challenged. Following the publication of a number of new works on various aspects of Hoover's career, including several on his presidential years, based on original research in the Hoover papers and other sources, the first scholarly biography of the man was published in 1979. David Burner's *Herbert Hoover: A Public Life* (New York, 1979) skillfully synthesized all of the published research on Hoover of recent decades by other scholars and joined it with the author's own original research to produce a landmark volume in the reassessment of the former president. But Burner's comprehensive treatment of Hoover's life ended with Hoover's departure from the White House in March 1933. The 31 years between the time of his departure from the presidency and Hoover's death in 1964 are dealt with only in a modest epilogue.

While Hoover scholars have been active in studying these postpresidential years, no comprehensive treatment has yet been attempted. The result has been that the myths and distortions concerning this period have not yet been dislodged and, in fact, are occasionally mirrored in the works of Hoover scholars themselves. Hoover's activities during these decades are often ignored even when he was important. His views are misrepresented, and the image perpetuated is that of a reactionary whose ideas were hopelessly out of date and who was shunned even by his fellow Republicans, who found his continued activities and public statements embarrassing to the Republican party and its political fortunes. For a generation of historians and writers to whom the New Deal was the Holy Grail of American political history, or for whom the twentieth century was to be the "American century," only those Republicans who sought to lead the GOP in these approved directions deserved any claim to attention or approval. Historians for whom the task of distinguishing between "non-interventionists" and "isolationists" was all too complex found it convenient to apply the latter epithet to all who opposed the Roosevelt–Truman foreign policies. So pervasive did the label become that even today it obscures Hoover's contribution to American entry into the United Nations and to other postwar foreign policies.

Perhaps the best commentary on the current state of the Hoover image for the postpresidential years is in a recent essay by historian George T. Mazuzan. Mazuzan argues that Hoover's image would have only benefited if he had died in 1933, for his activities after he left the White House further tarnished the already negative image produced by his presidential years. Consistently outside the mainstream in both domestic and foreign policies during these decades, Hoover became an "anachronism" after 1933. While noting the current interest of scholars in Hoover's postpresidential years, Mazuzan concluded that "it will still be some time before these scholarly interpretations filter out to either change or reinforce the general negative public image Hoover still represents."[4]

Mazuzan's gloomy prediction may be correct, but present political trends suggest that our definitions of what is anachronistic are changing rapidly. This alone would seem to warrant a closer look at a man whose message seems increasingly relevant to us today, even though it was at odds with the mainstream of thought during his lifetime. The modest intent of this book is to hasten the process to which Mazuzan refers. I have sought to survey the role of Herbert Hoover in American politics after he left the White House. Because Hoover remains a target for misinformation and distortion, I have sought to describe his postpresidential years as much as possible through his own words and actions. As Professor Burner has noted, much material that would be useful for a comprehensive study of the postpresidential years is still not available to scholars; but I have found enough, I believe, to illuminate Hoover's political views and activities during the period. A study of his family and personal life and his business and philanthropic activities must await the opening of other materials for use by scholars.

Volume One covers the years 1933–1945, a period when Hoover's public activities were largely devoted to analyzing and commenting on events. Volume Two, which chronicles Hoover's life from 1945 until his death in 1964, treats his postwar relief work and his service on the Hoover commissions.

Any researcher attempting a work such as this one incurs more obligations than can possibly be acknowledged. In the chapter on the research sources, which appears at the end of the second volume, I have listed the locations of the many archival collections that I consulted. The staff members of each of the listed repositories were unfailingly helpful, even when I dropped in with little or no advance warning. Most of my time was necessarily spent in the Hoover Presidential Library in West Branch, Iowa, and I gratefully acknowledge the contributions made to my research there by Thomas T. Thalken, director, Robert Wood, assistant director, Dwight Miller, senior archivist, and all the other employees of that institution who make working there such a delightful experience. Floyd and Darlene Christensen, and Heidi and Chris, made my many stays in that small Iowa town most enjoyable. I also thank Mr. Allan

Hoover and Dr. Felix Morley for helpful information that they furnished via correspondence, and Governor Alf Landon, Senator John Bricker, Mr. Samuel F. Pryor, and Ambassador Clare Boothe Luce for helpful interviews.

My work was also much assisted and expedited by the fantastic cooperation furnished by the University of Hawaii at Hilo Library, where special appreciation is due Kenneth Herrick, director, and Allyson Uratani, Sherie Gusukuma, and Junko Nowaki, as well as student helper Nora Takaki. I am also indebted to Professors Walter Johnson and Herbert Margulies, both of the University of Hawaii at Manoa, who read an early draft of this book and furnished useful criticism.

For their financial assistance I am grateful to the Penrose Fund of the American Philosophical Society for two summer grants, and to the Hoover Presidential Library Association and the Hoover Institution on War, Revolution and Peace.

A warm mahalo goes to Janis Shirai and Jennifer Doudna for their help in typing the manuscript.

Finally, a special debt of gratitude is due my wife, Matsue, whose unfailing willingness to abide my long absences during summer research trips, as well as months of relative inattentiveness while I attacked my Olivetti, made the research and writing of this book possible.

# Introduction

n 1932, in the midst of the worst depression in the nation's history, Americans voted in a presidential election. Despite all of the analyses and interpretations of that election, the only clear conclusion is that Herbert Hoover lost. History shows that the American electorate has not looked kindly upon presidents who presided during hard times. Faced with economic distress, the individual citizen can do little but vent his wrath on public officials for their alleged failures. The depressions of the 1870s and 1890s brought new faces to the White House, and prosperity followed. Economists in 1932 might offer theoretical explanations for the depression and proposals for its cure; the American people had a much more practical and proven solution to the problem. They elected a new president in 1932 and confidently awaited prosperity—and they waited, and waited, and waited. In 1940 labor leader John L. Lewis observed that the New Deal of Franklin Delano Roosevelt had made the depression a permanent fact of American life.

Given this reflex action of American voters toward their public officials in times of economic troubles (recently demonstrated in the 1980 presidential election), there seems little point in examining the issues raised in the 1932 presidential campaign. Roosevelt did not win the election, Herbert Hoover lost it. Nothing that either candidate said or promised in the campaign was likely to affect the election result. This is not to say that the result was foreordained.

By a variety of devices, Hoover might have used the federal government for political purposes—as his successors would do—in order to strengthen his candidacy. But Hoover would not, could not, do so. In this respect, at least, Hoover was the last of the "old" presidents; beginning with Roosevelt, the "new" presidents would find the temptation to use the growing powers of their office and the federal government as tools for the advancement of their own political fortunes too great to be resisted. This political use of the enhanced powers of the presidency, which began with Roosevelt, reached its crest in the Watergate Affair in the early 1970s, but seems only slightly to have abated.

The issues of the 1932 campaign are uninteresting for another reason. Rexford Tugwell wrote in 1953 that Roosevelt and Hoover "were—and are— the protagonists in an epic struggle of ideas,"[1] and so they remain today, as modifications of the ideas of the original protagonists of the early republic, Jefferson and Hamilton. But the clash of their philosophies is scarcely to be seen in the platforms or rhetoric of the 1932 campaign. Roosevelt pounded Hoover for his spending, unbalanced budgets, and bloated bureaucracy. If the presidential campaign of 1932 was a contest between an old order and a new order, then many voters had good reason to believe, if they cared, that it was Roosevelt who spoke for the old order of fiscal responsibility and limited government—orthodox Democratic views—and Hoover who spoke for a deficit spending, activist, and experimental (albeit unsuccessful) new order that must be repudiated. If the issues of the campaign of 1932 could be viewed as important to its result, then the success of an appeal to such old verities as the balanced budget, reduced federal spending, and smaller government, which won Roosevelt nearly 60 percent of the popular vote in 1932, could easily lead one to conclude that Hoover had gone too far with his innovations to suit the American people, rather than not far enough.

The New Deal that began on March 4, 1933, however, was not for long the New Deal that had been promised in the Democratic platform or the candidate's speeches in 1932. For those who espoused the traditional principles of the Democratic party, the New Deal was not Democratic at all, but a kind of ultra-Republicanism—Hooverism gone berserk. Many of those who now began to oppose Roosevelt had also opposed Hoover, and for much the same reasons. As Ralph West Robey, financial writer for the *Washington Post*, wrote in June 1934 of the "Old Deal" of Hoover: "One of the reasons that some of us have objections to the New Deal program is that to a great extent it consists of nothing but an aggravation of the policies of the Old Deal that we thought were bad."[2] Similarly, the Democratic *Baltimore Sun* found in much of the New Deal only more of the Hooverism that it had supported Roosevelt in order to escape. Of course there were profound differences between the Hoover and Roosevelt programs, but this sort of view of Hoover as a kind of "father" of the New Deal meant that he could win only limited support among Jeffersonian Democrats despite his attacks on the Roosevelt programs. They applauded his attacks on the New Deal, but not the man himself.

Hoover's standing with his fellow Republicans evidenced a similar ambivalence. Here one of his problems was of long standing and unrelated to the depression or his subsequent activities. Some historians have made much of Hoover's lack of popularity with Republican leaders after he left the White House, suggesting that it derived from the discredited and obsolete ideas contained in his speeches and writings. On the contrary, it is not remarkable that Hoover had few friends in the leadership of the GOP after he left the White House, for he had never had many before or during his presidency. This is not at all surprising. When he first appeared in public life during the Wilson administration, his political affiliation was unknown, but he certainly seemed a Democrat. He served as food administrator in the "war cabinet" of the Democrat Wilson, he supported Wilson's appeal for the election of a Democratic Congress in the 1918 mid-term elections, he went off to Paris with the president to make peace, and he was boomed for the 1920 Democratic presidential nomination by, among others, Franklin Delano Roosevelt. Such a political background was not calculated to make him popular with Republican leaders when he announced instead for the GOP nomination in 1920. Many of them regarded him as a "Trojan horse" for Wilsonian policies within the Republican party and were not at all pleased with his selection as secretary of commerce by President Warren G. Harding.

During the 1920s Hoover was widely regarded as a liberal in what was predominantly a conservative party. This did not endear Hoover to the conservative leadership, nor did the fact that he was not a professional politician and had not risen to the cabinet and then to the presidency after serving a long political apprenticeship. Instead, Hoover won the presidency in his first try at elective office, an interloper who scaled the heights as a result of his reputation as a humanitarian and administrator. These qualities, which ought to have won him support among the Western "progressive" wing of the party, did not. Among other complaints against him, Western progressives suspected Hoover of a Wilsonian, League of Nations variety of internationalism because of his support for the league when the issue was before the Senate in 1919–20. And no more than conservative professionals could they abide an interloper like Hoover, the more so since he had spent so much of his adult life outside America and was widely suspected of being at least as much English as he was American. The point is that Hoover was always something of a loner in the Republican party, and thus it was nothing new for him after he left the presidency; historians are in error in attributing what estrangement that existed between Hoover and Republican leaders to the record of his presidency or to his words and actions after he left the presidency. But it is true that Hoover's failures as president only served to confirm the misgivings that both progressive and conservative Republicans had harbored concerning him.

Hoover embarked upon his postpresidential years, therefore, without a great deal of support among either Republican leaders or Democratic opponents of the New Deal. And he had been soundly rejected by the American electorate. Many historians have assumed that because Hoover was discredited and unpopular, the ideas expressed in his speeches and writings must also have been unpopular. They are mistaken. Hoover, on the other hand, concluded that because his speeches and writings were popular, he must also be popular. Hoover was equally wrong.

While Hoover was shunned, his ideas were not. As a leading critic of the Roosevelt administration, and later of the Truman administration, his speeches and writings appealed to a wide constituency unhappy with the policies of twenty years of Democratic leaders. Outside of his own numerous and zealous followers, Hoover's message appealed particularly to four groups in American life: those who for partisan reasons sought to defeat the Democratic rule in Washington; those who were concerned about basic changes they saw being made in the American political, economic, and social system, especially under Roosevelt; those who did not oppose the New Deal on political or even philosophical grounds, but who viewed its programs as detrimental to economic recovery; and those who opposed the foreign policies of Roosevelt and Truman as leading inevitably to war.

But when Hoover lost the election in 1932, it seemed a tragic end to a distinguished public career. The tragedy was heightened by the events of the four months between the election and the inauguration of his successor. Rejected by the electorate, faced with a hostile Democratic Congress that was responsive only to the will of the president-elect, and unable to win Roosevelt's cooperation in meeting the mounting banking crisis of early 1933, Hoover watched the financial structure of the country come to a standstill as inauguration day approached. This final humiliation meant that as he left office on that gloomy March 4 in 1933, few would have expected that the 58-year-old former president would continue to take an active public role for 31 years more, performing a multitude of useful services for his party and for his country.

# 1

## Titular Leader

erbert Hoover left the White House a spent and exhausted man. The banking crisis, which brought much of the nation's economy to a standstill, had seemingly drained him of his last reserves of energy. Raymond Moley, Roosevelt's foremost "brain truster," found Hoover appearing "close to death," with the "look of being done, but still of going on and on, driven by some damned fury." Rexford Tugwell, another Roosevelt adviser, agreed that Hoover looked, "at the end, completely spent."[1] The contrast with the cheerful and optimistic Roosevelt was obvious on inauguration day and was captured by the popular photograph of the outgoing and incoming presidents as they motored to the ceremony—Hoover tight-lipped and expressionless, Roosevelt jaunty and cheerful.

Immediately following the inauguration, Hoover left for New York City with his son Allan, while his wife, Lou Henry, and other son, Herbert, Jr., traveled to the Hoover home on the Stanford University campus in California.[2] Hoover, who wished to be available in the event his help was sought, believed at this point that Roosevelt would begin with conservative legislation closely following his own program, and then, after gaining the confidence of business, would undertake more radical measures.[3]

Greeted by an estimated twenty-five hundred people at his arrival by train in New York City, the former president was obviously relieved by the lifting of the pressures of the White House. He slept twelve hours in his first night as a private citizen, then motored the next day, without police protection, to the Connecticut home of his old friend and associate Edgar Rickard for a visit.[4] On March 6 Hoover issued a short press statement calling on all Americans to cooperate in Roosevelt's closing of the banks.[5] The following day, he and his secretary, Lawrence Richey, were out at daybreak for a walk from the Waldorf-Astoria Hotel to Central Park and back, unaccompanied by Secret Service men. Those who recognized the former president in the light mist found him friendly and communicative.[6]

While Hoover recovered from the cares of the presidency, holdovers from his administration worked with the new arrivals of the Roosevelt regime in putting together legislation that would meet the banking crisis by isolating the strong banks from the weak and permitting the former to reopen. When the banking bill was introduced in Congress, Hoover wrote to Senator David Reed of Pennsylvania endorsing a statement that Reed had made in support of the legislation. But Hoover added that he hoped Reed would not get enthusiastic over the bill, since the need for it might have been prevented except for Roosevelt's refusal to cooperate with him in meeting the banking crisis during the preinaugural period.[7] Then, after having met with a steady stream of visitors in his apartment at the Waldorf-Astoria Hotel, Hoover departed for his home in Palo Alto in late March.

Reporters interviewing the former president as he alighted from the train in Oakland, California, wrote that "the years seemed to slip from his shoulders." Hoover planned, he told the press, to stay in Palo Alto for twenty years. "On economic and political questions I am silent," he declared. "Even on fishing I am silent." Moreover, he had no plans for the future.[8] But Hoover was not for long serene in these familiar, but far too quiet, surroundings. He chafed at the isolation and craved the type of news and inside information to which he had grown accustomed during a dozen years of service in the cabinet and the presidency. Removed by over three thousand miles from the action in Washington, Hoover began to confront his own and the Republican dilemma. The voters had given Franklin Delano Roosevelt and the Democratic party an overwhelming mandate to find solutions to the nation's economic distress. Could the Republicans fail to cooperate with the Democrats and thus risk incurring the charge of prolonging the distress by obstructionism? How was the party of opposition to function in such a situation? How important was an active Republican party organization if Republicans were not to oppose Democratic policies? Who was to lead the GOP in formulating its policies and strategies? Hoover could claim titular leadership of the party, but would Republicans listen? Should Hoover even venture to lead?

There was certainly no reason to expect that Herbert Hoover would ever again take an active role in American politics. Discredited by a depression and defeated soundly in his bid for reelection, any former president would have suffered justifiable pangs of doubt concerning his value as a political leader. And shy by nature, elected to the presidency because of his administrative abilities, Hoover had never impressed anyone with his political skills. His relations with the old guard politicians of the Republican party had never been close, largely because his very Republicanism had been suspect due to his service in the Wilson administration during World War I and his expression of support for Wilson's pleas for a Democratic Congress in 1918. Two weeks after Hoover's defeat in November 1932, a close friend, journalist Mark Sullivan, wrote in a letter:

> I am quite sure the Republican politicians, big and little, including the mass of little precinct workers, will be most disinclined to re-nominate Hoover. They will want to be through with him as a man and even more they will want to be through with him as a type. To them Hoover is an intruder, an outsider who came in from a world other than politics. To them Hoover does not belong to the politicians' union. Because of that they do not like him. They want to use the fact of Hoover's serious defeat as an excuse for not again nominating for the Presidency any man of Hoover's type. They will say that from now on they will insist on nominating for the Presidency only men whose careers have been political, such as Calvin Coolidge, for example. If Hoover is renominated, the pressure of it will have to come from the people, just as it did in 1928. The likelihood of that happening is, of course, intimately associated with what course Hoover follows in the next two or three years. I think it would decidedly be a mistake for Hoover to act as in the faintest degree conscious of himself as a possibility for future office holding. It would be decidedly a mistake for him to give the impression of trying to keep hold of the party organization. If he is to have weight in politics at all, it must be the weight of his ideas and of his voice.[9]

Yet Hoover did have certain advantages. As a former president, his words could capture the front pages of the nation's newspapers as those of few other Republicans. Through years of highly publicized service, as head of Belgian Relief, the U.S. Food Administration, and the American Relief Administration and as secretary of commerce and president, he had developed a large group of loyal supporters both in and outside of the Republican party. More followers would come to him because of his intellectual leadership as the principal exponent of a philosophy of traditional Americanism that was threatened by the policies of Roosevelt's New Deal. This threat was also a strong motivation for Hoover's decision to take up the role of leader of the opposition. Another force behind his decision was the desire for vindication. Rightly or wrongly, the former president did not believe that his administration had done, or had failed to do, anything for which apologies were needed. For the remainder of his life, Hoover would be convinced that the low point of the depression had been reached in the summer of 1932 (many economists and businessmen agreed with this) and that recovery had been arrested only by the presidential election and subsequent uncertainty concerning the policies of the president-elect. The depths to which the nation plunged in March and April of 1933 (and from which the Roosevelt administration would measure its contribution to recovery) were, to Hoover, a direct consequence of Roosevelt's failure to cooperate with him during the preinaugural period. Convinced that there was nothing in his administration for which Republicans needed to be ashamed, Hoover was equally positive that the party stood no chance of regaining control of the White House if it was trapped by the Democrats into regarding his administration as an embarrassment to the party.

As a result, Mark Sullivan found soon after the election that Hoover regarded himself as "the head of the Republican party and as the natural leader of those who may be dissatisfied with the programs of the Democrats."[10] Even before he left the White House, Hoover began to prepare for the political role he would play as a private citizen. He encouraged the organization and activities of a new political group known as the Republican Federal Associates. This organization, made up of appointees during Hoover's administration, was intended to operate as a political force in advancing the interests of the Republican party. Presumably, the members would be loyal to the former president who had appointed them to office, thus giving the group the flavor of a Hoover machine. In its early activities, however, Hoover suggested that the Associates should devote themselves primarily to the task of electing Republicans to Congress in 1934.[11] The leading figures in the Associates were former Hoover cabinet members Walter Brown and Ogden Mills.

Before leaving the White House, Hoover also laid plans for the defense of his administration. In late January, Edgar Rickard found him contemplating nine different publishing efforts by separate authors. Under French Strother, one of his secretaries who was acting as "editor-in-chief," Hoover was considering an article by Strother for the *New York Times* summarizing the accomplishments of his administration; a series of articles by Theodore Joslin for the North American Newspaper Alliance; a book of previously unpublished Hoover speeches to be edited by Theodore Joslin; articles for the *Saturday Evening Post* by Mark Sullivan; a book on the diplomatic accomplishments of the Hoover administration by former under secretary of state William R. Castle; a description of the public works achievements during Hoover's presidency; a study of the political attacks that had been made on Hoover for the previous dozen years; and, to further enhance the somewhat frayed Hoover image, a book on Hoover's many humanitarian activities, from the days of his

Belgian relief effort down to his inauguration, which was to be written by Burton J. Kendrick. Much of this public relations "blitz," however, had to be aborted when Strother died within days after Hoover left the White House.[12]

While in New York, Hoover also arranged to have a close personal friend, publisher John Callan O'Laughlin, join the Republican national committee headquarters in Washington as an unpaid assistant to Chairman Everett Sanders and to serve as liaison between the committee and Hoover.[13] Once established in Palo Alto, the former president quickly busied himself with funneling material through O'Laughlin for possible use by Republican senators and congressmen in opposing New Deal legislation, while lamenting the fact that Republicans seemed unwilling to stand up for Republican principles or to defend the record of the Hoover administration.[14]

Such activities made clear Hoover's determination to continue to exert an influence in the party, but did not indicate the extent of the role that he contemplated for himself. Shaken by the size of his defeat and by the dreary days before the inauguration of his successor, Hoover apparently left office with no aspirations regarding the 1936 nomination. Cautioned by O'Laughlin that he should "not leave the White House an obvious candidate [for 1936], but that the inevitable march of events will compel the Party to turn to you," Hoover responded that he had "not the remotest intention of such implication as you mention. . . . That is out of the calculations."[15] While many of his friends did not agree with Hoover's attitude relative to 1936, there was near unanimity among them on the policy he should follow in the months following the inauguration of Roosevelt. As George Akerson, a former Hoover secretary put it, the cause he represented would be best served if he stayed out of "the public prints for some time to come."[16] However, Hoover was also counseled to remain in readiness, since it would not be long before he would have to break his silence, go on the attack, and expose the fallacies of the New Deal.[17] Hoover agreed late in March: "The hysteria is still upon us and it ain't in my bones to sit down and see this destructive stuff going on forever. However, nothing would count now."[18] He believed that the public opposition to the New Deal's "march toward Moscow" should come from Republicans in Congress, aided by the GOP national committee.[19] Congressional leaders, however, took much the same view as Hoover of the desirability of silence; nor was the Republican national headquarters in any condition to exert the type of leadership or provide the kind of assistance that might have contributed to an effective opposition.

In the midst of the "hundred days," Hoover agonized privately over the march to dictatorship that he saw in the usurpation of congressional authority by the executive branch. There was little that escaped his criticism. Of the Civilian Conservation Corps (CCC), Hoover wrote that it "would be infinitely better to extend naval construction than to plant trees."[20] The Agricultural Adjustment Act (AAA), which granted unprecedented powers to the secretary of agriculture in order to limit production, was "a strong forward march to Moscow" and failed to touch the fundamental problem, which was to increase the consumption of agricultural goods.[21] It would also "diminish the purchasing power of the urban population by a billion five hundred million dollars a year" through increased agricultural prices. The Securities Act had "a fine demagogic flavor," but did not reach "the heart of the problem," which was "to prevent the issue of insecure foreign loans and loans for uneconomic purposes."[22] Roosevelt's inflation policies were "desperate measures" to which he had been driven only because of the "terrific deflation" caused by Roosevelt himself, and the Democratic leadership in Congress, through their policies since the November election. These policies Hoover listed as: (1) Roosevelt's refusal to direct congressional leaders to cooperate in Hoover's efforts to reduce expenditures, reorganize the government, and balance the budget; (2) the publicity given by Congress to Reconstruction Finance Corporation (RFC) loans to financial institutions that had precipitated the run on the banks; (3) Roosevelt's refusal to cooperate with him to stop the gold panic, which in Hoover's view was precipitated by public fear of Roosevelt's monetary policies; (4) Roosevelt's failure to cooperate in issuing a presidential proclamation against gold withdrawals; (5) Roosevelt's closure of the banks after his inauguration and the reopening of them in such a way as to put billions of dollars in deposits "out of action"; (6) and Roosevelt's "socialistic" proposals, which had stifled economic life in the nation.[23] In sum, Hoover regarded the inflation policies as "the greatest and most unnecessary gamble with the future of the American people ever taken or ever proposed in all our history."[24]

The National Industrial Recovery Act, which permitted business cooperation under governmental supervision, also came in for criticism. Hoover wrote that he could readily understand why big business was supportive of the legislation, since "their forty years of prayer to be relieved of the Sherman [Anti-Trust] Act seems to them realized, and visions of huge and secure profits are everywhere current."[25] Of the National Recovery Administration (NRA) codes, under which industries were to regulate themselves, Hoover wrote that he was not "in a position to criticize the code action because I have for years advocated building up of business codes and have, in fact, taken part in the construction of scores of them, but, of course, I have no patience with the attempts to control production and prices." It was all "a question of degree."[26] In his view, the NRA codes were "ruinous to small business and favored" big business while they added little or nothing to employment.[27] The system being created under the NRA was "likely to be worse than socialism itself and in any event will only lead to it."[28] When General Hugh Johnson, head of the NRA, went beyond the original intent of the legislation and sought to apply a blanket code to regulate the practices of all businesses in the nation by using the threat of a consumer boycott of businesses failing to comply, Hoover was even more appalled. In early August he wrote that in driving around California he had received many reports of the effects of Johnson's campaign on small business:

> The hideous immorality and tyranny of the boycott provisions, the stirring up of suspicion and hate between competitors in small business, conflicts between employers and employees in small businesses, and the burdens placed upon small business by which they are not able to compete with big business—all of them are creating a spirit in the community that is perfectly terrible. I have the most pathetic appeals for advice from people who wish to comply, and yet to whom it is ruin, or who have been subject to persecution in their communities. There has never been anything in our history that has so set neighbor against neighbor as this act.

The whole affair, Hoover confessed, was giving him "a great deal of anxiety on moral questions."[29] But still he felt that the American people were hopeful that the New Deal would deliver on its promises and that the time had not yet come when they would be willing to listen to the truth. Although he felt "so strongly sometimes that it is wrong to keep still when I see the country being misled that I cannot stand it any longer," he told O'Laughlin that "we must reserve our fire until we can make it effective."[30]

Hoover viewed the course of the United States as indistinguishable from that of European countries in their own recent march to totalitarianism.[31] Of press descriptions of the improved spirit in the country, he wrote Akerson: "The eulogies on the better spirit of the country do not take into account the revived antagonisms of employees and employers which we had so greatly mitigated, the terrorization of small businessmen, nor the motivation of all big business and investment by fear instead of confidence."[32] The resort to inflation, and the threat of more inflation, had fulfilled the New Deal's goal of raising prices, but since they had risen "through fear and not through confidence, the very processes set in motion will necessitate either more inflation or there will again sooner or later be a slump."[33] Such inflationary policies would eventually rob "the insurance policies, the savings, and bank deposits, endowments, the small investor, the wage and salary workers, for the benefit of speculators, bankers and foreigners, land holders and common stockholders."[34]

Hoover drew some consolation from the feeling that he had given the American people ample warning of what they could expect in the election of Roosevelt, even though the Democrats had been less than candid during the campaign about their intentions. As Hoover put it:

The country voted for the New Deal. What it was to be was not fully disclosed by the Democrats in the campaign. I appear now to have disclosed it very accurately in the campaign, especially in a speech at New York at the end of October. Senator [Carter] Glass and Owen D. Young were put up to deny it at the time and I hope they yet have the manhood to acknowledge the wrong they did the American people before they die. Always remember that careful, constructive handling of economic battles does not lend itself to the dramatic. Drama and headlines [are] what the people want just now. That can only be had by "turning to the left"—and the turn will be continuous until the public begins to taste the ballyhoo and the realities of it all.[35]

But that moment had not yet arrived. Ninety percent of the people, Hoover concluded, still believed that "the millennium has come," and critics would only be reviled if they attempted to break through the "hypnotism" of the people by the dramatic promises of the New Deal.[36] Not even a suggestion by Supreme Court Associate Justice James McReynolds that he speak out against inflation could induce Hoover to break his self-imposed silence.[37] In late April he wrote a friend: "I could explode; I could denounce; I could demonstrate and do a lot of things that would do no good. But anyway, we have come through before—but things could not be worse."[38]

In addition to his concern for the effect of the New Deal on American life was Hoover's worry over the future of the Republican party as a viable alternative to the new direction that the Democrats had taken under Roosevelt. Many Republicans in Congress were, as Senator Arthur Vandenberg of Michigan said of himself, "going along with the new administration as far as possible" because they wanted "the President to have his chance," even though it was apparent to Vandenberg that the Democrats virtually sought "to make a dictator of him."[39] For Hoover, Vandenberg's "as far as possible" was much too far. He argued that the GOP could not survive if it attempted to follow those leaders who sought to "compete in demagoguery and socialism" with the Democrats, nor could it survive if it followed other leaders who sought to compromise with the New Deal. He continued to believe that the Republican party could attract a majority if it continued to be a

defender of constitutional methods; of local responsibility, not centralization; of real liberty, not aborted by the glitter of radical dictatorship; regulation and not regimentation of men; the representative of sound economic thought, honest currency and honest private initiative; protection and upbuilding of our country before sloppy economic or political internationalism.

All of this, he conceded, "sounds old-fashioned just now, but it will sound new in a year." If the GOP failed to demonstrate its fidelity to these principles it would be "the end of this civilization." Eventually, Hoover said, more of the people would "return to the principles I have stated—and two million more of them [supporters] in the last election would have given a majority."[40] Little, however, was being done by Republicans in Congress, or by the GOP national committee, to stand up for the principles that Hoover espoused, and this inactivity made him "itch to make a few remarks," but, he continued, "I will keep still."[41]

Privately, Hoover admitted that some parts of the New Deal were good, that they were, in fact, "our own policies under new names." If restraint was observed, he thought that the fundamental forces of recovery, unleashed during his own administration, might carry the United States out of the depression with or without the New Deal.[42] In June Hoover wrote journalist Samuel Crowther that he believed there was "real recovery on a wide front," greater even than the recovery of the summer of 1932 under his own administration. Hoover worried, however, that such a recovery under the New Deal might pose a different kind of danger for the nation, since if the policies of the Roosevelt administration were credited with having produced the recovery, then "this new social philosophy may be fixed on to us with all its limitations and destructions of fundamental liberty." Yet none wished for the recovery to collapse. He encouraged Crowther:

> Keep your pen busy, for some time when the people have recovered from their money hysteria we will have to reconstruct their social views if America is not to ultimately decline and fall. It today stands with government pregnant with dictatorship—with the economic system pregnant with socialism (and the two must go together) and with its social system pregnant of servitude [*sic*] instead of freedom.[43]

As titular leader of the Republican party, but one who had chosen to maintain public silence, Hoover had two tasks before him. First, he must encourage others to make the public attacks on the New Deal that he had chosen not to initiate personally. Thus, in addition to expressing his views privately to those who could make use of them in editorials, publicity, and congressional debates, he encouraged those outside the party, like George Lorimer of the *Saturday Evening Post*, who were launching attacks on the New Deal.[44] Second, he was responsible for molding the Republican party into an effective vehicle for presenting to the country his view of the proper alternative principles and policies. This required that he must first confront the growing restiveness among Republicans over the lack of leadership being demonstrated by the GOP national headquarters and the shortage of money required for its effective operation.[45] In addition, there was the problem of Republican disunity created by those GOP members of Congress who either supported New Deal legislation or were chary about launching attacks on it, given the apparent popularity of Roosevelt and his programs among the voters.[46]

The result of Roosevelt's apparent popularity was that many Republicans, in and out of Congress, continued to consider it "good politics" to work with the Democrats to promote the president's program and thus, perhaps, restore prosperity to the nation.[47] This, in fact, appeared to be the view even of GOP chairman Everett Sanders.[48] Hoover's own view was that while the public might resent criticism from Republicans, such criticism was necessary for the very maintenance of democracy.[49] He remained unconvinced that the policies of the New Deal were producing economic recovery; on the contrary, he argued that they were retarding the "natural forces of recovery organized by the Republican administration," which had been "pressing for release during the past sixteen months and are strongly manifesting themselves."[50] When O'Laughlin lamented the unwillingness of the GOP national committee to attack the New Deal, Hoover agreed that the national committee "should begin stating facts, not destructive criticism, but in order that the country may have a full appreciation of what is going on."[51] However, all efforts to obtain leadership from the Republican national committee were now retarded by the illness of Chairman Sanders and his unwillingness to delegate responsibility.

For all of his own public inactivity, Hoover continued to be newspaper grist. When news of the creation of the Republican Federal Associates surfaced, the new organization was quickly linked to the former president and his political ambitions. That apparent linkage contributed to considerable opposition by some Republicans to the new organization. Even O'Laughlin wrote Hoover that he had been "very much embarrassed" by the publicity that had been given to the Associates in the press and that the organization was doing Hoover harm since it was being "looked upon as a movement to promote your candidacy in 1936, and particularly to get control of the southern delegates to that end."[52] Hoover responded that the creation of the Associates was "only a sign of the restlessness of Republicans under legislation and policies that are certainly inimical to the welfare of the country," and he denied that the Associates were working for him. He suggested that the organization might be "welded into the other groups" under the Republican national committee, because they represented "a large group who have no normal outlet of expression," but do have "the resolution to do something."[53] Hoover was "distressed at the charge that the Federal Associates are to promote me for office. I won't be promoted and I should like to find some opportunity to squash this notion."[54]

By May 1933, O'Laughlin's despair with the lack of activity on the part of the GOP national committee led him to conclude that he should resign and that Chairman Sanders should be replaced by a man "who will put some life and energy into the Republican Party."[55] He suggested former senator Walter Edge as "an excellent choice" for the chairmanship.[56] The sentiment against Sanders having thus been reinforced by the despair of his own man in the headquarters, Hoover was forced into action. A few days later he wrote to former postmaster general Walter Brown, now a leading figure in the Associates, that "the general movement against Sanders is making much headway and if the administration Republicans want to have [a] voice in party councils we better be ready with an alternative when Sanders resigns, as he is likely to do, under direct and indirect pressures."[57] By "administration Republicans," Hoover clearly meant his own supporters, such as those enrolled in the Federal Associates.

Republican national committeeman Charles Hilles of New York, a representative of the eastern GOP "establishment" with which Hoover had never felt comfortable and which had often viewed Hoover as an "interloper," now opposed any early replacement of Sanders as chairman, in part because of concern that it would be taken publicly as a slap at Hoover. Hilles did, however, advocate a change in advance of the 1934 off-year elections since Sanders was identified with the defeat of 1932 and could not give the energetic leadership that would be required in 1934. Walter Brown concluded that no change could be made in the chairmanship without the active support of Hilles, and Hoover agreed that "if Hilles does not join that effort nothing can come of it."[58] The policy of inaction seemed destined to continue, as Sanders showed no disposition to resign before the 1936 convention.[59]

In June, however, Sanders finally showed a willingness to undertake constructive activity by scheduling meetings with members of the national committee and chairmen of state committees in a number of cities across the nation. Hoover welcomed the regional meetings, believing they would "do much to rehabilitate spirit in the political organization."[60] Walter Brown, too, was encouraged that Sanders had begun to move.[61] But the Republican Federal Associates continued to be controversial, with strong animosity exhibited toward the group within the formal GOP organization. Moreover, the efforts of the Associates to organize appointees of the Hoover administration had been frustrated by Roosevelt's failure, during the first few months of his administration, to discharge Hoover appointees from postmaster jobs.[62]

The labeling of the Associates as a Hoover organization by the press did nothing to endear the group to those Republicans who were either opposed to

Hoover or did not wish to see him dominate the 1936 convention. In addition, some viewed it as a device for advancing the candidacy of Ogden Mills.[63] In mid-May of 1933 Walter Brown reported that efforts were under way to organize the group in New York and that satisfactory progress was also being made in Massachusetts, New Jersey, Ohio, Indiana, and Iowa. Efforts were also under way to organize in the western states all the way to the Pacific Coast. But Brown continued to lament the delays on the part of the new administration in replacing post office appointments. Postmaster General James Farley was dangling that patronage before Congress in an effort to get the president's legislative program through, while at the same time he denied to the Associates the most "fertile field" for recruits to their organization.[64]

The "fundamental purpose" behind the Associates, according to Ogden Mills, was to create "an organization equipped to function between elections to develop a Republican point of view and program and to prevent disintegration into groups advocating many different forms of political philosophy." Such an organization could best be built "around the many men and women who, during the past twelve years through service, have developed an understanding of, and an interest in, national government, or who, through their voluntary efforts, have become influential party leaders." He disclaimed interest on the part of the organization in the political fortunes of any individual. The purpose was to rebuild the Republican party.[65] In June, Mills and Brown lunched with GOP chairman Sanders and Congressman Bolton of the Republican congressional campaign committee to talk about cooperation between the Associates and the other two groups, but little was accomplished.[66] O'Laughlin counseled Hoover against attempting to "force" such cooperation, since it would lead only to further ill-feeling in the GOP national committee and "intensify the belief that we are really trying to displace the National Committee by the Associates."[67]

After an initial burst of activity, which culminated in a regional conference of Republican party leaders in Chicago on July 11, Chairman Sanders left for Europe on an extended vacation, arguing that politics were at a low ebb during the summer. Once again the GOP national headquarters lapsed into inaction.[68] In mid-August Sanders returned and seemed willing to undertake a renewed program to advance the party's interests. O'Laughlin now suggested to Hoover the desirability of "a bold declaration of Republican principles." The GOP platform of 1932 no longer seemed appropriate as a party standard, since it did not address itself to the program being undertaken by the Roosevelt administration. O'Laughlin argued, therefore, that Republicans "should formulate positive and emphatic expressions simple in language, which will apply to the new conditions and readily reach the mind and heart of the average citizen." Hilles and other national committeemen, he reported to Hoover, were pressing for a meeting to adopt such a declaration of principles.

O'Laughlin suggested that it might best be done by a meeting of a few Republican leaders, including those of the Senate and House.[69] Hoover had scheduled a visit to Chicago to tour the world's fair, and he now arranged for meetings with Sanders, O'Laughlin, and other GOP leaders during his stay in that city.[70]

The Hoovers spent ten days in Chicago taking in the fair, and the former president held his political meetings. He suggested to Sanders and financial chairman J. R. Nutt the appointment of a finance committee to obtain enough money to supply the current requirements of the party.[71] He also discussed with Ogden Mills "the desirability of a statement of a few fundamental principles by Republican leaders prior to the opening of Congress." Hoover suggested that any such declaration be confined to three subjects: "1. Restoration of constitutional practices; 2. Fiscal and monetary practices; 3. Opposition to socialistic programs." He and Mills did not, however, arrive at any decision on how such a statement should be issued, or even whether Hoover's name should be associated with it.[72]

During his ten busy days in Chicago, Hoover also conferred with close friend and businessman Arch Shaw regarding the establishment of a sound money league, to be made up of businessmen and economists, which would attack the New Deal's economic policies. These discussions eventually led to the creation of the Committee on Monetary Policies, which, through petitions, press releases, and publications, championed the cause of sound monetary policies against the inflationary tendencies of the Roosevelt administration.[73] Hoover also outlined for O'Laughlin a possible future course of action for himself—one that would gradually lead to his reappearance in the public arena. He proposed the enunciation of a set of Republican principles, lectures at several universities, and articles written for the daily press. O'Laughlin supported the plan since he felt that "the time for leadership in opposition to the menacing theories and acts of the Roosevelt Administration has arrived." The people were by now, he thought, ready to listen to opposing ideas and programs, and there was no one available but Hoover to rally the opposition. O'Laughlin proposed that 100 prominent Republicans should be recruited to address a letter to Hoover in November requesting from him an expression of the policies that he proposed for the nation. Hoover's reply "would constitute the declaration of principles for the Republican Party to observe."[74]

O'Laughlin soon learned, however, that others, including Ogden Mills and Elihu Root, were also drafting Republican principles, partly at Hoover's instigation. When all of the drafts, including Hoover's, had been received, Sanders planned to "develop a declaration for guidance of the Party." This obviously closed off the course that O'Laughlin had suggested, although he still thought his own plan to be preferable.[75] Sanders's activity in the formulation of a set of principles for the GOP was apparently an outgrowth of a meeting he held with Walter Brown, Senator David Reed, Congressman Bertram Snell, and Ogden Mills, all of whom were close friends of the former president. Mills, to whom Hoover had broached the subject in Chicago, urged at this meeting "the idea of a restatement of Republican principles, in view of the new issues created by the present administration," and all present had approved the idea. The plan, as formulated in the meeting, was to obtain one or two drafts, in addition to the one that Mills told the group Hoover was writing, and then to attempt "to reconcile the various statements, putting them in composite form, which can be shown to loyal members of the Senate and the House." Reed thought that about twenty senators could be expected to support such a declaration, and Snell believed that eighty to ninety congressmen would do likewise. The approval of the executive committee of the GOP national committee would be sought in order to give the declaration official status.[76]

Hoover quickly submitted a rough draft, which he admitted needed revision to give it "more force, and perhaps condensation." He suggested that the statement of principles might be released over the signatures of perhaps one hundred Republican leaders, with his own name, if it were included, in alphabetical order with the others.[77] Hoover's draft began with the statement: "The policies of the Democratic administration have violated principles which reach to the very foundation of our nation and race." It repeated the stock Hoover position that economic recovery had begun during his own administration only to be retarded by the panic of the winter months, which had resulted from "fear of the New Deal," and as a result of the Democrats' "departure from the sound economic policies" of his own administration. While acknowledging that there were many important issues between the Republican and Democratic positions, he confined his attention to "three fundamental questions that are so essential to our future." These he defined as the questions of "the restoration of the Constitution of the United States," "the re-establishment of a sound monetary, financial and fiscal system," and "the repeal or amendment of all emergency legislation that the country shall no longer be plunged into socialism and collectivism with its destruction of human liberty which pursuance of these measures are bringing." Hoover's draft offered little as an alternative to the New Deal, beyond insisting that progressive action must be taken "within the spirit and letter of the Constitution," and that the Constitution should be amended, if necessary. He also insisted that the nation must re-establish a sound currency and maintain honesty in the government's presentations of its expenditures, while also sustaining government credit. Rather than setting forth constructive alternatives, his draft concentrated on a call for abandonment of New Deal policies and methods.[78] Hoover sought a declaration of principles that would be "unanswerable" by the Democrats and that would not permit the Democrats "to consolidate their ranks and attack and thus make a smoke screen for obvious discontent among their own members."[79]

Hoover mailed copies of his draft to conference participants and others. He wrote Senator Reed that the declaration of principles "must be the method and basis on which we can secure the restoration of human liberty in the United States."[80] It was important, he wrote Senator Simeon Fess of Ohio, that the declaration, when issued, "should carry evidence of support by Republican leaders generally both in and out of Congress."[81] But while he was willing to participate as one of many signers of a declaration of Republican principles, Hoover was still unwilling to go publicly on the attack against the New Deal. Even the program he had outlined for himself to O'Laughlin in late September was abandoned as a result of a new Roosevelt initiative in mid-October. The administration's new tactic was to try to induce inflation by devaluing the dollar through the purchase of gold by the government at escalating prices. Hoover doubted that the action would have much effect but decided that he would go off to the Mexican coast for two weeks of fishing, as he believed the situation required "another two weeks' observation."[82]

O'Laughlin was growing increasingly urgent in his appeals to the former president to speak out. He had become utterly disgusted at the continued inactivity of the Republican organization and the missed opportunities. "There is," he wrote Hoover, "no rallying point, no leadership." He reminded Hoover that nearly sixteen million Americans had voted for him: "with them you continue to have commanding influence. The expression of your sane views will coalesce them once more, they will become a fighting force, and a real Party of opposition, which the Nation so sorely needs, will be developed."[83] Despite such urging, Hoover refused to speak out publicly, even though his correspondence reflects a greater sense of alarm with the passage of every week.

In mid-October Hoover was encouraged by signs of division within Democratic ranks over the New Deal. The discord, in his view, was between those who viewed the New Deal measures as emergency legislation and "the radicals who consider they have started a permanent revolution in the United States." The apparent conflict led him to question what the Republican response should be. On the one hand, it was desirable to leave the Democrats to their squabbles; but on the other hand, the nation had a right to expect some Republican leadership, for "if the party remains quiet too long we will be considered as having no leadership." Republicans, Hoover concluded, should not speak out until December, but in the meantime members of the party outside of Congress "should have a hand in formulating Republican policies and not leave it entirely to the Congressional Republicans who are very much divided amongst themselves."[84] The division within the GOP contributed to delays in the formulation of the planned declaration of principles, for, as Fess pointed out to Hoover, "the greatest obstacle lies within our ranks as represented in the legislative branches of the government where unity on fundamental principles may be impossible and at best only lukewarm."[85]

Meanwhile, Ogden Mills was pushing strongly for the declaration, incorporating Hoover's draft along with suggestions from Elihu Root and former secretary of state Henry L. Stimson. Root strongly favored such a statement in order to revive the Republican party, but he was unsure as to the proper timing for its issuance.[86] Hoover felt that no time should be lost in making the declaration.[87] The nation needed from the GOP some evidence "that its flag still leads in essential safeguards of our civilization."[88] Late in November another meeting was held in Washington between Walter Brown, Chairman Sanders, Senators Reed and Fess, and Congressman Snell. All agreed that there had recently been a decided swing in public sentiment against the New Deal, and there was some difference of opinion, therefore, as to the wisdom of issuing a declaration of principles under the circumstances. The group decided to delay the declaration until early in January. Reed, Fess, and Snell advocated that when the time did come the statement should be made by the executive committee of the GOP national committee, rather than by a group that would include senators and congressmen. They felt reasonably sure that Senator Charles McNary of Oregon, at least, "would not join in sponsoring any statement for sound money," and any dissent by individuals might leave an unfortunate impression on the public of division in the party. However, they believed that if an "authorized agency of the party," such as the executive committee, issued the statement, "comment by individual members of the party would not be so important."[89]

If such a declaration would present a picture of division rather than unity on the part of the GOP in its reaction to the New Deal, then it was perhaps best delayed. In early December, Hoover agreed that perhaps such a delay was not out of order, especially given the apparent discovery by many voters that a number of the New Deal policies were "erroneous both to American ideals and our everyday life." In such a situation, the Republicans could "afford to be patient."[90] But Hoover was also aware of the opposition within the GOP to such a declaration, and of the implications of that opposition for the success of such a statement. As he wrote Walter Brown, he had heard from a number of quarters "divided views as to getting out any statement of principles." Since it seemed that no declaration would have the solid backing of House and Senate Republicans, he concluded that it thrust "large responsibilities on Mr. Sanders."[91]

The declaration of principles having been temporarily placed on the back burner, Hoover now pressed more strenuously for public attacks on the New Deal by Republican members of the House and Senate, even while maintaining his own public silence.[92] Earlier, he had attempted to put the Republican Federal Associates under the GOP national committee as a field organization. However, Sanders had argued against the proposal since such an action would add "too much Hoover color to the National Committee." Hoover, of course, did not think that particularly objectionable, but his efforts came to naught.[93] By January 1934, the Associates were out of money and had decided to close up shop late in the month.[94] Other Republicans showed no disposition to speak out in defense of the Hoover administration against what Hoover described as the "continual misrepresentation" of it by the Democrats. Finally, on February 1, 1934, GOP minority leader Bertram Snell of New York rose in the House and in a brief speech defended the Hoover record during the depression, while excoriating the Democrat-controlled Seventy-second Congress for failing to support his programs, thus forcing Americans to wait two and a half years before obtaining relief. Snell declared that Hoover's antidepression policies had been:

> the most constructive, complete recovery program that has ever been presented during my service by any President to the American Congress. I want further to say that the basis of the great proportion of your recovery acts came from Republican President Hoover, whom you are trying to condemn in the eyes of the people at the present time. They were definite recommendations and he asked for cooperation of a Democratic Congress and did not get it. The depression was on then and I want someone to tell me where was your [the Democrats'] great interest in the people at that time? I know—you were absolutely unwilling for political reasons to give the chance to a Republican President you are now asking for a Democratic President. Except so far as the Reconstruction Finance Corporation is concerned, he never received a particle of cooperation. If you gentlemen had been as patriotic then as you are asking us to be patriotic now, the recovery would have begun a long time ago, and the delay in that is entirely up to you because you are absolutely responsible for the legislation in this House at that time.[95]

Hoover wired Snell: "I appreciate that."[96] But it was only one speech by one man.

Meanwhile, Hoover had begun writing a book. Scanning the reading list of books used for the "citizenship" class at Stanford University one day, he was disturbed that so few of the works on the list expounded what he regarded as the "American ideology."[97] At the same time, he had become increasingly angered at the distortions by the media of his own public philosophy, expressed a decade earlier in his small book *American Individualism*.[98] The distortions led him to wonder whether "instead of using the term 'American

Individualism' I should have expounded 'Controlled Individualism'—but the
former makes me feel more national pride, and some of that is justified in all of
us despite much gushing to the contrary."[99] In September 1933 Hoover wrote
to an old friend, writer Edward Eyre Hunt, that he had concluded that the
"impending battle in this country obviously will be between a properly regulated individualism (which I have always expounded as 'American Individualism') and sure socialism," while at the present time his own philosophy was
being misrepresented as "18th century *laissez faire* and other long-forgotten
social theses." Hoover concluded that before he could be "of much help in
advising the American people as to courses they should pursue, it seems to me
that my position must be clarified." He thought it would be appropriate now
to collect his speeches and other public statements outlining his philosophy and
to publish them "without comment." He believed it "might make a rallying
point for American thought."[100] The book was published late in 1934 and
entitled *The Challenge to Liberty*.

Late in January 1934 the press reported rumors that Hoover planned a
trip to the East, and speculation began that the purpose of his trip was to take a
more prominent role in the Republican party. Rumors were also circulating
that the former president planned to write for a national magazine. Responding to such rumors, Hoover wrote to longtime friend and writer Gertrude
Lane:

> My coming east was sheer newspaper speculation, as was the idea
> that I was to write for a magazine of national circulation, the title of
> which I have not yet learned.... I have no idea of writing for
> current publication. If I ever break loose on this situation, it will be
> an impulsive break and too sudden for prepared magazine articles.
> At the present moment I view it as hopeless because nothing I could
> say would correct it. Someday, I should hope to take part in the effort
> to restore representative government in the United States, but so
> long as the public is dominated solely by emotions vibrating between
> fear and hope, there is very little that one can do.[101]

He was "much amused," Hoover told O'Laughlin, by the published rumors
that he was traveling east, since the rumors generally followed the line that
"the present Republican delegation in Washington have shown no ability in
leadership and the welcoming of the idea that I [Hoover] should go back and
do something about it." Hoover did not, however, take this seriously. He still
considered it desirable that he should stay out of GOP matters until there was
"a general demand for a proper reorganization." He was disturbed by the
apparent desire of Republicans in Washington to forget that his administration had ever existed and by their attempts to gain votes through "partial

adherence to the planned economy and other features of the New Deal." It was a mystery to Hoover how any Republican considered that he could win as a partial New Dealer against a 100 percent New Dealer, rather than by opposing the New Deal on principle.[102]

But a year after the inauguration of the New Deal, Hoover was still unwilling to attack it publicly. As he told John Wheeler of the North American Newspaper Alliance, he was not convinced that any "reassertion" of his faith in "true American Liberalism would serve the national interest." He had, Hoover said, "resolved when I left the White House that no word of mine, nor any act, should weigh in even the slightest degree, directly or indirectly, against recovery," and he had adhered "faithfully to that resolution." His own efforts to bring about recovery having been "sabotaged for political ends at enormous losses to the American people," he was "determined that no such thing should happen to the present Administration."[103] In a more candid vein, he wrote Mark Sullivan that he did feel the necessity to "break into an entirely antagonistic audience in an endeavor to offer some opposition to disastrous action," but thought it better to "do nothing until the audience or some part of it demands some word from me." He was concerned that any action on his part this early would have no practical effect but to "destroy a more practical accomplishment at a later time." Nor was he certain that if he did go on the attack any others would come "energetically to my support and defense."[104] He continued to doubt, also, that there was an audience interested in what he might have to say.[105]

But the man in Palo Alto was finding new reasons to despise the regime in Washington. Hoover had evidence that his incoming and outgoing mail was being opened, which (to the detriment of later historians) led him to become more circumspect in his letter writing. When William Castle wrote that one of Hoover's letters to him "had been opened and rather crudely resealed," the former president replied that it was not the first time this had happened. In his letter to Castle, Hoover also added for the benefit of any snooper:

> If the gentleman who opens this letter would please transmit a copy of it to the President I should be greatly obliged to him. If he would make an adequate investigation as to what the Post Office Department is doing, or some other branch of government espionage, he will find a great many other complaints of tampering with the mails. A large amount of evidence is accumulating on this question which will sooner or later break loose and there will be a national demand for an investigation as to who is conducting the United States cheka.[106]

The other source of Hoover's outrage toward the New Deal was what he regarded as "the frantic attempts to smear my Administration and the industrious search for another Teapot Dome," which was most obvious in the investigation of former postmaster general Walter Brown by Senator Hugo Black's committee, the government's attempt to prosecute former secretary of the treasury Andrew Mellon for income tax evasion, and attacks that had been made on other Hoover cabinet members. With justified confidence, Hoover was sure that none of these maneuvers would prove fruitful for the Democrats. As he wrote one friend: "If there is anything I do know it was a four years of the highest probity and freedom from improper influence that the Federal Government has ever seen."[107]

The Hoover wing of Republicans continued to despair at the lack of activity being shown by the GOP national committee. O'Laughlin sought and received Hoover's permission to resign from his post as Sanders's assistant effective March 12, 1934. The national committee was still moribund, resulting in the House and Senate campaign committees becoming increasingly independent.[108] Republicans sought to invigorate the party in different ways. Blocked in his attempts to build the Republican Federal Associates into an effective national force, Ogden Mills turned to organizing a state group in New York known as the Republican Builders. As Hoover interpreted it, the new organization arose "from despair in the regular Republican organizations accomplishing anything except old-fashioned politics." Encouraged by the growth of the movement in New York, Hoover sought to stimulate interest in the formation of a similar organization "of young and new Republicans" in southern California and suggested that his former secretary of agriculture, Arthur Hyde, consider organizing something like it in the Midwest.[109]

However, changes were in store for the GOP national committee. Late in January 1934 the movement to oust Everett Sanders as chairman gained momentum when Senator Arthur Vandenberg of Michigan introduced a bill in the Senate that would prohibit the chairmen of the two national committees from practicing law before departments of the federal government. Sanders would now have to choose between the chairmanship and his livelihood.[110] In the search for a possible successor, Hoover initially supported former senator Walter Edge, who had earlier been suggested by O'Laughlin; but Hoover also was not averse to O'Laughlin's new choice, former diplomat Henry P. Fletcher, who Charles Hilles favored for the position.[111] O'Laughlin had been anxious for some time to bring Hilles and Hoover closer together for the sake of the party, and a first product of his efforts was their agreement on the choice for GOP chairman.[112] Hilles believed, he told O'Laughlin, that if he and Hoover could agree on a candidate, that person could be elected chairman.[113] Hoover preferred someone from the Midwest and a new, young face, rather than one of the party standbys, but he recognized that such a choice would "probably be too revolutionary for the National Committee."[114]

Early in May of 1934 Everett Sanders issued the call for a meeting of the national committee to be held on June 5. Hoover still hoped for the election of Edge or of a new possibility that had come to mind, former governor Kohler of Wisconsin. He still preferred a chairman from the Midwest, if possible, and Kohler met that qualification.[115] Hoover also shared the sentiment of those national committeemen who felt that the time had come for the release of a declaration of principles. Confiding in national committeeman R. B. Creager of Texas, he reiterated his belief that such a declaration should be "on the simple subjects of the constitution, the gold standard, a sound fiscal policy, and a complete rejection of all forms of regimentation."[116] Harrison Spangler, national committeeman from Iowa and a Hoover supporter, also believed that the meeting presented "an opportunity to do something really constructive toward revitalizing the party" in the form of a "resolution setting forth a short, concise and forward-looking declaration of principles." He sought suggestions from Hoover as to the form such a statement should take.[117]

At the June 5 meeting in Chicago, Charles Hilles quickly moved for the formation of a committee to prepare a statement of party principles, and the motion was seconded by Walter Brown. It was adopted by a unanimous vote, and Hilles was chosen to head the committee, which included in its membership Mark Requa of California, a Hoover Republican.[118] The next day the committee returned with a declaration of principles. Since Hilles (along with Mills, Root, Hoover, and others) had been involved in the earlier attempts to draft such a declaration, it is apparent that the draft presented to the national committee was the product of more hands than those on the drafting committee and of more time than the 24 hours that they had spent on the project.

The declaration began by sounding the warning that "American institutions and American civilization are in greater danger today than at any time since the foundation of the Republic." It described the choice before the people as between a democracy and the domination of an all-powerful central government. The statement disclaimed any intention to define "a detailed party program," but sought "to set forth the spirit and attitude in which our party should approach the problems of the day and to restate our principles of government." It reviewed the economic problems facing the nation and asserted that they must be dealt with "in a broad, liberal and progressive spirit, unhampered by dead formulas or too obstinately clinging to the past." Government must deal with social problems, but it must do so "within the framework of American institutions, in accordance with the spirit and principles of the founders of the Republic, without destruction of individual freedom." The policies of the Roosevelt administration were leading to "the chaos of unlimited inflation," with the savings and earnings of the people "being consumed recklessly by the government." The declaration warned:

A small group in Washington, vested with temporary authority, is seeking covertly to alter the framework of American institutions. They seek to expand to the utmost limit the powers of the central government. In place of individual initiative, they seek to substitute complete government control of all agricultural production, of all business activity.[119]

History recorded that such tyrannical attempts had always ended in failure—they had not only failed to bring prosperity but had crushed liberty and democracy. The declaration put the Republican party on record as opposed to repudiation of government obligations; in favor of freedom of speech, the press, and the radio for the discussion of national questions; and as for an economic system based upon free enterprise rather than upon "bureaucratic control and bureaucratic management." The party opposed "revolutionary change without popular mandate" and favored eliminating the emergency laws giving dictatorial powers to the president. It supported the "federal form of government with its system of state and local responsibilities." The nation could not spend its way to prosperity, but must maintain an "unassailable national credit and a balanced budget." The declaration called "upon all who believe in the maintenance of these principles to unite in the election of senators and representatives who will support them." The document was accepted by the GOP national committee.[120]

The *New York Times* described the declaration as "solemn emptiness," but the *New York Herald Tribune* found it "fresh in language and courageous in spirit." The *Tribune* approved the declaration's reluctance to "attempt to commit the party to a detailed program" and was encouraged that "it points the way and that way lies in the direction that the younger and more progressive elements in the party are convinced that it must lie if the party is to regain its prestige and leadership."[121] William Allen White celebrated the declaration as incorporating the "old Bull Moose program of 1912, with its 'social and industrial justice,' its plea for old-age pensions and job insurance, which was a quarter of a century ahead of its time." White added: "And who was back of all these liberal, highly democratic pronouncements? None other than the Hoover group. Led by Mark Requa of California, in the platform committee, and Ogden L. Mills, who sat in on the preliminary drafting committee, this platform was presented and adopted with scarcely a change of verbiage."[122]

The declaration of principles out of the way, the national committee turned to the business of electing a new chairman to replace Everett Sanders, who had resigned. Two candidates were nominated: Fletcher and Kansas GOP chairman John D. M. Hamilton. If Hoover had been serious in his stated wish for a Midwestern chairman, Hamilton would have filled the bill;

and he was also youthful enough to meet that qualification. But the choice of the Hoover wing of the party was early made apparent when those on the national committee who could be classified as Hooverites—Requa of California, Spangler of Iowa, Brown of Ohio, and Creager of Texas—went down the line in seconding Fletcher's nomination. Hilles also seconded the Fletcher nomination. The vote was 68 to 24 for Fletcher, after which Hamilton withdrew and asked that the vote be made unamimous.[123]

The election of Fletcher was far from a rebuff for Hoover, who wired his congratulations to Fletcher, describing him as a "most experienced and courageous leader."[124] Creager wired Hoover that Fletcher's election symbolized the "retention by you of powerful influence in [the] nation. I am delighted."[125] Hoover responded that he thought Creager and the rest of the committee had done "a good job at Chicago and distinctly you put the Republican party on its way."[126] William Allen White, who regarded Fletcher as "Hoover's personal friend and political protege," viewed the choice as a compromise between the conservative and liberal wings and as a Hoover victory.[127] The *New York Herald Tribune* agreed that Fletcher "has been known as a Hoover man," but applauded the choice since the new chairman "in a very real sense" could be described as "a neutral so far as the schisms and quarrels of the party go."[128]

In Palo Alto, Hoover was now devoting most of his time to the preparation of the book on his public philosophy. An early draft had been criticized as being too combative in its discussion of the Roosevelt administration,[129] and now a revised manuscript was mailed off to a number of close friends and writers for their comments. Hoover described the book and his state of mind in writing it:

> It is my last shot at public service, and must be made now before I go on to other occupations finally, and they [*sic*] do not contemplate a literary career. I do not overestimate the book's usefulness; but it clears my own conscience and does what I can for people groping in the dark. Privately, I have no expectation that a nation which has once cut loose from its moorings to definite human rights and places them at the disposal of the state will ever return to them. History does not move that way, and those who cling to such a philosophy are just part of the wreckage. We can nevertheless yell "help, help." With ten million unemployed and the destruction of business confidence after all this stuff, the most likely drive is toward more and more suppression of rights and more gospel from Walter Lippmann that it is the true interpretation of the forefathers; that it is all for our good; that it is deserved punishment for our sins; that it is the discovery by Hebraic philosophers of genius who can compound collectivism and individual rights and make the waters of life.[130]

Hoover wrote to Senator Warren Austin of Vermont in August: "You will see in a few days that I will bust loose into print. I hope it will do some good. At least it will relieve my pent-up feelings."[131] To O'Laughlin he wrote: "The book is on the way. I am looking for a storm cellar."[132] To George Akerson he confided the hope that his small contribution "would stand up in the storm it will invoke. My conscience would not stand further suppression, despite much contrary advice from friends."[133] Discussing the revisions he had made in the early, more combative draft, Hoover confessed to William Allen White that he had "originally written the book with more quip and epigram, but on consideration I concluded that wherever it could be interpreted as containing the slightest degree of bitterness that it should be eliminated." While the book was now duller, it was "perhaps more useful for its purpose."[134]

*The Challenge to Liberty* appeared in mid-September of 1934, preceded by articles in the *Saturday Evening Post* summarizing its major points.[135] Like Hoover's draft of a Republican declaration of principles, the book did not attack specific policies of the New Deal, nor set forth alternative policies. It was, instead, an appeal to the American people that they not abandon their philosophy of individual liberty to the destructive trend then current in the world toward the suppression of freedom. It was, in short, an appeal for liberty against tyranny, in which Hoover discussed the tradition of "American Liberalism" and the "American System," and contrasted them with the new forces of fascism, nazism, and communism in Europe and with similar tendencies that he found in the New Deal. As he put it in his summation:

> We cannot extend the mastery of government over the daily life of a people without somewhere making it master of people's souls and thoughts. That is going on today. It is part of all regimentation.
>
> Even if the government conduct of business could give us the maximum of efficiency instead of least efficiency, it would be purchased at the cost of freedom. It would increase rather than decrease abuse and corruption, stifle initiative and invention, undermine the development of leadership, cripple the mental and spiritual energies of our people, extinguish equality of opportunity, and dry up the spirit of liberty and the forces which make progress.
>
> It is a false liberalism that interprets itself into government dictation, or operation of commerce, industry and agriculture. Every move in that direction poisons the very springs of true Liberalism. It poisons political equality, free thought, free press, and equality of opportunity. It is the road not to liberty but to less liberty. True Liberalism is found not in striving to spread bureaucracy, but in striving to set bounds to it. Liberalism is a force proceeding from the deep realization that economic freedom cannot be sacrificed if politi-

cal freedom is to be preserved. True Liberalism seeks all legitimate freedom first in the confident belief that without such freedom the pursuit of other blessings is in vain.

The nation seeks for solutions of its many difficulties. These solutions can come alone through the constructive forces from the system built upon Liberty. They cannot be achieved by the destructive forces of Regimentation. The purification of Liberty from abuses, the restoration of confidence in the rights of men, the release of the dynamic forces of initiative and enterprise are alone the methods by which these solutions can be found and the purpose of American life assured.[136]

Hoover had some misgivings about publishing the book just before the 1934 off-year elections, but finally decided that if he waited until afterward "the Republicans would have a right to complain that I was shirking my responsibility." He consoled himself that the campaign might "enliven a discussion of the question, and that we have to have."[137]

Thanks to the recommendation of William Allen White, who was a member of the selection committee, *The Challenge to Liberty* was taken up as a Book-of-the-Month Club selection.[138] Hoover wrote the Kansas editor that he was "mightily obliged for all the help you are giving to spread the gospel according to Palo Alto." He also urged White to say something in the press about the book, since the opposition would "of course attempt to damn it as 'reactionary,' 'standpat,' etc., and your voice might give it more balance in the public mind."[139]

After the first of the *Saturday Evening Post* articles appeared, the *New York Herald Tribune* noted that Hoover's "silence has been broken at last, and as might have been expected, he offers to the nation the impersonal and philosophical reflections on politics of a thoughtful man in retirement." It noted that the article contained no mention of the New Deal, but that it pointed to the dangers of planning and centralization such as characterized the Roosevelt administration. It concluded:

> Mr. Hoover's views are those of an old-fashioned liberal, firmly devoted to the philosophy of government which evolved our Constitution and to the social philosophy under which the United States grew strong. In so far as he is unwilling to see either materially modified he will arouse the scorn of the New Dealers and the experimentalists. But no thoughtful student of American affairs can afford to ignore the reflections of a man who had four years of practical experience in the supervision of our constitutional and social system and whose knowledge of world problems is unequaled.[140]

Hoover and the *New York Herald Tribune* were correct in assuming that the book would not be welcomed universally. The reviews were more revealing of the political orientations of the reviewers and the journals in which they appeared than they were of the book. Broadus Mitchell, Socialist party candidate for governor of Maryland, wrote in the left-wing *Nation*: "The book is a sorry performance. It is worse than dull. It is numb. . . . Mr. Hoover's lips are automatically forming syllables which are familiar to him, but which have little enough application to what has recently taken place."[141] Even Arthur Krock described it in the *New York Times* as a "brooding book" and Hoover as a "writer of polemics," while he decried the fact that the former president had not outlined a platform for his party, which was "so needful of one."[142] The *Saturday Review* featured historian Allan Nevins's description of the book as "frankly an appeal to old standards, old aims, and old traditions; the traditions of Harrison and McKinley, of Taft, Harding and Coolidge—but not of Theodore Roosevelt and Woodrow Wilson, to say nothing of Franklin D. Roosevelt." Through it all, Nevins argued, the former president had almost totally ignored the crisis in which the nation was embroiled and was mistaken in treating "an emergency assumption of authority as a calculated and sustained assault on liberty."[143]

The negative reviews were balanced by more positive ones in such journals as *Management Review* and the *Political Science Quarterly*. Popular historian Will Durant wrote Hoover that he had found *The Challenge to Liberty* "amazingly eloquent and I cannot understand why the critics have not recognized its high literary quality."[144] Glenn Frank, president of the University of Wisconsin, called it "a great document! and," he continued, "it will so stand as the judgment of posterity. It has in it the sustained sense of moral power that one feels in Mazzini's 'Duties of Man.' "[145] O'Laughlin was "impressed by the profound stir which the breaking of your silence has created, the general appreciation of the vital importance of the subject you selected for treatment, and the moves made by the Administration to counteract the effect of your essay."[146] But columnist Elliott Thurston was probably correct when he wrote in the *Washington Post*: "An omniscient man from Mars might have written this book and been hailed as a prophet or a Moses. As a prophet in his own land, Mr. Hoover's fate at the moment seems to be the proverbial one. And the hour is not yet ripe for a popular uprising, even if Mr. Hoover were prepared to lead it."[147]

Hoover recognized that he had not offered an alternative program to the New Deal in his book, but as he wrote to one correspondent: "I am not entirely convinced of the fact that when a nation is about to jump out of a window it is necessary to offer him [*sic*] a constructive program. The main thing is to tell him to stop."[148] To another he wrote: "I have no idea that it is politically expedient but I have not enough interest in the political side to care. My conscience will not permit my sitting here any longer and not expressing my opinion on the dangerous courses that are in progress."[149] As for the reviewers:

> The New Deal reviewers, anxious to prevent the book from getting anywhere, are setting the unanimous cry that it is trivial, trite, badly written, stodgy, feudal, medieval, etc. The press away from the pink and sophisticated areas are giving it a good run. I wish that they [the New Deal] had the honesty to attack it front end on. It would circulate more books.[150]

But circulation of the book was not a problem. Through Hoover's efforts to distribute it among his friends and acquaintances (and they to their friends and acquaintances), as well as its selection as a book club offering, *The Challenge to Liberty* made the best-seller lists, and 135,000 copies were printed.[151] Furthermore, the *United States News* found that newspapers expressing an opinion on the book were divided 68 percent in favor of Hoover's position and 32 percent against.[152] Two decades later, Chadwick Hall (formerly of the *Nation*), in seeking to account for the return of businessmen to a position of dominance in public affairs through the Eisenhower victory in 1952, would date the beginning of the successful "businessmen's crusade against the New Deal" from "1934 with the publication of Herbert Hoover's *The Challenge to Liberty*."[153]

During the summer of 1934 Hoover made his annual visit to the Bohemian Club summer encampment amid the redwoods of northern California. This cathedral-like setting of 2,800 acres contained approximately 250 camps of from two to twenty congenial friends each, supplemented by guests and numerous common facilities. Its members and their guests included the elite from journalism, government, commerce, industry, and finance. Hoover's own affiliation was with Caveman's Camp, which included, in addition to Hoover, Hoover's two sons, Dr. Ray Lyman Wilbur, writers Clarence Kelland and Charles Fields, and oilman Bert Mattei. It was a time without care, devoted to conversation, speeches, golf, and theatrical productions; but it also was an opportunity for making important contacts.[154] Hoover would continue his visits there until his last appearance, in 1962, when he was nearly 88.

Columnist Raymond Clapper visited the former president in Palo Alto in July of 1934 and described for his readers the heavy mail that Hoover continued to receive—two hundred letters on an average day and up to fifteen hundred letters on days that an issue was before the country. Clapper wrote of Hoover's life on the Stanford campus and of his automobile trips into the surrounding area to keep in touch with grass-roots sentiment. He concluded:

> The outside world thinks of Mr. Hoover as a man brooding in
> silence. He is silent so far as the outside world is concerned and he
> has firmly rejected all offers to write or to discuss National affairs.
> But it is not a brooding silence. Nor the silence of a man who has lost
> his interest in life. It is the calm self-restraint of a man who is
> observing and thinking a great deal. It is a relaxed, attentive silence
> like that of a performer who has had his turn on the stage and is now
> watching the performance of others.[155]

During the summer of 1934 the American Liberty League was launched
by leading businessmen and political opponents of the New Deal. Prominent
in the organization were names anathema to Hoover because of their opposition to his reelection in 1932: industrialist Irénée Du Pont; John J. Raskob,
formerly a director of General Motors and chairman of the Democratic national committee; and Jouett Shouse, executive chairman of the Democratic
national committee under Raskob and the man who had hired Charles
Michelson as publicity director of the Democratic national committee to undertake the infamous smear campaign against Hoover as president.[156]

Hoover was not impressed with the new organization. While he agreed
that it might "serve a national purpose in creating a debate on fundamentals,"
Hoover was no advocate of "Liberty of the Wall Street model," and he could
not forget that the organizers of the Liberty League bore some responsibility,
at least, for the presence of the New Deal in Washington. He wrote O'Laughlin: "If this group had kept to the truth during my administration and had
devoted their vast expenditure of money and energies to the exposition of the
truth instead of slander, and if they had stated publicly what they all said
privately of the Democratic candidate, the country would not be writhing in
this situation." Some Republicans were attracted to the Liberty League, but
Hoover objected to its overemphasis on property rights, which in his view
ignored the true importance of the right to own property—"security of mind
and body and stimulus to effort, enterprise, and creativeness"—and ignored as
well the dangers to individual freedoms that could potentially be posed
through the power over property.[157]

Hoover liked the Liberty League's view of property no more than he did
the New Deal's belief that property could "be directly or indirectly confiscated
by the State without compensation, and further, that the State should drive
towards ownership and operation of property," since he viewed both attitudes
as "a negation of the whole spirit of Liberty." When the state gained possession of property, the power was used to "extinguish the other Liberties." The
role of the state should be to prevent "abuse of the right of property and to act
as an umpire between property holders to see that they do not do so." Hoover's
immediate concern was that *The Challenge to Liberty* should "not be classified

with either the interpretation that these gentlemen of the Liberty League apparently make of it, or that being made by the New Deal. I am neither for the Wall Street model nor the Pennsylvania Avenue model" of liberty.[158] He did not believe the Liberty League would have much influence, since "it is not a pulpit which is accredited by the American people with the bolts of pure patriotism."[159]

As the off-year elections approached, Hoover monitored the chances of Republicans in the congressional races and the issues they were taking up in their campaigns. Optimistically, he wrote in late August that the tide seemed to be running toward the Republicans, and that if it continued to do so the GOP could expect to gain some seats. He believed that if the Republicans could increase their number in the House by 50, it would "contribute very much to placing a check on destruction."[160] However, he was offended by the continued unwillingness of Republican candidates to stand up for his own administration. Ignoring Snell's defense in February, Hoover wrote Ogden Mills: "There has not been a single voice lifted in the Congress in defense of our administration." Many Republicans, he suggested, were unwilling to contribute campaign funds for candidates who refused to acknowledge that the Hoover administration "must represent the fundamental policies and principles of the Republican party," and who were unwilling to draw a contrast between the Hoover and Roosevelt policies. In Hoover's view, time had proven that "these policies of ours were right, and that the New Deal policies were wrong, but the whole attitude of the members of the House and Senate is to try to forget our administration; and therein lies the reason for the general feeling throughout the country that the Republican Party is dead."[161]

From Washington came disquieting word from GOP chairman Henry Fletcher in late August that he was handicapped by a lack of funds and a discouraging absence of interest or courage on the part of those who were in a position to help and who ought to be interested in preserving the free enterprise system. Nevertheless, Fletcher predicted that the GOP would preserve its strength in the Senate and make considerable gains in the House of Representatives.[162] Hoover, the titular leader of the party, planned to take no role in the campaign since he considered it "somewhat difficult for me to enter into a campaign where every effort has been made for my exclusion." He had concluded that the GOP campaign committees regarded him as a liability, and that they were probably right if the party's candidates were determined to run as partial New Dealers.[163] The image of the Hoover administration suffered, in Hoover's view, from two ideas that had "been smeared over the country." One was that his administration had done "nothing for the people," and the other was that it had been "the associate and tool of Wall Street and organized wealth." The result was that GOP candidates operated under the illusion that "they must scrupulously ignore or apologize for our administration." The "smears" could be easily rebutted, but no Republican seemed interested in doing so.[164]

While he bemoaned the unwillingness of Republican candidates to speak out in defense of his administration, and offered what he considered useful advice to some of the candidates, Hoover contributed no public leadership in the 1934 campaign other than his book. Privately he was concerned that the Republican party might be tracing the path to extinction that had been followed by the Whig party in the mid-nineteenth century. As he wrote to former governor of Kansas Henry Allen:

> I have been greatly shocked at the campaigns which many of our Republicans are carrying on. They are afraid of or are refusing to fight these questions out on principle. And, if the Republican Party does not, within the next twelve months, firmly announce itself as the protector of the Arc of the Covenant (details of which may be found in the "Challenge to Liberty") it will slide down the same precipice which engulfed the Whig Party in 1856.

Hoover realized the "difficulties of making a campaign of opposition where Santa Claus is visiting each household, and I realize that many people in this world would rather be elected than to be right."[165] Ironically, leaders of the party's "progressive" wing envisioned a similar future for the GOP if it continued to adhere to its traditional principles. As Senator William Borah of Idaho put it, "if the old regime continues to control" the Republican party, it would "die like the Whig Party died, of sheer political cowardice."[166] Neither Hoover nor Borah apparently included in their lamentations any consideration of the renewal of conservatism that had accompanied the decline of the Whig party and the rise of the Republicans.

As the congressional elections drew nearer, any early optimism concerning Republican chances dissipated. From House minority leader Bert Snell came pessimistic predictions resulting from a shortage of funds with which to carry on the House campaigns.[167] Senator Lester J. Dickinson of Iowa observed the campaigns in several states and wrote Hoover: "For the first time we are experiencing Tammany methods in national politics. They are buying favoritism."[168] Columnist David Lawrence concluded that the Democrats would gain, not lose, seats in the House of Representatives.[169] The week before the election Hoover wrote Senator Wallace H. White that the situation "does not look good either for recovery or for our party in these elections. But after this election the days of alibi for failure by laying it onto us will have passed." He pointed out that the number of unemployed in September 1934 was "about the same as September, 1932," but in 1932 the number had been decreasing, while in 1934 it was increasing.[170]

Republican pessimism was validated when the GOP lost more seats in the 1934 election in defiance of the tradition of off-year electoral gains by the opposition. It marked the third successive defeat for the Republican party. Hoover's reaction to the debacle was predictable. He wrote one correspondent:

> The election being over, it is possible of [*sic*] all kinds of interpretations, but the Santa Claus interpretation is unquestionably the soundest. It is very difficult for a Senator to stand up in his State against an opponent who points to the several hundred million dollars that has come into the State and the several hundred million more that is in prospect. He points out that it comes from his political party and that no Republican can have influence or weight with that party. The Republican, on the other hand, has to stand up and in effect denounce the very spending of money in his own State.[171]

Yet, if the election had to be fought on principles, Hoover, as titular leader of his party, had done little to present the issues to the voters. No doubt the former president felt some measure of responsibility for the size of the defeat because of his failure to speak out against the New Deal in the twenty months since he had left the White House. He would not make the same mistake in 1938.

In about November of 1933, Hoover began to receive reports of enthusiastic responses to his appearance in motion picture newsreels. The reports came from widely scattered parts of the country.[172] From Senator Thomas Schall of Minnesota came a typical report that Hoover was applauded enthusiastically in Minnesota by newsreel viewers "while scarcely any applause greets that [newsreel] of your former opponent."[173] Such reports led Hoover to question whether the negative attitude the press had for him was a true reflection of public opinion. "How is it," he wrote Arthur Hyde, "that movie houses universally report great applause? Does it mean anything?" If so, then perhaps there was after all an audience in America for the kind of attack that Hoover yearned to launch on the New Deal. Hoover now suggested to Hyde that a group of one hundred "representative men" from all over the country might be assembled to request that he "undertake a constructive debate of the measures before Congress during the winter as a needed public service." He suggested William Allen White as a possible organizer of the effort and proposed to discuss it with Hyde during his planned trip to the Midwest.[174]

Hoover's suggestion of White as a possible orchestrator of his reappearance on the public scene is interesting, because White's fellow Kansan, Governor Alf Landon, was already emerging as a potential contender for the 1936 GOP presidential nomination. Moreover, Hoover was already critical of the manner in which the Landon campaign was being handled since he considered the methods destructive of Republican unity. He complained that the Landon people "make the mistake of thinking that they gain strength by showing how antagonistic they are to Hoover and his many wickednesses, which offends good taste in many of my friends. They cannot be content to build up their man, but they must do it by blackening others who are not even rivals."[175]

Hoover was also concerned that some newspapers and columnists were suggesting that the Republican defeat in the 1934 elections was evidence that the party must swing to the left in order to attract votes. For Hoover, the election was confirmation of exactly the reverse argument. When, despite all of the material blandishments of the New Deal, 45 percent of voters cast their ballots against Democratic candidates, it was proof to him that this sizable segment of the population was "considerably to the 'Right' of the New Deal." From this and the vote in the 1932 election he concluded that "there would appear to be a staunch group in the Republican Party comprising probably 90% which is determined to remain to the 'Right,' and there would appear to be a very large group yet to be worked upon."[176] But Hoover was not optimistic that the hold of the New Deal on the American electorate would be easily or quickly broken. He told the Stanford University debate team in mid-January of 1935 that the use of direct federal relief funds had enabled the New Deal to build "an unbeatable political machine," and the Republican party would not be able to return to power "for two or three elections" because "they've got the people bought off for that long."[177]

Meanwhile, in October of 1934 Hoover had accepted an invitation to join the board of directors of New York Life Insurance Company.[178] Early in January he headed east from his Palo Alto home for a short visit to Chicago. Professor William Starr Myers called on Hoover there and found him "well, but mad and scrappy." Hoover was outspoken in his criticism of Roosevelt and the New Dealers.[179] After a brief return to California, Hoover traveled east again for his first meeting with the New York Life board. He had, Hoover wrote William Allen White, been "promoted to the life insurance business, which necessitates my going east once in a while and I shall thereby come nearer Emporia—and if the White family is not strongly insulated, I may be in to sell you a policy."[180] Hoover had decided that the record of his administration should be written by Myers and Walter Newton, and part of his railroad journey was spent in reviewing material for the book.[181]

On his arrival in New York City, Hoover received an enthusiastic welcome from old friends.[182] Ogden Mills hosted a large dinner for him, which included among its guests many former members of the Hoover cabinet and other officials from his administration, as well as a number of journalistic friends. The majority of the guests answered Mills's query as to whether the time was ripe for Hoover to reenter public life by agreeing that no one except the former president could get a hearing from the newspapers and the public for criticism of the New Deal. However, they agreed with Hoover that he should not go on the attack unless he and others were prepared to follow it up vigorously.[183] The following night Hoover attended the Lincoln Day dinner of the National Republican Club, at which an overflow crowd greeted him enthusiastically. In a few brief remarks, he lauded Abraham Lincoln and called for personal liberty, warning that people must be the masters of government rather than "the pawns of the state." Also while in New York he laid further plans with Myers and Newton for the book on the Hoover administration; and on February 14 Hoover left with Arthur Hyde for Palo Alto by way of Chicago.[184]

During Hoover's trip to the East, the Supreme Court was considering the constitutionality of the federal government's action in repudiating the clause requiring that government bonds be redeemable in gold upon maturity. At the dinner hosted by Mills, it was agreed that nothing should be said concerning the gold issue until the Supreme Court had issued its ruling.[185] When Hoover was returning to Palo Alto, the Supreme Court ruled that the government's repudiation of the gold clause had been unconstitutional, but it also denied recourse through the courts for those seeking bond redemption in gold.

As he drove through the towns of the West, Hoover was approached by newsmen for a statement on the decision. Finally, in Tucson, Arizona, he dictated a statement for the wire services.[186] Hoover called for restoration of confidence in the dollar by the removal of all threats of further devaluation. This could be done by immediately restoring the gold standard, but with the dollar convertible at its present value of 59 cents in gold. Hoover pointed out that most of the unemployment existed in the capital goods and construction industries, that these industries were dependent upon long-term capital for recovery, and that such capital would not be forthcoming so long as "people are hesitant to invest their savings and take long-term risks because there is uncertainty in what value they will be repaid." The restoration of the gold standard would, he argued, "put more men to work out of the twelve million who still remain unemployed than any other single action." Government spending programs could never produce 25 percent of the jobs that could be provided by recovery of the private capital goods industries. Moreover, the abandonment of inflationary policies would also benefit endowed universities and hospitals, as well as small savers, pension plans, and insurance policy owners. Hoover ended his statement with the observation:

> We can get in appearance a false prosperity out of inflation. There is much inflation poison in the national blood through the combined effect of the devaluation, expanded bank deposits through government borrowing, and the Federal Reserve credit policies. The fever

> may grow at any time. There is no real recovery on inflation medi-
> cine. If the currency were made convertible it would tend to check
> inflation, replace relief with real employment, and contribute mate-
> rially to a general recovery.[187]

The *New York Times*, which carried Hoover's statement on its front page, noted with understatement that it was "one of the few public pronouncements made by Mr. Hoover since leaving the White House in March, 1933."[188] The *New York Herald Tribune* found "much to be said for Hoover's solution," but wondered if it were feasible under the unsound economic policies of the Roosevelt administration. If the New Deal continued its unbalanced budgets and resorted to the issue of fiat money and fiat bonds, then "no amount of gold can save the dollar from depreciation or the country from currency inflation."[189] Hoover's statement also caused a flurry of speculation in both the House and the Senate. The chairmen of the House and Senate GOP campaign commit-tees both quickly followed his lead in declaring for the immediate restoration of the gold standard, to the embarrassment of "progressive" Republicans in both houses who had supported New Deal financial policies. Members of both political parties were quick to read into the former president's re-emergence a bid for leadership of the GOP as it approached the 1936 convention, and perhaps a desire for the nomination itself.[190]

Now that he was back in public life, Hoover resolved to stay there. He told Arthur Hyde:

> I will not keep still any longer, and I am going to periodically shoot
> at the situation, of which the gold statement is the first example. I am
> trying to get together some material to take a shot at the Relief bill
> and I hope to follow it with another with the NRA bill when it is
> brought up in Congress. Everybody says that it is not good politics,
> but I have not noticed any Republican in Washington or New York
> raise his voice in protest of the Moral issue.[191]

Indeed, his second public message, delivered the following month and written with greater deliberation than the impulsive statement at Tucson, signaled to the nation that Hoover was really on the attack. Sensing the drama of the occasion, the Associated Press requested a photograph of the former president, pen in hand, preparing to break his self-imposed two-year silence.[192]

Hoover's second statement took the form of a public letter to a meeting of the California Republican Assembly in Sacramento, and sounded a "call to arms" for Republicans. "The Republican Party," he told them, "today has the greatest responsibility that has come to it since the days of Abraham Lincoln." The GOP must furnish the "rallying point" for all Americans who continued to believe in "fundamental American principles." The issue was between the American "system of orderly individual liberty under constitutionally conducted government" and that "of the newly created system of regimentation and bureaucratic domination in which men and women are not master of government but are the pawns or dependents of a centralized and potentially self-perpetuating government." The prospect under the latter was that America would fall into "the sink into which first one great nation after another abroad is falling." Hoover listed the objectives that Republicans should champion:

> to upbuild and protect the family and the home, whether farmer, worker, or business man. . . . The fundamental protection of these homes is the spirit as well as the letter of the Bill of Rights, with the supports from the framework of the Constitution. They must be given peace with the world. There must be confidence in the security of the job, of the business, of the savings which sustain these homes. Increased standards of living, leisure, and security can come to that home through unshackling the productive genius of our people. The advancement of knowledge must be translated into increasing health and education for the children. There must be constantly improved safeguards to the family from the dislocations of economic life and of old age. With the growth of great industrial forces we must continue to add unceasing protections from abuse and exploitation. We must be liberal in reward to those who add service, material or spiritual wealth to these homes. . . . The windows of these homes must be bright with hope. Their doors must be open outward to initiative, enterprise, opportunity, unbounded by regimentation and socialism. Today there must be restoration of faith, the removal of fear and uncertainty that these ideals and these hopes will be open to those who strive.

The responsibility, he told Republicans, lay primarily with young men and women to ensure that liberty was preserved and responsible constitutional government restored in the United States, "as opposed to un-American regimentation and bureaucratic domination."[193]

The *New York Herald Tribune* predicted "blustering retorts to Mr. Hoover's Sacramento message," in anticipation that the "specialists in diatribe associated with the New Deal" would "make their usual scoffing comments." But it found Hoover's "dispassionate description of the present plight of the country" to be "unanswerable." The charges, while phrased in "calmness and fairness," and avoiding personalities, were "devastating," and "the solemn and inescapable truth is in every line."[194] A letter to the editor a few days later observed:

So many people have been saying of the Republican party, "Where are the leaders?"

Do we have to look further than Herbert Hoover? Does not his message to the Republican Assembly of California and his statement relative to the gold standard show sound leadership of true American principles—principles which made this country great?

Mr. Hoover has shown his willingness to lead. If he is willing also to carry the banner in 1936, then we should be grateful and get behind him. . . .

People said of Hoover during his term: "He is not a politician, he can get nowhere." Will some one please tell us what the arch politician now in the White House has done for us?[195]

If Republicans were seeking a leader, Hoover was willing to lead. If a sizable body of Americans shared his perception of the New Deal as alien to traditional Americanism and detrimental to economic recovery, then they would find their misgivings articulated in Hoover's speeches and writings. Having endured two years of public silence and private anguish, the former president clearly entered upon this new phase of his public career with relish, reclaiming the role of titular leader of the Republican party, which he had allowed to languish for two years. But whether silent or on the attack, Hoover continued to be discredited in many minds by depression and defeat, and as a man who seemed to call for sacrifice in the name of ideals while the New Deal offered relief in response to realities. These points, gleefully taken up by Democrats and anti-Hoover Republicans, took much of the force from his attacks. Subjected to years of smearing by the Democrats, a negative image of Hoover had been allowed, by default, to become deeply ingrained in the American public and even in his own party.

# 2
# Campaigning

he transformation in Hoover was remarkable in the early months of 1935. As late as mid-January he had remarked that he hesitated "greatly to make extemporaneous remarks" and was "too lazy to prepare an address." Moreover, he was disinclined "to give public advice until the country has come to a further realization as to this current nonsense." His book had made "the record" he wanted, and it seemed "about enough of a public contribution . . . to acquit my conscience in these matters."[1] He refused an invitation in February from William Allen White to speak in Kansas, pleading that he had "lately refused about 9,000 opportunities to speak" and was afraid of what would happen if he ever broke his rule against public addresses.[2] However, by the end of March, the reception of his first two forays encouraged Hoover to remain on the attack.[3]

Despairing, finally, at the apparent unwillingness of Republicans in Washington to oppose the New Deal, Hoover resolved to take up the fight himself, no matter how uncomfortable that course might be for the timid within his party. Discouraged by the apparent drift of the GOP and by the willingness of Republicans to desert traditional party principles in search of "alternative white rabbits," Hoover set out to steer the party back in the direction of his own definition of Republicanism. He was encouraged to find that "the audience is getting larger every day" for his public utterances;[4] and

he was convinced that his speeches were having a more powerful effect in
rallying Republicans than he had expected, despite the "smears" to which he
had been subjected by "Washington Republicans" for his "supposed ulterior
motives." Unimpressed by the level of courage being exhibited by Republicans
in Washington, Hoover concluded that there was nothing for him to do "but to
go on, simply because mine seems at the moment the only voice in the party
which carries nationally."[5] The "hurt surprise of the Old Guard and the
Republican Socialists that the newspapers would carry my governmental
views on the first page," he said, had led those elements of the party to indulge
unceasingly "in various kinds of political chatter, tender wishes, and abundant
smearing." One rumor being spread was that Hoover planned to make Ogden
Mills the 1936 GOP nominee. To Ashmun Brown, in the nation's capital,
Hoover wrote of such rumormongers:

> Have they not yet awakened to the fact that no New York and no
> Atlantic seaboard gentleman can be elected President on a Re-
> publican ticket? Would you not take it to yourself to whisper this
> important fact to them that Mr. Mills is not my candidate? In fact,
> he is not a candidate at all. Also suggest to them that I will be
> disposed to support some one, and if they know anything of present
> public opinion they would know that the man whom I do support
> will from that moment lead the race. It would be well that some of
> the eleven candidates now living in Washington were to be told this
> also.[6]

Even before his re-emergence into public life, Hoover had begun efforts to
chart the course of the Republican party for 1935–36. Early in January 1935
he suggested to Harrison Spangler that some constructive activity be inaugu-
rated to rebuild the GOP upon its midwestern foundation. In late January,
Spangler began to exert himself in this direction, with efforts that would
eventually lead to the calling of the midwestern Republican "grass-roots"
conference in June.[7] That Hoover was the moving force behind the conference, held in Springfield, Illinois, and other conferences held in various
regions of the country, seems clear.[8]

Hoover had definite ideas as to the form that the declaration of the midwest conference should take. In encouraging William Allen White to draft
such a declaration, he suggested that it should include: the assertion that the
depression was international in scope and a product of World War I; a statement that the nation had been on the road to recovery in 1932, but that
recovery had been aborted by the election of Roosevelt and the resultant bank
panic; "and a *detailed* blast of [sic] the New Deal actions—violation of the
constitution, including the Bill of Rights, NRA, AAA, relief, waste, politics

and corruption, failure to secure recovery, economy of scarcity, overwhelming expenditures, currency inflation, robbing bank deposits, ruin of foreign trade, violation of solemn promises." The declaration must point out, Hoover insisted, that the New Deal programs were leading "nowhere but to Fascism or Socialism." It must also imperatively state that the only real road to social and economic security lay in getting "people back to work on real jobs," in making them secure in their homes, savings, and other assets, and in preventing their governmental and private exploitation. "One thing is certain," he told White, "if we are to prevent the destruction of real Liberalism in the world we have to cry out and criticize the road we are traveling. We can at least create prejudice against practices which are driving us to the abysses with increasing speed. . . . The major word now is not 'plan,' but 'sanity.' "[9]

Despite urgings from Hoover, Spangler, Arthur Hyde, and others, White refused to draft a declaration of principles for the conference.[10] He explained to Frank Knox: "The Hoover people were particularly anxious for an indictment and I don't believe that we can win on an indictment." If the GOP did win on an indictment and without a constructive program, White feared it would simply mean "back to Coolidge," and he did not "want to go back to Coolidge."[11]

At the conference, held on June 10 and 11, Harrison Spangler, as temporary chairman, opened with an attack on the New Deal, which must have warmed Hoover's heart. Former Illinois governor Frank Lowden (the keynote speaker) and Kansas GOP chairman John Hamilton (chairman of the conference) followed with appeals for the defense of the Constitution. The platform of the conference was not, however, so forthright, being a mixture of attacks on the New Deal and tacit approval of some aspects of it.[12] Hoover sent a brief message to the conference and afterward pronounced it a "great success," but he cautioned that the device should not be used too often since its very novelty was what made it of such value.[13] The very discussion of the conference, he felt, would "keep the Republican lamp alight."[14]

While potential candidates for 1936 were not a topic for discussion at the midwestern conference, Hoover was told that he had "lots of friends and well-wishers among the delegates."[15] Buoyed by his contribution to the success of the midwestern conference, and by the response to his two public statements of early 1935, Hoover now began seriously to weigh the prospects of winning the Republican nomination in 1936. Dining with Hoover early in April, Edgar Rickard found him obviously exhilarated by his reappearance in the political arena and by the response to his statements. Rickard confided to his diary the hope that Hoover was not becoming too optimistic over the political trends, for he had no doubt that the "old guard" of the GOP would do all in its power to block his return to political leadership.[16] By June, however, it had become apparent to Rickard that Hoover wanted the 1936 nomination, even though he was unwilling to work openly to get it. Nor would Hoover give any open encouragement to the many who wanted to work in his behalf. Instead, in an attitude reminiscent of the strategy of his unsuccessful 1920 boom for the presidency, Hoover insisted that if his supporters felt strongly that he should be the nominee, it was up to them to create a movement for his nomination, for only if there was strong support manifested for him would he consent to carry the party's banner.[17]

Meanwhile, Hoover had resolved to keep up the attack. He was deriving, he told Chicago publisher Frank Knox, "a great deal of amusement out of the apoplexy of some of our Republicans in Washington whenever I move out of Palo Alto. It seems a pity that the Republican Party cannot show more cohesion. Nevertheless, they will have to suffer some more pains because I am going to have something further to say shortly."[18] He had resolved to "blast" the NRA and hoped that, at last, Republican officeholders would support his attack.[19] On May 15, in response to a press inquiry, Hoover reacted to House passage of an extension of the life of the NRA by calling upon the Senate to "abolish it entirely." He dismissed the entire code approach to regulation of business as "un-American in principle and a proved failure in practice." He charged the NRA with retarding recovery and acting as "a cloak for conspiracy against the public interest." Knowing that he would be pressed for an alternate policy, Hoover insisted that "the only substitute for an action that rests on definite and proved economic errors is to abandon it." The nation's economy could not be built "on a fundamental error."[20] A few days later he told the press that the use by the NRA of "bureaucratic coercion, intimidation and boycott are not American." He admitted that the NRA had accomplished some good in the area of minimum wages and hours, abolition of child labor, and the elimination of other unfair practices, but argued that "they should be accomplished by other than fascist methods if they are to be truly liberal and progressive."[21]

The response to his public comments from Republican newspapers and from rank and file members of the party convinced Hoover that "Republicans of the country are grateful for action on my part," despite the lack of support he received from the "Old Guard." He was getting "some constructive joy out of the doing, the grief of the opposition, and the silent tears of our machinest [sic] Republicans."[22] When shortly after his attacks on the NRA the Supreme Court found much of the NRA to be in violation of the Constitution, Hoover rejoiced that the decision had set the New Dealers "back a considerable distance"; but he was convinced that they would continue to pursue their goal by other means. That goal, as Hoover defined it, was "to make such fundamental shifts in the distribution of powers in our government as will enable them to establish their new system, whatever we call it, whether it is regimentation, national planning, fascism, or socialism." He saw no indication that Roosevelt had abandoned this goal, and concluded: "We have, therefore, before us the greatest struggle which we have seen in two generations."[23]

In the summer of 1935 a new star in the form of Alf Landon, was rising in the Republican party. Hoover's contacts with Governor Alf Landon of Kansas dated back to his presidency.[24] The two men occasionally corresponded with one another, and Landon expressed satisfaction with Hoover's attacks on the New Deal.[25] In 1935 Hoover invited the Kansan to be his guest at the annual summer Bohemian Club encampment in California. Landon at first accepted, but then, faced with labor difficulties in Kansas, was forced to cancel his visit.[26] Anxious that there should be no animosity between the two, William Allen White was careful to explain the reasons behind the cancellation, lest Hoover think that Landon was "sidestepping" the invitation.[27] White also sought to postpone any conflicts over the ambitions of the two men by suggesting to Hoover that Landon was not interested in the 1936 nomination, but instead was looking ahead to 1940.[28]

Meanwhile, Hoover strategists, including Walter Brown and Edgar Rickard were assessing the former president's prospects for gaining the 1936 nomination.[29] A major obstacle was Hoover's image as a "loser." As Frank Knox wrote one Hoover supporter, writer and former socialist John Spargo:

> In . . . the wide contacts which I have had recently with a great many of the active Republican leaders, I have found not one who was actively championing Hoover's nomination and almost invariably when the matter was discussed it was on the ground that to nominate Hoover would be unwise and inexpedient. Most of them, I should add, regard the feeling toward Mr. Hoover as utterly unjust and unwarranted, but nevertheless a very potent political fact that cannot be ignored.[30]

William Allen White lamented:

> This is a strange world in which we are living today, and one of the saddest and yet one of the most curious phenomenon is that the great mass of American people hold even after three years the rancor of 1932 which overcame Hoover. Nothing more terrible, more disheartening to our democratic ideals has ever happened in the history of this republic than this mob rage at an honest, earnest, courageous man. Yet it is here. It still hangs on. And everything he says, as well as everything his friends say, is discounted. It is unbelievable.[31]

Hoover's mail, and the newspaper editorials that his clipping service furnished him, revealed that the problem was not as great as White described it; but he did recognize that it existed. Part of it could be dealt with by the published account of the Hoover administration, which was being prepared by Walter Newton and William Starr Myers, and which Hoover regarded as a defense of his presidency.[32] Meanwhile, Rickard began efforts to woo back to the Hoover camp long-neglected associates from the old American Relief Administration and Food Administration days and to enlist engineers once again behind him.[33] Mailing lists were compiled for the distribution of *The Challenge to Liberty* and reprints of Hoover's articles and speeches.[34] By early October 1935 Rickard could record in his diary that Hoover was determined to recapture the presidency and was bending all of his efforts to that end.[35] However, he continued to refuse to seek the nomination openly.

Hoover's new public role as a leading critic of the New Deal, and his unwillingness to encourage a political movement in his own behalf confused many Hoover supporters who were unclear whether he sought to be king-maker or king. Whichever the choice, most agreed that Hoover could not wait until the Republican convention to act. Action would have to be taken soon, either to advance the candidacy of the man he favored for the nomination or to build his own campaign.[36] Others suggested that Hoover should forthrightly decline consideration for the nomination and then put all of his efforts into organizing opposition to the New Deal. From that point of stature Hoover could then "name the nominee" of the party in 1936.[37] Late in June 1935, D. M. Reynolds, the public relations man for Henry Robinson, who was a close Hoover friend and a financial backer of his political activities, suggested the course most suited to the former president's temperament: a repeat of the 1920 tactic of maintaining his availability for the nomination while not actively seeking it.[38] The tactic had not worked in 1920, but Hoover had not been a former president or titular head of his party in that year. Perhaps the tactic would work in 1936. Meanwhile, as letters came to Hoover expressing support for his nomination, they were forwarded to his "brains trust" with the suggestion that the writers be contacted and organized.[39]

While Hoover's intimates compiled mailing lists, distributed copies of his speeches and publications, arranged meetings for him, and sought to enlist new supporters under his banner, Hoover himself continued his public attacks on the New Deal and further aired his own philosophy. And his efforts seemed to have support among moviegoers, at least, for he continued to receive reports that his appearance in newsreels was receiving applause in the theaters.[40]

On October 5, 1935, Hoover lashed out at "spending, deficits, debts and their consequences" in a speech before the California Republican Assembly in Oakland and called upon Americans to "awake from the spell of hypnotic slogans." The issue in America, he declared, "is not a battle of phrases, but a battle between straight and crooked thinking." It was time for America "to return from muddling to sanity and reason." Common sense must be restored to the search for solutions to the nation's problems. By the test of common sense, the "gigantic spending" and "unbalanced budget" of the New Deal constituted "the most subtle and one of the most powerful dangers which has been set in motion by the administration."[41]

For those who had forgotten, Hoover recalled the Democratic promises of a balanced budget during the 1932 campaign and suggested that Roosevelt could not have won the election without such a promise. He lashed out at the waste in governmental expenditures and the great growth in the federal bureaucracy, the result of which was that "the Roosevelt administration is now clutched in the meshes of the gigantic spending bureaucracy which it has created." The enormous deficits must inevitably be paid by somebody, either through taxation, repudiation, or inflation. Americans already were taxed more heavily than anyone but the British. Repudiation or inflation would strike hard at every American. There was, in short, no way in which the American people could escape the consequences of the gigantic spending by the Roosevelt administration. "The folly and waste must be cut out of this expenditure and the Federal Budget balanced," Hoover declared, "or we shall see one of these three horsemen ravage the land—Taxation, or Repudiation, or Inflation." All aspects of the New Deal must be submitted to the test of common sense. Some would be found to be "of right objective and wrong method, such as the acts regulating securities, the old-age pensions, and unemployment insurance." Others would be found to be "destructive of every idea and aspiration of American life and will destroy the value of all the acts that are good—and more." But one test should be applied to all legislation: "Will these measures restore the prosperity of America? Will they restore agriculture? Will they give you real jobs instead of the dole? Will they make America a happier, a better place in which to live?"[42]

Many of Hoover's close friends refused to support his ambition for the 1936 nomination, which apparently hurt him deeply.[43] Others hoped he would not fight for the nomination, but out of loyalty to "the Chief" were willing to help him if he did so. H. Alexander Smith was one who counseled Hoover against becoming a candidate, writing him that "you should not be a candidate, because as I see it you can be of greater service to the party and to the country as a new leader of a very special kind in the period that lies ahead." Smith suggested that Hoover make a statement declining to accept the nomination even if it were tendered to him.[44] Hoover wrote Rickard that Smith's letter showed that Smith "must not participate in any action of our friends."[45] While much of the reluctance to see Hoover pursue the 1936 nomination doubtless stemmed from concern that the effort would be unsuccessful and "the Chief" would be hurt, Hoover refused to be deterred by such counsel and insisted that he wanted only the participation of those who were willing to give him their total support without any reservations.[46]

On November 16 Hoover addressed the Ohio Society dinner in New York City and took the occasion to follow up his October 5 attack on New Deal spending with one on the Roosevelt administration's economic planning. He divided opponents of New Deal planning into two categories: those who believed that it was "a deliberate plan for centralizing authority to a point where we the people can be made to do what starry-eyed young men in Washington think is good for us—whether it is good for us or not," and that the New Deal was only a cloak for the desire for power in the same sense that it had subverted liberty in Europe; and those who believed that the New Deal was an "attempt of a collegiate oligarchy to sanctify by a phrase a muddle of uncoordinated reckless adventures in government—flavored with unctuous claims to monopoly in devotion to their fellow men." These latter opponents held that New Deal planning possessed "neither philosophy nor consistency of action." Hoover's own view was that New Deal planning contained "any or all of these elements, depending upon which New Dealer is doing the Planning for the day."[47]

The only consistency that Hoover claimed to find in it all was that every bureaucracy created by the planners had "the habit of carefree scattering of public money" unfettered by the "old ghost of a balanced budget." He lashed out at the "planned scarcity" that planners had created "in the place of economic plenty, upon which America has grown great," and at the waste in federal administration of relief, as well as at the creation "of a great group of permanent dependents." The self-respect and responsibility of self-government were being destroyed, Hoover charged, by "turning the treasury into a national grab bag." The New Deal was not creating a more abundant life, but rather was raising the cost of living for all, eroding the purchasing power of wages, and creating strikes and class conflict. The intrusion of politics into the purchasing value of the dollar had led to a loss of confidence in it overseas and to a slowdown in recovery at home. Hoover told his listeners that he had come to the conclusion that

> a government should have in financial matters the same standards that an honorable man has. A government must realize that money must be earned before it is spent, that a nation's word in finance must be sacredly kept, that a nation is immoral if it repudiates its obligations or inflates its mediums of exchange or borrows without regard to posterity; and, finally, that a nation which violates these simple principles will, like a man, end in dishonor and disaster. A government cannot expect financial honor in its people unless it maintains honor itself. A large part of the world's misery in all ages has come from the acts of government that ignored these principles and entered upon policies of reckless spending and debasement and repudiation.

Hoover called for the abandonment of New Deal financial and fiscal policies, an end to unnecessary expenditures on public works, the return of relief responsibility to local authorities, an end to "spending for visionary and un-American experiments," reduction of the size of the bureaucracy, a balanced budget, the readoption of the gold standard, and an end to inflation of the currency, as well as other reforms.[48]

Ample provision had been made for distributing copies of the Ohio Society speech to all of the names on the Hoover mailing lists, and it attracted a good deal of attention. William Gross, editor of the *Fort Wayne News-Sentinel*, wrote Hoover to praise the speech and added: "If you can hold that same aggressively incisive, epigrammatic, hard-hitting, brass-tacks tone and tenor in succeeding addresses, you will not only be rendering a distinctly efficacious and patriotic service to the republic, but will also discover that (even if against your will) an increasing number of Americans will be committed to the proposition that you are the logical Republican standard bearer in 1936."[49] Hoover found that the reaction to the speech was "rather stupendous," and he decided to make two more speeches attacking other aspects of the New Deal.[50]

Though copies of Hoover's speeches were being disseminated by his campaigners through the mailing lists, these activities were inadequate to keep up with the demand. Even Charles Hilles, hardly a Hoover intimate, suggested to the GOP national committee that it print and distribute Hoover's speeches since there was such a call for them. GOP chairman Henry Fletcher had publicly commended Hoover's Ohio Society speech, and Hilles agreed that "it *was* an excellent speech and was most effective." Hoover was "doing a splendid service in debunking the New Deal," Hilles added, and the printing of his speeches by the national committee would be "a legitimate expenditure of the committee and will be invaluable in the preconvention campaign."[51] Walter Brown suggested that Hoover deliver another speech a few days before the December meeting of the GOP national committee, since it "would prove stimulating to the party leaders."[52]

Hoover's search for a topic for his next speech ended on November 29 when President Roosevelt responded to his critics with a speech in Atlanta, which the *New York Times* described as a comprehensive survey of his administration and especially of its fiscal affairs. Roosevelt argued that the "mechanics of civilization" had come to a "dead stop" by the day of his inauguration in March 1933, after spiraling ever downward from late 1929. Then, said Roosevelt, "America acted before it was too late, . . . we turned about and by a supreme, well-nigh unanimous national effort, started on the upward path again." Farm income, he claimed, had risen $3 billion since 1932, and this had contributed to "the rebirth of city business, the reopening of closed factories, the doubling of automobile production, the improvement of transportation and the giving of employment to millions of people." The worst of the depression had now passed. Revenues were increasing without new taxes, and expenditures were decreasing, so that the size of the national deficit would be reduced. The nation was in better condition now than in 1933. The national debt had only risen from the $21 billion when he came into office, to $29.5 billion now, and of the latter figure $1.5 billion was in the treasury and nearly $4.5 billion represented recoverable assets. In 1933, Roosevelt declared, the debt of Americans had exceeded the value of all the property they owned, but in 1935 property values had risen in relation to debt and America was in the "black." The quality of American life had improved in the past thirty months, Roosevelt concluded, and he was committed to further improvements.[53]

While Hoover was not mentioned by name, the speech was clearly a response to his attacks and, O'Laughlin wrote Hoover, "you should not fail to pick up the glove. . . . A situation has been created by Roosevelt where you and he are crossing swords; that is an excellent development."[54] Hoover agreed that he would "take the Atlanta speech for a trimming on December 16th at St. Louis."[55]

In his St. Louis speech Hoover noted that Roosevelt had made a sarcastic reference to his prediction during the depression that recovery was "just around the corner," Hoover responded in kind:

> There recently have been some premonitions of change. In that aspect I find a newspaper dispatch dated November 28 from Los Angeles. After announcing the naming of a new street as New Deal Avenue it says: "The new street is located near the Tugwell resettlement colony. . . . Because New Deal Avenue comes to a dead end the county supervisors will arrange ample room . . . to turn around.

Hoover sympathized, he said, with Roosevelt in his burdens and agreed with some of the actions of the Roosevelt administration, but disagreed with others "upon profound principles of human liberty." The conflict was between "the American system of liberty and New Deal collectivism." Three years of the New Deal had brought "the weakening of self-government by Federal centralization," "the abandonment of Congressional responsibility under Executive pressure," "executive orders, propaganda, and threats substituted for specific laws," "the color of despotism in the creation of a huge bureaucracy," "the color of Fascism in the attempt to impose government-directed monopolies," and "the color of Socialism by government in business competition with citizens." The government had repudiated its obligations and was "now speeding down the road of wasteful spending and debt, and unless we can escape we will be smashed in inflation."[56]

Hoover rebutted Roosevelt's assertion that the "mechanics of civilization" had come to a stop by March 3, 1933, arguing that the weeks before that date had seen "an induced hysteria of bank depositors" at the expense of a banking structure that was later proved to be largely sound. He then asserted again his contention that the depression had been turned in June and July of 1932 all over the world. That turn had been aided by the measures of Hoover's administration—measures which "were within the Constitution of the United States," and not the kind of "futile financial juggling which has violated economic law, morals, the Constitution, and the structure of American liberty," as under the New Deal. But after the 1932 election, he claimed, "we began a retreat." And only the United States had failed to continue the march upward. He added:

> We were the strongest and should have led the van. And we lagged behind for two years. The other countries of the world went forward without interruption. They adopted no New Deal. . . . It [the march upward] did not come to a stop even in the United States. It was meddled with. We have not got over it yet.

Why had the panic of bank depositors come in March of 1933? Hoover answered:

> Because they [the depositors] were scared. We had no bank panic from the crash of the boom in 1929. We had no panic at the financial collapse in Europe in 1931. We had no panic at the most dangerous point in the depression when our banks were weakest in the spring of 1932. There was no panic before the election of November 1932. When did they become frightened? They became scared a few weeks before the inauguration of the New Deal on March 4, 1933.

Obviously they had become frightened by the approach of the Roosevelt administration. Why? Because, Hoover argued, the people quickly awoke to the fact that the campaign pledges of the Democrats were going to be violated—that the gold standard would be abandoned, that the American currency would be tinkered with, and that "a wholesale orgy of spending of public money would be undertaken." Everyone sought to protect themselves. It was, Hoover declared, "the most political and the most unnecessary bank panic in all our history. It could have been prevented. It could have been cured by simple cooperation."[57]

Hoover then pointed out what he regarded as profound and misleading errors in Roosevelt's attempt to minimize the deficit of the New Deal. After defending his own administration's efforts to relieve the suffering of the depression, Hoover indicted the alphabet agencies of the New Deal, which he described as "a sort of rainmaker's cabalistic dance." He told his audience: "As each of these alphabetical organizations flares up in folly and waste its victims and its accounts have been buried by juggling of the alphabet. When they are all buried their spirit will live on as IOU." Nor did the urge to furnish employment seem to Hoover to be the primary motive behind many of the billions of dollars that were being poured into New Deal agencies. He charged:

> Part of these billions are going into wholesale sociological experi-
> ments. Most of them are already demonstrated failures. Part of these
> works are to take the government into business competition with the
> citizen. The government pays no taxes. The Treasury pays the
> losses. The constant threat of them retards enterprise and therefore
> jobs. One of the ideas in these spendings is to prime the economic
> pump. We might abandon this idea also for it dries up the well of
> enterprise.

But "the taxpayer had better not complain of these gigantic wastes. He will be told that he has murder in his heart through trying to starve his fellow citizens."[58]

Hoover also indicted the waste in relief, particularly the rise in overhead costs associated with the New Deal agencies. These costs alone, he concluded, amounted to "nearly one-half the whole cost of relief three years ago." And the great growth in the federal bureaucracy responsible for relief had not been through employment by the civil service, but through the spoils system, with those hired being chosen by Democratic politicians. He declared:

> The inevitable and driving purpose of any political bureaucracy is to
> use its powers to secure its jobs. The sudden appropriations to cities,
> counties, and states were singularly timed to elections. And this is
> not the only method of making politics out of human misery. Gover-
> nor [Al] Smith has said that nobody shoots Santa Claus. But the
> people may learn that there are other things moving around in the
> dark besides Santa Claus.

The administration of relief needed reform, and needed it immediately, not only in the interest of good government, but also "in the interest of the 85 percent of our citizens who have to pay for it" in one way or another. Hoover felt that wasteful federal public works projects should be terminated, and only those projects that met the needs of the nation should be continued; relief should be decentralized; the currency should be stabilized; and the budget should be balanced, so that the threat of inflation, which demoralized business and retarded recovery, could be eliminated and business could begin to provide productive jobs. "These people on relief have suffered enough from having playboys take America apart to see how the wheels go round," Hoover declared.[59] Thirty thousand copies of this speech were sent out to the Hoover mailing list.[60]

In his next speech, the fourth in the series he had planned, Hoover decided to attack New Deal agricultural policies, a course that many had been urging him to pursue for some time. As he wrote one correspondent: "I have the notion of taking up the whole agricultural question in the next address from some point in the midwest. A lot of people will not like it, but we have got to get this cadaver out on the table sometime, so we might as well begin the dissection now."[61] He thought it important "to get these things out in the open and force the hands of some of these pussyfooters."[62] Declining an invitation to spend some time sailfishing in Florida, Hoover regretted "enormously that I have to stick to my present task of inventing and delivering a blast against the New Deal about once a month."[63]

The agricultural speech was delivered in Lincoln, Nebraska, on January 16, 1936. Hoover began by acknowledging the existence of an agricultural problem that concerned the entire nation and that was still unresolved. The New Deal efforts to solve that problem had consisted, he charged, largely of attempts at "goosestepping the people under this pinkish banner of Planned Economy." "Step by step," Hoover told his audience, "the New Deal Agricultural Policies advanced from cajolery with a gentle rain of checks to open coercion. Men who planted on their own farms and sold in their own way . . . could have been sent to jail for doing just that. That is not liberty. That is collectivism." The emphasis on planned scarcity, the withdrawal of 50 million fertile acres from production, was not progress, which is based on producing more and more of varied things. The processing tax, levied to support the Agricultural Adjustment Administration (AAA), had been a burden on the homes of fifteen million workers and had "set boiling the witches' cauldron of class conflict of town against the farmers." The farmers' difficulties were a product of World War I, he observed, but when the world depression was "turned" in June and July of 1932, "agricultural prices arose in a start toward equality with industrial prices." That recovery, argued Hoover, had been retarded by the New Deal. The farmer would be especially hurt by higher taxes that must result from the torrent of government spending, unbalanced budgets, and debt under the New Deal, for the farmer "buys not alone for his family but also for his farm and is less able than any other production group to mark up the prices of his products and pass these taxes on to the consumer." The sum of the New Deal's agricultural policies was, said Hoover, "that the farmer has less to sell and pays more for what he buys. Labor pays for it in increased cost of living. By this device we have got the Economic Dog running around in circles chasing his tail." Exports of agricultural products had fallen, while imports of those products had risen. While American farmers were being discouraged from producing, the American market was being opened by reciprocity treaties to the farmers of foreign countries.[64]

After attacking the politics of the agricultural program, Hoover pointed out that the effect of the economy of scarcity and crop control had produced "a hideous poverty in the share croppers of the South." As alternatives to the waste and regimentation of the New Deal, he suggested increased consumption of food through the restoration of employment, which could come from a balanced budget, stable currency, and credit. The farmer should be allowed a monopoly of the home market and should be given assistance in exporting. Submarginal lands should be retired and cooperative marketing encouraged. Rather than paying farmers to curtail a particular crop, efforts should be made to help the farmer to develop another crop for which a market existed, or which would improve the fertility of the soil. "In order to secure these objectives," Hoover said, "I believe we must be prepared to subsidize directly such special crops until agriculture has again been brought into balance. At the end of such a road we could hope for a balanced agriculture in full production and increased fertility in our soils." By such devices farmers would not be regimented or controlled, and would be left entirely free to use their own skills and judgment. As for the administration of the special crop subsidies that he advocated, Hoover proposed that they be handled by the land-grant colleges and universities in order to free agriculture from politics. He added:

> Somebody will shy at the blunt word "subsidy." And, in fact, the American people have been going all around Robin Hood's barn, rather than use it. Over a century ago we began it in canals and turnpikes, since then we have kept it up. Railroads, highways, ships and aviation, and silver mines and land reclamation—agriculture— we usually do it under some other name than subsidy. We had better begin to use straight words and we will act straight. A subsidy is a burden on the taxpayer, but it does not regiment or destroy the initiative or freedom of the receiver—it is to stimulate that.

Under the present New Deal policies, the United States, Hoover concluded, was following "step by step the road through which . . . millions of people in foreign countries lost their liberties. . . . It was the farmers who fired the first shot at Lexington. It must be the farmers of America who defend that heritage. I ask you to stop, look, and listen."[65]

Privately, Hoover reiterated his belief that the solution to the agricultural problem did "not lie in taking the government entirely out of the field. We are already in it up to the eyes even outside of the AAA and agriculture is now sustained on the weakest props in the world and will require some kind of support during the intermediate period of transformation." What he strongly objected to, he repeated, was the "regimentation" of the New Deal approach to agriculture.[66]

In part because of the enthusiastic response to his agricultural speech, Hoover concluded early in 1936 that "the general tide is . . . running away from the New Deal."[67] In addition to a favorable reception of the speech by his audience, he found that the speech had attracted favorable editorial opinion throughout the nation. However, the speech received little support from Republicans in Washington, and of this Hoover wrote: "The only satisfaction I get out of the group of Republicans in Washington is that the country pays no attention to them."[68] He planned to continue to make speeches "about the middle of each month for awhile." The Republican old guard and the New Deal were united, he remarked, in their belief that his speeches were getting too much space in the newspapers and in their determination to spread the charge that the speeches were ghostwritten. Of this rumor, Hoover wrote: "I wish I could find a ghost of that sort. I could go fishing."[69] He was convinced that in addition to airing the issues his speeches would "force the candidates into the open when we can then form a better judgment as to their qualifications."[70] However, as Hoover clearly perceived, Roosevelt's personal image was a good deal more popular and stronger than his New Deal programs. It was an easy matter to attack those programs; but what was needed even more was to link the president with the programs, to drive home to the voters Roosevelt's responsibility for the New Deal.[71]

While Hoover unleashed his monthly attacks on the New Deal in late 1935, the campaign in behalf of his nomination was continuing. But the Hoover campaigners were finding much opposition to a Hoover nomination.[72] A part of the problem was the identification of Hoover in some minds with the "old guard" of the GOP. Hoover was aware of the necessity to somehow free himself of the image of "symbol of the Old Guard." As he wrote one friend:

> Some time some of our friends could help in this if they would get someone to stand up and say it. It would have to be someone whose voice would carry weight. To those of you who are familiar with the facts, that is not true. I have more occasion perhaps than any one of our friends to examine the public mind, and one thing appears clearer every day and that is the bitterness . . . does not exist so much in the people as it does in certain elements of business and this element perpetually fans it.[73]

Much of Hoover's time was spent in monitoring the progress of other potential Republican candidates and determining the highly fluid flow of support on the part of influential Republicans for those candidates.[74] By the end of 1935 it had become apparent that the leading possibilities for the nomination were Chicago newspaper publisher Frank Knox and Governor Alf Landon, with Senator William Borah a threat primarily because of his potential influence in driving the party in a more radical direction than was being preached from Palo Alto.[75] Hoover's own support did not seem promising. Even after his popular Lincoln, Nebraska, speech on agriculture, a poll of Nebraska farm voters showed Roosevelt the clear favorite for the presidency, with Hoover trailing both Landon and Borah among the Republican possibilities. Yet most of those responding to the poll simultaneously expressed disapproval of most aspects of the New Deal.[76]

Early in 1936, Landon emerged as the clear favorite for the GOP nomination. And those surrounding the Kansas governor continued to anger Hoover by their tactics. The former president wrote to Oklahoma newspaperman and Landon supporter Richard Lloyd Jones to complain of comments that Jones had reportedly made about him "and also some editorials from your paper which were circulated by the Landon group throughout the country." He objected to being used as "a whipping post" in order to gain support for other people. Three important questions were before the Republican party, he told Jones. The first was to make the American people "understand where this New Deal stuff is going to lead them." The second was "to set up a Republican Convention made up of men and women of such courage and independence of mind that they can establish the principles upon which this country can operate for the next twenty-five years," and not one made up of "third class politicians who are useful in carrying primaries and who will be traded about for purposes of selfish interest" as had been done in 1920.

> The third question is to find a man who has the guts to discharge 300,000 government officials, balance this budget within the first sixty days by whatever drastic means are necessary, and stabilize this currency; otherwise this democracy is going on the rocks through currency inflation. . . . By the time the new President has gotten through this initial program he will be as much disliked as any President who ever sat in the White House. But we have to find a man who has both the guts and the brains to bring this about.[77]

Although Hoover continued to disclaim any interest in the position, it is clear from his criteria that he viewed few others as possessed of the qualifications necessary.

William Randolph Hearst had swung the support of his newspapers behind Landon, a fact that was anathema to Hoover and other leading Republicans, such as William Allen White.[78] When the editor of the *Los Angeles Times* suggested to Hoover that it might be appropriate to publish a few articles on Hearst that would point out his reversals on various political candidates and issues in the past, Hoover responded that such an exposé would be "helpful, especially at the present time." Hoover believed that if the GOP press protested the Hearst-Landon association, especially in the midwest, "it might serve to bring Mr. Landon to a realization of where he is leading us."[79] Meanwhile, those who supported Hoover's renomination were growing restive at the absence of any apparent activity by those surrounding him. The former president's speeches, the distribution of those speeches and his publications, the writing of letters to newspaper editors by such supporters as former socialist John Spargo, and Hoover's meetings with dinner groups did not add up to an organized campaign. As one Hooverite expressed his concern:

> Various scattered people come in to see me or telephone to ask, "Isn't there something we can do about Hoover's nomination?" Were we in the open with an announced committee, a great deal of such support would evidence itself. If we don't have such a rallying point, the problem is how to bring out and evidence the support, and if we do not evidence it, how to convince the leaders that it exists. On the other hand, I fully appreciate the disadvantages of anything that looks like an organized movement. My mind is groping. We are restive at not coming out and doing something, but are doubtful what to do.[80]

Hoover apparently shared this concern, responding: "The main trouble with our army is that we have a great number of privates and officers, but as yet no general has emerged."[81] However, in January and February the Hoover "army" dispatched Arch Coleman for a swing through the southern states to develop delegate support there.[82]

On February 12, Hoover returned to the attack with a speech in response to Roosevelt's state of the union address. Recalling the president's inaugural statement that the only thing to fear was "fear itself," Hoover charged that the New Deal had, itself, been "a veritable fountain of fear," beginning with the period between the election and the inauguration. It was only "the Supreme Court decisions crashing through New Deal tyrannies which brought a gleam of confidence from the fears that had retarded recovery. The guiding spirit of the alphabet has not been love. It has been fear." He indicted such references by Roosevelt as that to "money-changers" as confusing the public and injecting class conflict. And he criticized again the growth of federal power through New Deal agencies, the coercive planning, and the massive spending and debt of the Roosevelt administration. In sum, this speech contained most of the points already expressed in Hoover's previous four major speeches on the New Deal. "Behind all this," he told his listeners, "is the great and fundamental conflict which has brought infinite confusion to the nation. That is a conflict between a philosophy of orderly individual liberty and a philosophy of government dictation," with the latter at odds with the Constitution of the United States.[83]

Two weeks later the inner circle of the Hoover campaign met at lunch in the offices of the banking firm of Kuhn, Loeb and Company in New York City. Present were banker Lewis Strauss, a veteran of Hoover's relief activities, as well as Edgar Rickard, Walter Brown, Larry Richey, and California oilman Bert Mattei. The latter reported failure in obtaining adequate funds to keep up the printing and distribution of Hoover's speeches. The GOP national committee had refused to help. All present agreed that Landon was in a strong position for the nomination, and Brown presented especially discouraging news from Ohio. A poll of 1,600 Republicans in that state had turned up only 4 percent support for Hoover as the nominee. Those at the meeting agreed that if the situation appeared hopeless as of May 1, Hoover should renounce any interest in the nomination and promise to back whichever candidate was selected.[84] Others, however, encouraged Hoover to fight to the end, believing that a deadlock would result and that the former president might emerge with the nomination. Even if he failed to win the nomination himself, his continued presence in the race must certainly exercise at least a strong influence in choosing the candidate.[85] Meanwhile, in Wisconsin a Hoover candidate entered the fight for election as a delegate to the Republican convention despite the former president's disapproval, and was soundly defeated.[86]

In March Hoover spoke before a meeting of Young Republicans in Colorado Springs. He began by reminding his listeners:

> The New Deal was not included in the Democratic platform of 1932. But the interpretation of political forces does not rest alone upon platforms. It rests also upon a knowledge of the motives and aims of men and the forces they represent. Eight days before that election I stated that the real intention of these men was to tinker with the currency. I said their program would raise government expenditures to nine billions a year. I said it was their intention to put the government into business. I said it was their intention to undermine State and local government by centralization in Washington. I said it was their intention to regiment our people and undermine the American System with imported European philosophies. That was all vociferously denied. All those interpretations have come true except as to that nine billion—it was only 95 percent correct.

Hoover deplored the degeneration in America toward personalized government at the expense of liberty, arguing that "almost every one of the world's mistakes had its origin in personal government. Violation of treaties, great wars, persecution of the Jews, and other religionists, and so on down to the fantastic laws by a Must Congress, and the slaughter of pigs."[87]

Young Americans, Hoover declared, should have the right to plan and live their lives as they chose, subject only to the limitation "that they shall not injure their neighbors." They should have the right to free and open competition with rewards to the winners, not to be "planed down to a pattern" by government. It was from such competition, he insisted, that there was produced "the national fiber of self-reliance and self-respect," which had made American greatness. The modern world required competent leadership, and such leadership could come only from "the ambition of free men and women against the polishing-wheels of competition. It comes in a system of rewards." It could not come from birth or wealth or be chosen by bureaucrats. To those who argued that individual liberty meant nothing to the poor or unemployed, Hoover responded that "it is alone through the creative impulses of free and confident spirits that redemption of their suffering must come. . . . Our job is not to pull down the great majority but to pull up those who lag behind."[88]

Hoover told his young audience that he saw three alternatives before America: unregulated business, government-regulated business, or government-dictated business. Government-regulated business he celebrated as the "American System." Government-dictated business was the New Deal way, and its "ideas are dipped from the cauldrons of European Fascism or Socialism." Unregulated business was unacceptable since "the vast tools of technology and mechanical power can be seized for purposes of oppression." In government-regulated business the government acted as "umpire," and regulation must be the least that would "preserve equality of opportunity and liberty itself." The major burden of such regulation, Hoover insisted, must fall upon state and local governments, and only when a problem was beyond their capabilities should it be undertaken by the federal government. Regulation should be by specific laws—"a government of laws and not of men." After indicting the planned economy of the New Deal in familiar terms, Hoover concluded his address by defining true liberalism as that which "seeks all legitimate freedom first, in the confident belief that without such freedom the pursuit of other blessings is in vain." It proceeded from "the deep realization that economic freedom cannot be sacrificed if political freedom is to be preserved."[89]

In late February Arch Coleman sent word from the south of some progress in recruiting delegates to the Republican convention who would "give the chief [Hoover] strong support if they get a chance."[90] Coleman noted considerable praise for Hoover's speeches and general agreement that Hoover had regained much of the ground lost in 1932; but Coleman also saw a widespread concern that, if Hoover were nominated, the campaign would turn into the mudslinging variety at which the Democrats had proven themselves so adept. Thus, despite a high regard for Hoover, the idea that he could not be elected was prevalent and deep-seated. Coleman concluded that if a move toward Hoover developed in the convention, many of the southern delegates would follow it "joyfully," but he saw no likelihood that the southern delegations would initiate such a movement.[91]

In mid-March, Edgar Rickard found Hoover gloomy as to his chances for the nomination. He was convinced that Roosevelt had gained in strength since the first of the year, so that the GOP nomination seemed of dubious value in any case, and he talked now of dropping entirely out of the picture. That evening a number of intimates met with Hoover and discussed conducting a poll to assess his strength.[92] Other supporters suggested that the time had come to attempt to build a movement behind his nomination, but one that would be "entirely divorced from you [Hoover] or any of your recognized political supporters." Walter Newton thought that there must be a number of business-men who would want to get behind such a movement, and he suggested that it was not "too early to get the lines formed and the organization under way."[93]

All of the talk, however, did not conceal the fact that there was very little action, and it was apparent that Hoover's drive for the nomination was limp-ing badly, despite his emergence as the leading Republican critic of the New Deal. At the same time, the campaign of Governor Alf Landon was gathering momentum. Typical of the comparisons made between Hoover and Landon was that by Senator Arthur Vandenberg, himself a Republican hopeful, who was impressed with the former president's ability but did not think that he could be elected. On the other hand, he believed that "Governor Landon is a newcomer but the fact remains that he has caught the public imagination." Vandenberg continued: "Even more important to my mind is the fact that everyone who meets him comes away impressed with his sincerity and his courage. I know of no exception to this."[94]

Hoover's nomination was even confronted with a Landon challenge in his home state of California. An uncommitted slate of delegates had been fash-ioned there, with Hoover's approval, and it included delegate-candidates who were favorable to a variety of potential nominees or to none at all. A Landon-for-President organization was active in California, but the impetus for the Landon challenge in the state came not from Landon or his group, but from California Governor Frank Merriam and newspaper publisher William Ran-dolph Hearst. A rival slate of Landon delegates was put up by Merriam and Hearst to contest the unpledged slate.[95] This was done despite the fact that Landon's California managers had promised that he would not contest for the state's delegates and over the opposition of the California Landon-for-President organization. Hoover, who was in New York at the time, made several telephone calls each day to California to monitor the situation.[96] When Landon refused to repudiate the Merriam-Hearst movement, Hoover resolved to return to California to fight for the unpledged slate in the primary. The feeling in the Hoover camp was that if Hearst succeeded in putting Landon over in Hoover's home state, the game would be up for Hoover's nomination hopes; but if Hoover could carry the unpledged delegation through against the Landon challenge, his own campaign would be very much ahead. Hoover's spirits were cheered by the prospect of the battle.[97]

Meanwhile, the former president had scheduled a speech at Fort Wayne, Indiana, on April 4, in which he planned to draw some comparisons between his administration and the New Deal. Much of the speech followed familiar ground, but then Hoover warmed to his work. After blaming Roosevelt for the bank panic because of his failure to cooperate with the outgoing administration, Hoover observed that Roosevelt's campaign for election in 1932 had been based "upon the implication that the depression was caused by me personally," and "continuously, day in and day out, before and even since the inauguration, and in the evening by the fireside, Mr. Roosevelt has condemned with great bitterness the policies and methods of the last Republican Administration." The "saddest blow of all," Hoover told his listeners, was that "certain New Dealers now arise and say that I was the father of the New Deal." And he admitted that: "Omitting their monetary and spending debauch, about all the agencies they will have left after the Supreme Court finishes cleaning up their unconstitutional actions will be the institutions and ideas they got from the Republican Administration." It was only fair to ask now, he said, after three years of the New Deal, whether Roosevelt had lived up to his promises and solved "our great national problems?" Hoover's answer was in the negative. The Roosevelt administration had not only failed to keep its promises, but it had not even done as well in solving the depression as Hoover's own administration. He would, Hoover said,

> be glad if the thinking American people would soberly consider if the Republican Elephant, even though he has made mistakes, is not more surefooted toward recovery and progress than the bounding white rabbits of the New Deal. I recommend that magician's animal as the symbol of the New Deal party. It travels in uncertain directions at high speed. It multiplies rapidly.[98]

Confronted with reports of increased headway being made nationally by the Landon campaign, Hoover recognized that the only hope of keeping his own prospects alive was to deal the Kansan a symbolic defeat in California.[99] Late in March, one Hoover supporter began a poll among the 31,087 names in *Who's Who in America*. [100] It was another tactic reminiscent of the unsuccessful 1920 campaign, and its results were sure to be as unreflecting in 1936 of sentiment among the general public as it had been on the earlier occasion. In mid-April the first returns showed Hoover and Landon running approximately even. However, another poll, by the regular Republican organization on Staten Island, showed Landon as first choice and ahead of Hoover by nearly a three to one margin, with the former president second among the first choices, but well down the list of second choices.[101] The results of the *Who's Who* poll among the "thinking" people, with whom Hoover thought he had the strongest appeal, was especially disheartening for Hoover, who concluded that "we had better hold up [releasing] the results of these polls until after the California primary."[102] Pessimistic now, in early May Hoover wrote John Spargo that he believed "the Republicans have determined upon new faces."[103]

Distressed not only at the sorry state of his own campaign, but also by a feeling that Republicans had generally lost ground, Hoover resolved to go back on the stump.[104] He had decided to deliver yet another speech, during May in Philadelphia, before the Republican convention.[105] He anticipated that this would be his last public address, since the "affront which Mr. Hearst and Governor Landon cooked up against me in this state [California] means that Governor Landon does not wish my assistance even if he is nominated." Since this might well be his last speech, Hoover proposed "to say my say on what this Republican Party ought to stand for."[106]

While the results of the *Who's Who* poll continued to show Landon and Hoover running almost even, Walter Brown suggested yet another poll designed to confront head-on the widely held assumption that the former president, even if nominated, could not win the election. The proposed poll would first query voters on their choice in the 1932 election, and then ask who they would vote for in 1936 if given the same choice. Alan Fox offered to try out such a poll "tentatively in a small way immediately," and then undertake it on a larger scale throughout the state of New York, sampling some 200,000 names.[107] Hoover delayed any consideration of the idea until after the California primary.[108] Fox was convinced that a satisfactory response on the poll could have an important effect in leading newspapers to take up discussion of a possible Hoover "draft."[109] The optimism in the Hoover camp increased when on May 5 the Landon slate of delegates in California went down to defeat before the uninstructed delegation backed by Hoover. The victory over Landon was perceived, by Hoover's supporters at least, as keeping him in the thick of the race for the nomination.[110]

Elated by the California result, Hoover nine days later delivered his "final" speech in Philadelphia. In this speech he set forth his concept of a proper Republican alternative to the New Deal. The GOP convention would assemble in a few weeks, he pointed out, and the Republican party was "the only available instrumentality through which an aroused people can act," because the Democratic party was "imprisoned by the New Deal." Disaffected Democrats should join with Republicans in putting "the republic on the road to safety." The Republican platform must be more than a party platform, it "must be a platform for the American people." The trend in America toward "personal government based upon collectivist theories" must be halted. The "five horsemen" of the New Deal Apocalypse—"Profligacy, Propaganda, Patronage, Politics, and Power"—or "Pork-barrel, Poppy-cock, Privileges, Panaceas, and Poverty"—must be reversed. The Republicans should pledge themselves to "reverse the whole New Deal planned scarcity into an economy of plenty" and to support a "constantly wider diffusion of property." The federal government should be restored to the role of umpire in its relations with business. The GOP should pledge its support for the abolition of child labor, the inauguration of old-age pensions, and provision of better housing. There must be moral regeneration in government and the elimination of the New Deal's emphasis on the spoils system. Trust in the federal government must be restored, especially faith in the government's financial policies.[111]

In the remaining weeks before the Republican convention Hoover alternated between buoyancy and pessimism. He regarded the primary election result in California as a repudiation of the efforts of his enemies to put an end to his public career.[112] But talks with Republican leaders could easily convince him that the Landon bandwagon was unstoppable and that his own public career was at an end.[113] Hoover obviously still hoped for a deadlock in the convention that would result in his renomination. Privy to the former president's desire, one correspondent extended to him his "best wishes to you for an intelligent outcome of the convention at Cleveland. I appreciate that your position is that they should wake up and ask you to lead them, but I am fearful of the lack of intelligence of selfish leaders leading helpless delegates."[114] As part of Hoover's strategy for creating a deadlock he apparently gave encouragement to Frank Knox's candidacy, leading the Chicago publisher to believe that he would swing the California delegation behind him.[115] According to an unpublished draft of Hoover's memoirs, the decision to encourage Knox resulted from a phone call from Harrison Spangler, a month before the convention, in which the Iowa GOP committeeman reported "that he had attended a meeting of prominent New York and Pennsylvania industrialists and bankers who had decided to support Landon" because they considered him "the best weapon against the New Deal." Spangler was disturbed at Landon's lack of qualifications for the presidency and asked Hoover to declare himself a candidate "to off-set this influence which he believed otherwise would be final with the Pennsylvania, New York, New Jersey and Delaware delegations." Hoover refused, but promised that he "would give what help [he] could to Frank Knox who seemed better fitted to make the fight."[116]

On May 18, nearly a month before the convention, Hoover took himself out of the active pursuit of the nomination by issuing a statement to the press.

> It should be evident by this time that I am not a candidate. I have stated many times that I have no interest but to get these critical issues before the country. I have rigidly prevented my friends from setting up any organization and from presenting my name in any state convention and so not a single delegate from California or any other state is pledged to me. That should end such discussion and get one thing straight, I am not opposing any of the candidates. My concern is with principles. The convention will be composed of a most unusual and able personnel. The seriousness of the convention is evidenced by the fact that the large majority of the delegates are being sent by the people of the states without other instructions than to find the right thing to do for our country in the greatest crisis we have met in two generations.[117]

Hoover later explained that he had made the statement "just to keep in line with the realities of the situation. The politicians in this country still run it." However, despite his disclaimer, efforts were still under way to influence the delegates in Hoover's behalf.[118]

The former president was determined that he would not go to the convention unless, as he put it, "I could go under proper auspices, as I do not want to be a hanger-on in that situation." Walter Brown and others were endeavoring, he reported, "to do something about it."[119] Specifically, Hoover hoped to be invited by the committee on arrangements to make a speech before the convention. But, he recorded in the unpublished draft of his memoirs, the idea "was violently opposed by the Old Guard of Watson, Martin, Fletcher, Pew, Vandenberg and company." Brown and other Hoover friends, however, won out, and the invitation was extended. Hoover later recalled that "the Convention managers tried to arrange my address on an afternoon when, due to Committee sessions, few would be present and the radio audience at its lowest." Hoover, however, refused to agree to the time, and his speech was scheduled for an evening hour.[120]

As he prepared to leave for the convention, Hoover still felt that it was impossible to "tell at this time just what is going to happen."[121] Some, like O'Laughlin, still harbored hopes for a Hoover nomination. In fact, he thought the former president was "in an exceptionally strong position." Although Hoover had no officially pledged delegates, O'Laughlin assumed that he could have the support of the California delegation and could also rely on other delegates from the western states, as well as some from the East. The Hoover campaigners, he told General Douglas MacArthur, were trying for a deadlock and, if successful, they expected the convention to try each of the possible candidates in turn. If none managed to attract the majority required, then Hoover was likely to be nominated. The strategy called for Landon, the front-runner, to be deadlocked through the third or fourth ballot, whereupon it was expected that his support would melt away.[122] To aid the effort, O'Laughlin sent Hoover detailed suggestions on how to handle his speech before the convention in order that he might "play upon the emotions" of the delegates. He had in mind, O'Laughlin said, a speech "along the lines of the liberty or death oration of Patrick Henry."[123]

In Cleveland with Hoover for the convention, Edgar Rickard thought he found little genuine enthusiasm for Landon. Many, he concluded, would have welcomed a contest if it were not already too late. The first note of enthusiasm he detected from the delegates was when the keynote speaker, Senator Frederick Steiwer, attacked Roosevelt for failing to cooperate with Hoover during the "interregnum." Throughout the evening and late into the night before the former president's arrival in Cleveland, a sound truck traveled the streets publicizing the time of his train's arrival. When he reached the railroad station at 9:30 A.M., he was greeted by a crowd estimated by Rickard, perhaps optimistically, at eight thousand. According to Rickard's diary, Hoover was visited during the day time on June 10 by representatives of Borah, Knox, and Vandenberg who urged him to join in a stop-Landon movement, but he refused.[124] At 8:30 that evening, Hoover appeared on the platform of the convention for his speech and was greeted by a wildly enthusiastic demonstration.[125]

Hoover's speech began by asserting that in the convention hall rested "the greatest responsibility that has come to a body of Americans in three generations." That responsibility was "to determine the fate of those ideals for which this nation was founded," and it transcended "all partisanship." Hoover took his audience through a survey of the New Deal and gave his conclusion of it:

> The New Deal may be a revolutionary design to replace the American System with despotism. It may be the dream stuff of a false liberalism. It may be the valor of muddle. Their relationship to each other, however, is exactly the sistership of the witches who brewed the cauldron of powerful trouble for Macbeth. Their product is the poisoning of Americanism.

The New Deal had failed, and it was now up to the Republican party "to set the country on the road of genuine recovery from the paths of instability." American freedoms must also be regenerated. The search for freedom had been man's eternal quest. The unborn generations must not be condemned to "fight again and to die for the right to be free." The principles of freedom must not be compromised. The Whig party had temporized and compromised over the issue of slavery for black people, and it had disappeared. The Republican party would deserve the same fate, Hoover declared, if it now compromised "upon the issue for all men, white as well as black." And then came the attempt at a Patrick Henry–like finish:

> Republicans and fellow Americans! This is your call. Stop the retreat. In the chaos of doubt, confusion, and fear, yours is the task to command. Stop the retreat, and turning the eyes of your fellow Americans to the sunlight of freedom, lead the attack to retake, recapture, and reman the citadels of liberty. Thus can America be preserved. Thus can the peace, plenty, and security be re-established and expanded. Thus can the opportunity, the inheritance, and the spiritual force of your children be guaranteed. And thus you will win the gratitude of posterity, and the blessing of Almighty God.[126]

Hoover's speech was followed by another enthusiastic demonstration and repeated cries of "We want Hoover!" Efforts to gavel the demonstration to silence and bring on the next speaker were fruitless. Even the announcement that Hoover had left the hall and was returning to New York failed to still the boisterous demonstrators. The convention had to be adjourned until the following day.

Citing a letter from Chester Rowell, a longtime Hoover friend and supporter, to his niece, historian George Mayer has written: "Misconceiving the demonstration as the prelude to a stampede, [Hoover] tried to bring it to a head by persuading Permanent Chairman Bertram Snell of New York to announce that he was leaving for New York."[127] But Rowell's letter does not support such a conclusion. His letter states: "The announcement from the stage was that he was already in the train and so could not come back, as the crowd was demanding. This was at his request. He was determined not to stage a scene which would look like a personal bid for himself. Who else in America would have done that, with the Presidency the prize? "[128] Mayer then writes, still citing the Rowell letter, that Hoover "returned to his hotel room and contacted Vandenberg and Knox," with Chester Rowell as the intermediary.[129] But again, the Rowell letter is at variance with Mayer's statement. According to Rowell: "Knox and Vandenberg finally—but far too late, reached the conclusion that they must make common cause or none. After the tremendous demonstration for Hoover . . . they got together and concluded to pass the buck to him."[130] Mayer infers that Hoover had contacted the two candidates in an effort to seek the nomination for himself.[131] But according to Rowell's letter, the negotiations were initiated by Knox and Vandenberg for the purpose of blocking Landon. Says Rowell: "They wanted him to announce that he was not a candidate and would not take the nomination, but that, as the titular head of the party, he proclaimed that Landon was not a fit candidate, and that the convention should resolve itself into a deliberate body to consider someone else—meaning themselves."[132]

According to the Rowell letter, Hoover's response was that

> he had not a single delegate in the convention to deliver—nothing but a situation, if tonight's demonstration constituted a situation. If they thought that a solution, he could not be the one to propose it, and it was for them to decide whether they cared to do so. He was not asking them to do it. They said they could not deliver their own delegates, but that they could deliver Borah for a joint anti-Landon statement (for their own benefit of course) if Hoover would make it. He said that, even if he made it, probably Landon would be nominated anyway, as both of them had already shot their bolt. Then he, as the former President, who had just reminded the party of its great mission, would have been the one who disrupted that party and prevented it from carrying out that mission.[133]

What Mayer has described as "Hoover's hint of availability," thus came only in response to the proposal by Knox and Vandenberg of a course of action by the former president that would have served their interests at the expense of Republican unity. Hoover desired the nomination—of that there is no doubt—but unlike Knox and Vandenberg he was not willing to risk disrupting the party's unity to get it.

Rowell's letter gives further testimony to the limits beyond which Hoover was unwilling to go in advancing his own political fortunes. Rowell had in his possession material that, he thought, "sprung at the right time, would have made [Landon's] nomination impossible, and which, sprung now, would make his election impossible." But Rowell had concluded that the material should not be released, even though he considered that he was doing "a very great disservice to my own honor, in concealing from the American people this information which it ought to be their right to know." When he counseled with Hoover, he found the former president in agreement that the material ought not to be made public.[134]

The nomination the next day was a cut-and-dried affair. In Rickard's view, however, the Hoover hopes for a deadlock and ultimate nomination might still have succeeded had it not been for the actions of his former secretary of the treasury, Ogden Mills. Some in the New York delegation had sought to postpone their caucus until after Hoover's speech. In Rickard's view, if the New York delegation had remained uncommitted to that point, it might have started a bandwagon for the former president after the speech. However, Mills had blocked the effort to postpone the caucus. It had been held before Hoover's speech, and the New York delegation was already committed by that caucus to deliver its votes to Landon on the first ballot when Hoover spoke. Rickard still hoped for a miracle as the balloting began, but it was a day without miracles. Landon was nominated, and Frank Knox was chosen as his running mate.[135] Although he attained second spot on the ticket, Knox apparently never forgave what he regarded as Hoover's "double cross" of his own attempt at the nomination.[136]

Despite Hoover's refusal to join with Knox and the others in a "stop Landon" effort, Drew Pearson and Robert Allen charged in their newspaper column that he had participated in such an effort. Hoover responded angrily in denying the charge to William Allen White:

> I just want you to know that a story put out by that scum of Washington, Allen and Pearson, as to my participating in a "stop Landon" movement at Cleveland has no truth except that some (no doubt unauthorized) fixers approached some of my friends with such ideas which I promptly directed these friends to turn down. I refused to see any of the fixers or any of the candidates. Any such action would have torn the party to shreds and I wished no part of it.[137]

Perhaps he also considered it in the interest of party unity not to mention the efforts of Knox and Vandenberg to enlist him in just such a movement.

Hoover was not pleased with Landon's nomination. At this point in the Kansan's political career, Hoover felt that he lacked adequate experience in the national and foreign fields to hold the office for which he had been nominated.[138] He also worried over the direction that Landon and his followers would lead the Republican party, fearing that they were out to reconstruct the party entirely, and in a way that would be contrary to Hoover's own ideals for the GOP. As part of his effort to block any such designs, Hoover sought to exert influence on the writing of the party platform, particularly insisting on an expression of support for the gold standard and a stable currency.[139] Responding to a request for his views on the currency plank in the platform, Hoover wired Chester Rowell on June 11 that the course for the GOP to pursue was: "(A) Repeal all Presidential powers over currency. (B) Guarantee that there will be no further devaluation. (C) Seek international agreement to stabilize currencies. (D) Resolute determination to restore gold convertibility of the currency either in coin or bullion . . . at the earliest practicable moment."[140] When Borah managed to prevent any mention of gold in the platform, Hoover insisted that he would not support the ticket unless it was included. The issue was settled when Landon wired his campaign chairman, John D. M. Hamilton, an interpretation of the platform to be read to the delegates, in which he interpreted the platform reference to "sound money" as meaning "a currency expressed in terms of gold and convertible into gold."[141]

Hoover received wide acclaim for his speech at the convention, and his supporters were pleased at the reception he had received from the delegates. One correspondent wired him:

> Revenge is sweet. Vindication complete. Public acclaim almost overwhelming. Best of all, your course of the last three years has been so wise, you are today, as formerly, our leading citizen, and more needed for the next few years than ever before. You will not be found wanting. You have led your party, kept the opposition guessing and last night you completed the cementing of all factions in our drive for victory.[142]

But despite the praise for his speech, and his success in helping to commit the candidate to the gold standard, Hoover was certain that he was out of step with the new faces of the Kansas group, and that they had no room for him in their councils. He resolved to help the nominee in the campaign only if Landon appealed for his assistance. Meanwhile, Hoover continued to seek to bolster his own image by having his speeches, including the convention address, printed and distributed in large numbers. If Hoover was no longer the titular leader of the Republican party, he obviously intended to continue as its conscience.[143] Some suggested that his speech and reception at the convention had laid the groundwork for another try in 1940. One Hoover enthusiast wrote: "1940 will arrive soon, and there will only be the necessity of picking out a vice presidential candidate to run with Mr. Hoover."[144]

Despite indirect feelers that he put out to the Landon camp, there came no requests either from Topeka or the GOP national committee for his assistance during the next few months, and whatever his intentions, Hoover was out of public life until the latter stages of the campaign.[145] He felt that the "drive of the Kansas group against all men formerly associated with us, and their junction with the real 'Old Guard,' of course, makes our ability to help somewhat complicated."[146] According to one Hoover intimate who had talked with Landon, the nominee was confident that he would attract the votes of all those who supported the former president, without Hoover's help. Apparently, Landon was reluctant to request Hoover's help, because the identification of his campaign with Hoover's presidency might drive away other voters who had been led by the Democrats to link Hoover with the cause of the depression. Hoover told John Hamilton, Landon's chairman of the GOP national committee, that he was willing to help in the campaign, but that the request must come from Landon himself.[147] Two weeks after the convention, Hoover wrote:

> The press has been most eulogistic in their obituaries over my politi-
> cal funeral. As a last flower on the grave, they have unanimously
> elected me Elder Statesman. I am considering accepting—and orga-
> nizing up the job. It has the possibility of surprise, humor, tribula-
> tion for evil doers, and pushing the weak onto the paths of
> rectitude.[148]

If he made the elder statesmanship into a "live, militant job," it "would surely chagrin the funeral directors and it might be made of some service to the American people."[149]

While Hoover was not asked to participate in the campaign during the summer months, he did attempt to bring about a defense of his administration by other Republicans in response to the continuing Democratic campaign attacks upon it. As he wrote to GOP chairman Hamilton late in June, it was obvious that the Democrats intended to campaign on the bank panic of March 1933, claiming that they had brought recovery. There would, he admitted, be no advantage in attacking the "recovery" as illusory since the people preferred to believe that it was real. Hoover suggested, therefore, that the "most effective Republican attack" would be to point out that recovery from the depression had begun during his own administration, and that the bank panic had resulted from "fear of the New Deal and their deliberate violation of their platform promises beginning immediately after the election."[150] Only if such groundwork were laid by the party, Hoover said, could he be of effective assistance in the campaign.[151] To Arch Shaw in Chicago, Hoover wrote: "I think that we have to keep forcing the hands of the Republican organization on this question of putting the last administration in the right light."[152]

Hamilton was conciliatory and quickly took up Hoover's point of attack in a speech in Chicago on July 2, while promising that he would continue to weave the theme into other speeches during the campaign.[153] Hoover was glad to see that Hamilton had "made a start."[154] But some Hoover supporters viewed Hamilton's speech as only a sop to satisfy him, rather than an indication that defense of the Hoover administration had become Republican strategy in the campaign.[155] Hoover agreed that this was probably true and would doubtless remain true as long as the Republican team thought that it was winning. However, "if at any moment they have a sinking spell, they will be crying for help."[156] He wrote Arthur Hyde:

> John Hamilton did not make any complete defense of my admin-
> istration. He made an attack on Mr. Roosevelt for not having coop-
> erated after the election. He did not even say that we had gotten
> recovery on the way before the election. However, I am not expect-
> ing very much these days. . . . What I am waiting for is for Governor

Landon himself to state the concrete fact that the depression was overcome in the last administration, that we were on our way, that the rest of the world was on its way, then we alone slipped back because of Mr. Roosevelt, that the increase of national debt during my administration was only 1,100,000,000 [dollars] after deducting the recoverable loans, and a few other tangible facts of this character; and with the addition of the fact that the greatest economic battle in the history of the world was fought and successfully won by our administration, and I don't expect that either, although it would be the truth and would be both grace and good politics on his part.[157]

Republicans friendly to both Hoover and Landon sought some basis for a compromise under which the former president would participate in the campaign. According to Charles P. Taft, in the Landon camp, the difficulty there resulted from the nominee's conviction that Hoover had tried to swing the Cleveland convention behind his own nomination, and that Hoover's people "certainly tried to get the Anti-Landon group to agree on him." As a consequence, Landon did "not feel enthusiastic about begging Mr. Hoover to help and Mr. Hoover on the other hand, as the only ex-President, thinks the approach should come from this end." Taft was at a loss over the impasse and asked his nephew Robert A. Taft for suggestions.[158]

Robert Taft, who had served with Hoover in the Food Administration and in the American Relief Administration (ARA) in Europe after World War I, agreed that his former boss had probably sought the nomination in Cleveland "and therefore was not particularly friendly to the man who was out in front." He had seen no evidence, however, of an organized campaign on the part of Hoover or anyone around him to derail Landon at the convention. As for Hoover's insistence on a defense of his administration, Taft wrote:

I agree with you that the Hoover position on the bank panic is extreme, but I hardly think it would be necessary for Landon to agree with him on that question. I do not think it would hurt Landon to refer to Hoover's fight against the depression, in friendly terms, and invite him, without begging, to speak during the campaign.[159]

By early August the nominee was making friendly overtures designed to bridge any animosities between himself and Hoover. On August 7 he sent Hoover an appreciative note concerning a statement that the former president had made about the improvement that could be expected in the unemployment problem with the election of a Republican president. Landon told Hoover: "I would appreciate your views as the campaign progresses, and I sincerely thank you for the help you already have so generously and effectively given."[160]

In mid-August, GOP chairman Hamilton began to urge Hoover to get into the campaign. After a meeting with Hamilton on the fourteenth, the former president confided that he had responded by asking the GOP chairman "to secure from Governor Landon a telegram inviting me to do so." He added:

> The time has arrived to have a showdown over all this gossip as to whether I am a liability to Governor Landon or not. I informed Hamilton that if I did not receive the telegram, form of which I gave him, I would take it that they did not want me in this campaign; that I prefer to stay out of it, that I would make no difficulties for them whatever, but that I was getting completely fed-up with the constant gossip that comes out of Topeka.[161]

Hamilton had asked for several speeches from him, and Hoover was convinced that Hamilton, at least, "was most desirous of major activity from myself in the campaign as he delivered many reasons for so doing."[162] For his part, Hoover yearned to go on the stump against Roosevelt. He regarded Roosevelt's acceptance speech to the Democratic convention as a reply to his own speech before the Cleveland convention, and he was anxious to devote himself "at least for one address to tearing that acceptance speech into small pieces."[163]

Finally, on September 2, Hoover and Landon found themselves on the telephone together, though it is not clear who placed the call, and the nominee asked for Hoover's assistance in the campaign, especially "in October when the fighting gets hard on the home stretch." According to Hoover's transcript of the telephone conversation, Landon agreed to make a public announcement of his request "when the time comes." The two also agreed that Hoover would stop off in Topeka to discuss the campaign with the nominee on his return from a trip he was making to New York.[164] After the telephone conversation, Hoover wrote Landon:

> I beg to confirm my answer to your telephone message of today that you urgently want my help and activity in this campaign. I shall be glad to help. Somewhere along the line I shall take occasion to indicate that you have made such a request as certain members of the Republican Publicity organization are giving a contrary color and are damaging the party and your interests. I will take up the question of visiting Topeka when I pass through Chicago on my way to New York.[165]

The atmosphere between the two men, as is evident from Hoover's letter, was distinctly not cordial.[166] The former president was greatly disappointed that he had not been given a greater role in the campaign. According to his information, Landon had been continually pressed to get in touch with him and had drafted at least eleven letters for that purpose, but had discarded them all before the telephone call. Hoover was convinced that the people around the nominee were determined that Landon should do nothing that would associate him with Hoover or the Hoover administration. Dispirited by his inactivity and his isolation in California, Hoover now resolved to move permanently to the East Coast after the election was over. He also hoped to visit Europe, making a triumphal tour through the countries that had benefited from his relief operations after World War I, and then return to the United States to be accepted as the elder statesman of the Republican party.[167]

Late in September, Walter Newton reported to Hoover on the results of a campaign swing by the nominee through Iowa and Minnesota and on his own conversation with Landon and his lieutenants. Newton found concern expressed by the Landon camp that Hoover was not actively involving himself in the campaign. Newton then reiterated for Landon the views of Hoover and pointed out that if he was not in the campaign it was their own fault. Newton emphasized the kind of hard-hitting speeches that Hoover could make, citing his preconvention attacks on the New Deal as examples; he told the Landon group that Hoover must be in the campaign, and if he were not, "they alone would be to blame."[168] Two days later Hoover was informed that Landon wished him to deliver his first speech in Philadelphia on October 16. Hoover was elated at the news.[169]

On October 1, Hoover traveled to visit the candidate in Topeka. Donald R. McCoy has written: "Whether political boon or boomerang, Hoover's visit was a bother to Landon."[170] After a discussion of the campaign, Landon and Hoover were entertained at a chicken dinner by newsmen and listened to a radio speech by Roosevelt. Hoover punctuated the president's speech with loud booing, much to the embarrassment of Landon and the newsmen present, which led the nominee to take early leave for the railroad station with his guest.[171] For his part, Hoover came away from his meeting with Landon convinced that the nominee was but little versed in either American political history or foreign affairs, and a man capable of little more than the management of a small business.[172]

On October 16, Hoover delivered the first of his two speeches in behalf of the Landon campaign. Speaking in Philadelphia, he lashed out at the "intellectual dishonesty" of the New Deal. He took up a Roosevelt speech from the 1932 campaign in which the latter had charged Hoover's spending with being "the most reckless and extravagant" he had ever been able to uncover in peacetime government anywhere or at any time. Hoover charged:

> He denied Republicans any mercy from the fact that Federal revenues had precipitously dropped off by two billion through a world-

wide calamity. He denied us any quarter because we had placed humanity first in the American budget and spent and loaned public funds to a people in distress. Now he claims a patent on that idea. He gave us no credit marks for fighting a Pork Barrel Democratic Congress to get a balanced budget. He has patented many improvements on that barrel. With solemnity he promised to save 25 percent a year from expenditures of the government and to at once balance the budget. And he tearfully appealed to the woman in her home struggling to balance her budget. And he vigorously asserted he would never conceal anything.

But in a 1936 speech in the same city, Hoover noted, Roosevelt had

omitted correction of his inexactitudes of four years before. He now dismisses his own immensely greater deficits and all the evidences of his wastes and follies by the pious remark [that] for him and his supine Congress to have balanced his budget would "have been a crime against the American people." Thus he changes the rules between these two innings.[173]

After attacking Roosevelt's claim that the New Deal had brought recovery from the depression and making his familiar case that the upturn had begun in 1932, Hoover zeroed in on the president's comparisons of the Hoover deficit with that of the Roosevelt administration. Instead of a $3 billion deficit by the Republicans and a $6.5 billion deficit by the New Deal, Hoover computed totals of $1 billion for his administration and nearly $10 billion for Roosevelt. He found similar errors in Roosevelt's depiction of the foreign debt owed to the United States. Moreover, he charged that by devaluing the American dollar Roosevelt had, in effect, canceled 41 percent of the debt owed to Americans by foreigners and thereby had "made a present to foreigners of another 4 billions of American dollars." After attacking other New Deal bookkeeping practices and waste, Hoover told his listeners that "to present hypocritical, misleading figures is a new deal in American public life. . . . If an income taxpayer or any corporation kept books like this administration, that is if they showed similar morals in juggling their accounts, they would be put in jail." He concluded that the American people should "resume congressional control of spending by the election of Republican Congressmen and Senators," and "drive these expenses down toward the Republican levels, balance the budget, put back the integrity of government accounting, and above all restore truth and morals in government by the election of these honest gentlemen, Alfred Landon and Frank Knox."[174]

On October 30, Hoover delivered his second and final speech of the campaign in Denver. It was on a familiar theme, "The Challenge to Liberty," and the contents had already been largely aired in his previous speeches against the New Deal. Hoover observed:

> Mr. Roosevelt on the eve of the election has started using the phrases of freedom. He talks sweetly of personal liberty, of individualism, of the American system, of the profit system. He says now that he thinks well of capitalism, and individual enterprise. His devotion to private property seems to be increasing. He has suddenly found some good economic royalists. And he is a staunch supporter of the Constitution. Two days ago he rededicated the Statue of Liberty in New York. She has been the forgotten woman.

But Roosevelt had also made many statements four years previously that had turned out "not to mean what they were thought to have meant." Roosevelt now ought to state "in plain words" whether he proposed to revive the acts that the Supreme Court had invalidated; whether he intented "to stuff the Court itself." "Why does the New Deal not really lay its cards on the table?" Hoover asked. Had Roosevelt abandoned "this 'new order,' this 'planned economy' that he has so often talked about? Will he discharge these associates of his who daily preached the 'new order' but whom he does not allow to appear in his campaign?"[175]

The ideas that now guided the New Deal had, Hoover pointed out, been pressed on his own Republican administration by "powerful groups" during his four years in the White House, but he had rejected them all—from stupendous spending to "prime the pump" to the centralization of power in Washington. Hoover had rejected them, he said, "because they would not only delay recovery but because I knew that in the end they would shackle free men." But all of "the ardent peddlers of these Trojan horses received sympathetic hearings from Mr. Roosevelt and joined vociferously in his election. Men are to be judged by the company they keep." Hoover then outlined his concept of the Republican philosophy in the social and economic fields in familiar terms and concluded:

> Many of the problems discussed in this campaign concern our material welfare. That is right. But there are things far more important to a nation than material welfare. It is possible to have a prosperous country under a dictatorship. It is not possible to have a free country. No great question will ever be settled in dollars and cents. Great

questions must be settled on moral grounds and the tests of what makes free men. What is the nation profited if it shall gain the whole world and lose its own soul?

The election was not alone a choice between two men, but "a contest between two philosophies of government," between "a system of personal centralized government" and "the ideals of liberty."[176]

In writing his memoirs years later, Hoover observed that the Denver speech had not been very useful for Landon "as it did not square with his program of 'me-too-but-cheaper,' " where the New Deal was concerned. He wrote further:

> However, together with the Convention speech, it reaped so many thousands of telegrams and letters from radio listeners over the country and so many editorials as to give me complete conviction that the rank and file of the Party realized the issue. If Governor Landon had made a speech along that line to open his campaign and had stuck to it, he might not have been elected, but he would have left the Republican Party with a substance of principle—and he would not have gone into quick oblivion.[177]

Whether Hoover's analysis of the Landon campaign was correct or not, several points should be made. The first has to do with the course of public opinion polls from the time of the convention down to election day. Disregarding the much-ridiculed and highly unscientific *Literary Digest* poll, which continued to show Landon winning the presidency right down to election day, all of the more respected and scientific pollsters, including Roosevelt's own opinion sampler, found the election to be virtually a toss-up in the weeks immediately following the conventions, with Roosevelt leading in the popular vote, but Landon leading slightly in the electoral vote.[178] Thereafter, however, in all but the *Literary Digest* poll there was a rapid deterioiration in Landon's standing so that by September it was clear that the election would be a landslide for Roosevelt. Clearly Hoover cannot be blamed for Landon's loss of popularity. His attacks on the New Deal came in late 1935 and early 1936, with the last one delivered at the GOP convention in June. Landon's high standing in the polls continued for weeks after Hoover's convention speech. Thereafter, Hoover was silent, a bystander until Landon called for his assistance in the final weeks of the campaign, when the GOP nominee was already far behind in the polls. As Hoover had predicted, the "sinking spell" had brought appeals for help. Perhaps nothing could have arrested Landon's steady decline in popularity and averted his landslide defeat in November. But

Landon certainly gained nothing by Hoover's absence from the campaign during the critical months, and he might have lost a great deal.

Could the Republicans have done better with Hoover as their nominee? Hoover's supporters, of course, thought so. But so did the president and vice-president. Raymond Moley has recorded that Roosevelt regarded Hoover as the only formidable challenger among the Republican possibilities and that the president made a bet with him that Hoover would be nominated.[179] Roosevelt, in fact, regarded Landon as the easiest of the GOP possibilities to beat and instructed members of his administration to say and do nothing that might make it difficult for him to be nominated.[180] Vice-President John Garner also thought that the "politically smart" thing for the Republicans to do in 1936 was to nominate Hoover. According to his biographer, Bascom N. Timmons, Garner was sure that Hoover couldn't win, but he believed Hoover "would carry more states than anyone else they can put up," and even in defeat "he might carry a number of other Republican candidates to victory." When Landon was nominated, Garner concluded that the Republican party had "set the stage for a party debacle."[181]

A debacle it was. The Landon campaign, Hoover concluded, had been a "mess" which had left the Republican party in shambles without "either principle or party spirit—at the moment." The GOP must now, he believed, move to create and organize a "constructive opposition based on real principles and realities."[182] This belief would guide Hoover in his actions during the next two years.

# 3

# A Bid for
# Leadership

n the aftermath of the 1936 election debacle there were renewed cries from Hoover's supporters that he should take
the leadership in steering the Republican party back to its
traditional principles. Attempts at coalition, and compromise with the New Deal, had, in the view of such Republicans, been exposed as folly by Landon's poor showing
against Roosevelt. Considerable disillusionment was expressed with what
some referred to as the "Kansas Gang," and even Landon's GOP national
chairman, fellow Kansan John D. M. Hamilton, expressed concern over the
confusion in Republican ranks caused by Landon's pro–New Deal positions
taken during the 1936 campaign in conflict with the platform of the party as
written at the Cleveland convention.[1]

For Hoover, Landon's defeat was traceable in large part to the candidate's
attempt to "out–New Deal the New Deal" rather than battle squarely against
the Democrats on behalf of more traditional Republican liberalism. Analyzing
the lesser contests, he concluded that Landon had not commanded the entire
Republican vote, since the total votes for Republican gubernatorial, senatorial,
and congressional candidates had exceeded Landon's total by some three to
five million.[2] Landon, as titular head of the party, could now be expected to
continue to steer the GOP in a New Deal direction unless an effort was made
to divert the party back to those traditional principles.[3] Throughout 1937 and

1938, Hoover and his supporters would carry on a major effort to do so against the opposition of the Landon forces and allies that the Kansan gradually recruited from congressional Republicans. The major battle would be fought over Hoover's attempt to bring about a mid-term Republican convention or general conference, which would restate the principles that should guide the GOP and at the same time, it was expected, restore Hoover to the position of leadership in the party.

Hoover had concluded that the GOP needed "some shaking up."[4] In mid-December of 1936 he traveled east to Chicago and New York, conferring with supporters and party leaders. When Professor William Starr Myers encouraged him to "jump in and raise hell" in the GOP, Hoover replied that at his age he did not want once again to go through the strain he had endured in 1935 and 1936 while seeking to revitalize the party.[5] But the disarray of the GOP and the urgings of his supporters had their effect. Early in January, Hoover wrote to his former secretary of agriculture, Arthur M. Hyde, that he and his followers had two alternatives before them. Hoover might "sit back like Cincinnatus, hoping to heaven that nobody will ever come near us," or he could adopt the role "of an evangelist in a world that does not wish to listen." He recoiled from the latter role, he told Hyde, because of the "deprivation of the normal joys of life which lies in it, and the mud that comes from it." Yet he felt "anxiety for the future of a misguided people." He would, however, take part in national affairs only if there was "on the part of some people an express desire that they would want it."[6] Hyde responded that the GOP "still flirts with New Dealism, still ogles the spoils of office, still slavers for party victory at whatever expense or compromise." Therefore, the Republican party was, itself, "a field for the evangelist." It was within the GOP that evangelism must begin.[7] From Hoover's friend Arch Shaw, in Chicago, came word that the "powers that be at national party headquarters, as well as men like Lowden," were turning to Hoover for "intellectual leadership" in these trying times.[8]

Hoover still harbored ill feelings toward Landon for the limited role he had been allowed to play in the campaign and for the conduct of the campaign, itself. In his view: "When the Republican party starts out to mix populism, oil, Hearst, munitions and the Liberty League, it is bound to come to grief." As for his future role in the party, he could see "no possibility of fighting a battle to organize a political party for good government with the knife of that party constantly in one's back."[9] And Landon's view of the future course of the party was still at variance with that of the former president. While Hoover contemplated with dread the role of Republican evangelist, Landon was proposing to Republicans and "Jeffersonian" Democrats a round table conference to be held during the summer of 1937 "to help formulate definite policies" that would be agreeable to both groups.[10] Thus, while Hoover saw a need to "purify" the Republican party, Landon sought to "taint" it further by compromising Republican principles by forming a coalition with non-Republicans, which might even produce a new political party. Landon's proposal, however, ran into early difficulties. "Progressive" Republicans like Gifford Pinchot objected to the participation in such a round table of "traditional" Republicans like Ogden Mills, Charles Hilles, or Hoover.[11] Lowden, too, expressed coolness toward the round table proposal, encouraging Landon to instead continue conversations with "the leaders of various groups" opposed to the New Deal in the hope that in this way a "set of principles" might be worked out that would be "acceptable to all who oppose the philosophy of the present regime."[12]

Lowden's response may well have resulted from a conference with Hoover, since he wrote to the Kansan on the day that he met with Hoover and a number of the former president's friends in Chandler, Arizona.[13] Arthur Hyde was one of those in attendance.[14] Lowden expressed the view that Hoover was the man best equipped for leadership of the party. He proposed inviting both Hoover and Landon to spend a day or two at his Sinnissippi farm in the expectation that this would convince the Kansan of Hoover's "inevitable leadership" and convince him to "fall in line."[15] After the Arizona discussions, Hoover traveled east to his apartment in the Waldorf-Astoria Hotel.

Not long after Hoover's arrival in New York, the news broke of Roosevelt's transparent attempt to curb the independence of the Supreme Court by "packing" the court with additional appointees of his own choosing. For those who opposed the New Deal, the Supreme Court was the last remaining bastion in defense of the Constitution against Roosevelt's tampering with American institutions. The elections of the 1930s had brought New Deal control of the legislative and executive branches of the government, but they had not altered the composition of the Supreme Court. Hundreds of cases involving New Deal legislation were fought in the courts, and in important instances, such as the Supreme Court decisions on the National Industrial Recovery Act and the Agricultural Adjustment Act, key elements of the New Deal were voided. Roosevelt, during the winter of 1936–37, decided to attempt to extend the New Deal mandate to the Supreme Court by seeking authority from Congress to appoint additional judges.[16] The president's grasp for power over the Supreme Court brought consternation to many, including members of his own party, and fears that Roosevelt was "driving steadily toward a dictatorship."[17] Hoover sprang quickly into action, telephoning political leaders and journalists of both parties from coast to coast and rallying them to fight Roosevelt's proposal. Wall Street lawyer and utility executive Wendell Willkie was one of those enlisted by the former president, and quickly impressed Hoover's close friend Edgar Rickard with his ability to propagandize.[18] With the skill and contacts born of years of organization and publicity work at the state and local level through the Commission for Relief in Belgium, the U.S. Food Administration, and the American Relief Administration, as well as through his political activities, Hoover was quickly able to organize groups in 30 states to arouse public opinion against Roosevelt's proposal.[19] Both former officeholders, like ex-governor Percival Baxter of Maine, and new emerging GOP hopefuls, like John Bricker of Ohio, were enlisted in the effort.[20]

Republican strategy in Congress was to leave the fight against the judiciary bill to Democratic opponents of the plan, lest GOP opposition drive Democrats to partisan support of the president. Strong Democratic opposition to Roosevelt's plan had developed, and Senators McNary, Borah, and Vandenberg on the Republican side decided that GOP criticism should be muted both in and out of Congress.[21] Special concern was expressed among Republican senators that Hoover might disrupt this strategy by an open attack on the bill, and Senator Vandenberg asked GOP chairman John Hamilton to try to restrain the former president. Hamilton, however, told Vandenberg that if the GOP senators did not want Hoover to go on the attack it was their responsibility to tell him so.[22]

Hoover had already issued a statement on February 5, deploring the implication in Roosevelt's proposal of an attempt to subordinate the court "to the personal power of the Executive" and describing the issue as one that "transcends any questions of partisanship."[23] He recognized that the issue must be approached in a nonpartisan fashion, and he discouraged Landon from taking up the Supreme Court issue as the main topic of his Lincoln Day speech.[24] Hoover was, however, working away at a speech of his own on the subject.[25] Journalist and close friend Mark Sullivan communicated to him Senator Borah's feeling that it was undesirable for Republicans to be "overconspicuous" in the court fight. Hoover responded that he agreed with that position, but he encouraged Borah to make an attack on the court plan "fairly early," since he felt that an attack from Borah was less likely to alienate Democrats than one from a more regular Republican.[26] The absence of Republican comment on the court plan, however, led the former president to despair at his party's timidity. On February 20 he unleashed his own attack on Roosevelt's proposal in a speech before the Union League Club of Chicago.

In his speech, Hoover called the court packing proposal "the greatest Constitutional question in . . . seventy years." He described the issue as a nonpartisan one and emphasized that he was speaking not as a Republican, but "as an American who has witnessed the decay and destruction of human liberty in many lands." It was not, he insisted, a problem for lawyers, but rather an issue for the people, since it reached to the very heart of their liberties. Hoover dismissed the arguments that had been advanced for the proposal. The reason, he said, was clear. If the Supreme Court had rubber-stamped all of the New Deal legislation, rather than found parts of it unconstitutional, Roosevelt would never have proposed such a "reform" of the court. He declared:

> If Mr. Roosevelt can change the Constitution to suit his purposes by adding to the members of the Court, any succeeding President can do it to suit his purposes. If a troop of "President's judges" can be sent into the halls of justice to capture political power, then his successor with the same device can also send a troop of new "President's judges" to capture some other power. That is not judicial process. That is force.

Such a practice, he argued, would result in the Constitution and the Supreme Court becoming "the tool of the Executive and not the sword of the people." The United States had "already gone far on the road of personal government. The American people must halt when it is proposed to lay hands on the independence of the Supreme Court. That is the ultimate security of every cottage. It is the last safeguard of free men." He left his listeners with a "watchword": "Hands off the Supreme Court."[27]

Hoover's speech was criticized by some Republicans as harmful to the cause of opposition to the Supreme Court plan.[28] Vandenberg telephoned Mark Sullivan a few hours before the speech to express his misgivings about Hoover's course. Borah, Vandenberg told Sullivan, was "raging around" at the news of what Hoover was going to say, and Vandenberg also reported that Senator Burton Wheeler, a Democrat, had expressed confidence that he could "line up three or four more" Democrats against the Roosevelt proposal "if the Republicans would continue to lay off a while." But after Sullivan convinced him that Hoover was determined to go ahead with the speech, Vandenberg said that he would "just tell Borah to wrap a wet towel around his head and stand it."[29] After Hoover delivered his speech, Borah claimed that because of the speech he had lost two potential opponents of the Roosevelt plan in the Senate, but the validity of the claim is doubtful.[30]

Meanwhile, Hoover was pursuing other possible strategies. Through Justice James McReynolds and Chief Justice Charles Evans Hughes, the former president tried to encourage Justice Louis Brandeis to retire from the bench and attack the court-packing scheme.[31] He also continued to encourage the organization of public opinion against the proposal and was sounding out public sentiment across the country.[32] While Landon was now willing to mute his own opposition to the court plan, Hoover had concluded: "If the 'hush-hush' people in Washington have their way, not only are we going to be defeated, but the Republican Party is going to give the greatest display of cowardice in all history."[33] He believed that the Roosevelt plan could only be defeated by an aroused public opinion, such as he was attempting to orchestrate nationwide, which would force the Congress to reject it. And he had, Hoover told O'Laughlin, received a greater response to his Chicago speech than to any other public statement he had ever made; furthermore, this response emanated from Democrats as well as Republicans. He asserted that when Republican candidates campaigned for election in 1938 they would "be grateful that at least one Republican had the courage to speak" out on the issue.[34] But he made no further speeches on the subject.

Hoover's supporters continued to urge him to take the leadership in rebuilding the Republican party. Professor William Starr Myers talked to the former president in early March and argued that he alone could save the country. Hoover continued to take the position that he would undertake the "evangelist" role only if he were assured of backing from others.[35] A week later, however, Myers found him in a fighting mood and looking well and came to the conclusion that "the Chief" was ready to lead a movement to rejuvenate the GOP. Hoover now urged the Republican national committee to call a national convention to give new life to the party through the formulation of a statement of Republican principles. Former Illinois governor Frank Lowden supported the proposal, but Landon did not.[36] On the contrary, Landon was still toying with the idea of his round table conference and wondering what effect the divisive court fight would have on the Democratic party.[37] Late in March, Hoover traveled to Florida for a few days of fishing, accompanied by Mark Sullivan and Arthur Hyde.[38] En route to Florida, Hoover conferred with Lowden in Chicago.[39]

Hoover was not alone in suggesting a meeting of Republicans. GOP national chairman John Hamilton had studied the example of the Conservative party in England and had concluded that the GOP should emulate that opposition party's practice of annual meetings and restatements of party policy. Judging from the disastrous results of the 1934 election, the GOP could not allow itself again to fall into inactivity between presidential election years, forcing the individual candidates to fend for themselves against the obvious popularity of the New Deal during off-year elections. Hamilton had consulted with Hoover about such a GOP meeting and had, of course, found the former president enthusiastic.[40] Hoover's concept, however, was somewhat broader than that envisioned by the national chairman. Hoover sought a formal convention that would include Republicans who had held public office or had been candidates at the national and state levels (as well as former cabinet officers, former chairmen of the Republican national committee, and others), with the call for such a convention to be signed by Lowden, Landon, and himself. Lowden had consented, and Hamilton was to approach Landon.[41]

On April 19 Hoover dined with Hamilton and outlined his proposal.[42] The GOP national chairman then took the matter up with his fellow Kansan, but Landon objected to the proposed convention. Disappointed, Hoover wrote Hamilton that he hoped Landon would, "in time, see the wisdom of our step." The purpose of such a convention, he wrote, would be "to secure a declaration of the fundamental principles of genuine American Liberalism—that is, 'conservatism,' as opposed to the collectivism of the New Deal." The Republicans must come up with a "program of constructive action to meet the dire and pressing problems which confront the nation." The preservation of democratic government required "effective party opposition." The GOP could not wait until the 1940 convention to act constructively. Hoover told Hamilton that he had discussed his proposal with 30 leaders of the party and only Landon was not enthusiastic about it. He suggested to Hamilton, therefore, that "we march ahead," without Landon, if necessary.[43]

By the end of April, however, Hoover's proposal for a mid-term convention lost momentum as Hamilton, too, failed to give the idea his full support.[44] According to his later reminiscences, Hamilton supported the concept of a conference and a policy statement, but he was cold toward holding a convention on the scale Hoover proposed because the party lacked the finances necessary to organize it. He preferred a statement by a smaller policy committee that could be named by the Republican national committee.[45] By early May Hoover had abandoned the original plan of issuing a call for the convention over the signatures of the three GOP leaders, because of Landon's opposition, but he was still insistent that there be a national convention.[46]

If Hoover lacked the strength in the Republican party to carry through his convention proposal, perhaps the answer was to increase his strength. In May the "express desire," which he had insisted upon before he would undertake the role of evangelist, began to be mobilized. On May 3, Arthur Hyde wrote to John Spargo in Vermont that the Republican party stood "in the presence of a great national peril, voiceless in leadership." Only Hoover could answer the party's need for leadership. "Whoever may be leader in 1938 or 1940," Hyde wrote, "there does not seem to be any leader except Hoover now." But, to be effective, a leader must "have a group with him who are [sic] loyal enough to defend him and to assist in gathering strength for his program." He asked if Spargo would "join a group in trying."[47] Two weeks later, William Starr Myers met with Dean Sommer and Professor Allison Reppy of New York University Law School, and these three also decided to begin a movement to restore Hoover's leadership in the Republican party. After the meeting, Reppy and Myers reported to Edgar Rickard with their plans.[48] Meanwhile, Spargo had expressed his support for Hyde's proposal and had also been in touch with the Reppy group.[49]

Landon's efforts to form a new party of Republicans and anti–New Deal Democrats continued to cause concern for Hoover.[50] Landon was in contact, directly and indirectly, with a number of Democrats, including Lewis Douglas, Newton D. Baker, and Raymond Moley. He found Ogden Mills in favor of his coalition idea over Hoover's proposed convention. The difference between Mills and Landon was over the method by which the coalition should be brought about. Mills supported a round robin declaration of principles supported by sixty or seventy Democratic and Republican signatures, while Landon insisted on a round table conference as the first objective.[51] William Hard, in Republican national headquarters, worked closely with Landon in the quest for a coalition, and arranged a meeting between Landon and Moley in June.[52]

Meanwhile, Hyde had written to some two hundred Republicans who were believed to be Hoover supporters in order to test their loyalty and to see if they would cooperate in the effort to draft Hoover as the "intellectual leader" of the GOP.[53] In his letters, Hyde argued that the former president should be tapped once again for leadership because he was a seasoned leader with a nationwide voice and a vast following of devoted supporters. Moreover, Hoover had a definite philosophy of individual liberty and an economic doctrine based upon the initiative of free men, while the nation was desperate for precisely such a man to lead them away from the collectivism of the New Deal. Hyde's effort was not, he said, an effort to promote Hoover for the 1940 nomination, but rather to place him in a position where he could rebuild the Republican party as an effective agency of opposition. The GOP was, Hyde argued, "the most effective instrument for the salvation of the country."[54] Later in the month, Hyde contemplated a mass mailing to approximately ten thousand members of Republican organizations throughout the nation.[55] The mass mailing, however, was held in abeyance, since Hoover objected to such a move as premature until a better foundation of support had been established from the earlier letters. Hoover also suggested that a "definite form of organization" be established in Chicago "at a later stage based on various satisfactory results of Hyde's own personal letters."[56]

Hoover viewed Landon's efforts to form a new coalition party with considerable disquietude, convinced that the Kansan was attempting to repudiate the Republican party's past and to freeze him out of political affairs.[57] He increasingly viewed his entire political future as dependent upon the efforts of Hyde and others to create support for his leadership of the party. By mid-May, however, these efforts had produced but scant results, to the discouragement of Hyde; Hoover concluded that if the effort failed he would retire from political life.[58] But Landon's efforts to form a coalition also suffered a setback in May, when Raymond Moley expressed his willingness to cooperate with Republicans on key questions, like the court fight, but also expressed his opposition to the creation of any new political party.[59]

The eastern group of Hoover supporters, under the leadership of Reppy and Myers, stepped up its work. As Reppy wrote to John Spargo:

> We agreed to form a center of support in this area for demanding the restoration of Mr. Hoover to the intellectual leadership of the Republican Party. . . . I quite agree with you that in anything we do we ought to keep away from the suggestion of candidature, limiting our agitation merely to a demand that Mr. Hoover resume the intellectual leadership of the party.

Spargo had suggested that the group formulate a "call" to Hoover that he assume that leadership, which would be signed by Republicans who felt that he was needed. Reppy agreed that the "call" idea was a good one and suggested a program to increase Hoover's popularity among the rank and file.[60] Spargo found the situation growing worse daily, with "the leadership of the Republican Party . . . so weak and incompetent that no hope can be derived from it." If the GOP were to survive "and be an effective medium for the opposition, there must be a change in leadership, and that change can only be brought about by action from below."[61] Hyde approved of the Spargo-Reppy efforts and reported that as of mid-June his own letters were beginning to gather encouraging responses, with "focal groups" forming in various areas, and with women especially interested in the Hoover campaign.[62]

Hoover was still attempting to generate support for his convention idea. Others were proselytizing in behalf of the concept and finding support for it.[63] In late May, Hoover left New York for Chicago, hoping to meet with Landon and other GOP leaders to press the convention proposal. He had not been able to make much progress in promoting the idea from New York, and he had started to despair that anything could be done before September. In the meantime he had begun to consider writing an article for the *Atlantic Monthly*.[64] In Chicago, Hoover conferred with Lowden, with both men discussing their concern over the movement toward a coalition party that was being orchestrated by Landon.[65] After a week in Chicago, Hoover left for California. Meanwhile, Landon's coalition effort was braking to a halt, as one after another of the leading Democrats he had counted on expressed the view that the time was not ripe for the kind of coalition he had in mind.[66] In mid-June, William Hard, who was privy to Landon's efforts, wired Hoover: "All immediate national coalition attempts abandoned and no talks on anything at all just now."[67] Hoover responded that the news would allow "us to pass the summer without great anxiety."[68]

In the midst of the Hyde and Spargo-Reppy letter-writing efforts, the "Washington Merry-go-Round" column of Drew Pearson and Robert Allen broke the news of their campaign for Hoover on June 25. Headlined as "Hyde Campaign Seeks Hoover as GOP Chief," the Pearson-Allen story described Hyde's "quiet movement to restore the former President to titular leadership of the Republican Party." Hyde's letters to prominent Republicans had urged "that they unite in a demand that Landon step out and make way for Hoover." The column went on to report that Hyde had laid the sad state of the GOP entirely at the door of Landon and his GOP national chairman John Hamilton.[69] Mark Sullivan cautioned Hoover: "If you make yourself the head of a movement to revitalize the party many will assume you are doing it for the purpose of being renominated in 1940; some others . . . will assume that if you revitalize the party, you can't help being renominated," and this would bring a renewal of the smear attacks by Charles Michelson and others. It was, as Sullivan noted, "a bedeviling paradox," since no one but Hoover could lead a revitalizing movement, and yet there was no way to dissociate it from talk of the nomination."[70]

While Hyde felt that the Pearson-Allen publicity would hinder their effort, the eastern group was undaunted, having targeted October as the occasion for the "new revival" of Hoover, although Spargo felt that "if we are going to get anywhere, we must have a great stirring of the rank and file in the ensuing six months." Without such a stirring the GOP would be unable to make any gains in the 1938 congressional elections, and without such gains the party would have no "important role in, or influence on the campaign of 1940."[71] Favorable responses, however, continued to pour in as a result of their letters.

In the face of Landon's unrelenting opposition to the convention idea, and his apparent devotion to a coalition, Hoover turned to a new arena to rally sentiment for his proposal, which would at the same time furnish new ammunition for those who were seeking to arouse support for his leadership of the GOP. The new vehicle would be the *Atlantic Monthly* article, which would seek to rally support for a Republican convention. As proofs of the article became available, Hoover mailed them off to his campaigners and to Harrison Spangler, Republican national committeeman from Iowa, who promised that he would do everything he could to secure newspaper publicity for the article.[72] Hoover's effort, published in the September issue, appeared on the newsstands in late August, and arrangements were quickly made by Hoover and his supporters to have 32,000 copies of the article distributed.[73]

In the article, Hoover wrote that his "concern with political parties today is that they perform their prime responsibility," which he defined as to "express their will as to the real issue of our times"—the issue of "personal liberty." The New Deal had exposed the Democratic party as the party of "coercion"—coercion of the economy, of Congress, of the Supreme Court, of local communities, and ultimately of the individual. The 1936 presidential campaign had obscured the real issues in America, Hoover said, in an obvious swipe at Landon, since the GOP had sought to out–New Deal the Democrats.

After reciting the historical achievements of the Republican party, Hoover found its present weakness to be primarily the result of its unwillingness to stand up "for its substantial record of service," its failure to replace with youth the deadwood accumulated through its years of victories, and "its failure to crystallize an affirmative and consistent body of principle in the face of this new situation." This had resulted in talk of a party realignment, but Hoover expressed opposition to a realignment of political parties (and to coalition) in a clear rebuttal of Landon's efforts.[74]

On the contrary, Hoover argued that the GOP should concentrate on providing a meaningful alternative to the New Deal in order to attract voters, rather than on meaningless "coalitions" with Democratic leaders who lacked any following. The voters were questioning what the parties stood for, and it was the clarification of this question that was "far more important to America." The nation, he insisted, needed a political party that would "clearly and courageously and constructively set out the affirmative alternative to the coercive direction of the New Deal." That alternative was an emphasis on the ideals of personal liberty, ideals that, he argued, were "deep in our American heritage." He then stated for his readers the "essentials" of a modern day creed of liberty: the Bill of Rights; government by laws, not by men; preparations for national defense; the maintenance of economic freedom since it was inseparable from spiritual and intellectual freedom, but a free enterprise that was regulated; economy in government and balanced budgets, as well as a sound dollar; the maintenance of equal opportunity for all; maximum production; the transfer of more wage earners to an annual earning basis to aid their security; economic fair play to spread, through taxation, the "swollen fortunes" to marginal groups; and an end to "any form of government or law or private action which coerces, intimidates, or regiments upright men." Hoover closed with a call for his proposed convention or conference to restate those principles for the Republican party. Such a conference, he wrote, could produce a declaration of principles that "would infuse a renewed fighting courage in the party's own ranks; it would inspire an organization with which free men could join in coalition; it would lift the hearts of free men and women." America, he concluded, needed "a new and flaming declaration of the rights and responsibilities of free men."[75]

Hoover followed up the *Atlantic Monthly* article by writing GOP national and state leaders in order to call it to their attention; meanwhile, his supporters mailed out thousands of copies to former delegates to national conventions, to national committeemen and committeewomen, and to others prominent in the party.[76] Through such methods, Hoover sought to build support for the type of convention or general conference that he favored. In some cases he asked state GOP leaders to see that resolutions were passed in favor of the conference, and that they send these resolutions to the Republican national committee and to other party leaders.[77]

Having been blocked by Landon in his earlier attempt to get the Kansan to join in the call for a mid-term convention, Hoover now made a new effort to enlist his support for a general conference. He counted heavily upon Lowden to convince Landon of the desirability of such a conference. Others, however, were also induced to make the trek to Topeka to attempt to persuade him.[78] The combination of Hoover's conference proposal and the visible work being done in behalf of Hoover's leadership of the Republican party by Hyde and the Reppy-Spargo group had, however, convinced Landon that "Hoover and the old guard" were "carrying on a deliberate organized campaign to get control of the Republican organization," using the former federal appointees of the Hoover administration as the nucleus for the effort.[79]

From Landon's fellow Kansan, Senator Arthur Capper, also came opposition to the idea of such a conference and statement of principles. Capper wrote Landon that he had talked over Hoover's proposal "with some of our best Republicans in Congress and they feel the same way about it."[80] Landon welcomed the news of negative sentiment in Congress, taking the position that "unless the Republican leadership in Congress would unanimously agree on the benefit of a convention of that kind, I would not be inclined to join in any such move."[81] Yet, Capper to the contrary, there was support for the proposed conference among the Republican leadership. House minority leader Bertram Snell wrote Hoover in early August that he favored such a conference, as it would do no harm and potentially accomplish a great deal of good.[82] And though the Senate minority leader, Charles McNary, was not consistently for the conference, neither was he consistently opposed to it.[83]

Hoover now hoped to issue the call for such a conference over the signatures of 30 prominent Republicans in order to meet the objections of those who associated it with him, and he sought Landon as one of the 30.[84] The news of Hoover's latest proposal, however, surfaced in the press in August, and the proposed conference was laid at Hoover's door with the result that both Landon and Hamilton denied having been consulted in the matter.[85] Hoover blamed Landon for the information leak, since Lowden had been seeking to arrange a meeting between Landon and Hoover at his Sinnissippi farm and the details of what was to be discussed were known only to Lowden and Landon. Hoover concluded:

> In any event, we will have to be guided by the reaction to the *Atlantic Monthly* article. Since it has been brought to the country that I am doing it [proposing the conference], I think Mr. Landon, if I meet

with him, will be in the position of having to take it or leave it. If he
refuses to go on, he will himself make the public break.

Of the organized effort by his supporters to restore him as the intellectual
leader of the Republican party, Hoover wrote that their tactics would have to
be altered. Since the Republican general conference had been associated with
him, he decided that "the drive now needs to be centered on this and the
creation of fundamental principles and not on leadership. If this idea carries, it
will have demonstrated leadership."[86]

Thus, Hoover now intended to gamble his bid for leadership of the Republican party solely on the issue of the general conference. To Jacob Allen, a
person involved in his "campaign," Hoover explained:

> The original object . . . was to establish a sampling of the people at
> the grassroots with the following up of points of influence. The
> situation has somewhat shifted. The premature leak of the discus-
> sions in respect to a general conference of the Republican Party has
> given a complexion of attempts at rival election as leader and has
> made it possible that this action would be interpreted and smeared
> up as purely an attempt to displace Mr. Landon. Our primary
> attempt is to save this country. That gentleman's position is only an
> incident for good or evil. I do not want to get in the position of
> running a campaign and having the whole centered on that outlook
> rather than the great issue. The first step is to get this great issue
> before the Republican Party, and it seems to me that this could be
> done in all directions, including making these cunning politicians
> wake up.[87]

The new tactic called for those who had been organizing sentiment in
Hoover's behalf to utilize their mailing lists to generate support for the conference idea. Copies of the *Atlantic Monthly* article were to be sent to the
people on the mailing lists along with a questionnaire asking if they favored a
general conference and soliciting their reaction to the program Hoover outlined in the article. Through such a questionnaire Hoover felt that he and his
supporters would "be able to determine what the intelligent grassroots think of
this proposal and what they think of these ideas, and thereby be able to prove
to the world, one way or the other" whether they supported Hoover's conference suggestion. And, incidentally, if people on the lists did support the
conference idea, the campaigners would have new "points of contact" for their
other Hoover work, and they "would probably get more of them than under
the first proposal."[88]

Hoover's campaigners did not welcome the emphasis they were to put on
the general conference, preferring instead their own "call" proposal; but

Hoover had made his decision, and during August he made a two-thousand-mile sweep through the western states talking to Republican leaders about his proposal.[89] In his travels, he found support not only for a conference, but also for a declaration of principles to furnish direction for the party, which was in chaos. The opposition he did receive arose "from people around Landon and others of the party politician type, who believe that by pussyfooting and opportunism we can win this election."[90] Such opposition meant that it was "going to be necessary to undertake some energetic work to get support" for the idea. Hoover had now incorporated into his strategy the creation of a "planning committee," which would consist of outstanding GOP leaders and would determine who should be invited to the general conference. The planning committee would also be responsible for drafting a set of Republican principles that would be submitted to the country a month before the general conference met.[91]

Hoover mobilized support for his plan on a variety of fronts. Spangler promised to take up the proposal at the next meeting of the executive committee of the GOP national committee and to ascertain in advance the views of the other members.[92] With numerous supporters on the executive committee (and in the national committee itself), Hoover had good reason to assume that his idea found approval there. However, to ensure a favorable result he worked personally to round up votes among national committeemen in the western states and early found support among those representing Wyoming, Montana, Washington, Oregon, California, and Arizona.[93] He also sought support from GOP organizations.[94] And, while he tried to silence opposition to the conference being expressed by some in the Republican national headquarters, he called upon others to do "missionary work among national committeemen" in behalf of the proposal.[95] Hoover also planned personally to undertake more such "missionary work," he told Spangler.[96] Early in September he wrote Chester Rowell:

> I am leaving tonight for the East. I may be back in a month. I may not be back for several. I am going out to make a battle on the question of a Republican conference. I have in the last month been in contact with Republican officials in many of our Western states and I have lined up South Dakota, Wyoming, Montana, Oregon, Washington, California, Nevada, Arizona, Utah and Texas and Iowa. I now propose to invade this type of folk in the East.[97]

The former president was clearly pulling out all the stops in his campaign for the Republican conference, and his prestige was on the line.

Not all who read Hoover's *Atlantic Monthly* article were impressed with the arguments it made. Landon, of course, was not impressed, and considered those who were agitating for Republican activity to be "just plain dumb." Any such activity would only furnish an opportunity for the Democratic leaders to divert public attention from their own turmoil over the Supreme Court and other questions.[98] Moreover, the agitation over the conference proposal remained in Landon's eyes simply symbolic of "the beginning of Hoover's campaign for the nomination in 1940."[99] From O. Glenn Saxon at GOP national headquarters came the disturbing news for Hoover that leading Republican senators opposed the plan and that Chairman Hamilton was not sure that the executive committee would support his proposal.[100] Frank Knox, who had seemed to support the proposal in the beginning, was now recorded in opposition to it.[101] From Spangler came word of a news bulletin that a poll of the GOP national committee had revealed "that the sentiment of Republican leaders was against holding a convention and that therefore nothing would be done along that line."[102] Obviously, the meeting of the executive committee scheduled for September 23 was going to provide a greater challenge than Hoover had earlier believed it would.

On his way east, Hoover stopped off in Chicago for conferences with his supporters and with Lowden.[103] To that point the replies to the questionnaires mailed out with his *Atlantic Monthly* article were running about 90 percent favorable to the conference proposal.[104] But from Saxon he learned that Republican members of Congress were cool toward the idea, since they preferred to run for reelection in 1938 on local issues rather than be tied down to any set of principles that might be adopted by a general conference.[105] Hoover now stepped up his efforts to flush Landon out into the open. In his view the project was "making headway and the very logic of it is bound to win out for us."[106] Landon, however, had not changed his mind. When William Hard wrote from the GOP national headquarters of his conclusion that "some sort of Republican gathering may be inevitable," and that the question now was of what character it should be, Landon responded that he could see no value in such a meeting and that what the GOP needed instead was the "quiet, efficient building up of our local organizations."[107] But the sentiment in favor of a conference was strong, and both Landon and Knox began to express the view that the situation might be appropriate for such a conference in the spring of 1938, but they continued to oppose a decision at the present time with matters in a state of "flux."[108]

If public opinion was any guide, Hoover more nearly reflected the temper of the country than Landon. Polls showed that sizable majorities believed the Republican party would revive without being replaced by a new party.[109] And a Gallup Poll released on September 18 gave a resounding push to Hoover's conference proposal when 88 percent of a cross section of Republicans responded in favor of holding a national convention in the spring of 1938 "to strengthen the party for the Congressional campaign of next year." Hoover must have found grounds for disappointment, however, in the fact that only 22 percent listed him as their choice "to guide the policies of the Republican party" between then and 1940. Landon, however, was the only Republican to run ahead of Hoover, with 31 percent.[110] Hoover's own sampling of sentiment, made by his campaigners, revealed an even higher percentage in favor of the conference proposal, 94.2 percent, and only 3.14 percent opposed; but his poll was admittedly an unscientifically administered sounding. The figures were based on 5,692 replies, which had been received from 11,047 questionnaires.[111] All of this seemed to buoy Hoover's spirits, although his close friend Edgar Rickard worried that Hoover underestimated the opposition and overestimated the influence of his friends.[112]

Upon reaching New York, Hoover met with Spangler on September 22, and on the following day Spangler issued a press statement saying that he would urge the executive committee, in its meeting later that day, "to call a meeting of the full National Committee at an early date to determine the advisability of calling a General Republican Conference within the next two months, for the purpose of uniting upon a declaration of fundamental principles." Hoover's proposal had, he noted, "met with an extraordinary response," with the support arising not only from many GOP leaders, but also from rank and file all over the country. Spangler cited both the Gallup Poll and the samplings by Hoover's own campaigners, as well as resolutions that had been passed in support of a conference by various Republican groups nationally. The specific steps that Spangler recommended for bringing the conference into operation were those outlined by Hoover earlier: the appointment of a planning committee to work out the details and to formulate a draft set of principles, followed by the convening of the conference itself.[113] The gauntlet was down. Would Landon and other opponents of the Hoover proposal defy approximately 90 percent of the Republican party by seeking to block the holding of a conference?

One difficulty the conference proposal faced was its identification with Hoover, which aroused hostility among those Republican leaders who were opposed to the former president but were not necessarily opposed to the principle of the conference. In the executive committee meeting, Texas national committeeman R. B. Creager, a Hoover supporter, sought to meet this criticism by arguing that the proposal for such a conference had not originated with the former president, but had been suggested even earlier by others, including former senator Walter Edge, GOP chairman Hamilton, and Creager himself. The movement had become identified with Hoover, Creager suggested, only because of the *Atlantic Monthly* article.[114] However, Hoover was denied the victory he sought in the executive committee meeting, when the committee failed to recommend the conference proposal but instead referred the matter to the meeting of the whole GOP national committee, which was to be held in November. The *New York Times*, however, reported that "thirteen of the sixteen members" of the executive committee had favored such a gathering, and it expected that the national commitee, "accepting the decided trend in the executive committee, will call such a convention some time in the Summer of 1938."[115]

If Hoover's proposal had not won a victory it had at least cleared a hurdle. He now enlisted journalistic support from such columnists as David Lawrence and Arthur Krock for his proposal in preparation for the meeting of the national committee.[116] One product of his efforts was a column by Boake Carter, which appeared at the end of September and attacked the "old guard" for their opposition to new ideas in the party, and especially their opposition to Hoover's proposal. Carter wrote:

> So far their chief effort . . . is to chant inanely that Hoover is leading the party revolt because he wants to take another crack at the Presidency. Instead of using what little brains they have left and examining the proposals made on their merits; instead of weighing the significance of the poll results among Republican citizens of the country; instead of taking stock of themselves, they descend to personal attacks.[117]

Other newspaper comments concerning the proposal tended to center on the conflict between Hoover and Landon for leadership of the party.[118] Columnist Frank Kent, like Carter, equated the opposition with the "old guard" and argued that they were obstructing the conference proposal because they "seemed to fear that in some way the convention may redound to the credit of Mr. Hoover and apparently some of them are small enough to prefer scuttling the whole idea, shutting the door of hope on the party and on the country, as well, rather than have that happen."[119]

Lowden, meanwhile, had finally succeeded in arranging the meeting with Landon that he and Hoover had long sought. On October 2, Hoover left New York City for a strategy conference with Spangler and Hyde in Chicago before traveling on to Lowden's farm for the meeting with Lowden and Landon.[120] The results of the GOP "summit" meeting were interpreted quite differently by at least two of the participants—Hoover and Landon—with considerable resulting controversy. According to Lowden's memorandum of the meeting, the discussion centered on the personnel who should participate in the general conference, the role of the GOP national committee in arranging for it, and the choice of members for the planning committee. Hoover apparently made no objection to Landon's insistence that state GOP office-holders and county chairmen should be included, nor did Landon object to Hoover's proposal that the planning committee should consist of Hoover, Lowden, Landon, Knox,

Vandenberg, possibly Borah, and such others as the initial members should decide to add. Lowden, like Hoover, apparently left the meeting in the belief that the three men had reached agreement.[121] Hoover wrote to Hamilton two days later saying that, as a result of the meeting, Landon had agreed that Hoover was to notify the chairman that they jointly favored the creation by the national committee of a group to draft a declaration of fundamental principles of the party, which would then be submitted to a conference of party leaders in the spring of 1938. He then listed for Hamilton the names of GOP leaders who had, he said, "authorized me to indicate their support" of the proposal; included in that list were both Lowden and Landon.[122]

Despite the impressions Hoover and Lowden carried away from the conference, the third member, Landon, did not recall giving the general conference proposal his unqualified support. According to Landon's account of the meeting, he had stipulated three conditions that would have to be satisfied before he could agree to the proposal: (1) the committee that selected the personnel of the general conference must be representative of all interests in the GOP, (2) that he must ascertain the attitude of congressional leaders before giving the proposal his support, and (3) that he must have clarification of exactly what the general conference was to do—he wanted "full accord on the plans and programs." Under such conditions Landon was willing to support the proposal, but only if the Republican national committee voted to go ahead with the conference.[123]

It seems curious that three such specific conditions as Landon claimed he had insisted upon could have escaped the attention of Hoover and Lowden. But whatever the position Landon had taken in the meeting, the Kansan now made every effort to ensure that the GOP national committee did not adopt the general conference proposal. He continued to express his misgivings about the appropriateness of such a conference and continued to encourage opposition to it.[124] Landon also sought to delay the meeting of the GOP national committee for a month, but failed.[125] In such ways did Landon attempt to snatch from Hoover the victory that the latter thought he had won in their meeting with Lowden.

Hoover sought to confront the opposition of Washington Republicans to the conference proposal in a meeting with Senator Vandenberg. He found the Michigan senator opposed to a mid-term conference on the grounds that it might embarrass the local stances of congressional candidates. Hoover's view, by contrast, was that "every Republican candidate for Congress is beaten to a frazzle on local issues before he starts." New Deal candidates could promise the sky and show evidence that they delivered. In Hoover's opinion, the only hope of Republican candidates was to run on national issues "beyond the narrow vision of local benefits."[126] However, Landon's "new" conditions, coupled with the refusal of such GOP leaders as Vandenberg to support the mid-term conference, seriously damaged the prospect that the conference would be held, since it was apparent that any constructive action by the Republican party that did not have the party leaders' active support would present a picture to the nation of a badly divided GOP.[127]

While Landon voiced specific and strong arguments against the conference proposal, it is apparent that a good part of his opposition was based on his resistance to Hoover's attempt to re-establish himself as leader of the Republican party. The motive behind Hoover's effort in advancing the conference proposal, and the extent of his campaign for intellectual leadership, became joined in Landon's mind as a drive by Hoover to dominate the GOP and to win the nomination in 1940. It was apparent to Landon, from the Hyde and Reppy efforts, that Hoover was determined to become the dominant figure in the party, and the Kansan professed to worry about the effect that such Hoover dominance would have on the GOP, since the former president was "too inept as a politician."[128] Landon frequently drew contrasts between Hoover's apparent organization and expenditure of funds and his own lack of money or organization.[129] Landon was not worried over the prospect of a Hoover nomination in 1940, he said, because he considered both Hoover's and his own prospects as "nil," but he worried over the effect on the party's standing with the people if Hoover appeared to be its dominant figure.[130]

Hoover had delayed his return to California until after the GOP national committee meeting so that he could continue to exert pressure for the passage of his proposal. As he put it, he had "to try to get some stamina into the Republican party. I am gradually forcing the various leaders into line, but it is a tedious job. There are many pinheads to deal with."[131] He wrote Ray Lyman Wilbur: "If I had any opinions before on the pigmy minds of some recent notables, I have stronger opinions now and include more persons in it [sic]."[132] Hoover had scheduled a speech in Boston for late October, and some of his campaigners urged him to use the opportunity to set forth his own principles for the Republican party and thus defy opponents of the mid-term conference plan.[133] Hoover refused to do so, however, arguing that he had urged a mid-term conference to debate a statement of principles and that it would be unfair for him to publicize his own views in advance.[134] His strategy in October was to continue to break down the resistance to his leadership and to control the conference, when it was formed, because, in his view, he would have the only program to offer it.[135] If Landon thought that Hoover was interested in the 1940 nomination, Hoover was equally certain that Landon had the same object in mind.[136]

As both Landon and Hoover marshaled their forces for the November national committee meeting, the press increasingly viewed the mid-term conference proposal as a test of strength between them. The North American

Newspaper Alliance (NANA) opined that unless Landon and Hoover could "work out a meeting of minds before the Republican National Committee" met, there was "likely to be an explosion among the party leaders." Pointedly, it observed that neither of the two had declared that he would not accept the 1940 nomination if it were tendered, and the NANA article concluded: "Apparently each is seeking recognition as the titular leader of the party."[137] The *New York Times* reported that Landon was rallying congressional opposition to the conference proposal and added: "The hostility between Mr. Hoover and Mr. Landon, both of whom appear to be determined to be the mouthpiece of the party, is reported to be deep seated."[138] Senator Arthur Vandenberg, however, now approached Landon with a proposed compromise. Under Vandenberg's proposal the national committee would appoint a special committee to consider a declaration of principles, but without any commitment regarding a 1938 general conference. Landon promised to take up the idea with GOP chairman John Hamilton.[139]

In mid-October, Landon sought to reassert his titular leadership of the Republican party by going on the air with a nationwide speech. Contrary to expectations, especially of Hoover supporters, that he would devote the speech to an attack on the mid-term conference proposal, Landon ignored the issue. Instead, he lambasted the New Deal in a fashion befitting the leader of the opposition party.[140] The press quickly grasped the significance of the speech. The *New York Times* wrote that it represented an attempt by Landon "to assert his leadership of the Republican party and put himself in the role of titular leader," while columnist Delbert Clark described it as "the crisis in the half-hidden struggle between ex-Governor Landon and ex-President Hoover for supremacy in the councils of the party."[141] *Time* magazine concluded that "Alf Landon decided the time had come to reassert his position."[142]

Hoover pronounced the Landon effort a "good speech" and busied himself with making sure that Republican leaders tuned into his own Boston effort on October 26.[143] In that speech, delivered before the Massachusetts State Republican Club, Hoover spoke of the necessity for the GOP to have "a fighting cause," "an affirmative program," "effective methods," "a forward purpose," "idealism," and to be responsive "to the needs and crises of the people." Of the charges that he was seeking to advance his own political career, Hoover reassured his listeners that he was not seeking public office, but would "keep on fighting for those things vital to the American people." Such activities would necessarily lead to charges that he was seeking the nomination because "the accusation of seeking office seems to be the highest intellectual level to which the opposition can rise when they are made uncomfortable by argument and new proposals." The time had come, he reiterated, "when the Republican Party should be reoriented to . . . fundamental issues. No civilization is static. It must move forward or die. Therefore no party can be static. It must move forward with the times." He described the efforts being made in behalf of the convening of a general conference to formulate GOP principles. He was not, he said, "concerned over details," but he was "deeply concerned that people who are losing their way shall be given a banner of moral and intellectual leadership around which they can rally as the inevitable day of disillusionment comes to them." It was not enough, he argued, to follow the theory that most people voted against something and it was adequate for the GOP to wait until the Democrats made enough mistakes to deliver the nation back to the stewardship of the Republicans. That had been the tactic of the Whig party, and it had died. Nor was mere talk of fusion and coalition enough, because "the people fuse or coalesce around ideas and ideals, not around political bargains or stratagems. If the Republican Party meets the needs and aspirations of the people who are opposed to the New Deal, they will fuse and coalesce and not before."[144]

Hoover's speech was featured on the front page of the *New York Times*, which took special note of his disclaimer concerning any interest in public office.[145] Hoover was encouraged by the general press reaction to his speech and by the letters he received.[146] Columnist Boake Carter congratulated him on the speech, but urged that he go on the attack with even more blunt and pointed attacks that would "hit hard and shock the party and shock the old guard." Carter found a feeling of despair among Republicans "that nobody in the Republican Party will get up and hit. The feeling is that it's the same old talking in riddles." Landon, he observed, had "tried to hit and bumped himself in the nose" with a speech that had been "like a windmill trying to go to work." But Hoover, Carter insisted, was capable of the kind of bluntness the times required.[147] Hoover agreed, but he pointed out that the object of his Boston speech had been to influence the passage of the mid-term conference resolution through the national committee "and to set the direction of ideas." He told Carter: "I know something of the individual men and what will help them fight that battle. I may be wrong. There is time to change if these methods do not win."[148]

Caught between the conflicting ambitions of Hoover and Landon, GOP chairman Hamilton sought a compromise that would be acceptable to both camps. Stymied in one such attempt by Landon, Hamilton submitted to both leaders two proposed resolutions on November 2.[149] The first resolution would establish a policy committee "to consider and report to the Chairman of the Republican National Committee its conclusions upon the pertinent questions now before the American people, said Committee to be composed of not less than one hundred members." The policy committee would "ascertain as fully as possible the different views held by national and local leaders" upon the questions that came before it for consideration. The second resolution proposed a committee of arrangements, made up of 25 members, "to determine the place, time and method of determining the membership" of a general conference to which the report of the policy committee would be submitted by the national chairman.[150]

Hoover and Landon alternated between pessimism and optimism as a final barrage of pros and cons on the conference proposal filled the newspapers on the eve of the GOP national committee meeting.[151] At this meeting, the national committee adopted a resolution that was a compromise, although it substantially met Hoover's desires. The proposed committee on arrangements was dropped. The policy committee, however, was formed to undertake the work contemplated in the Hamilton compromise, although it was renamed the program committee. The recommendations of the program committee would still go to the national chairman who, under the new plan, would then call a meeting of the GOP national committee "to determine the most effective and practical manner (a national general forum, conference, or otherwise) of presenting a report of the recommendations for the consideration of the nation."[152]

Hamilton had drawn up the final resolution after consulting with Hoover and Landon and receiving input from "well over half" the members of the GOP national committee. The motion for adoption of the compromise resolution was made by Congressman Joseph Martin, a strong opponent of the midterm conference proposal, and it was carried without a dissenting vote, although Hooverite R. B. Creager of Texas expressed disappointment with the compromise and stated his intention to fight "till the last for a quick and early calling" of a general conference once the committee had submitted its recommendations.[153]

As Landon's biographer, Donald R. McCoy, has pointed out, the compromise reached by the national committee amounted to a "rebuff" for Hoover.[154] Still, the former president had achieved much of what he had sought. He had already expressed the opinion, before the meeting, that the policy committee was the most important element in the proposal, and he reiterated this belief in his public response to the national committee's decision. The rank and file of the party had, he told reporters, pushed the Republican party "the larger half of a strong movement forward from a policy of negation." He added:

> The program committee of 100 is to be appointed as proposed by myself and associates to formulate a declaration of convictions and an affirmative program for the party. General conference or no conference, the declaration is the thing. The rank and file will probably take care of the conference question in time. The program committee can perform a great national service if it is appointed from unafraid men and women who will stand up and be

counted. . . . The program committee will have a great opportunity
to give life and vigor; to unify the Republican party; to realign it to
the needs of the people; to lay the foundations of fusion to all forces
who not only oppose many New Deal methods but who want a way
out of the crisis.[155]

By whatever name—program committee, general conference, or mid-
term convention—Hoover had succeeded in his goal of getting a representative
group of Republicans to work on formulating principles for the Republican
party. This was what he had sought from the beginning, some constructive
activity on the part of the GOP. While a decision on any general conference
was held in abeyance, no such conference would have been convened in any
case until the program committee completed its deliberations; and the role of
the general conference would have been simply to consider and act upon the
declaration of principles already drawn up by the program committee.

Since the concept of the general conference had come to be associated with
Hoover, rather than with the ends such a conference would achieve for the
party, the former president was denied something of a victory by the national
committee's action. Hoover knew that despite the appearance of a personal
defeat, he had actually achieved a victory, and he was upset by attempts to
paint the national committee's action as a setback for him. When Frank Knox
did so in his *Chicago Daily News*, Hoover responded bitterly that the most
important thing for him had always been the declaration of principles, not the
general conference:

> The National Committee did adopt that more important thing.
> After having been for months practically the sole voice of insurgency
> in the party against rotting inaction, you do not even mention the
> major thing that I have stood for but depict the minor thing. The
> result was to plaster me all over the country as having been defeated
> and turned down and generally humiliated. I presume that it is
> satisfactory enough to some of you, but I question whether it is for
> the good of the country.[156]

Hoover was correct, but so was Knox in responding that it was the mid-term
convention or general conference idea that had become associated with Hoover
in the popular mind, and in that sense he had, indeed, the image of one who
had been defeated.[157]

For those like Spargo and Reppy, whose attempt to organize a call for
Hoover's restoration to leadership of the GOP had been aborted by his concentration on the conference fight, the compromise on the conference proposal
was a bitter pill. Spargo saw their efforts as "left pretty well stranded by the

action of the national committee," and felt the only possibility of action now lay in going "back to where we started" and issuing "the call precisely as we had originally planned," an action that "would serve the original purpose of providing the Chief with a perfectly respectable and unassailable platform upon which to stand." Spargo had never favored the general conference idea and had gone along only because of Hoover's insistence, nor did Spargo feel that anything constructive would now emerge from the program committee.[158] He continued to feel that if Hoover had consented to the original plan for a call, "it might well have made a sufficient stir and its publication have brought out a sufficient demonstration of strength to have forced the timid souls on the other side to face the music." In that case, the Landon forces would not "have dared sidetrack the convention in the face of uprising."[159] However, the evidence from the correspondence in the Landon papers suggests that their efforts were having the contrary effect. In attempting to build Hoover's "intellectual leadership" they kindled suspicion that the conference proposal was but one element in a campaign to build the former president for the 1940 nomination. Thus, their efforts led to opposition to the conference proposal on the part of those who might otherwise have favored it. The issuance of a call would doubtless only have confirmed further this suspicion and stiffened the opposition even more.

The program committee now became an arena of contention between Hoover and Landon as both sought to ensure that the committee would be staffed with members representative of their views.[160] The two GOP leaders would naturally seek to influence the deliberations of the committee as much as possible. The key questions to be answered were: Would the program committee complete its deliberations early enough in 1938 for a general conference to be called, as Hoover wished, or would it be delayed into 1940, as Landon preferred? If the deliberations were completed in 1938, would a general conference, in fact, be called? Predictably, Hoover pushed for rapid action by the program committee, while Landon sought to delay its deliberations and thus stalemate the possibility of a general conference.[161] Despite Hoover's prodding, the program committee, under Dr. Glenn Frank, did not move quickly to formulate the program he sought.

Frustrated at the slow progress of the program committee, Hoover took to the speaking circuit to give further force to his effort to reinvigorate the Republican party. On November 8 he delivered an address at Colby College on freedom of speech and press. In the previous fifteen years, he observed, "increasing darkness has descended upon free expression and free criticism in the world." Dictators used free speech and free press to attain power and then suppressed all free speech except their own. The durability of free speech and a free press rested upon a commitment to truth. A "special breed of cultivated untruth" was propaganda. It had been perfected by use in wartime and was now used to "create bias and inflame the minds of men" even in the area of politics. The responsibility lay upon newspaper editors to discriminate between "propaganda and real news, between untruth and truth." This responsibility was greater and more difficult with radio than it was for the newspapers. Hoover did not call for new laws or the extension of governmental control over free speech, but he did call for a reform "in the morals of the users of untruth"; and he noted that the best refutation of untruths and half-truths was truth. "This antidote," he admitted, "works with discouraging slowness at times, but unless we maintain faith in our medicine civilization will despair."[162] Four days after his Colby address, Hoover spoke at Syracuse University on "training for public service," and called upon those trained in public service by the universities to get involved in "the hurly burly of political conflict," since it, too, was an aspect of public service.[163]

The campaigners for a call for Hoover felt they had "thoroughly scared" the Washington Republicans "with relatively little effort" and were eager to undertake anew their efforts in Hoover's behalf.[164] Hoover was now totally absorbed with his speaking efforts and with monitoring the progress of the program committee, and he instructed his campaigners to limit their drive.[165] He was, however, aware of the dissatisfaction the campaigners felt over his concentration on the conference proposal and the declaration of principles at the expense of their efforts to boom him for the intellectual leadership of the party. As he prepared to leave for Chicago to deliver a speech there, Hoover wrote John Spargo a lengthy letter explaining his reasons for pursuing the course he had followed:

> I know that you have not felt comfortable under the tactics which I have been following. After all, what we are fighting for is to hold certain precious fundamentals of personal liberty to the American people in the midst of a crumbling world. The time we have in which to do this is limited. It is not as if we could take years and years to build up. I came to a realization that despite all of the efforts of such devoted friends as yourself, there was little hope of building up, in the time we have, a personal leadership of these ideas which would dominate the American mind and control the direction which they would take. I felt that in this limited time, we must get some great instrumentality pledged, or we would not succeed. The only possibility is the Republican Party. I realize that if the leadership and these ideas are handed over to a party, one gives over the role of John the Baptist, to become the supporter of a political mechanism. But I have thought it was in the interest of the country that it should be done this way. I have had to fight every inch of the way against pinhead politicians whose sole object is to get to the public trough by the easiest route. They, of course, attack me as a means to destroy the

idea of the hard road. Whether the policy committee . . . will serve effectually for this purpose or not, no one of us can tell. I am, of course, a great deal discouraged with what is going on. But anything that does come of it, is to the good in the great cause we have to fight. I have no intention of retiring for one minute from the battle and, of course, one accomplishes nothing unless one has a group of strong men such as you, who are willing to wade in at every moment to support such leadership as I can give. But peoples' ideas of leadership are still crystallized in the terms of ambition for political office, and they are not disposed to rally around people other than those they think are making a fight to secure office. Whether we can succeed in this sheer fighting for the ideas as distinguished from personal ambitions I do not know. At the present, I have very great doubts about it.[166]

On December 16, 1937, Hoover delivered his Chicago speech on the economic situation. In the summer of 1937 there had been a dramatic downturn in the nation's economy that was being called a "recession." In September production fell by 5 percent and the decline continued in subsequent months. Between September of 1937 and the following June, industrial production fell 33 percent, national income dropped 13 percent, profits plummeted by 78 percent, payrolls declined 35 percent, industrial stock averages fell by over 50 percent, and manufacturing employment dropped by 23 percent. It was the severest decline in American economic history.[167] It was in the midst of this recession that Hoover addressed his audience.

Hoover found Americans "torn with dissension and feelings of insecurity and even fear." The concern did not stem from external causes, but from something "far deeper in our national life than this immediate business recession." He preferred the new word "recession," and he could "be wholly objective on this depression because certainly I did not create it." The recession, however, was only one indication of deeper currents in America's economic troubles. Under the New Deal, the entire economic system had been "condemned without discrimination as to its strengths or its faults," and a planned economy had been instituted. This "brought a conflict between two fundamentally opposite philosophies of government and economics in operation at the same time." The central idea of the new planned economy was "the gigantic shift of government from the function of umpire to the function of directing, dictating and competing in our economic life" through such weapons as "politically managed currency, managed credit, managed interest rates, huge expenditures in pump priming and inflation of bank deposits," as well as the use of "relief funds to build the government into competitive business," the use of taxing powers to control business conduct, and the use of regulatory powers to dictate to business. The result had been "obvious violations of common sense."[168]

Hoover warned that when "the government expands into business then in order to protect itself it is driven irresistibly toward control of men's thoughts and the press." Group conflicts had been magnified by government policies; nothing done by the administration had provided either economic security or equal opportunity. Hoover championed free enterprise because, he argued, it was the only economic system that did not limit intellectual and spiritual liberty. In the operation of the economic system, there must be full utilization of each new development in technology and the elimination of waste in order to maximize production and bring costs down so that people could purchase goods and so that well-paying jobs could be created. Government's role must be limited to regulation; economic groups must voluntarily cooperate with one another and with noneconomic groups, including the government. The taxing powers should be utilized by government to ensure that no group got either too much or too little of the abundance produced. Greater cooperation was needed between labor and management, and there should be more research into the causes of booms and slumps in the economy. "It is difficult," Hoover told his listeners, "for timid minds to believe that free men can work out their own salvation. Arrogant minds seeking for power live upon this timidity."[169]

On his arrival in California from Chicago, reporters found Hoover "in a jovial mood" and describing the program committee as a "move in the right direction."[170] He quickly busied himself in the California political situation, looking ahead to the 1938 off-year elections. The basis for a political organization existed in the groups that had been created at Hoover's instigation to fight the court-packing bill, as well as in the list of names that had been unearthed through the questionnaire on the mid-term conference proposal.[171]

Foreign affairs, however, began to intrude into Hoover's activities. The eruption of a full-scale war between Japan and China was followed in late December by the Japanese bombing of the American gunboat U.S.S. *Panay*, on the Yangtze River. When Alf Landon wired Roosevelt to offer his support in whatever action the president took, he was roundly criticized by other Republicans.[172] Hoover agreed that the Kansan's wire had been foolish. He wrote Woodrow Wilson's secretary of state, Bainbridge Colby, that Landon had "no authority from any citizen or the Republican Party to give a blank check to any President to take the United States into war." In Hoover's view, there were many ways short of war by which the United States could establish its honor in such situations, and war "should be reserved as the answer to assaults upon our national freedom and this alone."[173]

Before he left New York for the West Coast, Hoover wrote Gertrude Lane at *Collier's* to suggest an editorial supporting the Republican program committee: "There is nothing the country needs more than to have a definite banner erected by the Republican Party to get it out of pure negation and pinhead politics into the field of constructive statesmanship." He sought support from *Collier's* in his drive to expedite the work of the committee.[174] Now, in California, he monitored the work of the committee through Arch Shaw, one of the Hooverite members of the committee.[175] As other Hoover supporters and potential supporters were named to the committee, he sent them his congratulations.[176] He also ensured that the members of the committee all received copies of the Wilbur and Hyde book on the Hoover administration; he commented on this practice in a letter to committee member H. Alexander Smith: "It certainly makes a better background for new policies if they know what really has taken place under the Republicans, not what the New Deal says has taken place."[177] He warned his supporters on the committee:

> There is a definite drive on the part of the Congressional and Topeka groups to defer any statement until after the Congressional election. The rank and file of the Republican Party would be disgusted with any such measures and the committee on policy would be hopelessly lost. Everywhere I go I find that the hope of the party lies in this committee and the disgust is chiefly centralized in the opposition group.[178]

On January 15, 1938, Hoover made a radio speech to the Republican women's clubs of New York, Chicago, and San Francisco. The darkening international situation in both Europe and Asia led him to address the question of "American Policies for Peace." He found the world "filled with increasing distrust and rising disorder," with armies increasing in size and international economic life demoralized. America, like other nations, was torn by confusion over what policies should be followed, but it should have learned some lessons from the Great War it had fought less than a generation earlier. It should have learned that the winners suffered almost equally with the losers, that wars inevitably produced inflation, that democratic government in the United States "probably could not stand the shock of another great war and survive as a democracy." The United States should fight only to defend its own independence and against violations of the Monroe Doctrine in the western hemisphere.[179]

Hoover also expressed his opposition to the Ludlow Amendment, a proposed amendment offered by Congressman Louis Ludlow of Indiana, which would have required a nationwide referendum in support of American participation in war, except in the event of an invasion of the United States, before a congressional declaration of war could be made. He argued that such a device was workable only if all nations of the world were democracies and agreed to a similar type of referendum. The greatest assurance that the United

States would not be attacked by another nation lay in preparedness for defense and the determination of the nation to use its arms "solely to repel aggression against the Western Hemisphere." In any other situation the United States must preserve its neutrality. Hoover was opposed to economic sanctions, embargoes, or boycotts to try to force peace on other countries at war, because he was convinced "that the use of such measures is the stepping-stone to war and not to peace." Instead, the United States should "cooperate in every sane international effort to advance the economic and social welfare of the world," since the "prosperity of nations is the best sedative to hate." International economic cooperation had been the goal in arranging for the 1933 World Economic Conference, but that conference had been sabotaged by the Roosevelt administration. Such conferences remained the best answer to international economic friction. The United States, Hoover concluded, should also exert all moral force to preserve peace through such devices as international disarmament, treaties of conciliation and arbitration, and other acts to advance "the moral foundations of the peace in the world."[180]

Having largely ignored foreign affairs for nearly five years since leaving the White House, Hoover's short and relatively minor speech to the GOP women launched him into an area that would loom increasingly important in his public career for the next fifteen years. And his first discourse laid down in sketchy outline most of the principles he would espouse regarding American foreign relations throughout this coming period. The speech aroused a good deal of favorable comment, and Congressman Hamilton Fish, Jr. inserted it into the *Congressional Record*, noting in a telegram to Hoover that he was happy to see that the former president did not agree with the internationalism of Hoover's former secretary of state, Henry Stimson, who supported the use of embargoes, armed force, and the "quarantining" of other nations.[181] Hoover's future pronouncements on foreign policy would gain further authority as a result of a visit he would make to Europe early in 1938.

Arrangements for Hoover's European trip had originally been made in 1935, but the death of the queen of Belgium had forced a postponement.[182] Late in 1936 the planned trip was taken up once again, and Hoover sought an invitation from the Belgian government to revisit the nation he had fed during the early years of World War I.[183] That trip, too, fell through when it became apparent that the Belgian government did not wish to offend the Roosevelt administration by extending an invitation to one so obviously in disfavor in Washington.[184] The reluctance of the Belgians to make an event of his return, the crisis over the Supreme Court, and Hoover's involvement in the fight over the mid-term conference proposal, all led to a delay of the trip until 1938.

En route to the East for his departure for Europe, Hoover stopped in Chicago for a visit with GOP program committee chairman Glenn Frank. Hoover had grown anxious over the direction the committee was taking.

While Landon rejoiced that Frank had determined "to limit the work of the committee to simply one of inquiry," Hoover regarded such an approach as entirely contrary to the intent in setting up the committee.[185] As he wrote H. Alexander Smith, the committee had "no use on earth unless it is prepared to make a bold direction of principles at this time."[186] Congressman Bert Snell likewise hoped that the committee would "do something that attracts the attention of the country."[187] Landon had met with Frank late in January, and Hoover was determined that the chairman should be equally certain of his own views concerning the committee's work.[188] At his meeting with Frank, early in February, Hoover argued for the desirability of getting out "a short, pungent statement of steps which, if taken immediately, would restore employment to millions of men, distinguishing between this and the long view program," which would follow later. He also suggested a similar short statement "on keeping the peace and keeping away from entanglements in either Asia or Europe."[189]

After impressing his views on Frank as to the necessity for somewhat prompter action than that advocated by Landon, Hoover left for Europe, arriving in France on February 16, 1938. The Hoover party motored to Belgium for a week of feting, then returned to France before traveling on to Switzerland, Austria, and Czechoslovakia. Early in March he arrived in Germany, and at noon on March 8 he had a forty- to fifty-minute conversation with Adolf Hitler. The following day he lunched at the hunting lodge of Hermann Göring. Thereafter, the Hoover group traveled to Poland, Latvia, and Estonia before visiting Finland and Sweden. Hoover ended his European visit with a few days in England, where he was interviewed by the press. He observed that he had discussed the European situation "with the leading men of fifteen nations" and had "a deep consciousness of the many menaces to peace," yet did not "believe that a widespread war is probable in the immediate future."[190] Hoover and his party returned to New York City on March 29. In almost all of the countries visited he had met with the top government officials, U.S. diplomatic representatives, and the press.[191]

Scarcely debarked in the United States, Hoover addressed the Foreign Policy Association in New York on March 31. His speech, entitled "Foreign Policies for America," was nationally braodcast. Hoover opened the speech by pointing out that since World War I he had received numerous invitations from European governments, cities, and universities to visit, but this had been the first opportunity for him to accept. He had "welcomed the opportunity to observe at first hand the political, social, and economic forces now in motion nineteen years after my last day in Europe." He recounted for his listeners his earlier experiences in Europe and described his return to those nations "to discuss the forces in motion with more than a hundred leaders whose friendship I had enjoyed in the past and probably another hundred whom I met for

the first time." Europe had experienced a rise of dictatorships and was caught
up in an arms race that had resulted in "increased government debts and
deficits." Each nation was striving for the maximum of self-sufficiency in
industrial and food production. The League of Nations had failed and had
been replaced by a renewed reliance on the old concept of the balance of power.
The result was fear, and a steady increase in some nations "of brutality, of
terrorism, and disregard for both life and justice." It was, Hoover reflected,
"an alarming and disheartening picture." He reiterated his belief that a general war was not an "immediate prospect." Military preparations were not
complete, and the thinking was still primarily defensive rather than offensive.
Beneath the visible aspects of the situation there were "still deeper currents."
These included the "injustices and unrealities of the Peace Treaties," the
economic chaos that led to the European financial collapse of the early 1930s,
and the racially mixed populations of Europe with their age-old hatreds and
aspirations. Hoover traced the rise of totalitarianism in Europe from the
economic chaos of the 1930s and sought to analyze what "should be the
American attitude toward all this maze of forces."[192]

The United States, he concluded, should make clear that it would not take
part in another general European war, not even in alliance with the democracies against totalitarianism, for such a conflict would "have all the hideous
elements of the old religious wars." America should have none of it. "If the
world is to keep the peace, then we must keep peace with dictatorships as well
as with popular governments. The forms of government which other peoples
pass through in working out their destinies is not our business." The United
States should limit itself to organizing and joining "in the collective moral
forces to prevent war." As for economic relations, Hoover reiterated his belief
that the "prosperity of nations is the best antidote for the poisons of fear and
hate." The United States should encourage international economic cooperation. Other than that, he felt the great mission of the United States was to
"keep alight the flame of true liberalism." He added:

> The protection of democracy is that we live it, that we revitalize it
> within our own borders, that we keep it clean of infection, that we
> wipe out its corruptions, that we incessantly fight its abuses, that we
> insist upon intellectual honesty, that we build its morals, that we
> keep out of war.

This, Hoover concluded, was "the greatest service that this nation can give to
the future of humanity."[193]

In April 1938, Hoover's attention was drawn to Roosevelt's bill for reorganization of the executive branch of the government, then being debated in
the House. The proposed legislation would have permitted the streamlining of

the executive branch in the interest of efficiency, something that Hoover might be expected to applaud, but for opponents of the New Deal it represented another power grab by the man in the White House. Hoover wired Congressman J. William Ditter that the bill was "an attempt by indirection to increase the Presidential authority over legislative and judicial functions and to bring about an extension of the spoils system, which should render this bill wholly objectionable to the American people."[194] En route back to his California home, he told the press in Chicago that the administration's bill represented "the reintroduction of the spoils system after 75 years of battle to set up the civil service commission" and "a grab for more power by the President."[195] By the time he reached San Francisco, the bill had become to Hoover a step toward fascism. "Any encroachment upon the judicial and legislative areas of our government," he told reporters, "is an attempt to break down the democracy under which we live." The United States seemed to be "moving in the direction taken by every European state that has lost its liberty as the result of economic misery."[196] A few days later the bill was defeated in the House of Representatives by a vote of 204 to 196, with 108 Democrats bolting the president.[197] Hoover hailed GOP minority leader Bert Snell for his "grand fight." He wrote: "You cannot appreciate in Washington, what a tremendous effect it has been [*sic*] throughout the country. It has lifted the spirits of everybody who has any devotion to the American form of government."[198] To William Castle he admitted: "The defeat of the reorganization bill is of much more importance than the bill itself, because it indicates the turning of the public mind of this country from centralized authority."[199]

On April 8, Hoover returned to the subject of foreign policy with a speech in San Francisco. He tried to give his listeners some sense of the conditions in Europe by comparing California to a European country:

> If we had 500,000 troops and 2,000 aeroplanes looking at us hatefully from over the Oregon line, another 400,000 men and 2,000 planes ready to march over the Nevada line, and another few hundred thousand being drilled in Arizona ready to pounce upon us, this would be a less comfortable place. And if we had to pay taxes for about 400,000 men in our own State to make faces at these sister States, then it would be still more uncomfortable.

He described the living conditions in Europe, which resulted from such constant threats, as well as conditions in the authoritarian states of Europe, where if one did not agree with the state, one ended up in a concentration camp. Altogether, Hoover concluded, he was happy California was 7,200 miles from Europe. After discussing his European trip, Hoover surveyed the American scene and indicted the Roosevelt administration for the United States' slow recovery from the depression as compared with the recoveries of democratic, as well as totalitarian, countries in Europe. America, he said, "must restore genuine self-respecting jobs in productive enterprises." That could only be accomplished by discarding the "Planned Economy" of the New Deal and restoring free enterprise. The most prosperous democracies in Europe, he told his listeners, were those that had "refused to adopt these courses of Planned Economy."[200]

Hoover's speeches on foreign relations sought to preserve reason in the American approach to international affairs. After his first speech in New York on returning from Europe, he wrote Hugh Wilson, U.S. Ambassador to Germany, that he had sought "to be fair and yet to express my own conclusions honestly. I do not expect it was overwhelmingly approved over there [in Germany], but if the German officials had any idea of the attitude taken by most Americans they would consider this with some relief." His purpose in the New York speech had been to bring "our people to a realization that we must live with other nations," and he felt that his goal had been achieved, judging from the reactions to the speech.[201] Wilson responded that he had read the speech with satisfaction "and these people over here have done so as well." He added:

> I wish our people in general could understand how little is gained in scolding other people, and how much is gained by trying to work with them. We accomplish nothing by the scolding except to irritate the other fellow and make business harder. If we were willing to stop him, that's a different matter, but we obviously are not.[202]

The foreign policy speeches had apparently struck a responsive chord among the American people. Professor Allison Reppy wrote Hoover in early April that his trip abroad, and the subsequent speeches, had "worked a profound change among the classes and groups of our people whom it was desirable to reach and who have been in the toils of the New Deal." This applied especially, he said, to the foreign born, who had been affected by the spectacle of Hoover being feted by the governments of the countries from which they had emigrated. He found that even German- and Italian-Americans did not seem offended by Hoover's criticism of the totalitarian governments in their native countries because he had emphasized that the United States must preserve peace with them no matter what their form of government.[203] A number of others remarked upon the continuing renaissance in Hoover's popularity in movie theaters, with applause greeting his appearance in newsreels. William Allen White applauded the March 31 speech and wrote that when Hoover appeared in a newsreel in a Kansas City theater, "the audience burst into a cheer."[204] Columnist Raymond Clapper reported the same occurrence in "widely scattered parts of the country" and concluded: "Obviously something is going on in this country, but I still am not quite certain what it is."[205]

Late in April, Hoover attacked the morals of the New Deal in a speech in Fresno, California. The greatness of nations, he averred, depended upon their moral stature, "not the size of their population or their wealth," and when government was dishonest it affected the morals of the people. Morality in government required that public officials be selected under the merit system, but the Roosevelt administration had disregarded "seventy years' effort to build up a national system of merit service." Government funds should not be used to influence elections, but the New Deal had used federal funds to pressure members of Congress, to influence voters in "politically doubtful districts," and to aid corrupt urban political machines. Morality required an honest accounting of public funds, but the Roosevelt administration juggled accounts to deceive the American people. "Manipulation of budgets and obscuring the nature of government expenditures always precedes the rise of dictatorships," Hoover warned. The government should be "scrupulous in its financial transactions with the citizen," but the New Deal had welshed on its promises, used "public funds to manipulate its own bond market, rigged the currency." Government expenditures should be used to build up the character of the people, and not to "undermine the responsibility, the self-respect, the dignity that marks free men." But New Deal policies had led every community into "a conspiracy to get its share from the Federal grab bag," undermining the responsibility of states, communities, and individuals. Government officials had connived "at lawlessness and sit-down strikes" and had stirred up class animosity, setting one group against another, dividing the people by hate. Under the Roosevelt administration intellectual dishonesty had "become an art under the heading of propaganda." He told his listeners:

> These are grave hours. We are in a moral recession in government. Beyond this we have for five years listened to a continuous defamation of everything that has gone before. Honest achievement of men has been belittled and attributed to improper motives. Ideals embedded in our patriotism are smeared with contempt. We are told that the frontiers of initiative and enterprise are closed. We are told that we are in ruins and we must begin anew. We are told the government must do it for us.

But Hoover concluded that with a restoration of morals the nation could do even more in another generation.[206]

Hoover continued the attack a few days later in Oklahoma City. Made before a "grass-roots" Republican meeting, this speech was on the "Dangerous Road for Democracy." He pointed out that none of the fourteen Euro-

pean nations under authoritarian governments had set out to surrender their
liberties, but each had undertaken "New Deals under some title, usually
Planned Economy," and gradually, by the same course the United States
seemed to be following, they had "sapped the vitality of free enterprise by
government experiments in dictation and socialistic competition." They had
sacrificed free enterprise to pursue the utopias of both fascism and socialism,
with each step "accompanied by greater corruption of the electorate, increasing intellectual and moral dishonesty in government." Permanent economic
recovery was impossible under such a situation, and only further collapse
resulted, leading "desperate people" to surrender more liberties to "some man
or group of men who promised security, moral regeneration, discipline, and
hope." It was only a short easy step "from experimental dictation by government to farmers, workers and business into a full Fascist system," when free
enterprise, "having been demoralized by fear," had to be compelled to produce
"by more fear and coercion." By contrast, the surviving democracies in Europe
had practiced belt tightening, balanced budgets, and had "refused new deals
and planned economies." They were now the most prosperous nations in the
world, Hoover maintained. But the United States was following those nations
that had ended in fascism, and already, Hoover asserted, "it would startle this
country if our people had a detailed list of the powers over their daily life they
have surrendered to the President and his bureaucracy." The "creeping collectivism" of the New Deal had aborted the beginnings of recovery that had been
seen in 1932. "A few drops of Socialism or Fascism" was poison to private
enterprise, he argued, just as surely as "a drop of typhoid in a barrel of water
will sicken a whole village." The mixture would not work, and the American
example was proving that it did not work. It had only sickened initiative and
enterprise, substituted fear, and destroyed millions of jobs. Now, faced with a
depression of its own making, the New Deal could propose only "more bureaucratic dictation to business, more inflation, more pump-priming, more
Planned Economy." The devices of the New Deal must be discarded totally so
that confidence could be restored and the initiative and enterprise of men
released once again. The emphasis on scarcity must be abandoned for abundance, morals must be restored to government, the budget must be balanced,
and control over the economy must be taken from the hands of politicians. By
such measures, Hoover insisted, the nation would be started "on a saner and
more cheerful road."[207]

In June 1938, Hoover and his supporters on the Republican program
committee began to press Glenn Frank to move on an early preliminary
declaration of principles.[208] Despite obvious reluctance, in late June Chairman Frank began to work on a preliminary statement in consultation with the
former president.[209] Frank's draft, however, was unacceptable to Hoover as
lacking force, so Hoover asked Chester Rowell to revise it.[210] He hoped that

such a preliminary declaration could be ready for a meeting of the full committee, which was scheduled for August 1.[211] Late in July Hoover sought to
further spur the movement toward a preliminary statement of principles by
sending to his supporters on the committee copies of a letter in which he wrote:

> One of the most discouraging things going on in the Republican
> Party is the constant apology being made for it. The attitude on the
> part of many speakers implies that the party has no record of eco-
> nomic reform or humanitarian actions; that we must debase our-
> selves in sack cloth and apologies for the failure of our party; that we
> must acknowledge that the New Deal has the only righteousness in
> that field; that we must adopt New Deal methods; and that we will
> do it a little cheaper. If the Republican Party has been the kind of
> party that our apologists would have us believe, it does not warrant
> public confidence. It can never win on that foundation. The most
> heartening thing to Republicans that could take place is for the
> policy committee to make a strong statement of Republican accom-
> plishments of the past, for there lies the evidence to the people that it
> is a party of progressive understanding of economic and social
> changes.[212]

Hoover had clearly marked out in his letter the direction he thought the
preliminary declaration of principles should take. However, the declaration
encountered a rocky road through the executive committee and the program
committee itself; and it emerged in a form quite disappointing to Hoover and
his supporters.[213] Issued in a press release on August 5, the statement declared:

> The Committee has the conviction that, under present trends in
> legislation and administration, the United States may suffer the
> two-fold disaster which has overtaken peoples quite as sure of their
> destiny as we have been—the breakdown of an elaborate economic
> system and the disintegration of responsible and effective govern-
> ment.

The declaration continued, explaining that despite five years of New Deal
spending and "a freedom to act without parallel in our political history," there
were still twelve million Americans unemployed. The "continuance of unemployment on this scale threatens the continued employment and income of
every American who now has a job." Certainly these twelve million were not
unemployed because there was no work to be done in America. Rather, the
statement charged, they were unemployed because of "the confusion and
uncertainty in which the present Administration has plunged us" through
untested policies that were "hastily conceived, wastefully financed, ineffec-

tively administered," and in conflict with one another. No solution would be possible until there was "complete assurance that the nation's life and enterprise are to be operated under a program founded on the principles of a balanced representative government, an adequately regulated and just system of private enterprise, a workable economics of plenty, and an inviolate code of civil liberties." Having stated the principles, the press release concluded, the Republican program committee would now set to work on the remainder of its task, the formulation of specific policies that would implement these principles. The statement made it clear that it did not commit the GOP national committee or any candidates for office to the principles expressed.[214]

Hooverites on the committee wrote of "strenuous nights" spent in getting any declaration at all released and congratulated themselves on having attained even the statement that resulted.[215] Chester Rowell was not so charitable in his appraisal of the document, writing Hoover that the mountains had labored and brought forth a mouse, which "has so little vitality that it is barely able to squeak." The document, he charged, was largely "an apology for saying anything, with the defense that it really does not say anything important nor bind anybody." There was no hint, Rowell complained, that the committee recognized "that we are at a crisis in American life, which may determine toward which way of liberty, of political and economic structure, and of place in the world, the American people are to be committed, perhaps irrevocably," nor any assertion of leadership by the Republican party "of those who wish to go forward on the basis of what has been, until now, universally recognized as the American way." Americans needed to be told "that we are at the parting of the ways between one system, political and economic, and another," and that the choice must be made by 1940 "or it may be forever too late to choose at all." Since the committee had defaulted in that responsibility, Rowell concluded that it was up to Hoover to continue to put the issue before the American people.[216]

Though in many ways the declaration read like a Hoover speech, Hoover himself shared Rowell's disappointment with it. But Hoover also was charitable toward his supporters, who had labored with much difficulty to achieve any statement at all. As he wrote to one of them:

> Considering the opposition which you encountered, I think you did well to get a statement of any kind through. Of course, it is far from what you would have and what many of our friends would have, but I am never disposed to quarrel with fine men because they do not win everything. We have to bear in mind that those destroying the Republican Party, either through determination or ineptitude, had started out deliberately to lick this Program Committee, and that they had done considerable work in advance to prevent the August meeting from having importance or value.[217]

A few days later Hoover wrote Arch Shaw: "Having read and reread the text of the committee's statement, I think better and better of it. You and Alex [Smith] certainly went down into the pit to rescue this much from that crowd." He was now considering distilling the principles enunciated in the statement into a speech.[218] Hoover's long battle for a declaration of Republican principles before the 1938 elections had been capped with at least this minor accomplishment.

Hoover now turned his attention to the rapidly approaching mid-term elections. Silent in the 1934 race, he decided to deliver three speeches during the 1938 campaign.[219] "One of the difficulties of the whole situation," he wrote Mark Sullivan in mid-July,

> is the fact that Roosevelt is more popular than the New Deal. This is due in considerable extent to the fact that the responsibility for the New Deal has not been laid to him, and that he has succeeded in completely divorcing himself from its failure and its more malevolent acts. I am beginning to have the belief that if we are going to get rid of him we are going to have to associate him with the responsibility that is really his. I agree with you as to the weight of this flood of money and its influence on the voters. While millions of people will agree collectively that it is wrong, the personal benefit they receive still holds them within the Roosevelt ranks. It may be that there will be no relief except bankruptcy. The difficulty with bankruptcy in a democracy is that it is the end of democracy. If it were only the money involved I could view it with more complacency.[220]

To John Spargo, Hoover directed the question of how far he "should go in bringing personal responsibility on Mr. Roosevelt."[221] Spargo encouraged him: "Bold and uncompromising attack upon Mr. Roosevelt himself is the best political strategy."[222]

Hoover did slightly toughen his approach to the president in a speech before Montana Republicans early in August. He listed seven reasons why there should be "a radical change in the membership of the next Congress":

1. To restore the independence of the legislative arm of government, which had been abandoned by the "rubber-stamp majority" in Congress for the previous six years.
2. To restore "sober consideration and effective debate of legislation." This, Hoover declared, could only be accomplished by the presence in Congress of "a substantial opposition" which could delay legislation until it had been duly considered.
3. To restore legislative control of the national purse.

4. The Congress needed "responsible law makers" and not "rubber stamps."

5. The rubber-stamp Congress had "frightened and scared" the business community and had thus been "a potent agency for producing unemployment."

6. To defend independent-minded members of Congress against attack by the president. Hoover described what he regarded as the new Roosevelt doctrine: "If Congress is not subjective to the Executive then the Executive Branch may use its vast powers and its control of expenditures to defeat candidates who have dared respect their responsibilities and conscience."

7. "If the people do not want centralization, personal power and dictation in this government, now is the time to act."[223]

Hoover clearly believed that the congressional elections of 1938 were of critical importance for the nation and for the GOP. If the small Republican minorities in the House and Senate slipped even further, there would be virtually no check any longer on Roosevelt's apparent thirst for power. After successive defeats in 1930, 1932, 1934, and 1936, a defeat in 1938 might well be the end of the Republican party. Hoover described the 1938 election as the most important for America since that of 1860.[224] In August he worked his way through the western states, meeting with GOP leaders and seeking to invigorate the congressional campaigns of Republicans in Idaho, Montana, and Utah, where he concluded that the party might pick up four seats in Congress.[225] He was, he told a friend, "working like a dog" on the speeches he had planned for the campaign.[226]

In the first of these speeches, delivered in Kansas City in late September, Hoover described the plan he had constructed for his participation in the campaign. He proposed to make three speeches, which would explore Roosevelt's New Deal, using as a yardstick "the test of the greatest Leader humanity has ever known [Jesus Christ], who said: 'By their fruits ye shall know them.' " The first speech would deal with "morals in government," the second would be about the "destruction of government of free men," and the third would describe the "economic consequences." In this first speech, Hoover attacked the New Deal for its "alphabetical morals," which he described as "the G.E.A.A.—Get Elected Anyhow Anyway." The Roosevelt administration was using the spoils system in appointing 300,000 officeholders for whom their political affiliation had been the first test of merit. Federal agencies like the Works Progress Administration (WPA) had been shamelessly used for political purposes, and the administration was coercing corporations into making political contributions. The New Deal demonstrated no morals in its financial practices, was deceptive in its dealings with the public, and was actively propagandizing itself at the taxpayers' expense. It preached class hatred. Hoover concluded: "Mr. Roosevelt denounces and accuses all of us who do not believe in these methods and these actions as conservatives. If being conservative on dragging America into the morass of political immorality or into the Dead Sea of reaction is Conservative then I cheerfully join that party."[227]

In his second speech, made in Hartford, Connecticut, on October 17, Hoover found the familiar faults with the New Deal: the degeneration of political morals, "the malignant growth of personal power," the fostering of class divisions, "a creeping collectivism," and failure, despite all that it had inflicted upon the country, in curing the depression. He concluded:

> The New Deal and its yes-yes men in Congress have been experimenting with the American way of life for six years at dreadful cost in human misery and despair. It would seem that the experiment has not been a success.
>
> The voter might well experiment for himself for once. He might vote for men who would halt this whole movement. For a nation to take the next two years to stop, look, and listen is an experiment that could not make the situation worse. It is not a very great risk for the voter to take. . . .
>
> It might prove the experiment that saved the freedom of the men and women of a great nation.[228]

Hoover reserved his most biting remarks for the third speech, delivered in Philadelphia on November 5. The previous night, Roosevelt had delivered a speech in which he claimed success in "creating economic stability, prosperity, and security for the average man." Hoover leaped at the president's claims, retorting: "Naturally he did not mention the 11,000,000 unemployed, or farmers' prices, or some other instabilities and insecurities." Hoover would demonstrate, he declared, "that the consequences of New Deal morals, their undermining of representative government and their economic policies not only cancel out the humanitarian objectives which it professes and to which all Americans aspire, but that they undermine all hopes for progress in standards of living to all our people." The two methods of providing the necessities of a people were through an economy of liberty and through an economy of compulsion by the government. Hoover argued for an economy of liberty "because I know it is inseparable from intellectual and spiritual liberty," and the "only road to higher standards of living," as well as "the only system under which morals and self-respect of men can survive." There were weaknesses, he admitted, in the free enterprise system, but "from an economic point of view there is a superlative quality which makes that system worth fighting for." Free enterprise stimulated technology and efficiency, and resulted in productivity and a high standard of living. "Free enterprise," Hoover observed, "can well be called the economy of plenty."[229]

Roosevelt, however, had introduced a conflict between the two types of systems through the adoption of the planned economy, and after six years of the New Deal, Hoover asserted, America alone of all the surviving democracies was still mired in depression. New Deal policies had undermined the long-term confidence of men. The humanitarian objectives of the New Deal had been distorted by the growth in personal power and the lack of morality in government. "The people grow poor in personal liberty when its officials grow rich in personal power," Hoover charged. "You wonder if idealism can live in the same land with moral debauchery. What has a nation profited if to gain any objective it has lost its own soul?" He called upon his listeners to make Congress independent. "That will be a sign to America that we have changed our national road from compelled men to free men. It will bring new confidence in the future and will quickly make jobs." He pleaded for the "election of a new Congress of independent men," and with that, he said, America would "come back."[230]

In September of 1938, Europe teetered on the brink of war over German aspirations in the Sudeten region of Czechoslovakia. War was averted by a settlement at Munich that provided for the incorporation of the Sudetenland into Germany. Hoover dealt with the world crisis in a speech on foreign policy made to the Forum on Current Problems in New York City on October 26. His theme was already familiar. The question that Americans must ask themselves, he said, was: "Do these totalitarian governments threaten our safety?" Hoover answered this question in the negative and opposed any American involvement in a European war. The United States should give "moral force" to the principle that international relations should be based on law and free agreement, rather than on force, and should aid international economic cooperation to bring prosperity to the world. Economic improvement would not only contribute to peace, but would also "relax these philosophies of despotism" and "remove their brutalities" more "than all of the armies and navies in the world."[231]

As the elections approached, Hoover was deeply troubled by an issue on the California political scene. A proposition had been placed on the California ballot that was described as a "Labor Peace Initiative," but which was clearly designed to curb the power and activities of labor unions in that state by severely restricting strikes and boycotting activities.[232] Hoover had friends who were deeply committed on each side of the issue. His own disposition was to oppose the proposition: "In the broad sense, I have always felt that laws which step over the line of mere correction of obvious abuse and enter the field of dictating conduct are in themselves a contradiction of true American ideals." Hoover placed some aspects of the proposition in this category.[233] He briefly considered issuing a statement in opposition if the presidents of Stanford University and the University of California would join in a request for his views on the proposition, but he was dissuaded by President Ray Lyman Wilbur of Stanford, who argued: "No matter what the merit or demerits are, I see no good come [sic] from bringing you in."[234] In the end, Hoover concluded that he "had better keep still and hope to be of service later."[235]

The 1938 mid-term elections brought spectacular victories to a party that had become unaccustomed to success. The Republicans captured 81 seats in the House and 7 in the Senate, as well as new governorships. The sense of crisis, based on the attrition of GOP officeholders through four successive elections, was somewhat lessened. Both the Landon and Hoover camps found in the election results vindication of the courses they had followed in 1937 and 1938. For Landonites, it was confirmation that they had been correct in their opposition to a mid-term Republican convention or conference.[236] For Hoover and his followers, the gains were directly attributable to the former president's speeches and articles attacking the New Deal and putting forth Republican principles, as well as his successful and well-publicized efforts to bring about some constructive activity on the part of the party organization.[237] The Republican party, in which Hoover had sought to play the role of evangelist, had demonstrated durability and vigor, defying the views of those like Landon, who had believed its only future lay in coalition. Whatever factors contributed to the Republican resurgence in 1938—the court fight, the recession of 1937–38, or the international crisis of late 1938, to name a few—Hoover had good reason to believe that his vision of the party's future had been vindicated and that he had aided in the resurgence of the Republican party in 1938.

# 4

# The World Intervenes

oover was encouraged by the Republican gains in the 1938 elections, but was disappointed at Thomas Dewey's defeat in the New York gubernatorial election since he felt that a GOP victory there "would have been practically a final blow to the New Deal."[1] In a press statement issued after the election he declared:

The returns indicate that a majority of the American people voted for Governors, Senators or Congressmen, either Republicans or Democrats, who are opposed to the New Deal. This protest should enable the beginning of the end of this waste of public money, these policies of coercion, political corruption and undermining of representative government. The reinvigorated Republican party is now in a position to join effectively with the anti-New Deal Democrats to check these policies in the Congress and thereby contribute to restore employment and agriculture, to reestablish confidence in business and above all to restore faith in America. Over the next two years, it is the duty of the Republican party not alone to join in this check, but to develop a constructive program which will commend itself to the country for 1940.[2]

He was optimistic, saying: "If we keep up the battle for the next two years, I believe we shall end this episode in American life in its destructive aspects."[3] Others were not as confident. H. L. Mencken wrote William Allen White: "Roosevelt got a beating on election day, but he still has two years to go, and in that time he may convert the boobs all over again. In particular I suspect him of a scheme to get the country into war. The trick will be easy if he really wants to perform it."[4]

Nevertheless, the Republican victories in the 1938 congressional races did suggest the possibility that a conservative trend was abroad in the land. While the 1936 Republican presidential nomination had been considered by many to be of doubtful value, the 1940 nomination seemed to offer greater promise. Other elements, too, made the 1940 nomination seem attractive. The Republican candidate would be facing either a new Democratic contender or a Roosevelt campaign that would be burdened by the third-term issue. The chaotic world situation seemed to offer additional opportunity, especially for Hoover's own ambitions. No one in the Republican party could approach the former president's experience in world affairs. Only Hoover, it seemed, could offer the prospect of experienced world leadership as an alternative to the Democrats in the White House. The "thinking" people in the GOP must surely grasp this essential truth and rally to the Hoover banner. The question was, however, Would Hoover make a more determined bid for the nomination in 1940 than he had in 1936? If so, the groundwork must be laid in 1939.

Hoover's efforts to wrest control of the party from Landon in 1937 and 1938 had failed; however, they had given him tremendous visibility, and he entered 1939 as a leading figure in the GOP. Many party members wrote to the former president, commending him for his contribution to the turnaround in the party's fortunes in 1938. Hoover wrote Will Irwin: "I am getting an enormous amount of mail insisting that I carried the election, but I haven't seen any account of that in the newspapers."[5] But Julius Klein called his attention to such an observation in the *Washington Post* and added: "There's no doubt whatever but that a goodly portion of the avalanche which swept down on our 'red' friends last Tuesday was started by your forceful blows during the campaign."[6]

Under the circumstances it would have been easy for Hoover to overestimate his contribution to the Republican success, if indeed he did overestimate it. He was much sought after as a speaker; he maintained a loyal following and close ties with Republican leaders both in and out of Congress and the Republican party.[7] During 1939, as the international situation resulted in the introduction of various defense and foreign affairs proposals in Congress, the former president found himself increasingly consulted by Republicans in both houses of Congress. Relations with Landon, however, remained strained, despite Hoover's attempts to extend a "long arm" to the Kansan in the midst of the 1938 campaign.

By late 1938, Hoover and Landon were not the only possibilities for the GOP nomination in 1940. One of the brightest stars rising in the party, despite his defeat in the New York gubernatorial election, was the dynamic young New York district attorney, Thomas E. Dewey. Both Landon and Hoover interested themselves in Dewey early in his political career. As Dewey campaigned for governor in 1938, his supporters appealed to the former president for assistance in raising funds. But at the same time, Dewey himself maintained distance from Hoover and was reported to have said that he was divorced from the Hoover "old guard" and viewed himself as representative of an entirely new brand of Republicanism.[8] While Dewey lost the race for governor, he did attract a considerable vote and remained a potential nominee for the party in 1940. Hoover continued to encourage Dewey's political activity, acting through Lewis Strauss, of Kuhn, Loeb and Company, as intermediary.[9] It was part of Hoover's deepening interest in New York politics now that New York City had increasingly become his residence.

More than any other single factor, Hoover's prominence in the debates over foreign policy kept him before the American public and contributed to the rise in his popularity in 1939 and 1940. His 1938 speeches in response to the growing crisis in Europe had already established the basic outlines of the position he would maintain, with only slight modifications, in the remaining years before the Japanese attack on Pearl Harbor. While the Roosevelt administration apparently believed that the Munich settlement had averted war in Europe, Hoover was less optimistic. "I do not think the world has anything to congratulate itself about at any point over the whole European episode," he wrote a friend, "and of course my impression is that it is only a portend [sic] of worse to come. I would like to persuade myself otherwise."[10] In February 1939 he outlined for the Council of Foreign Relations what he regarded as the traditional foreign policy of the United States. This policy included: (1) remaining free of foreign entanglements and of other peoples' wars; (2) concentrating on defense, not on intervention in others' wars; (3) including the western hemisphere in that defense under the Monroe Doctrine; (4) protecting the lives of Americans abroad by force, if necessary, but relying upon peaceful negotiations to protect American rights and property; (5) cooperating in "peaceful movements to promote peace and in economic movements to promote world prosperity," but without threats of force to attain those objects; and (6) prohibiting, under the neutrality law, the purchase of armaments in the United States by belligerents.[11]

In Hoover's view, President Roosevelt had deviated from these traditional policies, and the logical result of Roosevelt's policies, if carried further in their practical application, must certainly be the involvement of the United States in war. Hoover saw no danger to the United States or to the western hemisphere that justified the administration's policies, and he worried that personal liberty and economic freedom could not be maintained in the United States under the conditions of modern warfare. Thus, he maintained that one inevitable outcome of an American war against fascism must be the transformation of the United States itself "into practically a Fascist state." America should, on the contrary, stand as a beacon of liberty for the rest of the world.[12]

Hoover's speech was hailed by the editor of the *Los Angeles Times* as "the most illuminating and penetrating analysis of our mis-called foreign policy yet made by anyone," and he suggested that the former president undertake a syndicated weekly column on world affairs.[13] Frederick J. Libby, executive secretary of the American Council for Prevention of War, believed that the speech had "checked temporarily [the] war trend [of the] Roosevelt administration" and told Hoover that he was distributing 25,000 copies.[14]

In December of 1938, Hoover began to counsel congressional Republicans on foreign policy, traveling to Washington early that month for a breakfast meeting with them arranged by his former under secretary of state, William Castle.[15] The following month, Republicans in Congress formed a GOP Policy Committee for National Defense and sought Hoover's counsel.[16] Senator Styles Bridges, of New Hampshire, was one who echoed the Hoover position in the Senate, delivering a speech on the floor of that body in February along lines he had discussed with the former president. Bridges argued that the United States must stay out of war and follow a realistic foreign policy "based upon fundamental proven principles and maintained for a longer time than necessary to deliver a 'fireside chat.' " The United States should not, he asserted, "act in the cause of peace as though we intended to fight."[17]

Others, including Democratic Senator Thomas Walsh, also expressed approval of what Walsh called Hoover's "militant pro-American views and his broad liberal and patriotic attitude."[18] The former president was pleased to find allies in the struggle to keep America out of war regardless of where these allies came from and regardless of their motives. He wrote O'Laughlin that he was "rather astonished to find an article by that left-winger, Professor [Charles] Beard in the 'American Mercury.' It is worth reading. He is opposed to our going into war from a rather different point of view, but any point of view is good now."[19]

Hoover pinned his hopes in early 1939 on the British desire for peace. He was no critic of appeasement of Germany by such European leaders as British Prime Minister Neville Chamberlain. As Hoover stated his position:

> Probably the only thing that will keep us out of war is the British.
> They have sanity. They do not want to go to war. And they are today
> the only outstanding skillful group of world diplomats. If Roosevelt

had maintained at least the tone of voice of Chamberlain in this situation, he might have been in a position, at the proper moment, to have been of great service to the world in bringing these people around a council table.[20]

Since foreign affairs had begun to loom importantly on the political scene, Hoover was all the more anxious that his own record in foreign policy as president should get wider dissemination. William Starr Myers now replaced William Castle as the person designated to bring out a book on the foreign policies of the Hoover administration.[21]

Elaborate preparations went into Hoover's Lincoln Day speech in New York. Shunning suggestions that he appear folksy and humorous, he lashed out at Roosevelt in a reply to the president's state of the union message.[22] In a speech on "The Real State of the Union," Hoover charged that the nation was "more sadly divided and confused than at any since Lincoln's time." The 1938 elections had brought improvement, however, by demonstrating that Americans were willing to use the ballot box to safeguard their liberties. The independence of Congress had been partially restored and champions of the independence of the courts had been returned to office. "The people," he concluded, "have proved that elections cannot be controlled by government subsidies," Defining the "first chore of a political party out of power" as "corrective opposition" and the "exposure of the witchery of half-truth and the curb of arrogant and extreme action," Hoover pointed out that the Democrats had failed to bring about recovery from the depression. Their only solution for their failure, he charged, was to call for even greater spending on a scale that meant "the most startling budget proposals ever laid before the American people in peace-time." Hoover concluded that the Republican party had three great missions before it: the preservation of the principles of freedom, which were being undermined by the New Deal; the economic recovery of the United States; and the avoidance by the United States of any entanglement in a foreign war.[23]

A few days after the speech, Edgar Rickard found Hoover totally absorbed in weighing his prospects for the 1940 nomination and for attaining recognition as the leading figure in the Republican party.[24] There was no doubt in Alf Landon's mind that Hoover was after the nomination and that, if he didn't receive it himself, he wanted to be able to select the nominee.[25] The two men continued to be rivals, with part of that rivalry manifesting itself in their mutual attempts to build close relations with Dewey. The Hoovers had developed something of a social relationship with the Deweys in New York City, while Landon sought to steer Dewey away from being identified as a "Hoover" man.[26] Landon had supported the efforts of New York GOP national committeeman Kenneth Simpson in creating fusion tickets in New York in which Republicans and the left-wing American Labor party cooperated to defeat the Democrats.[27] Predictably, Hoover had opposed those efforts. When Dewey broke with Simpson early in 1939, it could well have been regarded as a rebuff for Landon, although among those advising Dewey to make the break were not only Hoover but also Landon's fellow Kansan William Allen White.[28]

Unlike 1936, when the Hoover effort to win the nomination lacked any attempt to organize the grass roots, 1939 saw such an attempt launched in the form of a group known as the Republican Circles. While ostensibly designed simply to impart new vigor into the Republican party in the western states, it is clear that Hoover's supporters intended that the Circles should support the former president's ambitions, whatever those turned out to be.[29] By late February 1939, Circles had been organized in California from San Luis Obispo to the Mexican border, with each county having ten initial members, who, in turn, were creating new Circles. One inducement to join the Circles was the promise of an opportunity to meet with Hoover in "informal, confidential" conferences.[30] In mid-March, Hoover left New York City for California to hold a series of such meetings.[31] That the Circles were intended to function as Hoover "shock troops" is clear from Ben Allen's remark: "Every man selected in this Circle had to be a Hoover devotee and pledge himself simply to a belief in the political philosophy and principles of the Chief and support of his leadership."[32]

Early in 1939 another potential candidate was beginning to make his presence felt. Robert A. Taft, son of former president William Howard Taft and a close Hoover friend since his association with Hoover's food and relief work during and after World War I, had been elected in November 1938 to represent Ohio in the Senate. By the end of that year Hoover was already convinced that the new senator was determined to make a bid for the 1940 presidential nomination. Concerned that he would suffer a challenge from his own wing of the party, Hoover sought to discourage Taft's ambitions as premature in view of his lack of a record in the Senate. In early 1939 there was increasing talk of a possible Taft nomination.[33] However, there was also a good deal of speculation concerning Hoover's own plans and prospects for 1940. One of his supporters suggested a ticket with Hoover as the presidential nominee and one of the younger hopefuls as his running mate, with an agreement that Hoover would step down after four years to clear the way for the experienced vice-president to move into the White House.[34]

Hoover definitely considered the 1940 nomination worth attaining. He sensed that the political trend in the nation in 1939 was in the direction of the GOP and "if the ball is not fumbled and we can keep up the battle, the 1940 election can be won."[35] But his own ambitions aside, Hoover was concerned that the Republican party should return to its traditional principles in 1940—

principles he believed had been deserted in 1936 by Landon. Thus, while he was concerned about the threat to his own nomination, posed by Thomas Dewey's rising prominence in the party, he was also disturbed by the prospect that the Landon group might "control" Dewey and continue to steer the party away from traditional Republicanism.[36] The break between Dewey and Simpson somewhat lessened this latter concern, but Hoover continued to work to ensure that the GOP would reflect his own philosophy in 1940. Throughout 1939 he sought to shape the declaration of the Republican policy committee, which was to be made in 1940, but his efforts had scant effect.[37]

Both to disseminate his philosophy and to advance his own standing in the party, Hoover now began to hold small meetings with local groups of 50 to 150 members at the site of each of his speeches. Included in these gatherings were local civic leaders and molders of public opinion including, usually, the publisher of the local newspaper.[38] These small meetings appeared to be successful, with the former president proving particularly adept at making a favorable impression on groups of that size.[39] One outcome of these meetings was that Hoover found among those he talked to a deep sentiment against American participation in another war; but these emotions were, to him, dangerous and contradictory. He found that "99% vociferously denounce our going into war; but almost 75% think we ought 'to do something to the dictators.' " Hoover recognized that the latter attitude, if followed, could lead the United States "on the road to being entangled in war' " despite the strength of the former view. "It is a poor national policy to go around the world sticking pins in rattlesnakes," Hoover argued. "The British and French, who are realists, do not do that."[40]

In April Hoover supplemented his speeches with an article on foreign policy for *Liberty* magazine. He suggested that the United States could respond to a world crisis in two ways, neither of which he judged as isolationist. The first was to maintain neutrality and to seek to bring about a settlement of world tensions through peaceful methods, including economic cooperation. The other was "to depart from neutrality in the controversies between other nations and to exert the physical force of the United States on one side of a conflict." The latter course must result in American involvement in war. The path of neutrality he defined as "the long view and the realistic view," while the use of force he regarded as "the short view and the emotional view." Hoover argued that the fascist states had no intention of attacking the Western democracies, but that if an attack came the Western democracies were entirely capable of their own defense.[41]

Hoover was opposed to allying the United States with France, since in his view that meant this country must also align itself with the Soviet Union, a nation which had sought for twenty years to undermine the American government. Fascist though it might be, Italy had never done that. Hoover also argued that the destructive philosophies of Germany and the Soviet Union could not much longer survive. Then he added:

> Moreover, the whole theory of stopping aggression is in fact an attempt to maintain the *status quo* in national boundaries all over the world. We need only to look back even one hundred years of history to see how many fights we could get into. In fact, we have been aggressive in our time. Otherwise parts of the Rocky Mountains and California would belong to Mexico today.

Hoover concluded: "We cannot become the world's policeman unless we are prepared to sacrifice millions of American lives—and probably some day see all the world against us. In time they would envisage us as the world's greatest bully, not as the world's greatest idealist." World War I, he reminded his readers, had shown the folly of trying to "make the world safe for democracy."[42]

When not writing or speaking, Hoover was monitoring the grass-roots efforts of the Republican Circles and others in the western states.[43] By the middle of 1939, Circles had been formed in Montana, Idaho, Washington, Oregon, and Colorado, in addition to California, and the group was cooperating with similar organizations in Arizona and Nevada.[44] Hoover busied himself raising funds to put men into the field in the western states to further promote the Circles. Thomas Campbell, former governor of Arizona, was entrusted with the task of organizing groups in Arizona and New Mexico.[45] Hoover also wrote to political leaders in the western states to encourage their cooperation in the organization efforts. He wrote C. C. Moore, former governor of Idaho, that the Republican Circles were "the only satisfactory form of Republican organization to fight the New Deal in 1940 that I have seen. It mobilizes the responsible men in each county and town for active campaigning and at the same time supports the regular organization and all other Republican organizations."[46]

Back on the stump, Hoover told the graduates of Lincoln University (Harrogate, Tennessee) on June 4 that they were "about to enter a world more confused as to its ideas and principles of life than has been the case for a long time." One of those confusions was over how to protect "personal liberty in the changing economic and social pressures." The American system of free enterprise, based on liberty, brought greater productivity, more progress, and was the only system with humor, he argued. It was impossible, however, for the voluntary cooperation of the free enterprise system to survive when mixed with compulsion. Hoover told the graduates:

> Voluntary cooperation moves from a delicate mainspring. That mainspring is the initiative, enterprise and confidence of men. The moment any part of compulsion or coercion is directed at free men their fears rise, their energies slacken, their productivity slows down, and the people suffer. Coercion feeds upon more coercion. Either out of desperation or design, governments apply more and more coercion once they have started. And they demand more and more power over men.

Noting the fears of war in the United States, he asserted that the real danger to America was not from "violent invasion of these systems from abroad," but rather from "the subtle growth of these compulsory ideas as a means to remedy war dislocation and depression."[47]

Eight days later, Hoover sought to clarify for the graduates of Earlham College in Indiana the confused thinking on political labels like "reactionary, conservative, liberal, and radical." America, he pointed out, had no political parties organized under such labels. He told his listeners:

> We use these terms politically mostly for slogans and oratory. They are used for eulogy and defamation. If you do not like somebody you consign him to the complexion most hated by your listener. These terms are used as refuges from ignorance or intellectual dishonesty. They are set up as pigeon-holes for men and groups to imply they are righteous, stingy, public-spirited, opposed to public interest, or generally sinful. They are dumdum words to assassinate men and then to plant bitter onions on their graves.

Hoover defined for the graduates his concept of American liberalism, in familiar terms, and then explored for them the "impure" forms of liberalism then current in America. Hoover recommended to his listeners that they shun all such labels as liberal, reactionary, radical, or conservative, and devote themselves instead to the American system of liberty. Where defense of that system called for them to be liberal or conservative or reactionary or radical, they should not hesitate to be whatever was required.[48]

During his trips into Tennessee and Indiana for the commencement addresses, Hoover met with small local groups, sounded public opinion, and made useful political contacts.[49] Traveling back to California, he concluded that "the general shift is toward the Republican party, but I think it is going to be more of a battle than most of our people believe at the moment."[50] Dining with him in New York before his departure for the Indiana speech, Rickard found Hoover still totally absorbed in his political ambitions, monitoring the grass-roots efforts in the West, and writing and revising his speeches.[51]

Hoover knew that if he were seriously considered for the 1940 nomination

it would rekindle the old "smear" attacks against him, and he had already
begun to consider ways in which such smears could be met.[52] His determination to confront such attacks head-on was tested in the summer of 1939. On
July 30, Hoover tuned his radio to the University of Chicago "Sunday Roundtable." In the course of the radio discussion, journalist Drew Pearson alluded
to reports he had received of the former president buying up convention
delegates for 1940 in Mississippi and Louisiana. Hoover immediately consulted with friends on the action that should be taken in response to this
slander. The draft of a telegram to the president of the University of Chicago,
Dr. Robert Hutchins, was approved by Hoover's intimates, and a copy was
also sent to the president of the radio network.[53] In his telegram to Hutchins,
Hoover demanded "an immediate public disavowal" of Pearson's statement as
"a rank untruth," and also "a full and approved apology" to be made on the
"Sunday Roundtable" at its next broadcast. Hoover did not want any reference made to Pearson in the apology since, as he wrote to his attorney, Frank
Hogan: "We will take care of him separately and we cannot allow them to
devise any method which protects Pearson."[54] After a series of wires and
letters between Hoover and the university, agreement was reached on a public
statement by the university.[55] Hoover then decided not to pursue any libel
action against Pearson. Although he was certain that a suit "would result in an
unquestionable conviction," he felt it was "not worth while going after such
cattle."[56]

In July Hoover published an article in *American Magazine* pointedly
titled "Shall We Send Our Youth to War?" Europe, he wrote, was once again
engaged in a historic power conflict, and the United States must ensure that it
did not again become, as in 1917–18, a pawn of European power politics,
whether as a result of foreign propaganda, the mistakes of Americans in
making preachments echoing such propaganda, or official blunders that might
entangle the United States in the European morass. Propaganda, Hoover
pointed out, was already seeking to "fertilize our soil for our entry into war."
Hostile words were being fired at "the nations we don't like" by government
officials. And the policies of President Roosevelt meant that he had "taken a
seat at the table where power politics is being played. He has joined in the
chessboard of Europe." Hoover reiterated his belief that the country could
"never go through another great war without becoming a totalitarian state in
order to fight effectively such a war. When we have finished we shall not have
established peace in the world. We shall have sacrificed liberty for generations
in the United States." The United States could keep out of any European war
only if its people had "the resolute will to do so." He told his readers:

> Staying out is a matter of tactics and strategy almost as difficult as
> the strategy and tactics of war. And, if there is not the adamant will

to stay out, no amount of law can keep us out. The first thing
required is a vigorous, definite statement from all who have responsibility, both publicly and privately, that we are not going to war
with anybody in Europe unless they attack the Western Hemisphere. The second thing is not to sit in this game of power politics.
These are the American policies that will make sure that we do not
send our youth to Europe for war.[57]

On July 5, Hoover gave a summary of his *American Magazine* article
over the radio on the "American Magazine Hour," and the following day he
expanded upon the article with a speech before the International Convention
of Christian Endeavor Societies in Cleveland.[58] In this speech he touched upon
the inhumane and destructive aspects of modern warfare and proposed that all
nations agree (1) that food ships should be as immune to attack as hospitals,
and that they should not be subject to blockade; (2) that there should be no
bombing of civilian populations; and (3) that bombing should be restricted to
"the field of actual fighting men on land or sea, and at works devoted strictly to
munitions." Neutral nations should be responsible for ensuring that the agreement was not violated through their management of the shipment of food
supplies and by monitoring conditions in belligerent countries "to determine
the facts of any killing of civilians from the air." Moral force, the power of
world public opinion, would be the "teeth" of enforcement, since under conditions of modern warfare, Hoover maintained, "one of the utmost anxieties of
both sides is to hold the good will of neutrals" in order to avoid influencing
them to "aid or join the enemy." At the very least, the arousal of ill will in the
neutral countries by violations of these conditions could lead to "informal
boycotts of credit and supplies even though they go no further."[59]

From popular historian Will Durant came encouragement and the hope
that Hoover would "continue to arouse the country to the fact that it is once
more being made the pawn and joke of British policy."[60] John Callan
O'Laughlin reported that the speeches and magazine articles had "created
great interest in Washington" and that Republican members of Congress had
admitted to him that in their statements and votes "they were inspired by
you."[61] Hoover had made certain that copies of his speeches were being sent to
selected members of Congress.[62]

Hoover was sure, however, that Roosevelt's policies had brought Europe
to the brink of war by giving the European democracies confidence that the
United States would support them. As a result, Hoover believed, these democracies had abandoned appeasement and had begun to take a more aggressive
stance toward Germany and Italy, despite the fact that neither had shown any
intention of attacking the democracies. Thus, in Hoover's view, Roosevelt's
policies had "measurably advanced the possibilities of war in the world, and

the end of that war to save democracy will be that there will be no democracy left."[63]

As Hoover's activities became increasingly dominated by his efforts to keep the United States out of war, some of his supporters voiced the suspicion that the international situation was being made into an issue by the Democrats in order to divert public attention from Roosevelt's failures in domestic policy; and they expressed concern that Republicans, obviously including Hoover, were "falling into the trap."[64] For the former president, however, the dominant issue in 1939 was keeping the United States out of war.[65] In late August, as the situation in Europe worsened, Hoover voiced concern that if war did break out there, it would change "the color of American attitudes and interests" and make the fight to keep America neutral even more difficult.[66]

When Hitler's army invaded Poland in September 1939, triggering a general European conflagration, Hoover issued a statement describing the time as "one of the saddest weeks that has come to humanity in a hundred years." It was, he declared, a "senseless war," which was being "inevitably forced upon hundreds of millions of people," and would result in the deaths of many in combat and through starvation, only to be followed by "another quarter of a century of impoverishment to the whole world." He foresaw a long war of slow attrition and feared that "there may come a time of desperation when all restraints go to the winds." Then it would likely become "the most barbarous war that we have ever known." Nazism was repugnant to the American people, he observed, and American sympathies would be with the Allies, but "whatever our sympathies are, we cannot solve the problems of Europe." He concluded:

> America must keep out of this war. The President and Congress should be supported in their every effort to keep us out. We can keep out if we have the resolute national will to do so. We can be of more service to Europe and to humanity if we preserve the vitality and strength of the United States for use in the period of peace which must sometime come, and we must keep out if we are to preserve for civilization the foundations of democracy and free men.[67]

In August of 1939, Senator Robert A. Taft announced that he would be a candidate for the 1940 GOP presidential nomination. Hoover's contacts with grass-roots feeling in the western states had convinced him, however, that there was no real enthusiasm for Taft or any of the other apparent Republican candidates. He did find, though, "a sense of seriousness and resolution to make the fight," one "such as we have not seen in 70 years."[68] The Taft campaign quickly put out feelers to the former president concerning the possibility of attracting delegates in California. Hoover expressed appreciation for Taft's consistent opposition to the New Deal and voiced his doubts about Dewey and Vandenberg. He insisted, however, that the California delegation to the convention must be uninstructed, and the Taft camp concluded that it would be "suicide" to oppose Hoover in this.[69] Others visiting the former president came away with the impression that he intended to have a prominent voice in the selection of the Republican nominee, and that he might well be interested in obtaining the nomination himself.[70]

Meanwhile, Hoover was continuing the campaign against the smearing that he anticipated in 1940. His swift response to Pearson's remarks on the University of Chicago's "Sunday Roundtable" had been the opening gun in this effort. In mid-August he wrote to journalistic friends suggesting that they write articles attacking the general tendency toward smearing, which had become so apparent in American politics, especially in the speeches and writings of the New Dealers and their allies. As he wrote to Boake Carter:

> The whole art of smearing has been developed in the last 10 years to a major strategy of the Left Wing. We have seen the President smear the whole business world—bad and good alike. We have seen the administration smear the doctors. We have seen them smear the lawyers. We have seen the President smear the publishers and editors. We have seen authors such as Steinbeck smear the whole people of California. We have seen Senate committees do nothing else. We have seen the smearing of George Washington by supposed biographers. We have seen the whole Left Wing using the technique of smearing as their reply to sober argument. Basically, it is the method by which they are creating class conflict in this country. It is more than mere demagoguery. It is aimed at the destruction of every individual or group who offer opposition.[71]

Frank Kent, at least, responded positively to Hoover's suggestion, by writing a column on smearing that appeared in the *Baltimore Sun* on August 23, 1939.[72] Hoover wrote Kent that his article "filled me with enthusiasm. If we could get a number of people harping away on this, we may do something."[73]

With the Republican convention less than a year away, the Hoover campaign for the nomination seemed much farther along in August 1939 than it had been at the same time in 1935. Strong grass-roots organizations in the western states seemed to offer the prospect that he would go to the 1940 convention with a solid core of support within uninstructed delegations from those states. His writings and speeches continued to maintain him at the forefront of Republican criticism of the New Deal. Copies of his speeches and publications continued to be distributed through his mailing lists. He had carefully cultivated friendly relations with each of the emerging potential candidates, which offered the prospect that if their own bids for the nomination were halted they would not be unfriendly to a Hoover candidacy. Moreover, he had demonstrated in the Pearson instance that he would not idly permit smears against him.

In addition, the German-Soviet invasion of Poland in September provided new opportunities for Hoover in the public arena. Hoover's impact as a leading opponent of the New Deal had been blunted by the popularity of Roosevelt and many of the New Deal programs Hoover attacked. But as a leading voice in opposition to American involvement in the European war, Hoover could expect to appeal to larger numbers of Americans, who, for whatever reasons, were opposed to a repeat of the country's experience in 1917–1918. As the only living Republican ex-president, and having international expertise gained both in and out of that office, Hoover could expect to be looked to for leadership by Republicans and non-Republicans alike who were concerned about the war issue. The former president recognized that international questions would likely outweigh domestic ones in the campaign and election of 1940, and he determined to bend all of his efforts to establishing himself as the leader in the fight to prevent American entry into the war.[74]

But as the countdown began for the last year before the convention, the question had to be answered whether there was anything more that ought to be done to strengthen Hoover's bid for the nomination. Hoover posed this question to several of his supporters. Chief Justice Robert Simmons, of the Nebraska Supreme Court, counseled him against allowing his friends to openly seek the nomination for him. To do so, Simmons argued, would detract from his attacks on the New Deal, since those attacks would then appear to be designed solely to advance his candidacy. Moreover, to go openly in pursuit of the nomination would likely disrupt Hoover's cordial relations with the other candidates and make it less likely that they would throw their support to him once their own efforts had failed. An openly avowed candidacy would also make it apparent that his efforts to get a largely uninstructed convention were motivated by his own ambitions, and this would lead the other candidates to seek instructed delegations. Hoover would also lose, Simmons warned, the immense esteem in which he was held by the American people—esteem that might very well have led to his nomination in 1936 had the convention not already been committed to Landon. Thus, the Nebraskan recommended that Hoover continue to operate very much as he had in 1936, clarifying the issues before the American people, staying out of the way of other potential candidates, "and being in a position to inherit their strength and support" while continuing to seek a largely uninstructed convention.[75]

Others, though, were looking for ways to increase Hoover's influence at the convention. Public relations man James Selvage wrote Hoover in August to suggest the formation of a group to "do a propaganda job favorable to you, designed to increase your influence at the convention." It had been suggested

that with twenty to twenty-five thousand dollars the operation could be inau-
gurated.[76] Hoover, who was always extremely reluctant to put his political
objectives or machinations down in correspondence, responded that he would
be in New York the following month, "and we can discuss the various things
about which you have written to me."[77]

Meanwhile, Hoover had embarked on a combined fishing and political
trip through Wyoming and Montana where he had scheduled three meetings
with political leaders, but had been forced to increase the number of meetings
to eleven because of their popularity. In fact, the demand for his appearances
had been so great that his difficulty, he reported, "was to get out of that
region." Each of the meetings had been with groups of 200 to 400 men and
women. "There can be no doubt," Hoover wrote Robert Simmons, "that
Republicans are deeply moved and they are going to make a more determined
campaign than ever before."[78]

By mid-September Hoover was back in New York and holding meetings
at his apartment concerning his future plan of action. The proposal that
Selvage had mentioned for advancing his influence at the Republican convention was now launched.[79] From Norman Davis, head of the Red Cross, came
an intimation that Roosevelt wished Hoover to take over the handling of
private European war relief, a suggestion that struck the former president as
an effort by the White House to sidetrack him from politics into relief.[80] A few
days after Hoover's return to New York, Kenneth Simpson called on him, and
thereafter, relations between the two men were amicable.[81] Perhaps it was
reflective of Hoover's rising stature in the country, in part a result of the
international situation, that Republican leaders like Simpson suddenly found
reasons to build bridges to him. A good deal of evidence was accumulating that
pro-Hoover sentiment was on the increase at the grass-roots level.[82] Landon
supporters were aware of the trend and were concerned. One supporter wrote
Landon that he had found that the "men in the street" were saying "we need
Hoover—too many of them," and because of this, he wrote, "we've got to walk
carefully for some time, Alf."[83]

The rapidly changing world situation led to calls for a reconsideration of
the American neutrality law. President Roosevelt sought from Congress a
repeal of the provisions embargoing arms sales, asking that the "cash-and-
carry" provisions of the existing law be extended to munitions as well as raw
materials. Hoover was quickly drawn into the debate. On September 14, 1939,
he set forth his views in a letter to William Castle. The principal issue, he
argued, was how best to keep the United States out of the war. "We must judge
[our] every action in foreign relations from that standpoint alone, not only in
the immediate setting but over a few years to come." Both sides in the controversy—that seeking repeal of the munitions embargo and that opposing it—
believed, he said, that their method was "best designed to meet our major issue

of keeping us out of war." There were, however, "grave dangers in either course proposed." The answer was to try to find a middle ground between the two extremes, which would lessen those dangers. Hoover proposed "a different point of view from either of the present alternatives of embargo or no embargo."[84]

Hoover suggested that the Neutrality Act then being debated in the Senate be amended to forbid "the sale and shipment of bombing airplanes, aerial bombs, large mobile guns, submarines, tanks and poison gas," since these were offensive weapons, and the United States "should not sell aggressive weapons to anybody at any time, whether they be at war or peace." Sales should be limited solely to weapons that would enable nations to defend themselves against attack. Hoover believed his proposal

> would largely remove this legislation from any genuine charge of favoritism or unneutrality or intervention in this war. Such action as I propose would be the enactment of fundamental principals which we have already laid down to the world, which have nothing to do with the declaration of wars. Their purpose is at all times to decrease the barbarous practices of modern warfare; to confine war activities to purely military objectives; never to support the idea of offense; and to discourage aggression.

He considered it vital, too, that the preamble of the bill "be revised into an emphatic declaration of policy by the United States of keeping out of war, in order that there may be no misapprehension on the part of any of the belligerents of our determination."[85] Hoover was not opposed to selling defensive arms to the Allies under such cash-and-carry provisions, since he recognized that such assistance "would give an emotional outlet to the American people," while to deny such assistance to the Allies would "only dam up the tide which will break loose in a demand for participation."[86]

In September Hoover was confronted with a political problem in his own state. In Los Angeles a movement had begun among some Republicans to restrict to virtually nil the influence of the former president in the selection of the state's delegates to the 1940 convention. Hoover and his supporters moved quickly to confront the situation, developing a strategy for the application of pressure where it would be the most effective.[87] By late in the month the Los Angeles movement had been thwarted.[88] Meanwhile, the organization of Republican Circles had spread to Utah, but as a result of the challenge in Los Angeles, Hoover decided that further development of the Circles was needed in California.[89] As he put it in mid-September, the necessity had arisen "for directing all resources at the moment to building up the manpower in the California situation. We must have this manpower before the end of November when we may have to begin a battle against the forces of evil."[90] The development effort concentrated especially on Los Angeles, where Hoover's strength had been revealed as weak, with the goal of recruiting 5,000 members in Los Angeles county by the middle of October.[91] But organizing activities in the northern part of California also disappointed Hoover, and he found financial support being spread thin. There was a real likelihood that unless additional sources of funds were found, the Circles movement might collapse by the middle of November.[92] Thus, Hoover's once-promising grass-roots organization did not present a hopeful prospect as of the end of September 1939. Dining with the former president early in October, Edgar Rickard found him gloomy and uncommunicative.[93]

Hoover's own wealth was not so substantial that it could support his political activities. Yet it was true, as Landon so frequently observed, that considerable money was spent in the former president's behalf. Such financial support came from Hoover faithfuls located in many parts of the country, but a large part of it came from wealthy Californians like mining engineers Harvey Mudd and William Honnold, oilman A. C. (Bert) Mattei, and financier and industrialist Henry M. Robinson. During the Hoover administration, Robinson was frequently referred to in the press as "Hoover's Colonel House" because of his intimate role as an advisor.[94] As the tempo of the former president's activities picked up in late 1935 and early 1936, a group of his friends organized Constitutional Publications, Incorporated, to print and distribute Hoover's speeches and publications and to furnish funds for his other political acitvities.[95] Cereals magnate W. K. Kellogg also aided Hoover's efforts by underwriting the expense of publishing his speeches in the *Addresses Upon the American Road* series.[96] The direct link between Hoover and the Republican Circles organization was made clear in September 1939, when, at Hoover's request, the Constitutional Publications group paid some of the bills of the Circle organization.[97]

Shortly after the outbreak of war in Europe, President Roosevelt began to consider emulating the British example by organizing a bipartisan administration, which would include cabinet members from the Republican party. Several editors and columnists had suggested the desirability of such a move. On September 20, 1939, the president met with legislators from both parties and with Landon and Knox, the 1936 nominees, to seek bipartisan support for the repeal of the embargo clause in the neutrality law. After the meeting, Roosevelt met privately with Knox and informed him of his intention to form a coalition cabinet, as Knox's newspaper, among others, had been advocating.[98]

Responding to the suggestions and rumors of a coalition cabinet, Hoover wrote to Senator Charles W. Tobey late in the month on "the partisanship and coalition question" and suggested that Tobey put the letter in his files "as against the day when this subject may become a live one and we may need an attack." He asked the senator to contact him whenever Tobey felt the letter should be released, and if Hoover agreed, it would be released.[99] In the letter, Hoover expressed his views "on the position the Republican Party should take on the adjournment of partisanship and coalition government." If by adjournment of partisanship it was intended that "party action" should cease, Hoover wrote, "then a most serious question is raised. Virile organization of political parties has a vital function in sustaining the processes of free government" and could "only be suspended if self-government had been abandoned." The nation would be confronted with monumental issues in the 1940 election, which must be debated and decided at the ballot box. Even in foreign policy there was need for debate and decision by the people. "If there is to be no debate upon foreign policies when there is difference of opinion, then we have again lost free government." If the purpose of coalition government was to suspend party action, then it would mean one-party government and "the start of totalitarian government." Coalition was of doubtful utility even in wartime, Hoover asserted, and the United States was not at war. If Republicans did enter the administration, they would not represent the Republican party or Republicans in Congress. Hoover continued:

> If, to obtain greater skill in the Cabinet or greater confidence for his Administration, the President desires to select Republicans for those posts, there is not the slightest objection. If he desires to obtain advice from Republicans, likewise, there can be no objection. If he desires to explore what unity could be obtained upon special questions, that also is good. But these individuals would give this advice and sit in those positions solely for their skill and merit. They would not be acting for their party.

While the United States remained at peace, Republicans should support the administration in its efforts to keep the nation out of war and to prepare for the defense of the nation, but political activity could not be adjourned since it would "adjourn free government in the United States."[100]

The European war not only affected Hoover's political life, but also brought him new responsibilities in the form of relief work. And this role, too, led to publicity, as the experienced director of relief relied on tested public relations techniques to generate support for his efforts. These relief activities, however, were not as successful as they had been in the years before America's entry into World War I. In part, this was due to the antipathy toward him on the part of the Roosevelt administration and the effect that antipathy had in lessening his influence with foreign governments, such as Great Britain, whose cooperation was needed for effective relief. Such governments were unwilling to irritate the Roosevelt administration by cooperating with Hoover even if the will to do so was present. Thus, Hoover's public role as an opponent of Roosevelt's policies worked to the detriment of his relief efforts.[101] Nor did Hoover receive the support of his own government in his efforts to moderate British opposition to the lowering of their blockade of Europe in order to permit food supplies to go through.

Meanwhile, Hoover was ensuring that his own position on the war and on American policies related to it was being publicized by columnists and inserted into congressional debates.[102] He was also busy writing more magazine articles. When Christian Herter suggested that he should write a book based on the *American Magazine* article, Hoover responded that articles were preferable since they could reach four or five million readers, while the best that a serious book could obtain was a readership of ten or twelve thousand.[103]

Late in October his article "We Must Keep Out" appeared in the *Saturday Evening Post*. Again he described the contradictory attitudes of Americans—their desire to stay out of the war on the one hand, and their sympathy for the European democracies and indignation toward the dictatorships on the other hand. The former was the attitude of reason, the latter that of emotion, and Hoover defined the danger to America as the possibility that "our indignation will displace our reason." He reiterated his theme that the United States could not "create liberty and self-government in Europe." He said: "We cannot reconstruct Europe. The social regeneration of nations must come from within. It cannot come from without." European nations had always put their own interests first during times of peace. They had not repaid the loans from America, while at the same time they had "accumulated balances and assets in this country several times the amount of payments." And when World War I ended, the Europeans had tried to avoid purchasing the great agricultural surplus that had been created for them in the United States during the war years and had rushed to buy cheaper food from other nations. It was time, Hoover argued, that Americans recognized that other nations put their own interests first and that Americans started doing the same. His mail, he wrote, was full of the concern of parents that their sons not be sacrificed for "a useless hope." American sympathies for the European democracies would "be drawn upon heavily in the days to come," but America's duty to its sons was "to hold reason in power over emotion. It is to hold the long vision of America's future. It is to keep out of these wars."[104]

Hoover remained confident that Britain and France could not be defeated and that, at worst, the war in Europe would resolve into stalemate.[105] Partly for this reason, no doubt, he exerted his energies against repeal of the embargo provisions in the neutrality laws. On October 5 he wrote that he was "in day and night conferences with a great many national leaders over the very dangerous situation into which we are drifting over this neutrality legislation." He had been obliged to postpone his return to California because of the insistence of some advisors that he remain close to the action in order to assist in the fight.[106] Roosevelt was not only seeking to free himself from restrictions on the cash-and-carry sale of munitions, but was also seeking a flexible law that would permit him to discriminate between aggressor and victim. Failing that, he sought repeal of the embargo provisions altogether, so that arms and munitions could be sold to belligerents, at least on a cash-and-carry basis like other exports. Hoover had found support for his own proposal (to limit such sales strictly to defensive items) from popular aviation heroes Charles Lindbergh and Eddie Rickenbacker, and he believed that at least six senators could be expected to support his plan.[107] But he also found opposition to his plan voiced by many upon whom he had counted for support.[108] For many of Hoover's friends there seemed to be no safe middle ground between repeal of the neutrality law and no law at all, and the law must be preserved in toto as the only guarantee that America would not be drawn into the war.[109] As Hoover had already observed, he considered the particular legislation in force as less critical than the will of the administration and of the people. He advocated the sale of "defensive" weapons, hoping this would be an outlet for the emotions of a people who overwhelmingly supported the Allies and that, thus appeased, the public would oppose actual American intervention in the war.

On October 11, Hoover responded to a request from Senator Styles Bridges by sending him proposed changes to a preamble, which Bridges intended to add to the neutrality amendment before the Senate. Bridges' version read:

> WHEREAS it is the determination of the people that the United States remain at peace, and WHEREAS it is the determination of the people that the United States remain wholly neutral in all foreign wars not effecting [*sic*] the defense of the United States, and WHEREAS the United States stands for restoring and strengthening the rights of neutrality at the earliest practicable time, and WHEREAS the risk of this Nation becoming involved in foreign wars can be diminished by restricting the exercise of certain neutral rights of our citizens; Therefore be it. . . .[110]

Hoover's proposed changes made the message even clearer to the Europeans: "It is hereby declared to be the policy of the United States to remain absolutely neutral in wars between other nations. Whereas, in accordance with this policy the risks of becoming involved can be diminished by restricting the exercise of certain neutral rights of our citizens; Therefore be it. . . ."[111] Bridges incorporated Hoover's proposal into his amendment.

On the same date, Hoover released his views on the proposed changes in the neutrality law, also solicited by Bridges. He again offered his compromise.

Pointing out that much of modern warfare centered around the intimidation or attack of civilian populations from the air, Hoover proposed that bombing planes and other weapons that could be and were used against civilian populations should be embargoed by the United States. At the same time, the weapons by which nations protected themselves from such attacks should be sold—including pursuit aircraft, antiaircraft guns, "and any other instruments of defense against attacks on civilians." He believed that his proposal would "meet many of the difficulties and dangers enunciated by both the opponents and supporters of the embargo." It would not mean that the United States would take sides in the wars or that the nation was moving toward participation in them. The United States would not be contributing "the weapons of mass murder," nor would this approach "inflate American industry" and contribute to "the creation of industrial and financial pressure groups interested in going deeper into war"; it would not lead to the "after-war collapse and unemployment" that always resulted from wartime "inflated industry." It would not be an unneutral action, and it would be consistent with the ideals of the United States. It was not directed "for or against nations who may be at war, as it would apply at all times against neutrals as well as combatants, before and after war occurs." The United States "would be again raising a standard against barbaric action," and rather than moving "deeper into the war," it would be "stepping away from pitfalls that may lead into it." The proposal would keep "both our conscience and our neutrality right." In other respects, Hoover found the proposed neutrality bill generally "constructive."[112] Hoover also stated his proposal succinctly for the movie newsreels on the same date, declaring that his compromise would shift "this whole issue from power politics to foundations in morals and humanity. It is the only safe ground upon which to maintain American neutrality and to keep out of this war."[113]

William Allen White took a prominent role in organizing and chairing the Non-Partisan Committee for Peace through the Revision of the Neutrality Law, but privately he supported Hoover's proposal to embargo offensive weapons.[114] Senator Arthur Vandenberg thought there was "much to be said" for the Hoover compromise, and he asked him to draft into legislative form the ideas contained in his memorandum.[115] Hoover complied. He had, he told Vandenberg, received a "very large response, particularly a seeming surprise that our Administration would dare propose to sell bombing planes, poison gas, and submarines."[116] Vandenberg placed Hoover's statement in the *Congressional Record* and asked for any further thoughts he might have as to the precise form that an amendment along this line might take. He would, Vandenberg told Hoover, "see what can be done at this end of the line."[117]

Hoover was discouraged, however, by the fact that his proposal had done nothing to alter the balance of the division in the Senate over the repeal question. A substantial majority still favored repeal of the embargo, some of them under prodding from the White House. The compromise Hoover sought could only appeal to some of those in the minority who sought, thereby, a ground for blocking total repeal. He received pessimistic reports on the prospects for his compromise and was not pleased with the reception given his proposal by the press.[118] One difficulty lay, obviously, in defining precisely what were defensive and offensive weapons, since the demarcation was not as clear as Hoover supposed it to be.[119] Seeking to arouse public support for his proposal, on October 20 the former president went on the radio.[120] He did not expect to "change the course of events," he told Vandenberg, "but it does seem to me that somebody has got to voice moral standards in this country if we are not to slide down the same barbaric road that Europe has tread."[121]

In his radio address, Hoover called for national unity in the face of the crisis abroad. He outlined his compromise, explaining that its object was to prohibit the sale of those weapons used primarily against civilians. Every child in Europe, he insisted, could make the distinction between the bombing planes and poison gas that were being used against them and the "pursuit planes, observation planes, search-lights, anti-aircraft guns and gas masks," which were used in defense against such destruction. The bombing of civilians from the air meant "that the world has gone back to savagery, where armed men killed women and children and burned cities." Brave men, he argued, did not "sneak around and kill unarmed men, women and children, and destroy their homes. . . . Chivalry is certainly dying in our world." Hoover, therefore, not only opposed the sale of weapons to commit such deeds, but also sought to make the use of such weapons as ineffective as possible by freely selling the devices that could be used in defense against them. It would be a purely neutral action, and it would, he hoped, restore unity among the American people. The conflict in Europe, he warned, had "begun to take on a bitterness that threatens our national solidarity in [the] face of dangers." Americans were denouncing one another as pro-German or pro-British when in reality their only "crime" was in being pro-American. "Gradually," he warned, "we are dividing into two camps over a question that is after all very secondary to the dominant question of keeping America out of this war." His proposal, Hoover insisted, would avoid many dangers and above all would contribute "something constructive to the world by way of humanity and moral standards."[122]

Even before his appearance in front of the microphones, however, Hoover had been disappointed by the reaction of some of his friends to advance drafts of the speech.[123] Typical was the response of one friend, who was "gravely disappointed and saddened beyond measure" over Hoover's willingness to relax the embargo for such defensive weapons. Whether defensive weapons or not, he argued, there were "deadly dangers" in any "ammunitions traffic." According to this view there was no real distinction between one soldier killing another with a rifle and the murder of children by bombing planes—both were equally abhorrent. The only hope lay in extending and strengthening the embargo on all weapons of war.[124] As a Quaker, Hoover no doubt agreed with the idealism expressed in this position, but he argued that the reality of the situation was that in a straight vote on repeal of the embargo it would be repealed in the Senate by at least 60 votes, and by a vote of about 235 to 180 in the House. There were, however, a number of members of the House, where the vote would be close, who favored repeal but might, he felt, support his plan if only those members who supported a continuation of the embargo were willing to compromise. In the interest of practicality, then, as well as idealism, blind support of the embargo would accomplish nothing, while support for Hoover's proposal might, in his opinion, rescue something from the situation.[125]

Hoover was not sanguine, however, that his proposal would be adopted. Although he received considerable praise for his radio address, the rigid position in Congress on both sides of the embargo question did not augur well for a compromise.[126] When his substitute plan was introduced as an amendment in the Senate, it was defeated on October 26 by a vote of 56 to 36.[127] Hoover now looked to the House, where he expected the vote to be closer. On October 28 he wrote:

> While it may be too late, Republican leaders in the House have concluded that their best hope of handling this embargo is to ask the members to vote against the Senate report so as to give an opportunity to amend it to prohibit the export of poison gas and bombing planes. There is a bare possibility that they might get a majority on this basis. Otherwise they are licked by about twenty votes.[128]

Other GOP leaders, including Frank Knox, argued that the injection of partisanship into what they felt should be a nonpartisan issue was unwise and not in accord with public opinion. The Republican position on the embargo, Knox said, had led him to "wonder whether our party has not lost through inept and stupid leadership even the right to come back into dominance."[129] With public opinion clearly in favor of the repeal of the embargo, the GOP was being saddled with the blame for delaying that repeal.[130] Because the fight was so obviously lost, other GOP leaders, including Alf Landon, tried to ensure that "the Republicans would not line up solidly against the bill" and encouraged Republicans in the House to vote for repeal.[131] But Landon refused to come out publicly in favor of repeal despite urgings from William Allen White that he do so.[132] Although Landon apparently favored repeal, he was reluctant to take a public position at odds with the sentiment of most Republicans in Congress.[133]

Both the Senate and the House voted overwhelmingly for a new Neutrality Act along the lines Roosevelt had requested, and on November 4, 1939, the president signed the new bill into law. Opponents of the bill had obtained some concessions. While the cash-and-carry provision was extended to arms and munitions, American citizens were barred from sailing on belligerent vessels, and American ships were barred from sailing into belligerent ports. Thus, the prospect that the United States might be drawn into incidents such as those that had precipitated American entry into World War I seemed reduced. Nevertheless, the vote on the bill followed markedly along party lines, with only a few Republicans in either the House or the Senate voting for the president's proposal.[134]

For Hoover, the failure to get his compromise proposal adopted was a defeat, but he still regarded the question of American involvement in the European war as hinging not on the enactment or repeal of laws, but on the will of the American people and their leaders. Vandenberg reported that while he had tried to get Hoover's compromise adopted, the administration had been in such complete command of the Senate that he had not been able to get even a vote against the export of poison gas. The Michigan senator did, however, believe that the expressions of opposition to American involvement in the war, uttered by both proponents and opponents of the embargo repeal, had set back the plans of the Roosevelt administration to involve the United States in the war, and he sensed that the administration was backing away. "It remains to be seen how long the administration will be content to wear its latest disguise," he wrote Hoover. "Let us hope and pray that it may be permanent."[135]

Hoover was less optimistic about the intentions of the Roosevelt administration. "We must now await the next step toward taking us into war," he wrote O'Laughlin. "I imagine it will revolve around either extending government credit to the Allies or presenting them with ammunitions."[136] To Vandenberg he wrote that he agreed that the debate in Congress had crystallized the anti-intervention group in the nation, but also that it had done the same for the pro-intervention group. At the moment the anti-intervention group was in the majority, "but it is in danger from an emotional invasion at any time."[137] Accurately, Hoover predicted that the war in Europe was "likely to go to bed in the military sense until spring and that we will be deluged on the diplomatic front until that time. If there is no success in that direction, then we can expect to see a serious war that may last for many years."[138]

In the midst of his activities in connection with the Neutrality Act, Hoover was meeting with intimates in New York City in October and discussing with them whether the time had not come for him to launch his campaign for the Republican nomination.[139] Later in the month, Alan Fox, who had sampled public opinion for Hoover in the 1936 campaign, prepared to launch yet another effort. The plan was to sample approximately forty different groups in New York state with some four thousand questionnaires.[140] As the questionnaires began to come back, Fox found that more were "favorable to Hoover than any other one candidate and a good many of those who favor Hoover say they voted for Roosevelt last time."[141] Fox was convinced that a poll on a larger scale could be "quite influential."[142] Hoover pronounced himself as "much interested in the poll."[143] However, he continued to maintain to all but his most intimate associates that he was not interested in the nomination. When Daniel Willard, president of the Baltimore and Ohio Railway, wrote Hoover that "of all the names mentioned as possible candidates for the Republican nomination for the presidency in 1940, you personally stand so high above any of them as to be distinctly in a class by yourself," Hoover responded that he was "not seeking for any such job—and one of the cardinals of politics is if you do not seek, nothing comes to you. Therefore, I am able to sleep nights."[144]

In the view of some, Hoover was the ideal figure to mediate an end to the war in Europe. In November of 1939, the editor of *Zion's Herald*, a Methodist weekly, wrote that he was prepared to publish a plea for Hoover to take the leadership in such a mediation and that a number of New England churches had already passed resolutions to that end. He asked for Hoover's approval of the publication of such an appeal.[145] Hoover replied that he preferred not to "make any public statement on the matter." While he agreed that an early end to the war would be the "greatest blessing that can come to civilization and no effort should be spared that has hope of constructive success," he did not feel that the time was ripe for such an effort. No one could tell, Hoover said, "when a new situation might arise that would be more favorable," but for the present, "the first obligation in this matter rests upon the administration in Washington." Moreover, he pointed out to the Methodist editor, "the law forbids any negotiations with foreign governments by private citizens."[146]

It is apparent, however, that Hoover was not opposed to the movement in behalf of such a mediation effort. On November 10 he had already met with Howard P. Davis and had apparently not discouraged Davis's attempt to generate a mass appeal for Hoover to take steps to end the war in Europe. Davis's movement was taking the form of petitions to be utilized in churches throughout the United States, and through newspaper and magazine publicity. Davis wrote Hoover late in November: "Presently you will hear this faint cry for your services in the greatest of world crises swell into a mighty roar."[147] True to his word, Davis was soon deluging Hoover with petitions and resolutions from churches all across the United States. After reciting the reasons why the war should be stopped, the petitions went on to say:

> Whereas we believe that Herbert Hoover by virtue of his internationally known record as director of relief to all nations involved in

the World War is the one world figure qualified to call the leaders of
Europe to a reconsideration of the tragic steps which lie before them
if this war is continued, be it therefore resolved that we the under-
signed, people of a neutral state, hereby implore Herbert Hoover as
a private citizen of a neutral nation to use his offices and influence as
the world's outstanding humanitarian to the end that the responsible
leaders of the belligerent nations may agree to an immediate truce
pointing to an international conference dedicated to the peaceful
solution of international problems.[148]

As nothing, quite obviously, could come of such an appeal, one can only
speculate on Hoover's motives in failing to squelch it. Perhaps he felt that such
an outpouring of evidence of the desire for peace in Europe would be a useful
tool in opposing the administration's policies leaning toward intervention. And
perhaps the movement could also be useful to Hoover in gaining the 1940
nomination.

The invasion of Finland by the Soviet Union late in November 1939
immediately aroused great sympathy in the United States for the plight of the
Finns, the only Europeans who had repaid their World War I obligations to
the United States. Hoover's response was to suggest the withdrawal of the
American ambassador from Moscow in order to register American disapproval for the Soviet act of aggression. He wondered aloud "why we are so
tender towards communist Russia, especially in view of the rough treatment
this present administration gave to Nazi Germany. We ought to express our
national indignation both ways."[149] Hoover quickly took the lead in organizing relief for the Finns by reassembling many of his old relief hands and
launching a public appeal for relief funds.[150] The drive rapidly attracted
widespread support from those prominent in public life and from the press.
Rather than establish local committees as in past efforts, in the interest of
speed and publicity Hoover enlisted local newspapers to drive the appeal and
to receive cash contributions, while acknowledging the contributors in their
columns. By late December he could report over twelve hundred newspapers
actively engaged in appealing for funds for his Finnish Relief Fund, Inc.[151]

Such activities were double-edged, however. While they gave further
publicity to Hoover and enhanced his image as a humanitarian and director of
such works, they also detracted from the time and energy that he could otherwise devote to politics. The diary of Edgar Rickard, filled with the topics
discussed around the dinner table in Hoover's apartment at the Waldorf-
Astoria Hotel, became increasingly devoted, late in 1939, to the details of the
relief effort, with political discussions rare. More and more Hoover's concerns
were with the raising of private funds for the Finnish relief work and with
disputes he was having with Norman Davis of the Red Cross over demarcating

the responsibilities between that group and Hoover's organization. Thus, during the critical months of late 1939 and early 1940, politics became a minor concern of the former president, and his own campaign suffered neglect.

In mid-December, Hoover decided to move permanently to the East Coast after the 1940 Republican convention and, if he were not the nominee, to retire from all political activities.[152] According to Rickard, Hoover had been growing increasingly restless in late 1939 over what he regarded as the sabotage of his political ambitions by the professional politicians, and the Finnish relief activities had furnished a welcome diversion and outlet for his prodigious energies, so that he ended the year in good spirits and health.[153] When journalist George Sokolsky questioned, early in January 1940, how Hoover's name might be kept before the American people in 1940 in preparation for the convention, Rickard found the former president totally uninterested in such political matters since he was completely absorbed with the relief problem.[154] During these critical winter months, Hoover's nomination campaign was limping along without his active involvement.

# 5

# The Last Try

hile 1939 witnessed the outbreak of war in Europe, the winter months saw the conflict quickly settle into a "phony war." During the spring of 1940, however, the war escalated as German troops poured into most of western and northern Europe until even the British Isles seemed threatened. American politics would be buffeted by the events in Europe, and by midyear two Republicans would sit in the Democratic cabinet of President Franklin Delano Roosevelt, responsible for directing the two agencies most concerned with mobilization—the War Department and the Navy Department. Even more than in 1939, Hoover's activities in 1940 would be shaped by the disintegrating international situation.

Hoover began the year 1940 totally preoccupied with relief matters. Nevertheless, Hoover supporters continued to report a "revolutionary change of attitude" in the country toward Hoover.[1] For anyone who was sitting on the fence, Hoover's rising popularity posed a problem. If those upon whom Hoover was counting for support allied themselves to another candidate, and it turned out that Hoover won the nomination, they knew that their disloyalty to "the Chief" would incur his wrath. On the other hand, such fence sitters obviously hoped to have a hand in the nomination and election of the next president, and despite his apparent rise in popularity, Hoover appeared to be little interested in the nomination and to offer only an outside chance at best.[2]

While critical decisions were being made over which candidate to support, Hoover declined all invitations to speak during the month of January, preferring to confine his activities during that month exclusively to Finnish relief.[3] Thus, Hoover continued to look less and less like a serious possibility for the nomination.

The question of whether or not the United States should offer financial aid to beleaguered Finland was dropped in the lap of Congress by President Roosevelt. There seems little doubt that the president was sympathetic to the plight of the Finns and favored financial aid, but the administration recognized the opposition that would doubtless be aroused against such financial aid to a warring nation if Roosevelt were to support it. Very likely, any discussion of financial aid to Finland would be viewed by opponents of the administration as a backdoor for extending similar aid to Great Britain and France. But ironically, despite their opposition to financial aid to these latter (due to the precedent of World War I), such Republican leaders as Taft and Hoover favored a loan to the Finns because, in Taft's words, "there is no conceivable excuse for the Russian attack, and America has always favored, and often aided, those who are fighting for their freedom."[4] Yet the same argument could as easily be made in behalf of financial assistance to the British and French. It is apparent that those who advocated financial aid to victims of Soviet aggression, and not to victims of German aggression, were practicing a double standard while at the same time they criticized the administration for its double standard where German and Soviet aggression was concerned. The loan, when passed by the House and Senate, was limited to 30 million dollars, did not mention Finland by name, and excluded the purchase of "arms, ammunitions, or implements of war" with the money, under the provisions of the Neutrality Act. It was also passed too late to be of any assistance to the Finns, as that war was already in its closing phase.[5]

With the fall of Finland to the Soviet army, Hoover began in February to give renewed attention to his political future, dividing his time now between political activities and Polish relief. Edgar Rickard found him convinced early in the month that none of the other GOP hopefuls was making much headway and that his own prospects for the nomination, therefore, remained good.[6] Alan Fox had discussed his polls with several people and reported to Hoover the sentiment he had found:

> There would be nothing to the nomination if the leaders [of the party] could be convinced that you did have popular support and [there is] . . . no better way to evidence this than by the type of polls on which we are working . . . all the leaders recognize that you are incomparably the best fitted but still have the impression that you could not get popular support.

Hoover, then, still suffered from the image of a loser, and in the view of his supporters, this alone could prevent his nomination. If the polls could demonstrate that he possessed enough popular support to win, then presumably the "leaders" would support his nomination. Fox now had in mind a poll of 20,000 voters in the state of New York and was looking for money to finance it.[7] A week later Fox wrote excitedly that his questionnaires were turning up more support for Hoover in New York City than for any other candidate. Again he pressed for a wider scale poll, saying, "I know of no way to prove this popular support except by the method I am freely attempting."[8]

In mid-February, two polls in New York City showed very different results. In one poll, Thomas Dewey outpolled Hoover nearly 2 to 1, and a very definite shift away from Roosevelt and toward the Republican party was revealed. In the other poll, which was confined to the Queens area of the city, Hoover barely edged out Dewey 159 to 157, with no other candidates even close.[9] Neither of these polls bore out the results Fox was reporting from his own efforts. Another poll, taken in Indiana, asked two questions: Who was most qualified to be President of the United States? and Who should be nominated by the Republican party in 1940? To the first question, the response was overwhelmingly for Hoover, with 86 percent, while his nearest rival, Senator Arthur Vandenberg, polled only 10 percent. To the second question, however, the response was 36 percent for Vandenberg, 26 percent for Dewey, 23 percent for Taft, and only 9 percent for Hoover. Clearly, qualifications were not counting heavily with the voters of Indiana.[10] Hoover, however, derived some encouragement from both the New York and Indiana polls.[11]

Hoover's Lincoln Day address was delivered to Republicans in Omaha. Having been distracted for months by relief and foreign affairs, he now returned to domestic policies, where he found the principal problem to be the continued high unemployment. Getting the American people back to work was "the greatest humanitarian action of our day and age," he told his listeners. Pending solution of the problem, the government must provide relief, but relief could not go on forever because of the expense. The taxes that must pay for the borrowing of relief dollars would eventually "asphyxiate the whole productive system." The problem derived not from the free enterprise system, or laborsaving devices, or foreign causes, or any of the other stock explanations; it derived from the fact that "certain dynamic forces" must be combined in order to create jobs. These forces were, Hoover asserted, ". . . intellectual, spiritual and economic liberty; The moral strength of a people; Natural resources; Constant new scientific discoveries and inventions." America possessed all of these, and "when these great forces are firing on all four motors, they can make employment for all of our people." However, there were three "notions" that, in recent years, had paralyzed these forces. First was the notion that "the whole system is wrong and must be made over." Second was the notion that government officials should "plan, direct or operate the economic life of the people." Third was the notion that "governments can spend and spend and borrow and borrow without thought of tomorrow." What the nation needed was "a vigorous shift in ideas,—of point of view in the nation." The drift toward statism must be reversed. Solutions must be sought not in transforming the entire system, but in correcting faults that "are marginal around a heart and hearth which are well founded." New emphasis must be placed on productivity as the only way to progress. Thrift must be emphasized, not government spending. Morals and intellectual integrity must be re-established in government. Unity must be sought instead of class conflict and disunity. And finally, the American people must stay out of the war. Then the unemployment problem could be solved in America.[12]

Late in 1939, Hoover found new financial support for the Republican Circles. By this time he could report 85,000 members in the western states.[13] When western Republicans gathered to hold a regional conference in Salt Lake City in December 1939, Circle members and other Hoover supporters were well represented and, according to one report Hoover received, "strongly dominated" the conference.[14] Hoover was told that the conference had been "completely satisfactory" from his standpoint.[15] All but Oregon, Arizona, and New Mexico were represented in the Salt Lake City conference, and the Hoover supporters experienced little difficulty in persuading the meeting to express itself in favor of uninstructed delegations to the 1940 GOP convention.[16] The earlier struggle in California had also ended on a satisfactory note, and early in February Hoover was told that he could count on 32 of the 44 California delegates to the convention.[17] The former president congratulated his supporters for "a fine job considering the manipulations and disloyalties" with which they "had to contend." He thought that he could influence one or two more of the delegates and hoped "that we may be able to do something to the people who have not played the game."[18] It was apparent that Hoover was approaching the 1940 convention in a spirit far different from that of 1936.

The Taft campaigners were not happy at Hoover's apparent control over the "uninstructed" California delegation, since they felt that if it were not for him they could line up most of the delegates behind the senator "within 48 hours." As one put it: if Hoover "would pass the word around, or by public announcement state that he in no way directly or indirectly seeks to interfere with the vote of the uninstructed delegation, and that he is not opposed to Taft, in my opinion it would be easy to line up the whole delegation for the Senator." But, the same Taft compaigner observed, rumor had it that Hoover was opposed to the nomination of any senator or congressman, and favored, instead, "some good Republican governor."[19] Some believed that a deal had been struck between Hoover and Ohio governor John Bricker, with the latter presenting Hoover to the convention and perhaps getting the nod for the vice-presidential slot if Hoover were the presidential nominee.[20]

Meanwhile, Hoover sought to discourage the mounting of any challenges in California to the uninstructed slate by the Dewey and Vandenberg camps, occasionally taking the opportunity to remind others of the fate that had befallen the Landon challenge in that state four years earlier.[21] In mid-February, Hoover wrote Arch Shaw that he did "not think any of the political candidates are getting anywhere. They are all claiming the earth which is a sign of weakness."[22] He found it interesting that, in contrast with 1936, he now appeared to be regarded as "a desirable ally for all candidates because one time or another each one of their political managers starts the story that I am for his man." However, he had "preserved an absolute and complete independence from the whole business and this goes for ever since the beginning."[23]

Late in February Hoover traveled to Washington to confer with the State Department concerning Polish relief and to testify before the House Foreign Affairs Committee in support of financial aid for Poland to buy relief supplies.[24] During his stay in the nation's capital, Hoover talked with Secretary of State Hull and also held meetings with the Polish ambassador and others concerning the problems that would be encountered in administering relief to that country if financial assistance were arranged.[25] Throughout the month of March, Hoover was again almost totally absorbed with relief matters.[26] Despite attempts to keep in operation the Finnish relief effort to aid refugees from that country, the Soviet occupation of Finland had led American interest in the Finns to ebb, and funds were reduced to a trickle.[27]

Hoover was encouraged in March by a poll of midwestern and eastern newspapers, which showed that 50 percent of the Republican papers considered him the candidate best qualified to handle the problems of the presidency.[28] Others suggested that he could probably do better in New York City in a presidential election than Dewey or any of the other potential GOP candidates, in part because he was likely to take more of the normally Democratic foreign-born vote.[29] Meanwhile, Alan Fox continued his New York polls, with Hoover continually a leader or close second.[30] Hoover's efforts to get uninstructed delegations to the convention from other states were also bearing fruit.[31] In early April, Rickard found Hoover optimistic about his political prospects.[32]

Efforts continued to keep the Republican Circles alive in the western states.[33] A poll was also taken in California, similar to those which Alan Fox was taking in the East. It consisted of a double postcard (half to be torn off and returned) mailed to 20,000 Californians randomly selected from the Democratic and Republican registration lists. The postcard asked the questions: Whom did you vote for in 1932 and in 1936?; and, If Hoover and FDR were the candidates in 1940, which would you vote for?[34] The first returns showed a slight shift in sentiment from Roosevelt to Hoover compared with the 1932 vote.[35] The cards had, however, been mailed only to middle-class districts.[36] Other Hoover supporters encouraged Dr. George Gallup to take a poll ascertaining public sentiment on the qualifications of the various candidates, especially their qualifications for handling foreign policy questions.[37] As the fast moving events in Europe were making foreign relations loom even more important for the 1940 nomination and election, Hoover urged that William Starr Myers complete the book on the Hoover administration's foreign policies by spring.[38]

In mid-April, Rickard found the former president mapping his strategy for the pursuit of delegates at the convention. Hoover was convinced that many of the delegates would turn to him after the third ballot.[39] Pleased with the initial results from the Fox polls, Hoover now decided to pursue them on a larger scale, while also arranging for "educational" material to be mailed to each of the delegates.[40] Furthermore, he was exploring the possibility of using some newspapers to initiate a "call" for a Hoover draft during the month of May.[41] Public relations man James Selvage outlined the thinking in the Hoover camp:

> It seems to some of us here that the time has come, or will have come early in May, to begin to activate the demand for the Chief which we know is there, and almost on every side you hear today that he is the ablest man and should be in the White House, coupled with that silly followup, "but he can't be elected." That is the thing that must be broken down and we have the feeling that if we concentrate our fire over a period of six or seven weeks before the convention, that a grass-roots demand can be built that will catch fire. In this connection . . . a survey has been made in New York in the vicinity of more than 10,000 voters—names taken from the official voting list. . . . In all but one election district, Mr. Hoover is running ahead of Dewey by a sizable margin and on the first choice for head of the ticket he is far in front. . . . A poll of the bar association went heavily for the Chief and against Dewey. If we know the demand is there under the surface, we must bring it upward and, by letting it be known that there are many who feel that the Chief is the man, give courage to those who are hesitant about speaking out. With this in view, several of us are writing to everyone we know and can trust, suggesting that starting soon after May 1st they do everything in their power to stir talk about the Chief.[42]

As part of the "information" campaign, John Spargo was again pressed into service, with letters and articles being distributed to the mailing lists; but the effort in this area was much reduced from its level in the 1936 campaign."[43] Efforts to actually influence delegates, however, were obviously greater than they had been four years earlier. A Hoover supporter in the Texas delegation who had lobbied with Republican leaders and likely delegates in Arkansas, Louisiana, New Mexico, Oklahoma, and Georgia reported his conclusions:

> I believe the majority of all these delegates want to see the Chief nominated. . . . The worst thing we have to combat is the adverse psychology of the average voter which includes delegates. I have only talked to one Republican in the past two years who did not say that Mr. Hoover was better qualified than any other man in our party and that he would like to see him nominated, but they always wind up with the statement that he cannot be elected. . . . Of course this is an adverse psychology which must be met, and the results of the polls which you enclosed are very heartening indeed to me.[44]

Late in April, Hoover estimated that he would attract approximately ten votes on the first ballot in the convention, but pick up sixty votes on the second ballot due to shifts from California, New York, New Jersey, and Illinois.[45] This did not include votes from Ohio, where he had been told by Governor Bricker that if Taft failed, the governor would try to carry the Ohio delegation into the Hoover camp.[46] From a delegate who was part of the North Carolina contingent came an inquiry as to Hoover's availablity for the nomination and the news that the North Carolina delegation was "in the most part open-minded," while Senator Bailey of that state had paid Hoover the compliment of being "the smartest and best informed man in the United States today."[47] From every direction, Hoover was being told that the grass roots were for him if only they could be convinced that he was electable. Thus, it seemed at the end of April that merely by publicizing the results of the opinion polls that were being conducted, Hoover's potential strength could be brought to the fore and his nomination be assured. In late April yet another of the Hoover polls (one seeking to compare voters' behavior in 1932 with their preference in 1940) showed the former president gaining substantially at Roosevelt's expense.[48]

It is also clear that Hoover was once again attempting to keep all of the other candidates in the race in order to prevent any one from gaining a clear majority. A memorandum in the O'Laughlin papers recounts a telephone call of April 28, in which Hoover asked O'Laughlin to take a message from him to Vandenberg encouraging the Michigan senator to make two major speeches in the middle or latter part of May. Hoover wanted Vandenberg told that Dewey had not nearly the delegate strength that he claimed and that it was desirable for every candidate to stay in the battle, including Vandenberg, who "should not cease to battle and to battle hard." O'Laughlin did pass Hoover's message to Vandenberg, but found the senator discouraged. He got the impression that Vandenberg was inclining more and more to the idea of returning to the Senate. O'Laughlin suggested to Hoover that the only way to keep Dewey and Vandenberg "in line" was to encourage Vandenberg further and try to get the 40 anti-Dewey delegates from New York together to announce their opposition to him.[49]     Vandenberg, however, continued to be discouraged, and O'Laughlin reiterated to Hoover that "in order to keep him in the race, he must receive a shot in the arm every once in a while."[50]

Meanwhile, Hoover continued to air his views on the international situation. His longtime hatred and suspicion of the communist regime in Russia had been confirmed by the Soviet invasions of Poland and Finland. In April, in an article for *Collier's*, he expressed his displeasure with the Soviet government and lashed out at the Roosevelt administration for having extended diplomatic recogntion to that government in 1933. Hoover took a moralistic approach to diplomatic recognition that echoed Woodrow Wilson:

> When our neighbors choose to live a life of disrepute, we do not shoot them up. But we can hold up the moral and social standards in the country a little better if we do not associate with them. Or take part in their parties. Or invite them in our homes. Or present them to our children.
>
> Recognition of new governments is thus more than reestablishment of legalistic or trade relations. It is a sign that we believe they are respectable members of the family of nations. It gives them the right of entry into our homes. It gives them a recommendation to our neighbors.

Hoover wrote that the communist regime had been immoral since its inception. The revolution had not been against the czar, but had been a "liquidation" of liberalism in Russia. Ever since, the communist regime had been characterized by terror, bloodshed, and murder within the country, and by attempts to undermine democratic governments abroad. Four successive presidents and their secretaries of state had concurred in the view that such a government ought not be recognized by the United States, but the Roosevelt administration had extended it recognition. In exchange for recognition, the Soviet Union had promised, according to Roosevelt, that it would not seek to undermine the government of the United States. The Soviets had not kept their word, as the six years subsequent to the agreement had been filled with instances of Soviet conspiracy against the Constitution of the United States. Furthermore, the USSR had revealed its utter lack of morality in foreign affairs by its rape of Poland, the destruction of the independence of Latvia and Estonia, and the invasion of Finland. "The recognition of Soviet Russia was a gigantic political and moral mistake," Hoover concluded. "It was not a mistake proved from change of circumstance. It was a mistake obvious from the beginning." Once again he called for the recall of the U.S. ambassador to the Soviet Union. Hoover did not advocate severing relations with the USSR, however, since such an act might be interpreted "at this time of a world aflame . . . as warlike."[51]

Senator Vandenberg and Hoover continued to consult on questions of foreign affairs and to harbor similar viewpoints. Responding to the *Collier's* article, the Michigan senator pointed out that he had written a similar article for *Liberty* magazine that would soon appear. "We are presenting substantially the same indictment and we reach substantially the same conclusion," he told Hoover. "I have been urging this viewpoint on the floor of the Senate for a long time."[52] Hoover responded that his idea was "the same as yours and that is to ventilate the follies of the foreign policies of this administration. It is not often in foreign policies that one is able to point to the direct consequences of wrong such as we are in this case."[53] The two continued to consult on foreign policy both by letter and in personal meetings.[54]

In May the Hoover campaign for the nomination consisted of the polls, letters mailed to delegates and GOP officeholders, and fieldwork on Hoover's behalf in the eastern and southern states.[55] Work was also being done in the western states by Ross Laird, who had been instrumental in setting up Republican Circles outside California. In the middle of the month, Laird reported that work in Colorado was "progressing nicely." Two "ardent followers" of the former president had been enlisted in the Colorado delegation, and they would endeavor to convert the others. Laird found the Utah delegation "not entirely to my liking, but we do have one good friend on it and one other delegate is beginning to come our way."[56] Later in the month, Laird assured Hoover that he would have "a trifle over a majority" of the delegates in the western states. Idaho and Washington were not very satisfactory, but he was hopeful that they, too, would come along when they saw where "the wind is blowing."[57] Dining with Hoover in mid-May, Rickard found him almost every evening occupied with analyzing the polls conducted by his supporters to find further proof of grass-roots support for his candidacy.[58]

Hoover's confidence, however, was gradually undermined during the month of May. His expectations of winning the nomination were based largely on the inability of the other candidates to arouse enthusiasm. Given the results of his polls and his obvious qualifications to handle the presidency during an international crisis, Hoover had good reason to believe that the delegates would turn to him once the other candidates failed to gain the required majority. In May, however, a new and unforeseen challenge to his ambitions began to surface. The name of Wendell Willkie began increasingly to appear in Hoover's correspondence and in Rickard's accounts of their conversations. At first Hoover attached little importance to the boom for this former anti–New Deal Democrat, who was now a candidate for the Republican nomination. Early in the month he concluded that on the first ballot in the convention there would be about thirty votes scattered between Congressman Joseph Martin, Wendell Willkie, and himself.[59] However, he was receiving reports of enthusiastic receptions for Willkie.[60] On May 11 he wrote to Walter Newton that he agreed with the latter's assessment of the Willkie movement as little more than "a sort of reaction from disappointment as to candidates." He could not "conceive that it will get anywhere in the convention, although it is very popular in business circles. Many of the people who have been backing Dewey financially have now switched over."[61] But by the end of the month, Rickard found Hoover disturbed over Willkie's growing popularity and considering the organization of some draft-Hoover groups.[62] A few days later Hoover was even forced to acknowledge that there had been numerous defections from among his own supporters to Willkie.[63]

While Hoover tried to keep Vandenberg in the race, Robert Taft sought the former president's support for his own candidacy. Early in May, Hoover received word through Mark Sullivan that Taft, if elected, wanted Hoover to be his secretary of state.[64] Hoover dismissed the idea as "not particularly new," since it had "been suggested from each one of the leading candidates." He regarded it as "wholly infeasible and . . . nothing more than preconvention stuff."[65] Hoover's estimate of delegate counts in early May showed Taft leading the other candidates, but well short of the number needed for nomination.[66] His own preference among the other candidates was well concealed. Hoover graciously consented to entertain each of the aspirants who sought to call on him either in New York or in California, and rumors abounded in the press after each such meeting, but he gave no indication of a favorite.

It was apparent, however, that if Hoover had no preference, many of his supporters favored Taft over the other candidates. In late May, one of Taft's lieutenants in California reported to the senator a conversation with Herbert Clark, one of Hoover's key strategists there, in which Clark promised that the Hoover supporters in the California delegation would not withhold their votes from Taft, if the senator had a chance of nomination, simply to promote a stalemate from which Hoover might emerge as a compromise.[67] If the conversation was accurately reported, Clark had committed himself to a course at considerable variance with Hoover's own strategy. For his part, Hoover was counting heavily on Taft's delegates to come to him once it became clear that the senator could not win the nomination.[68] Taft, himself, was confident that Hoover "would rather have me in than any other of the active candidates."[69]

After struggling for the first five months of 1940 with the problem of Polish relief, Hoover found his efforts complicated and sought even more as a result of the successful German thrust westward in the spring of 1940. As country after country fell before the German juggernaut, the number of nations requesting relief grew. Soon Poland was joined by Belgium in requesting assistance, then by the Netherlands and, later, by Norway.[70] These demands for relief continued throughout 1940 to bring Hoover into contact with his own and the British governments, and they also brought difficulties in the competing appeals for funds of such agencies as the Red Cross.[71] However, by the summer of 1940 the effort to get relief to the occupied European nations remained so thoroughly blocked by the war that when W. K. Kellogg, of cereals fame, offered to contribute $20,000 for "the care of children in some European country," Hoover was forced to turn it down, since, he replied, "in the present situation there is no opportunity to do a constructive service such as you mention in your letter." It was, he told Kellogg, "impossible to land supplies anywhere on the European continent of importance, and there is no more than normal destitution in England." He hoped, however, that in the fall the opportunity would arise for such relief activities as Kellogg sought to assist.[72]

Hoover was also concerning himself with the question of defense mobilization. On May 17, 1940, he issued a press statement arguing that there could "be no partisanship upon the principle of national defense." He called for "thoughtful and scientific" armament of the United States based on the experience gained from the current war in Europe. "Undue haste" in actual production must be avoided, but the nation must move forward rapidly with the "creation of facilities for production, which must be first in any event." Industry must furnish the skill to direct industrial production, not the army and navy. "The job should be directed by a staff of tried leaders chosen from actual industrial production," Hoover insisted. "That is, not the financial leaders of the industry but the men who have come to the top through actual production experience of a large scale."[73]

Hoover wrote to Congressman Joseph Martin on the same date, saying that if American industry could be "mobilized under some nonpartisan government agency in which they [industry] had confidence," industry could almost instantly double the production of aircraft. He suggested that the government encourage the expansion of equipment by permitting tax write-offs when wartime use of the equipment ended and by coordination of subcontracting. He suggested also that automobile manufacturers be encouraged to suspend new models for a year, thus turning "over their machine tool capacity and their machine tool machinists to making machine tools for expansion in the aviation field." What was vital, he told Martin, was "to set up some sort of an agency that would have control of the entire production of all munitions of every kind. We finally had to come to that in the last war. Every other country in the world has done it long since." He favored overall control by one man, rather than by a board, since "no board ever functions properly in executive matters unless all the powers are vested in the chairman and even then it is inefficient." He added that with such a system in force there no longer would be any "justification whatever for appropriating money on blank checks to the President and it is the only way that Congress can keep control of the purse."[74]

While Congressional Republicans did press for such an organization of the defense effort, Roosevelt chose, instead, an advisory defense commission. Moreover, the assistant secretary of war, Louis Johnson, attacked Hoover's suggestion of a one-man defense administrator in a radio address on May 28. Hoover responded the following day with a press statement criticizing both the president's action and the Johnson speech. Said the former president:

> In view of the crisis we face and all the exposures of the past month, the country will be disappointed that President Roosevelt has chosen to set up another advisory committee instead of reorganizing the war and navy departments and appointing somebody from industry for the production of munitions. There are three or four good men on this committee, and the country will gain confidence in it if it boldly insists that these things be done at once. Certainly Assistant Secretary of War Johnson last night demonstrated that his capacities at political smearing exceed the capacities he has shown in past years in production of airplanes and guns. We need action now and not advisory reports for the file.[75]

In the midst of the deteriorating situation for the democracies of Europe, the Republican convention was fast approaching. The Hoover campaigners continued to gamble heavily on the effect they believed the Fox polls would have in demonstrating to the delegates that the most qualified Republican for the presidency was also the man most likely to be able to win in November. However, late in May this keystone of the Hoover strategy collapsed. The credibility of the Fox polls was shattered when the results of the Gallup Poll taken in May were released. Instead of polling for opinions concerning the qualifications of the candidates, as Hoover's supporters had urged, Gallup had simply tested their popularity. The poll showed a slight trend away from the Democrats and toward the Republicans, but it still found the Democrats supported by 54 percent of the people. Trial results showed both Roosevelt and Hull capable of beating any of the potential Republican candidates. Most important for the fate of the Hoover campaign was the finding by the Gallup organization that Dewey was the leading GOP choice, favored by 62 percent of those polled and gaining in strength, while Hoover was not a factor, lagging behind as the choice of only 2 percent.[76] All of the potential in the Alan Fox polls for influencing delegates at the convention had been destroyed by a single Gallup Poll.

Disappointed, Hoover now counted heavily on the speech he was to deliver before the convention, and in early June, Rickard found him absorbed in writing it.[77] On June 4 the former president lunched with Dewey and learned that the New Yorker claimed over four hundred delegates.[78] This was nothing like Hoover's assessment of the situation. Renewed efforts were made at this late moment to mobilize the support of the old Belgian Relief and American Relief Administration crowd, as well as of those involved in the newer Finnish relief effort.[79] The Willkie challenge was appearing more threatening. In early June Mrs. Ogden Reid, wife of the editor of the *New York Herald Tribune*, sought Hoover's support for the Willkie candidacy,[80] Hoover had now concluded that Willkie was his chief rival for the Republican nomination.[81] He was receiving alarming reports about the new challenger. As one of his correspondents wrote in mid-June:

> A local minor official of the local utility company brought me downtown yesterday morning. He swung right into Willkie talk. It ran something like this: "We have had our orders. At the right time our employees, stockholders and bondholders will go to work. We have a nationwide campaign committee ready to go, and the heads are now laying the groundwork."

The writer concluded that the Willkie boom was part of an "effort of the utilities to control things Republican."[82]

Hoover continued to maintain his visibility as the leading GOP opponent of American entry into the war. Hitler's conquest of the Western European democracies, despite Hoover's prediction that they would be able to defend themselves, created new alarm. The former president continued to maintain close contact with Republicans in and out of Congress for the development of a partisan resistance to what he perceived as Roosevelt's goal to involve the United States in the conflict. On June 7 Hoover wrote to Governor John Bricker that he had been following Bricker's "vigorous attacks on the President's notion that opposition" to his foreign policies "should cease" and added that Bricker's speeches had "done a lot of good."[83] Early in June Hoover published an article in *Liberty* magazine in which he reiterated his warning against American participation in the war. The responsibility of Americans, he insisted, was to "use our unimpaired resources, our courage, our moral strength to do mankind infinite service" in allaying "the destruction of war, and the ravages of Famine and Pestilence" after the war was ended, rather than become involved in fighting it.[84] Congressman Karl Mundt of South Dakota congratulated Hoover on the article and added:

> Our minority group in Congress has gradually—too gradually, in my opinion—gotten back its fighting spirit and from now on until adjournment I hope we shall have power enough and policy enough to wage a head-on attack on FDR's steady usurpation of Congressional powers and his sure march toward American involvement in the war. . . . I am convinced if we can keep out of war until next November, we can rid this country of Roosevelt and rescue it from the permanent loss of its own democratic processes and privileges.[85]

While other GOP leaders, including Landon and Knox, the 1936 nominees, favored bipartisanship in foreign policy, Hoover called for determined Republican opposition to the administration's march toward involvement in the war. As an articulate spokesman for a foreign policy based on reason rather than emotion, he won the support of many Republicans in and out of Congress, as well as the support of many others who were opposed to war. As one editorial expressed the Hoover position:

> Mr. Hoover sees our foreign policy marching with our preparations for defense. He is not isolationist. He firmly believes that isolation is impossible. He wants intensely to keep America out of war, but armed effectively to keep any threat away from this hemisphere. To keep out of war he wants America to act realistically and without emotion. He wants only cool, deliberate action. It is clear that he is not a man who would ever try to sweep America off its feet and into war. He sees only folly in talk offensive to other nations. The President's first responsibility, he says, is to evade war, not to stimulate it.[86]

Throughout the month of June, Hoover concentrated most of his attention on the campaign for the nomination. One issue before the convention drew his attention and his intervention, however. Amidst headlined stories describing the German advance into western Europe, the delegates to the convention divided over the question of whether the GOP should take a stand in its platform favoring support for the beleaguered democracies.[87] On June 18, the *New York Times* reported:

> A strong current toward a declaration of sympathy for the forces still battling Nazi domination of Europe, as well as for all possible mate-

rial aid "short of war" developed quickly among the forty-odd members of the Republican Resolutions Committee as it convened informally today to begin drafting a platform to be presented to the national convention next week. Led openly by Alfred M. Landon of Kansas, Presidential nominee in 1936, and Walter E. Edge, former Senator from New Jersey and later Ambassador to France, the so-called "Aid-to-the-Allies" movement pushed into the background, for the time being at least, any serious agitation for a restatement of the traditional isolation policy for which the Republican party has been noted in recent years.[88]

Landon was subsequently named chairman of the subcommittee to draft the plank on foreign policy and national defense.[89]

The efforts of Landon and others to develop a pro-Allies plank for the GOP platform were complicated, however, when on June 20 the White House announced that Republicans Frank Knox and Henry Stimson were joining the Roosevelt cabinet to head the Navy and War Departments, respectively. The move was not unexpected. In late May it had seemed so imminent that Hoover consented to the release by Senator Charles Tobey of his letter of September 27, 1939, on the subject of nonpartisanship and coalition government.[90] When the letter was revealed to the press on May 23, 1940, Hoover felt that "the release of the letter did some good."[91] What shocked the Republicans about Roosevelt's appointments was the timing, which was practically on the eve of the GOP convention and at the very moment the Resolutions Committee was debating the foreign policy plank of the platform. As a result, Knox and Stimson were "virtually read out of the Republican Party" by some party leaders, for, as the *New York Times* reported, "party leaders, convention delegates and committee members regarded their course as an act of party treachery." The president's action was denounced as "petty politics" and as a step toward dictatorship and war. There was considerable feeling, briefly, that Roosevelt had virtually forced the GOP into a position of opposition, as the party of peace as against Roosevelt's apparent warlike intentions.[92]

Hoover's public response to the appointment of Knox and Stimson was temperate and followed the line of his letter to Tobey. He told the press: "Messrs. Stimson and Knox are, of course, entering the Cabinet to give personal service, and not representing the Republican Party. There is no question of coalition involved. It has no effect on the 1940 campaign. The national issues remain exactly what they were."[93]

At the same time, Hoover's intimates were seeking to overcome the baneful effects of the Gallup Poll results, released in May, by announcing, on June 21, the results of the Alan Fox polls. The press release reported that in polls matching Hoover against Roosevelt, voters in fourteen states had demonstrated that the former president would gain 16.7 percent over his 1932 vote, while Roosevelt would lose 14.2 percent of his vote in the same election. In every community sampled, "Mr. Roosevelt's vote as compared with 1932 would be smaller, and that of Mr. Hoover larger, although Mr. Hoover is not a candidate." The results of the poll were released by Richard Lawrence, the publisher of *Printers' Ink*, Mrs. Ruth Pratt, a former congresswoman, Everett Colby, the former GOP national committeeman from New Jersey, and John J. Hopkins, the former assistant to the secretary of the treasury in Hoover's cabinet.[94] The press release did not confide that the polls had been limited to middle-class suburban areas, where Hoover's support could be expected to be strongest.

As the convention drew nearer, Hoover, perhaps from wishful thinking, began to downplay the Willkie challenge despite increasing evidence that the recent convert to Republicanism was gathering momentum in his bid for the nomination. To Robert Simmons, Hoover wrote that the Willkie boom seemed to have dealt a mortal blow to Dewey's chances because "the big business people have gone over to Willkie," but he still considered it doubtful that the latter would have many delegates. He now estimated that Willkie would have "perhaps 40 at the start and 100 maximum."[95] From Simmons came the disquieting news that in his Nebraska speech Willkie had lumped the Republican administrations of 1921 to 1933 in the same category as Roosevelt's, distinguishing them only in attacking the Roosevelt administration by name. "This," reported Simmons, "is not only my reaction on the situation, but the reaction of others who listened to his address with whom I talked after the meeting."[96] For Hoover this was "certainly an unhappy development in the Willkie attitude."[97]

From Christian Herter in Massachusetts came word that the Massachusetts delegation would most likely opt for Hoover or Willkie, with sentiment for Dewey and Taft on the wane.[98] Industrialist Edgar M. Queeny sent Hoover the results of a poll he had conducted among party contributors in Missouri, which showed Willkie was supported by 82 percent of those responding, with Dewey and Taft each receiving the support of only 5 percent. Although a close friend of the former president's, Queeny wrote that he would support Willkie and that Willkie thought highly of Hoover and would seek his counsel. Queeny closed by adding: "I know but a word from you would assure his nomination, and it is my earnest hope that at the proper time you will lend him support."[99] Dining alone with Hoover on June 21, however, Rickard found him still convinced that Willkie would fail to gain the nomination, and more concerned about the effect that a Taft–Dewey combination might have on his own chances. Rickard despaired at the very uncoordinated state of the

Hoover arrangements for the convention and doubted that order could be brought out of the chaos.[100]

Adding to the confusion was the fact that Hoover had urged even supporters who were not delegates or alternate delegates to converge on Philadelphia to aid in proselytizing the delegates.[101] The pursuit of support included letters urging the delegates to vote for Hoover; some delegates also received copies of the latest collection of Hoover speeches.[102] A working committee had been formed to direct matters at the convention; it consisted of Arch Coleman, Walter Newton, Arthur Hyde, and Herbert Clark as chairman. The possibility that Clark's loyalties were divided has already been noted. Even with the committee established, there was no formal Hoover headquarters such as existed for the other candidates.[103]

In the week before the balloting began, the Willkie camp was predicting the nomination of their candidate on the sixth or seventh ballot, and there was growing evidence of defections in his direction from the other candidates.[104] Rumors abounded of combinations being formed among the other candidates in an effort to block the Willkie bandwagon.[105] A seeming boost to Hoover's candidacy came from labor leader John L. Lewis. In his testimony before the GOP platform committee on June 18, Lewis defended Hoover's administration against the charges that it had brought on the depression and had done nothing to alleviate its effects. The labor leader supported Hoover's claim that recovery from the depression had begun in 1932, but that the New Deal had prolonged it and transformed it into a chronic condition by its policies and weaknesses. According to the *New York Times*, Lewis had also suggested to numerous people that Hoover was the best qualified candidate to attack the New Deal in the campaign and to deal with the critical international problems which would face the next president.[106]

James A. Hagerty, writing for the *New York Times*, now listed Hoover with Willkie in the "dark horse" category, since he considered that Lewis's testimony had "brought the former President decidedly into the convention picture."[107] Much would clearly depend upon the effect of Hoover's speech to the convention. Would it evoke the demonstration of support that his 1936 effort had? As the *New York Times* put it: "On the effect of his speech, more than anything else, will depend the possibility that Mr. Hoover may be put forward for the Presidential nomination."[108] A few days later the same newspaper opined:

> A decided threat to the candidates already in the field is seen in the scheduled appearance of former President Herbert Hoover before the convention tomorrow night. Friends who have read Mr. Hoover's speech declare that it will be the best and most forceful he

ever has made. It is regarded as significant that Mr. Hoover will not leave Philadelphia immediately after his speech, as he did after addressing the national convention at Cleveland four years ago. Friends of Mr. Hoover—and they are in many State delegations— expect the speech to make a great impression, and possibly to make Mr. Hoover a candidate before the convention. With no candidate having a majority of the delegates and no one of those under present consideration entirely satisfactory to a majority, the situation is ripe for something in the nature of a stampede. It may not and probably will not be for Mr. Hoover, but if he chooses, his influence would be a powerful aid to any candidate.[109]

There was also a great deal of speculation over the effect Hoover's speech would have on the foreign policy plank in the platform. Support for an aid-the-Allies declaration in the platform had quickly resurfaced after the initial furor over the Knox–Stimson appointments had subsided. A great deal, then, seemed to be hinging on Hoover's speech when he entered the convention hall at 9:37 P.M. on June 25. Samuel F. Pryor, GOP national committeeman from Connecticut, chaired the committee on arrangements for the 1940 convention. Pryor was a dedicated supporter of Willkie for the nomination, but also an admirer of the former president. According to Pryor's recollection in 1980, Hoover began the evening badly by jumping the gun in making his way to the podium. Pryor recalled: "When he came up to speak on the platform, he didn't wait for the signal to the television people, the signal from me to the people, he just walked up. All I heard was a lot of clapping, and I said, oh my God, is that Mr. Hoover coming? And he was walking up the aisle!"[110]

After the initial ovation, and the introduction by convention chairman Joseph Martin, there was a demonstration for the former president that lasted for several minutes—the first real demonstration of the convention. Hoover stood in his familiar blue suit, self-consciously putting his hands in his pockets and then withdrawing them while he watched the demonstration before him. Then, as Martin gaveled the demonstration into silence, Hoover ceased smiling, and with a serious expression on his face he launched into his speech. He told the delegates:

> We are faced with the task of saving America for free men. Two-thirds of the world is at war. Twenty nations have become the stamping ground of militant despotisms. Almost everywhere in the Old World the light of liberty for which men have struggled and died has gone into a long night. Men and nations have lost their moral and spiritual moorings. Even in America our system of liberty has been weakened. We are divided in mind and fearful. And confusion

in liberal nations is made worse by the spread of incompetence in governments everywhere.

The greatest threat to America was the loss of liberty, not hostile armies or fifth columns. The major problem was the growing reliance on government as the answer to all economic problems in liberal nations. Governments, however, could not dictate economic policies without also destroying "free speech, orderly justice and free government." The inevitable failures of governmental economic dictation led only to cries for greater power and to further disruption of the free enterprise system. The failures of these "totalitarian liberals," as Hoover referred to them, led inevitably to unemployment and class division and, finally, to the curtain dropping on liberty altogether, because "frustrating and despairing these hundreds of millions of people voluntarily voted the powers of government to the man on horseback as the only way out." Such had been the case in Europe, and America had now experienced eight years of the same type of confused thought, which crippled free enterprise while failing to recognize that free enterprise was "the one dynamic force by which we can restore jobs to our people." Relief was necessary for those who were destitute, but Hoover warned that the nation could not "exist two-thirds workers and one-third dependents." People must be restored "to self-support before the money fails." That could come about only through a change in the occupant of the White House.[111]

Hoover also indicted the lack of morals in the New Deal, the misuse of relief, the support of Democratic urban machines through federal funds, and the use of taxpayers' money for partisan political propaganda. He lambasted the New Deal spending policies, which included deficits, debts, and inflation and he pointedly called attention to the handicap that such a heavy debt posed on America's ability to defend itself. America must avoid becoming involved in the wars in Europe and Asia and must concentrate on industrial preparedness while creating a strong army in reserve. Meanwhile, America should supply materials and munitions to "those nations who are fighting for their freedom"; but Hoover approved of such aid only with provisions, "first, that it involves no action which takes us to war, and second, that as liberty lives by law we must act within the law." The United States should involve itself in war only if the western hemisphere was threatened. Participation in another foreign war could only lead to the extinction of liberty in America, and it would be generations before it could be restored. Four more years of the New Deal would be a disaster for America. Said Hoover:

> The New Deal has contributed to sapping of our stamina and making us soft. In quest of security they [the New Deal] have retreated

from liberty. In quest of reform they have abandoned justice and stirred class hate. In quest of relief they have injured self-reliance. In quest of an easy way out they have lessened the vision of America. The road to regeneration is burdensome and hard. It is straight and simple. It is a road paved with work and with sacrifice and consecration to the indefinable spirit that is America.

This was the road along which Republicans must lead the nation.[112]

Following the speech, Hoover was rewarded with applause and another demonstration. One reporter wrote that the convention had "found its lungs" in response to the speech, which had "provided a much-needed blood transfusion for what had been until then an anemic gathering of the Grand Old Party." But the hoped-for stampede did not come about.[113] James Hagerty wrote that the Hoover speech had "virtually challenged the delegates to the Republican National Convention to nominate him for President if they had the courage to make a real fight at the election in November. . . . Indications that Mr. Hoover might be the leader for whom the convention is searching came from the warmth of his reception." However, the enthusiasm in 1940 was, Hagerty found, somewhat milder than in 1936, [114] Yet another observer wrote: "Through all of the political atmosphere . . . ran a new factor based on the sudden realization that the speech delivered tonight by Mr. Hoover automatically put him among the contenders for the nomination." No demonstration comparable to that for Hoover had yet been seen for any of the other candidates.[115]

Hoover's speech, however, had suffered from poor sound amplification and many of the delegates could barely hear him. There were frequent calls for the former president to speak louder. This, of course, was particularly disastrous because Hoover was counting so heavily upon the speech to create a bandwagon for his nomination. As James P. Selvage recounted the situation years later: "Instead of his speech going over big, as it would have, there began to be cries from all over the auditorium— 'We can't hear you—louder.' . . . Well, his speech was a flop. Instead of being a good speech, it was a flop, and I am convinced—all of us were—that this had been deliberately rigged and the loudspeaker cut off."[116] Hoover and his secretary, Larry Richey, were also convinced that the sound system had been tampered with.[117] Pryor, who was suspected by some, had a different explanation for the poor sound quality when interviewed in 1980. He recalled that Hoover had not spoken into the microphone:

I had to go out and get the microphone and put it in his hand. He wouldn't pay any attention to the microphone. . . . The microphone was perfectly all right. But he wouldn't talk into it. He would talk over this way and the microphone would be here, and I'd go out and bring the microphone over and put it in front of him.

Another difficulty was that Hoover ignored the television cameras, much to the consternation of the cameramen and of Pryor.[118] Since Hoover had years of experience speaking into microphones, it seems incredible that he could have encountered the difficulties described by Pryor. In view of other Willkie tactics that transpired at the convention, it is within the realm of possibility that Hoover's microphone was tampered with.

Hoover's speech touched only briefly on foreign affairs, but what he said was judged to be of no comfort to the "isolationists" in the party. The *New York Times* editorialized:

> What [Hoover] had to say on the subject of foreign relations was clearly awaited with special interest by the audience which honored him with its reception. But what he had to say will not resolve the doubts now present in the minds of his fellow countrymen. For his discussion on foreign policy was not free from inherent contradictions, and it contained at least a little of something that will be pleasing to all sections of his party. But in one important respect— the matter of giving aid to European democracies, provided this is done within our law and provided it involves no risk of war—Mr. Hoover went much farther than the plank which is apparently to be recommended to the convention.[119]

The foreign policy plank adopted by the convention was, in fact, virtually a statement of Hoover's views. It declared for nonintervention in foreign wars, attacked the Roosevelt administration for its foreign policies and lack of preparedness in national defense, and supported the extension of "such aid as shall not be in violation of international law or inconsistent with the requirements of our own national defense" to all peoples fighting for freedom or whose liberty was threatened. It also called for orderly and realistic preparations for the defense of the United States, its possessions, and outposts and for upholding the Monroe Doctrine.[120]

The day following his convention speech, Hoover held a press conference for approximately one hundred and fifty newsmen. When questioned concerning his availability for the nomination, Hoover maintained his now-familiar pretense. He had, he pointed out, announced two years earlier that he would not again seek public office, and he did not think that they would find any evidence at Philadelphia that he had changed his mind. He had, however, advocated an open convention because "of the seriousness of the times and the shifting problems that the country has to meet." The delegates were meeting in an open convention and had before them a number of able candidates from whom they would make their own choice for the nominee. Whichever candidate they decided upon, Hoover promised he would do his best to support the ticket. When pressed to answer whether he would accept the nomination if it were offered to him, Hoover responded that he would "have no further comment to make upon it." To the end, then, Hoover openly refused even to make himself available for the nomination, although he also refused to slam the door absolutely shut upon the possibility.[121] It is unlikely that Hoover's press conference did anything to advance his prospects for the nomination.

The *New York Times*, however, still thought Hoover a possible nominee, though it conceded that the modest reception accorded his speech made him now a viable prospect only in the event of a prolonged deadlock.[122] The delegates continued to receive Hoover material, including copies of the Alan Fox polls, but reports from delegates to the Hoover camp were not encouraging. If a move developed in the former president's direction, many delegates expressed an interest in joining it, but as in 1936 there was no indication that any significant body of delegates would initiate such a move.[123] Rickard confided to his diary that the Hoover forces believed they had 150 to 200 delegates, but would hold them back with only a few votes shown on the first two ballots. The hope was that the convention could then be adjourned, the Hoover forces mustered, and Hoover's nomination put over in subsequent roll calls. The desired adjournment, however, never took place.[124]

On the first ballot, Hoover received 17 votes; his total rose to 21 on the second ballot, to 32 on the third, and then began to decline. Dewey led all candidates on the first ballot and then steadily lost strength. Taft gained steadily, but Willkie, who began with 105 votes on the first ballot, gained more rapidly than Taft and reached 659 votes on the sixth ballot, thus winning the nomination. By that time, even Hoover, with 9 votes, was ahead of Dewey, who finished with 8. Most obvious from Hoover's tally was the fact that the efforts of the Republican Circles in the western states had been ineffective. Hoover received 7 votes from California on the first ballot, a total that increased gradually to 13 by the fourth ballot, but thereafter declined. And of the other western states, only Colorado, with 3 votes, supported him on the first ballot. On the third ballot Hoover gained 1 additional vote from Utah. Clearly the "western strategy" had failed miserably.[125]

The *New York Times* reported that on the day of balloting Hoover went to work seeking actively to corral delegates to support his nomination.[126] If he was less active than the *Times* described, Hoover did, at least, encourage Dewey to stay in the race, advising him to hang on to the bitter end and not release any of his delegates. Dewey later began to suspect, accurately, that Hoover had his own interests in mind in giving the advice.[127] But every aspect of Hoover's strategy failed. The Republican Circles had failed to deliver on their optimistic predictions. From all the western states combined, they failed to produce even the vote total they had claimed to control in California alone. The Fox polls had lost their credibility in the face of the Gallup results. And the impact of the speech on which Hoover counted so heavily was undercut by poor sound transmission, regardless of whether this resulted from sabotage or his own errors in front of the microphone. But despite his loss, Hoover's analysis of the situation before the convention was correct—neither of the leading candidates did, indeed, arouse enough enthusiasm to win the nomination. And as he had predicted, a dark horse was nominated by the convention. However, the horse was Wendell Willkie and not Herbert Hoover.

Understandably, the former president was profoundly disappointed by the nomination result and by the disloyalty of those delegates who had promised to support him and did not.[128] Alan Fox suggested that a more effective strategy might have been to show more Hoover votes in the earlier ballots rather than to hold them back for later ballots. He thought such a tactic might have resulted in Hoover, rather than Taft, becoming the rallying point for those who were opposed to Willkie, and that the delegates had more enthusiasm for Hoover than for Taft.[129] Fox's analysis, however, was predicated on the belief that there were 150 potential Hoover votes to be manipulated. However, this was highly unlikely in view of the 32 vote maximum he had received on the third ballot. From his disappointment, Hoover now proposed to remain outside the campaign completely unless he was begged to participate, and unless Willkie agreed to defend his administration and to give him a voice in political appointments in California.[130]

Part of Hoover's antagonism toward Willkie stemmed from the methods that the nominee, or his overzealous supporters, had used to gain the nomination. This included not only the suspected tampering with the sound system for Hoover's speech but also the apparent printing of duplicate tickets so that the convention galleries could be packed with spectators chanting "We want Willkie" throughout the convention.[131] There was also the staggering volume of telegrams that Hoover and other GOP leaders and delegates were inundated with before and during the convention. Landon, who threw the support of Kansas to Willkie on the crucial and deciding sixth ballot, returned home to Topeka to find that many of the telegrams he had received were fabricated, as some eighteen mail sacks containing his acknowledgments to these telegrams awaited him with their contents stamped "Addressee Unknown."[132] Another part of Hoover's alienation stemmed from his concern that Willkie's nomination signaled a further turn away from the ideals he felt should be championed by the Republican party.[133] As Walter Brown expressed the disquietude in the Hoover camp: "I fear the Republican party as we have known it, is gone forever. Under the leadership of anti–New Deal Democrats there will be little to interest real Republicans."[134] Another wrote: "I feel that if the American people want a renegade Democrat and a representative of Wall Street as their leader, they are welcome to him."[135]

In the beginning of the presidential race, Hoover was noncommittal in public toward the GOP nominee. After Willkie's nomination, Hoover wired his congratulations and expressed confidence that he would win in November.[136] However, when he arrived in San Francisco a few days later en route to his Stanford home, the former president told reporters that he would not "like to make any statement about Mr. Willkie without giving more careful thought to the matter."[137] From his home in California, Hoover addressed a reflective and warm letter to the defeated Tom Dewey. He wrote:

> In a large sense not only is the pattern of the world changing but the pattern of American life is making deep and fundamental shifts. Among these shifts there is a substantial realignment in our political parties. That this realignment be held to two party organization and to certain fundamental principles is of transcendent importance to the American people. It is a time of effervescent public moods, of short distance thought instead of long distance deliberation, of rapid shifts to meet emergencies of the moment rather than the deeper currents of national life.
>
> A great responsibility is going to fall on the young leaders of the Party of which you are the outstanding person. And my anxiety, which I am trying to express here, is that you are going to remain alert and active in public life. I feel this more especially because you have the fundamental sense of the long view rather than the transitory.[138]

Some of those close to Hoover expressed disappointment at the chilliness of his reaction to Willkie's nomination and the lack of support shown for the nominee.[139] Others encouraged Hoover to campaign actively for the ticket.[140] Given Hoover's concern that Roosevelt and the New Deal should be evicted from Washington, it followed that he would not long maintain his neutrality. He was encouraged by the early progress of Willkie's campaign, writing: "Mr. Willkie has gotten off to a good start and we now have a chance to get rid of that Blum administration in Washington."[141] But no overtures came from the candidate seeking Hoover's assistance in the campaign. Hoover wrote Walter Brown late in July that he had received "a number of indirect and verbal messages but no direct communications from Mr. Willkie." Hoover thought it best "to await his directly expressed wishes." He added: "There are many people among his friends who have the same feeling that Landon had in 1936. Having had one experience I shall not be put to the same humiliation."[142]

In mid-August, however, Hoover's attitude changed. Willkie invited Hoover on a fishing trip. When this trip had to be canceled, the nominee, instead, invited Hoover to visit him in Colorado Springs. While the meeting between the two men was marred by Willkie's incredible faux pas of inviting Elliott Roosevelt, son of the president, to dine with them, Hoover apparently decided that Willkie was preferable to Roosevelt in the White House.[143] He now wrote O'Laughlin: "I believe Mr. Willkie is making a good candidate and I have a good deal of confidence that if nothing intervenes in world affairs or from some unexpected quarter that we will be able to get him over."[144] Hoover had suggested to Willkie that he actively seek the support of Hoover's followers in the campaign.[145] At the Colorado Springs meeting Hoover also consented to make some speeches in Willkie's behalf.[146] He tentatively planned a speech for mid-September and set to work researching some attacks on the New Deal.[147]

Hoover regarded the Willkie campaign, however, as disorganized and chaotic. The nominee had antagonized the party regulars with impulsive and ill-advised remarks, and, in Hoover's view, did not seem to have any definite ideas on any subject. Moreover, he found in the Willkie group the same disposition to ignore Hoover and his followers that had been manifested by the Landon campaign in 1936, though to a lesser extent.[148] But his coolness toward the nominee did not divert Hoover from the primary objective, which was the defeat of Roosevelt. He wrote one correspondent who had criticized Willkie:

> As to your political observations, I have one central thought at this moment. We must make the maximum effort to get this Blum regime out of Washington. A rebuke of these present policies and a change are of vast importance to the whole future of the country. I shall do any proper thing they want me to do. I don't think it will be very much.[149]

From an old friend in Kansas, William Allen White, came approval of Hoover's support of Willkie and the observation that Willkie could win if only he made no mistakes.[150]

During the summer of 1940, Hoover became increasingly concerned over the likelihood that Roosevelt's policies toward Japan would result in war in the Pacific. Roosevelt was following a course of applying economic pressure upon the Japanese in the expectation that it would discourage them from their expansionist aims, but Hoover wrote O'Laughlin early in August:

> Shutting down scrap iron and octane gas exports to Japan is again only sticking a pin in a rattlesnake. As a great majority of her trade

will go on anyway, she can obtain these supplies elsewhere. Either we should leave this thing alone, or we will be drawn into real trouble. However, there does not seem to be anything to be done about it at the moment.[151]

For the former president, who had opposed his secretary of state, Henry L. Stimson, over the question of economic sanctions against Japan in response to the Manchurian incident of 1931–1932, this was a consistent position. In 1940, as in 1931–1932, Hoover viewed economic sanctions as leading inevitably to war.

The question of the proposed destroyers-for-bases deal between the United States and Great Britain occupied much of Hoover's attention in August and September. While no one doubted that the situation was critical for Great Britain, opponents of American participation in the war argued that to give such vitally needed military assistance to one side could easily be regarded as a hostile act by the other and must lead inevitably to American entry into the war. Hoover's public position was neither for nor against such a transfer. He did, however, believe that Republicans should not support the proposal, and he counseled Willkie to resist the pressure being applied on him by the Roosevelt administration, through such Republicans as William Allen White, to support the destroyer deal.[152] Hoover felt in his "bones" that the British would be able to stand off the Germans.[153] When the destroyers were exchanged to the British for bases in the western hemisphere, Hoover issued a statement that omitted reference to the destroyer part of the arrangement:

The new naval and air bases are important contributions to our defense. The only criticism of the transaction is that it was not submitted to the Congress for approval. There can be no sound reason why that should not have been done. The American government has sought such bases in the Caribbean but hitherto the British refused. I am very glad to see that all of these bases have been acquired.[154]

While the presidential campaign proceeded without Hoover's participation, he remained active. On September 18 he delivered a 30-minute speech at the University of Pennsylvania bicentennial conference. The affair was nonpartisan, and he prefaced his remarks by giving "advance notice that this is not a partisan discussion, despite the intellectual climate of a national campaign." He noted, though, that there were "disabled minds, of course, who would imagine that I was making attack on the New Deal if I were to read the Ten Commandments during such a period as this. But I will not do even that."

Instead, Hoover argued against American involvement in the wars in Europe and Asia by asserting that the United States could exist with a free economy even in a world awash with totalitarianism. On the other hand, he argued, a free economy would disappear from the United States for a generation if the nation did enter the war, and totalitarian dictatorship would be inevitable. The United States could, however, defend itself economically without adopting totalitarian methods. It could compete with cheaply produced goods from the totalitarian countries by increasing industrial efficiency. Such efficiency could come through technological advances produced through support of pure and applied scientific research, as well as through the upgrading of plant equipment and elimination of waste, the application of laborsaving devices, and the removal of every sort of restriction upon capital and labor that impeded or penalized efficiency. Hoover also advocated reciprocal quotas to protect American jobs and to secure markets abroad for American goods. America's "service to humanity," he concluded, "is to make this industrial revolution serve free men. We must prove that here in America free men are the only basis of prosperity and progress. We must prove that the purpose of science is to save mankind and not to destroy it. And we must prove that we can defend ourselves."[155]

The *New York Times* editorialized that Hoover's speech was "not only one of the most thoughtful statements to come from any American statesman in recent months but one of the most impressive speeches of his own career." The newspaper found his call for support of pure and applied scientific research in order to increase industrial efficiency "a proposal that deserves immediate study."[156]

As Hoover spoke in Pennsylvania, Willkie was traversing California in search of votes. In all of his speeches in California, the GOP candidate lauded Senator Hiram Johnson as a man who had "fought for the cause of true liberalism against all comers," and he said that Johnson had been his "boyhood idol and he is my hero now." James Hagerty suggested that Willkie was being careful to avoid the experience of Charles Evans Hughes in 1916: Hughes had ignored Johnson while campaigning in California and had lost the state in the presidential election, only to lose the election itself to Woodrow Wilson.[157] What Hagerty failed to note was that in ignoring Hoover, a California favorite son, Willkie was following a course at least as perilous as that of Hughes in 1916. While Willkie sought to woo the support of Johnson and his followers, his studied refusal to mention Hoover's name was alienating the former president and his supporters. And despite Willkie's effusive praise for him, Johnson still refused to commit his support to the nominee.[158] The combination of Willkie's slight in California and the continued neglect of his potential service in the campaign led Hoover to briefly consider issuing a statement taking himself out of the campaign entirely. He was dissuaded, however, by Edgar Rickard, who convinced him that to do so would be to eliminate any chance of a Willkie victory.[159]

Hiram Johnson sent word to Hoover through O'Laughlin that he had not been in contact with Willkie, that he had not known beforehand of Willkie's intentions during his campaign in California, and that he considered the nominee's failure to mention Hoover during the California swing as an "outrage." But, like Hoover, Johnson felt that he must support Willkie in order to see Roosevelt defeated.[160] Coincidentally, Willkie was visiting in New York City and spent the entire day in that city without paying even a courtesy call on the Republican former president, although Hoover anticipated that he would do so.[161] By now, perhaps because of his own absence from the campaign, Hoover was beginning to be pessimistic about Willkie's chances in the November election.[162]

Early in October, the former president was under the impression that he was to make two national radio broadcasts in Willkie's behalf during the final month of the campaign. No money, however, was forthcoming from the campaign to pay for the broadcasting of the Hoover speeches, as all campaign money had been allotted for the nominee's own speeches.[163] If Hoover was to participate in the campaign, it was apparent that he would have to raise the money to pay for his own radio broadcasts, and he set to work to do so. He also sought, unsuccessfully, to arrange for a joint appearance with Senator Hiram Johnson, as he thought this "would represent the final healing of all Republican wounds in California and would create enthusiasm amongst the people." He also believed it was the only way Willkie could carry the state.[164]

In late October, Hoover delivered the first of his speeches for Willkie in Columbus, Ohio. He devoted his talk to the third-term issue, reviewing the tradition in American history of a two-term limitation to deal with the implications of a third term for America in 1940. Under Roosevelt, he pointed out, there had been a great growth in presidential power, such as had undermined democratic government in the rest of the world. He did not mean, Hoover added, to "suggest that Mr. Roosevelt aspires to be a dictator." But it was apparent that Roosevelt's power had been built "to a dangerous point in this Republic" and that there were those around him who were "implacably pushing further and further in that direction." Hoover questioned whether "any single person in America . . . is so ignorant that he does not know the gigantic growth of the personal power of the President during this last seven years." That growth, Hoover declared, had been at the expense of the people and of Congress. It reached into every aspect of American life. And at no time had any powers been surrendered back to the people or the Congress. The two-term tradition was a check on the growth of such personal power. "Is this any time for America to surrender forever this vital check upon power?" he asked.[165]

Hoover went on to charge that the New Deal had engaged in intimidation and smearing of those who had opposed this grab of power and had sought to purge those from office who did not agree with it. He added:

> In building up these powers the independence of the Supreme Court, the Congress, and the local government has been degraded. Methods of intellectual dishonesty have been used in creating this personal power. A political machine has been built which places all free election in jeopardy. An economic system is being created which drifts steadily away from free men and free enterprise down the suicide road of National Socialism.

And this personal power, he warned, was now being used to steer the United States toward war. It was time, Hoover declared, for the American people to take a stand against this growth of personal power through the election of Wendell Willkie.[166]

Now that he was actively in the campaign Hoover concluded that the tide was running in Willkie's favor "and unless something revolutionary happens during the next week we ought to get him over."[167] On October 31 Hoover attacked Roosevelt's foreign policies in a speech in Lincoln, Nebraska. He indicted the president for aiming "billingsgate" at foreign heads of government, a practice that had destroyed the moral influence of the United States and stimulated enmity toward the nation everywhere in the world. Roosevelt's involvement of the United States in the "power politics" of Europe had led to the creation of an international alliance against the United States for the first time in history. Hoover lashed out at Roosevelt for sabotage of the London Economic Conference in 1933, the collapse of the Geneva disarmament conference, recognition of the USSR, and for the whole conduct of American foreign policy since the Munich Agreement in 1938. The threat to the United States in 1940 was minimal, Hoover argued, for if Germany could not cross the 25 miles of the English Channel to invade Britain, how could Hitler contemplate an invasion of the western hemisphere thousands of miles away. The argument that Roosevelt should be reelected because of his expertise in foreign relations was, Hoover insisted, patently ridiculous, for all the president had demonstrated was his incompetence in that area. Hoover concluded for his listeners: "You are far more likely to get into war with Franklin Roosevelt as president than with Wendell Willkie."[168]

The following night, Hoover spoke in Salt Lake City and tried to summarize the major issues of the campaign. The principal task before America, he concluded, was the preservation of democracy. The New Deal had started with three economic ideas, which he enumerated: (1) "the whole American system was a wreck and wrong and must be made over"; (2) "new frontiers of enterprise were gone and the job was to divide the existing pot"; and (3) the federal government should control all economic life through the planned economy. These ideas, Hoover charged, had led to "attempts to control our courts, to control our Congress, to control our elections, to control our public opinion with mass propaganda and slogans, and finally to demand a third term." All of that, Hoover warned his listeners, had "a pronounced odor of totalitarian government." The New Deal had succeeded in making economic depression "a chronic way of American life." By contrast, Willkie's intention, he said, was "to get this economic machine functioning, produce, give jobs, make a market for farm products in full stomachs instead of half-full stomachs, build up national income, create the production out of which taxes can be paid and deficits overcome."[169]

Though Hoover felt Willkie did not come forth emphatically enough against American intervention in the European war, he nevertheless counted heavily on Willkie's election to reverse Roosevelt's foreign policies and also to support his efforts to get relief to the people of Europe. Of this latter, Hoover wrote Hugh Gibson:

> . . . the future of our [relief] work depends much upon the American election. It looks at the moment to me as if Mr. Willkie will be elected. He would naturally be favorable to relief of these people. Mr. Roosevelt will follow American public opinion. I cannot let the fate of these 30 millions of people rest where it is. I have, therefore, been devoting my time to arranging with the spiritual and moral leadership in the United States for a widespread American demand that agreement be brought about by which they can be saved. I find universal support amongst these leaders and a resolution to put on an active campaign to stir up American opinion. I am making no statements in the press and I am exerting myself everywhere to keep this campaign from taking anti-British form. But I shall break loose as soon as the election is over.[170]

Hoover had long since come to the conclusion that Roosevelt was sabotaging his every effort to furnish food relief to Europe.[171]

Another source of opposition to his relief efforts, however, came from an old friend, William Allen White, whose Committee to Defend America by Aiding the Allies regarded Hoover's relief plans as a source of assistance to the German war effort against the Allies, and therefore was against any relaxation of the British blockade of the European continent. While the United

States had furnished such relief to Belgium and northern France during the early years of World War I, White argued that the situation was different in 1940 because the Germans now were systematically forcing the conquered people of Europe "to produce for Germany munitions, ships, planes, and other supplies to be used to destroy England and eventually menace America." Accordingly, White did not feel that it was "wise to feed those enslaved populations actually engaged in producing implements and munitions that threaten our safety." He told Hoover that his committee was, nevertheless, interested in finding "some formula under which . . . humanitarian relief medical and food supplies may enter the conquered countries." White continued: "There is no black here and no white. We have all got to move in a gray area."[172]

As election day approached, Hoover predicted that either Roosevelt would be elected by a small majority or that Willkie would win by a "handsome" one. All depended, he concluded, "upon what the movement of the silent vote of the country is going to be."[173] Like many Americans he was unprepared for the size of Roosevelt's convincing victory.[174] Analyzing the returns, however, he concluded that the Republican party had "capacity in it yet."[175] He noted that GOP candidates for governor, senator, and congressman had run ahead of Willkie in their total vote, while they had been closer to traditional Republicanism than the presidential candidate.[176] And if Willkie had obtained even one-half percent more of the votes in Ohio and the states farther east, Hoover concluded, he would have won the presidency.[177]

Hoover decided that this "phenomena of running behind the regular Republican candidates stands out in this campaign even more vividly than it did in the Landon campaign. The aggregate vote was from 1 to 2 million greater than the vote for Willkie." From this he concluded again, as in 1936, that in courting the votes of anti–New Deal Democrats, independents, and New Dealers, Willkie had lost the votes of a significant number of Republicans.[178] The lesson of 1936 was re-emphasized for Hoover—GOP presidential candidates must stand for traditional Republican principles or they could not be elected.

# 6

# Fight Against Intervention

oover recognized that Roosevelt's reelection represented a setback for the cause of peace. However, of more immediate concern to Hoover was the obstacle that Roosevelt's presence in the White House would pose to his plans to furnish food relief to the people of occupied Europe. Hoover quickly redoubled his efforts to sign on as members of his relief committee such prominent Americans that the demand for relaxing the British blockade would be difficult to resist. He sought to keep his efforts confidential until there had been gathered sufficient names to "carry weight."[1] His goal was to recruit for his committee "four or five ambassadors to these occupied countries, leading prelates, rabbis, bishops, business leaders and substantial sympathetic intellectuals and writers."[2] For Hoover, whose sympathies were with the British in their moment of trial against the Germans, it was difficult to apply pressure for his relief activities, but he considered the British "dumb to their own interests; to the terrible and unnecessary suffering in the small democracies, and to American reactions." He concluded: "That being so, I must pursue a course which they will think against them until they become intelligent."[3]

But Hoover experienced less success than he had expected in attracting prominent Americans to his cause. He received letter after letter responding negatively to the idea of furnishing food to malnourished people in Europe who might be of use to Hitler. Presidents of many major American univer-sities, for example, refused to serve on the committee because of their disagree-ment with Hoover over this question.[4] Humaneness, under the test of war, suffered from many "isolationists." Moreover, Hoover found the opponents of his relief efforts were "making things . . . lively" for him. Although he was successful in recruiting General Pershing as a member of the committee, he could not overcome the resistance of the British to his relief proposals.[5] In late December he left for a fishing trip in Florida in search of "ease of mind," but determined to push on with his efforts after the first of the year.[6]

Meanwhile, Hoover had been continuing his efforts to keep the United States out of the war. In late November 1940, he discussed with Joseph Kennedy, U.S. Ambassador to Great Britain, the British resistance to his relief plans. He found Kennedy in agreement that the United States must stay out of the war since the only result of American intervention would be the triumph of fascism in the United States. Kennedy confided to Hoover that he intended to resign from his post within a few weeks in order to devote himself entirely to opposition to American entry into the war. The ambassador promised to maintain close contact with Hoover, as they had a joint mission to keep America at peace.[7] Although Hoover welcomed allies from any source, he refused to align himself with the America First movement. Responding to an invitation to join the committee, he wrote:

> In view of my obligation to organize a movement in the United States to break down the barriers against food to the five small democracies, I think it is desirable that for the present I should keep free of other connections. I am completely possessed with the neces-sity of making clear the facts and the truth of the relations of the United States to the European situation. It is indeed a difficult job in view of the furious emotions and the enormous amount of propa-ganda that is flooding the country. This is injected to destroy even so humane a question of trying to save the lives of millions of innocent people from famine.[8]

On December 17, 1940, President Roosevelt floated the concept of lend-lease assistance to the Allies at a press conference, and on January 6, 1941, he offered the program to Congress in his annual address. Hoover did not oppose granting assistance to the Allies, but he was concerned with the precise nature of whatever legislation was enacted. He wrote Senator Taft that there were several questions that ought to be asked by the Senate before it gave approval to lend-lease. Some of the questions concerned payment for materials that had already been contracted for, payment for future supplies, and other payments. Another category of questions dealt with defining Britain's war objectives.

Specifically, Hoover sought clarification of what the British proposed as a peace settlement, their intentions regarding disarmament after the war, and what measures they proposed for bringing about permanent peace in the world when the fighting had stopped.[9]

Hoover's primary concern with the lend-lease proposal, however, was voiced in his press statement of January 10, 1941, in which he questioned the necessity for the "enormous surrender" of congressional responsibilities to Roosevelt specified in the proposal. Such a surrender of powers, he warned, had implications for the very preservation of democracy in America.[10] Press reports indicated that Congressman Sol Bloom sought the testimony of the former president concerning the lend-lease proposal before the House Foreign Affairs Committee. Responding to these reports, Hoover wrote a public letter to Bloom expressing his views on the proposed legislation. He wrote that he was "in favor of extending every practicable aid, short of war, to Britain to enable her to maintain her independence," but that he was opposed to American intervention in the war. There were, Hoover told Bloom, many questions about the proposed legislation and great confusion over what it would include. He suggested that Congress should "at once draft into the bill positive definitions of what these powers are and specifically exclude what they are not" and thereby provide for "concrete debate and eliminate much controversy and bitterness."[11]

Already convinced that President Roosevelt was bent on taking the United States into the European war, Hoover hoped that the Republican minority in Congress would be able to reduce, through amendments to the bill, Roosevelt's freedom of action in using lend-lease for that purpose.[12] The former president took an active role in rallying the Republican effort to that end. As he described his efforts to one correspondent:

> I have been in constant communication with Republicans in the House and Senate. We are developing a definite program. We have secured a continuous stream of able radio speakers and have more coming up. I think we are going to defeat the big issue in this bill, that is giving the President the power to make war.[13]

From the America First Committee came requests that he go on the national radio networks to oppose lend-lease in a speech, together with promises of assistance to obtain broadcast time for such a speech.[14] Hoover, however, responded that he was "exerting" himself "in this matter day and night" and that rather than go on the radio he preferred to "let this situation develop a little."[15]

The lend-lease bill caused the GOP's 1936 presidential nominee, Alf Landon, to defect from support of Roosevelt's foreign policies. While Landon had lukewarmly supported the president up to now, he refused to follow Roosevelt on the lend-lease proposal because he regarded it as a step toward involvement in the war and as following the pattern that had preceded American entry into World War I. In a nationwide radio broadcast on January 11, 1941, Landon asserted that Willkie, who supported the lend-lease proposal, would not have been nominated by the Republicans in 1940, nor would Roosevelt have been elected, if the American people had known then what Willkie and Roosevelt would be saying now.[16] From his friends, like columnist Raymond Clapper, came expressions of concern that Landon might "drift into a position of general opposition and get . . . tagged as one of the Hoover-Lindbergh crowd, and . . . that would be unfortunate."[17] Landon responded, however, that he had "no illusions as to the popularity of my course." He had been willing to help England "in all material ways and in ways that will not involve us in actual combat," but the Lend-Lease Act he regarded as a step toward the latter.[18]

For Hoover and Landon, bitter political adversaries since 1936, the ground was now laid for cooperation in opposing Roosevelt's foreign policies during the remaining months until Pearl Harbor. At the same time, however, Hoover was seeing defections from his own camp, some by those among his most dedicated political supporters. John Spargo, for example, joined Wendell Willkie in wholeheartedly supporting lend-lease, though assuring Hoover that "[my] profound admiration for you and my loyalty to you are not and will not be in the least measure lessened."[19]

On January 24, 1941, Hoover sent Senator Vandenberg four proposed amendments for the lend-lease bill. He told Vandenberg that it seemed to him "obvious that the minority opposition can only move effectually by amendments and by amendments we would aggregate great support from the public and possibly in Congress that cannot be had by attempts at substitute legislation." Hoover proposed amendments that would make explicit that nothing in the Lend-Lease Act authorized the president to convoy ships with the American navy, repair the ships of belligerent nations in American harbors, transfer American naval vessels to other nations, or expend funds outside the United States.[20] Vandenberg responded that he could "use a great deal of this helpful material." Vandenberg was meeting with Hoover in a few days, but wanted Hoover in the meantime to phone if he had further suggestions since, Vandenberg said, he was "always most happy to have your [Hoover's] effective cooperation."[21] Senator Robert Taft was inclined toward offering a substitute bill in place of the Lend-Lease Act; but Hoover believed that the amendments he had proposed would make the issues clear to the American public and that sufficient support could be obtained from public opinion to amend the bill in its most vital provisions, thus eliminating the grant of such power that the president could involve the United States in war.[22]

Willkie's support of Roosevelt's foreign policy in late 1940 and early 1941 only increased the suspicion and opposition toward him on the part of other Republicans. Immediately after Willkie's defeat by Roosevelt in early November, efforts were begun by Republicans to ensure that the 1940 nominee would not carry the mantle of titular leader during the next four years. One group of Republicans asked Hoover to state publicly that "as a matter of practical reality, principal Republican leadership [in] this country now resides or should reside in Republican members of Congress where extremely slight loss compares most favorably with [the] presidential verdict." Republicans in Congress, therefore, represented the "only Republican voice truly national in character and possessing [a] mandate denied to both Landon and Willkie."[23] Hoover did issue a press statement on November 11, 1940, commending the two party system.[24] While it did not take the form suggested, it was nevertheless commended by anti-Willkie Republicans for having made no mention of him.[25]

Privately, Hoover agreed that the responsibility for formulating GOP policies must rest with congressional Republicans "for the simple reason that they have to vote on these questions and they have to answer to their constituents for their vote." That did not mean, however, that they could not consult with GOP leaders outside of Congress, as they were doing with Hoover.[26] This, of course, was a far cry from his attitude in the first years of the New Deal, the difference being accounted for, no doubt, by the fact that Republicans in Congress were now generally consulting with Hoover and taking positions approved by him. For others, the fact that Willkie had been defeated meant that Hoover must again "point the way" for Republicans in the years ahead.[27] This the former president obviously intended to do. As part of the effort to reduce or eliminate Willkie's influence in the party, Hoover and his followers in California sought to eliminate the 1940 nominee's supporters from any influence in that state's Republican politics.[28]

Congressional Republicans were especially disturbed over the fact that they were leading the fight against Roosevelt's foreign policies, while their supposed titular leader seemed to have gone over to the side of the opposition.[29] In the first months of 1941 this added further fuel to the movement to purge Willkieites of their influence in the party, a movement in which Hoover took part.[30] Landon agreed that congressional Republicans should plot the party's future for the next four years, especially "in these times and with a titular leader who is not much inclined to work with the party leadership in Congress."[31] So critical was the Kansan's view of the situation that, despite his reluctance to travel to Washington, he consented to Senator Taft's appeal that he testify against the Lend-Lease Act before the Senate Foreign Relations Committee because, Taft told him, he was "the only Republican leader whose testimony will combat the idea that Willkie speaks for the party."[32]

The fight in Congress to amend the Lend-Lease Act continued on through February and into March of 1941. Although he frequently considered delivering a public attack on the bill, Hoover was restrained by O'Laughlin's counsel.[33] But he continued to counsel Republicans in Congress on ways to blunt the administration's proposal.[34] Returning from Washington in late January, after seeking to rally Republicans in behalf of a united front against what he regarded as the worst features of the lend-lease proposal, Hoover expressed concern that each of the congressional Republicans seemed to be going his own way and that they had also lost the cooperation of conservative Democrats, which had existed in the previous sessions.[35] By mid-February Hoover confided to O'Laughlin that there was no doubt in his mind "that the country is losing interest in any amendments to the Lend-Lease Bill. It is unquestionably going to pass, and therefore a very large number of people have become discouraged and have given up the fight against it."[36]

By March Hoover had given up hope that the bill could be amended. His concern, he wrote William Castle, was that "it is a war bill, yet 95 per cent of the people think it is only aid to Britain." He added:

> The bill [a] surrenders to the President the power to make war, any subsequent action by Congress will be rubber stamp work; [b] empowers the President to drive the country still further toward a national socialistic state; [c] empowers the President to become real dictator of opposition policies to the Axis. He can determine who, in what way and how much aid any nation may receive from the United States.

Hoover preferred a policy that would give the British "all of our accumulated defense material which we could spare" and "an appropriation of anywhere from two to three billions [of dollars] with which to buy other things," allowing them "to spend the money directly themselves and to conduct their own war in the way that seems to them to be the wisest." He concluded: "All that we can do is to use our energies and influence to keep down emotions and to hold the President to his promises not to spill American blood."[37]

On March 11, 1941, the bill was passed, but it contained only one of the amendments Hoover had sought. That amendment stated: "Nothing in this Act shall be construed to authorize or to permit the authorization of convoying vessels by naval vessels of the United States." Another amendment added: "Nothing in this Act shall be construed to authorize or to permit the authorization of any American vessel into a combat area in violation of section 3 of the Neutrality Act of 1939."[38] These amendments were small consolation for Hoover and other opponents of American involvement in the war who recognized that passage of the lend-lease bill had, even more clearly than the destroyer-for-bases deal, committed the United States to one side in the war. Under Roosevelt's prodding, the pattern of 1914–1917 had advanced another giant step.

The principal reason for Hoover's reticence about publicly attacking the lend-lease bill during the early months of 1941 was his continuing effort to get food relief to the occupied areas of Europe. Throughout the debate over the lend-lease bill he was confronted [1] by the dilemma posed by his opposition to aspects of a bill that provided aid for Britain at the same time that he sought British cooperation in his food relief plans and by [2] the dilemma of his opposition to the Roosevelt administration's bill at the same time that he was seeking assistance from the State Department in breaking down British resistance to relief. Late in January, Hoover relief representatives H. Alexander Smith and William H. Tuck met with State Department officials on behalf of the relief effort and found the department, including Secretary of State Hull, "interested and sympathetic in the maintenance of the effort, but at the same time" of the opinion "that everything should be done to have the Germans do their share of any relief work that might be decided upon." The problem, they were told, was to search for "a formula which . . . would be acceptable to the British government." Smith and Tuck concluded that Hoover's relief efforts were "not being actively opposed by the State Department, but that on the contrary they are watching the situation with interest."[39]

By mid-February Hoover had formulated a plan he felt sure would meet every objection the British had raised to his previous proposals. It called for soup kitchens that would take care of only the destitute and children and would "exclude all those working for Germany and all that sort of claptrap," which the British and other critics of food relief had raised as objections.[40] Meanwhile, Hoover's efforts to rally public support behind relief seemed to be showing results, as he found editorial opinion "running 7 or 8 to 1 in our favor" and only a few newspapers of importance in opposition.[41] Late in February, however, he complained: "We are now getting a deluge of British propaganda against us, and . . . the Administration has joined in the chorus." He now proposed to turn his fire on the Roosevelt administration once the lend-lease bill had been passed because the "responsibility now belongs to them, as they are in a position to carry it through with the British."[42] Through his control of the lend-lease effort, Roosevelt could, Hoover felt, force the British to lower their blockade if the American government insisted.

O'Laughlin, who was in close touch with Hull, counseled Hoover to withhold his attacks on the administration, however, lest such attacks give a political complexion to the relief movement. O'Laughlin's impression was that Hull was sympathetic, but that Roosevelt and Under Secretary of State Sumner Welles were "the most virulent in opposition to your [Hoover's] work.

They are encouraging the British in their refusal to open the blockade." His advice was for Hoover to continue his course of "presenting the facts to the people and letting them place the responsibility where it belongs. As time goes on, and starvation increases abroad, the feeling thus aroused will force Administration action."[43]

Hoover's proposal to the British, which he laid before the American people in a speech on February 16 in Chicago, called for (1) an initial experiment in Belgium to test whether food relief could be conducted without military benefit to either side; (2) soup kitchens "where the people come to get their food and thus there can be no question of feeding Germans"; (3) an initial feeding of one million adults and two million children with bread and soup; (4) agreement from the German government not to requisition native food; (5) promises from both the British and Germans that relief ships would be safe from attacks; and (6) supervision of the entire relief effort by some neutral body. There was, Hoover argued, no possibility of military advantage to either side and no question of charity. The small democracies possessed reserves in the free world with which to pay for the food, and no appropriations from the American government were needed. Nor would food relief deprive any Americans of food. The humanitarian reasons for feeding destitute Europeans were obvious enough, but Hoover repeated them for his listeners. American self-interest was also involved, he argued, for Americans would have to live with the European nations after the war and needed their goodwill. He concluded by describing his own experiences with famine in Europe and told his listeners: "I know starvation in the last war had a large part in the causes of the world's agony today. I had hoped it would never again come to the world. But it has come, and I would be untrue to myself and to my country if I did not fight it to the end."[44]

On February 28 Hoover traveled to Washington to meet with Hull and to lobby in behalf of administration support for his relief plan. Much of the conversation with the secretary of state, however, dealt with national and international affairs. Hull told Hoover that he was convinced the Germans were out to conquer the entire world and that if England fell, the Germans would first take South America into their "economic or political axis," and then attack the United States. Hoover responded that he had an entirely different theory, based on his discussions with German leaders, including Hitler, in 1938. He viewed Germany as determined to dominate Russia after Hitler had finished with Britain, because Russia and the Balkan states together "possessed far greater undeveloped resources than the whole Western Hemisphere, that the Germans were a land people, a soldier people not a sea people, that Russia could be had with two Army Corps, while the Western Hemisphere would require gigantic sea equipment."[45]

Hoover regarded the meeting with Hull as "satisfactory."[46] But if he had any expectations that his talk with the secretary of state would end British resistance to food relief, he was not long in being disappointed. Optimism that opposition to the feeding plan was breaking down was dampened on March 7 by a press release from the British embassy, which rejected all appeals to lift the blockade of the continent.[47] Rickard regarded it as the worst blow yet to the relief efforts.[48] On March 10 Hoover issued a press release in response to the British statement. He argued again that his relief plan would not impair any British war effort, but instead would "uphold the ideals of democracy to the world and these little nations" and would "save the lives of multitudes of children and others." The food situation, he insisted, was worse on the continent than the British assumed.[49]

On March 25, Hoover and his chief lieutenants gathered to consider a letter he proposed to send to Secretary of State Hull.[50] The following day, Sir Gerald Campbell, British minister to the United States under Ambassador Lord Halifax, called on Hoover to explain Britain's position once again. One thousand British children and women were being killed every day by German air attacks, he told Hoover, and he did not feel that Hoover was considering their interests. Hoover argued that the deaths of British children at the hands of the German enemy could not be avenged by British complicity in the starvation of the children of Allies. Campbell criticized the propaganda of Hoover's committee as "distinctly anti-British and . . . injurious to their cause." Hoover responded that the British had attacked him without giving him the opportunity to explain to the British people exactly what his proposed plan entailed. When Campbell reiterated that the committee was anti-British in its propaganda, Hoover said: "To disagree with British policies was a right even of Englishmen and certainly I had not surrendered that right by being an American."[51]

Hoover repeated these points in his letter to Hull the next day. He told the secretary of state:

> The passage of the lend lease act obviously involves us deeply in the consequences of the war. But it also gives our government a measure of responsibility to see that the policies pursued by the British are in the interest of both winning the war and winning a peace, and in the interests of the United States. The British have opened the blockade on food to southern France [via the Red Cross] and with that event 95% of all the so-called principles they have advanced for the absolute wall of food blockade to the democracies is negatived [*sic*]. I have considered the humanitarian question of saving millions of lives as the transcendent purpose and so long as our government had no responsibilities I felt it should be solved by private actions. But it now has other important and different aspects. In view of this

changed situation I would like to present the bearings of this use of
food control to aid in winning the war and the peace and in the
special interest of the United States.

Hoover argued that if Germany would give the requisite guarantees, which
the United States and Britain demanded, then the British should be pressed by
the United States government to allow the food relief in. As an extra inducement, Hoover added: "I know it would bring to the British cause support [in
the United States] that is now lukewarm or doubtful."[52]

On March 28, however, two Hoover aides visited the British embassy in
Washington and received the same response Hoover had heard from Campbell. Under no circumstances, they were told, would the British lift the blockade on food to the European continent. Rickard and the others now decided to
propose to Hoover that the efforts of the relief committee be curtailed.[53]
Reluctantly, the former president decided to concentrate on educating Congress concerning the proposal while withdrawing the relief committee representatives from Europe.[54] By the end of April, Hoover had decided to
"gracefully" close up the relief efforts, but not yet acknowledge defeat because
he recognized that relief was now a matter for governments to resolve since
private efforts were hopeless in the face of British opposition and unremitting
British propaganda against relief.[55]

If the U.S. and British governments could not be induced to support his
efforts to relieve famine on the European continent, then Hoover was freed
from the need for restraint in dealing with foreign relations questions and
could resume his attack on the march of the United States toward intervention
in the war. He feared that the passage of the lend-lease bill, "aside from its
direct purpose, will further channel the public mind into the rapids which lead
inevitably to military war. The British propaganda, our natural sympathies,
our indignations and fears over the Nazi regime have already conditioned
thought to a readiness for that definite action." Hoover still clung to the hope,
however, that war might be avoided.[56] For Alf Landon, who had moved ever
closer to Hoover's position on international affairs, the talk that the lend-lease
bill signified the end of an "era of isolation" was inaccurate. The Kansan
recognized that the "only real period of isolation we have had" that he knew
anything about "is the period under Roosevelt, from the time we abandoned
the London economic conference down to and including the signing of the
neutrality act." The Republican party had been labeled as isolationist in the
1920s because of its opposition to American participation in the League of
Nations, but as Landon well knew, the foreign policies of Harding, Coolidge,
and Hoover had, in other respects, been anything but isolationist.[57]

On March 19 William Castle wrote Hoover:

A good many people have said to me they feel the time has come for you to make one or two nationwide radio speeches. There is a tremendous groping for the truth, or for something approaching the truth, among Congressmen and Senators just at this time. It seems to me, and to a good many others, that if you should now make a calmly reasoned speech which would show this country just where we are going, it might give a kind of leadership which is utterly lacking at the present time.[58]

Hoover responded that he was planning a speech for March 28 in which he was "trying to find a new approach to this problem that will utimately cause the American people to stop, look and listen.[59]

In that speech, delivered in New Haven, Connecticut, Hoover returned to the attack. The passage of the Lend-Lease Act, he pointed out, had "enormously changed the shape of things," and the United States was fast "driving into the psychosis of war." America was faced with the same choice as in 1914–1917. He asked his listeners to confront a number of issues before making up their minds on the question of war. Was the United States determined to remake the world? Was it going to impose its will on the world by becoming a world policeman? If the United States entered the war, how would it be able to restore economic prosperity to the world and to its own people with reduced resources after the war? How would it be able to "save a world ravaged by famine and pestilence?" How would the United States be able to restore liberty in its own land after the inevitable adoption of wartime socialism and fascism? How could a peace be made that would be any more permanent than the last one? Hoover's view was that the United States ought not to spend its young men and resources in war, but ought to preserve the "sanity and compassion" of a noncombatant for the peace table after the war, and should maintain its resources intact so that with the end of the war "we may be able to contribute something to restore another and better world."[60] Hoover had, however, no "expectations of stopping the American people from going to war or to stop them from making a mess out of peace. I do not know that any prophetic warning has ever had any importance in history. I am, however, going to die with my conscience alive."[61]

Some Hoover admirers counseled that he "should pipe down for a while," lest he ruin any chance of his being called upon by the government for service if war did come.[62] Hoover recognized that his position was growing unpopular as public sentiment moved closer toward support of American participation in the war. He was convinced in early April that the United States would be in the war within 90 days.[63] The nation, he told Arthur Hyde on April 5, was "backing into this war through a series of intellectual dishonesties. But so long as the people like to be fooled and are willing to be fooled by persons, I do not see what an isolated voice in the wilderness can do."[64]

A few days later, on April 7, Hoover made a stab at predicting what the next six months would bring and concluded that if he were just 50 percent correct he would be "a qualified prophet." During that six-month period he expected that every American would come to want a British victory and a German defeat. The Germans would not be successful at invading England, but neither would the British air attacks on Germany break that country's morale. In the meantime, millions of men and women in the occupied European democracies would "die of starvation or become stunted in mind and body, which will be as bad for themselves and the world as actual death— unless help is brought to them." The Germans would overrun Yugoslavia and Greece, while the British would defeat the Italians in Ethiopia and control East Africa and the Mediterranean. He predicted that the United States would begin to convoy ships to Britain and that there would be incidents involving the sinking of American ships and the deaths of American sailors. The United States would likely send an expeditionary force to assist the British in their control of East Africa and the Mediterranean Sea. Hoover did not believe that Japan would join the war within the next six months because he thought they would wait to be sure that Hitler had won before they entered. In the United States, he predicted, the rising war psychosis would cause "every word of caution uttered by honest Americans" to be "denounced as being 'A call from Hitler.' " Free speech would disappear. Only the ballot box was capable of reversing the trend, but there would be no elections in the next six months. "Western civilization," Hoover concluded, "has consecrated itself to making the world safe for Stalin."[65] He despaired that "nothing can stop this landslide towards war now except a great reaction from the middle west, which has no way of expressing itself as there is no meeting at the ballot box in time."[66]

The crucial issue, as Hoover saw it, was convoying. If the American people expressed their opposition to convoying vehemently enough, then the type of incidents that could precipitate American involvement in the war might be avoided. But, he concluded, the situation in 1941 was quite different from that in 1917 because the American people were now more divided, confused, and uncertain. Organization for defense was still lagging, and, Hoover believed, the United States could not hope to have adequate armed forces for one and a half to four years. However, he was sure there was little likelihood that Hitler would go to war with the United States unless this nation committed "an overt act or shooting [*sic*] his men." Thus, if the United States avoided such a "shooting" situation as convoy duty, there remained a possibility of staying out of the war. Viewing the situation in Europe, he concluded that the war was, at best, a stalemate and that the odds of this stalemate being broken in Britain's favor were not the best. The defense of Britain could not be improved by American entry into the war; however, entry would cause the American people to suffer from a lowering of their standard of living and the adoption of "totalitarian methods" to fight a war against totalitarianism. Moreover, the economic dislocations after the war were likely to be tremendous. "A long war means revolution in the end to all countries engaged in war," he concluded. "The net effect is to make the world safe for Stalin."[67]

On May 9 Hoover wrote to Senator Charles Tobey calling attention to a speech he was to deliver over the radio on May 11. He told Tobey that in this speech he was going "to do the best" he could "in this situation." He also asked Tobey to try once again to unite Senate Republicans for a "team fight" against Roosevelt's foreign policies.[68] In his speech Hoover made one of his strongest appeals against intervention. During his campaign for reelection, Roosevelt had promised on October 23 that if he were elected, the United States would not participate in foreign wars and would not send its servicemen to fight in foreign lands except in case of attack. But now, Hoover insisted, Roosevelt's pledge could no longer be believed. In the first ten days of May, the American people had been deluged with speeches and propaganda "the meaning of which is to drive the American people into this war." Hoover advocated giving Britain "the maximum tools of war," but he was convinced that this could be done only if the United States stayed out of the war. This country was unprepared even for its own defense, he charged, and yet the use of American naval ships for convoy duty must inevitably lead to war. "To go in now," Hoover told his listeners, "is neither wise nor for the interest of either Britain or ourselves." The situation was very different in 1941 than it was in 1917. In 1917, Japan had been on the Allied side, and there had existed no need for the United States to consider defense in the Pacific. Now Japan was "openly allied to the Axis" powers, and if the United States entered the war it must provide for the defense of the Pacific as well. Hoover reviewed for his listeners the price he believed America must inevitably pay if it participated in the war—the sacrifice of lives and liberty and the inevitable postwar bankruptcy.[69]

Hoover's speech was hailed by opponents of American intervention. Charles Dawes, whose assistance had been recruited by Hoover for the fight against intervention, issued a statement to the *Chicago Tribune* strongly endorsing Hoover's "voice of reason, of experience, of patriotism, and of statesmanship." Dawes continued, saying that the speech "is also the voice of wisdom and will be a guide to his [Hoover's] fellow countrymen."[70] Senator Alexander Wiley praised the speech as "a polestar for an unemotional appraisal of the situation" and inserted it in the *Congressional Record*.[71] Raymond Moley called it "a magnificent summation of the reasons why the American people ought to put a restraining hand on their government." He told Hoover: "Whatever happens, you have made the record and it is a record with which you, your children, and your childrens' children can live in the sober years to come."[72] Robert Wood, head of the America First Committee, thought Hoover's speech "one of the very best utterances that has ever been given on the subject of our entry into the war." He added: "From all sides I hear that it had a very powerful effect." He asked Hoover to make another speech in June, as the America First Committee planned "to throw everything we have into the fight in June."[73]

In June of 1941 the German armies poured into the Soviet Union, just as Hoover had predicted to Hull that they would. This invasion furnished Hoover and other opponents of American intervention with a powerful new reason for the United States to remain out of the war. The Russian revolution in 1917 had affected the perceptions of many Americans concerning World War I. So long as one of the nations allied against the Kaiser had been the widely despised and autocratic czarist regime in Russia, slogans supporting a war in defense of democracy had a hollow ring. But the revolution of 1917 changed the perception of Russia from that of an autocracy to a democracy, and to many people the war became more acceptable. In 1941 the events in Russia again contributed to altering the perception of the war. Once perceived as totalitarianism against freedom, the war was now transformed, in the eyes of Hoover and others, into one in which the principal antagonists were two equally reprehensible totalitarian dictatorships—Nazi Germany and Communist Russia—neither of whom the United States should ally itself with.

One of the first to raise this new issue was a Democrat, Senator Harry S. Truman of Missouri, who urged that the United States should back whichever side seemed to be losing: "If we see Germany is winning we ought to help Russia, and if we see Russia is winning, we ought to help Germany, and in that way, let them kill as many as possible, although I wouldn't want to see Hitler win under any circumstances. Neither of them think anything of their pledged word."[74]

Senator Robert A. Taft addressed the changed situation in a speech on June 25 in which he pointed out that the war was now primarily between two totalitarian states, despite Roosevelt's attempts to convince the American public that the Soviet Union was a democracy. How, Taft asked, could the United States ally itself with the Soviet Union when "no country was more responsible for the present war and Germany's aggression than Russia itself"? It was the Russian nonaggression pact with Germany that had freed Hitler to undertake his aggression against Poland and the war with Britain and France. What's more, "Russia proved to be as much of an aggressor as Germany itself," with its invasions of Poland, Latvia, Estonia, and Finland. How could the United States, in the name of democracy, make an alliance "with the most ruthless dictator in the world?" If Germany won, it would be a victory for fascism. If Stalin won, it would be a victory for communism. If the United States would but stay out of the conflict, the German invasion of the Soviet Union might well turn out to be the solution to many of the problems of the world. Let the two totalitarian ideologies waste their energies fighting one another. Taft concluded: "The Russian war has weakened every argument for intervention."[75]

Hoover followed with a speech four days later. He noted it was curious that the German invasion of the Soviet Union had intensified the "propaganda of fear or hate" designed to force the United States into the war. He recognized that it was sensible for Great Britain and the Soviet Union to cooperate against their common enemy; but, like Taft, Hoover pointed out that the new situation made "the whole argument of our joining the war to bring the four freedoms to mankind a gargantuan jest." The Soviets had demonstrated over and over again that they were "one of the bloodiest tyrannies and terrors ever erected in history"; they had "carried on a world conspiracy against all democracies including the United States," despite pledges to the United States at the time Roosevelt had extended them diplomatic recognition in 1933. "Is the word of Stalin any better than the word of Hitler?" Hoover asked his listeners. Stalin had joined Hitler in destroying the freedom of Poland, then had invaded Latvia, Lithuania, Estonia, and Finland. If the United States now aided the Soviet Union, it would win "for Stalin the grip of communism on Russia, the enslavement of nations, and more opportunity for it to extend in the world." On the contrary, the United States, Hoover said, should adopt a policy of "watchful waiting, armed to the teeth, while these men exhaust themselves."[76]

Hoover's belief that Germany and the Soviet Union would "exhaust themselves" was undoubtedly buttressed by a conversation he had with Colonel Truman Smith, of Army Intelligence, in mid-May, just before the German invasion of the Soviet Union. At that time, Smith told Hoover, according to the latter's memorandum of their conversation, that "every indication is that Roosevelt intends to get into the war" and that "no member of the General Staff wants to go to war but that they bring no great influence to bear on this situation." Smith also dismissed any German threat to the United States and predicted that Hitler would invade the Soviet Union. He added that the Germans and Russians "would destroy each other if left alone."[77]

Explaining his purpose in delivering the speech, Hoover wrote: "For what my life and conscience are worth, they become valueless to me or anyone else if I do not persist in what I so deeply believe." He would welcome the opportunity not to have to deal with the international problem, but "as long as my voice will be heard I shall do the best with it that I can." He was convinced that Germany would make short work of Russia "and dispose of that infecting center of Communism," and that when this had been accomplished, Hitler would seek peace with the British. Meanwhile, he hoped that his speech would "help stay our hands from the trigger until these events arrive."[78]

Hoover was obviously wearying from the fight against intervention and from his failures with the relief effort. But he recognized that his was one of the few influential voices still protesting the course of the president's policies, and he could not turn from that responsibility. Early in June he replied to an invitation to go on a welcome fishing trip into Canada that he doubted he would be able to make it:

> I am trying to fry a great number of fish—among them to keep this country from going into the war. I do not want to get away very far from the center of things so that I may use what little influence I have in that direction. If this country does get into war I would go out and fish for the balance of the war. But as long as there is the remotest possibility that we will stay out of it, I feel I must do what I can.[79]

Hoover's "educational campaign" in behalf of his relief effort had brought a number of additional congressmen to its support but had done nothing to lessen the Roosevelt administration's opposition to relief.[80] Gradually the work of the National Committee on Food for the Small Democracies was liquidated as a result of inaction and lack of finances.[81] Early in June Hoover addressed an angry letter to Secretary of State Hull:

> Not only am I deeply shocked at the present attitude of our government, but I know tens of millions of Americans would also be shocked. History will never justify the government of the United States siding with the starvation of these millions. What you have said, in effect, is that the American government accepts the view of Britain in this matter; that you will not even attempt to moderate those policies so as to save the lives of literally millions of women and children in these small democracies. Yet these countries have sacrificed their all for Britain and the cause against aggression which you properly state is also an American cause. . . . We now apparently abandon these peoples to their fate and that without consideration of the sacrifice they have made against aggression or the importance of preserving among them confidence in the ideals of democracy itself. The fundamental question to be answered by our government is not whether the Germans are primarily responsible or the British blockade is responsible, but whether our government refuses to secure from these governments the remedy which it has the duty to urge and thus avert disaster from these peoples and their millions of children.[82]

But in his reply, over three weeks later, the secretary of state was obdurate. He told Hoover that he could not accept his "interpretation of the attitude of this Government toward the spectacle of millions of people in want of food because of the arbitrary action of the German Government." The responsibility for supplying food rested with the occupation authorities, and in the case of occupied Europe, the Germans had removed vast quantities of foodstuffs for the use of those working in behalf of the German war efforts. This was the cause for the shortage of food in the occupied countries, Hull asserted, and Hoover's proposals would only "replace the stocks removed by the occupying authorities" and would naturally be welcomed by the Germans since they "would in fact release labor now required for food production to be used in furtherance of the German military effort." The fundamental problem, Hull argued, was the "overthrow of Hitlerism unless all Europe is soon to starve. It is this broader and more basic viewpoint that many of us visualize."[83] It was a viewpoint that did not put food in hungry stomachs. Clearly Hoover's committee was to get no assistance from the U.S. government, without which its activities could not be carried on.

Late in May a journalist suggested to Alf Landon that, to counter the united front that had been forged in support of Roosevelt's interventionist policies, a counterpart united front should be formed in opposition to those policies. He suggested that Hoover, Landon, and former vice-president Charles Dawes go on the radio from different parts of the country and during the same half hour of radio time attack the administration's foreign policies.[84] Also at this time, Landon was being asked by Frank Knox, his former running mate of 1936 and now one of Roosevelt's in-house Republicans, to come out in support of Roosevelt's policies. Knox argued that Landon could contribute greatly to much-needed national unity.[85] Landon agreed with Knox on the need for such unity, but blamed its lack on Roosevelt.[86] Rather than pursuing the joint radio address that had been suggested, Landon apparently raised with Raymond Moley the possibility of a joint statement to accomplish the same purpose. Moley passed Landon's suggestion along to Hoover, and the former president wrote Landon on June 27 that he had considered the same idea a month or two earlier but had dropped it. Hoover now agreed with Landon that the time for such a statement had come, and he agreed to join in making it. He suggested that Raymond Moley organize the statement. Hoover told Landon that he would talk with Dawes, and he also suggested that University of Chicago president Robert Hutchins and Ambassador Joseph Kennedy participate in the statement, as well as others of "that caliber." He thought the statement could be very effective but said that members of Congress should be omitted "so as to make it entirely a common or garden variety citizen statement."[87]

At Hoover's request, Robert Hutchins quickly prepared a draft statement that contained most of the points Hoover had made in his speeches—the changed situation caused by the German invasion of the Soviet Union, which left "little to choose between the domination of Europe by a Nazi dictatorship and its domination by a communistic dictatorship," as well as the assertion that "American participation in this war is far more likely to destroy democracy in this country than it is to establish it in Europe and Asia." America, the draft argued, would be justified in entering such a war only if its own independence were at stake, but nobody seriously believed that Hitler was then, or would be in the near future, in a position to threaten the United States. Hutchins's draft statement put the signers on the side of continued aid to China and Great Britain, but argued that "American lives should be sacrificed only for American independence." American energies should be "devoted to preparing the defense of this hemisphere," and the president should "abstain from further war-like and provocative deeds, and . . . recognize that the country wants to aid Britain and China, defend itself—and stay out of war."[88]

The draft was circulated among potential signers, with suggestions incorporated, and the Republican leaders considered various possibilities for the role of organizer of the movement and issuer of the statement. Felix Morley, former editor of the *Washington Post*, and the current president of Haverford College, was finally chosen.[89] A number of Democrats were suggested as possible signers, in addition to Joseph Kennedy.[90] All concerned agreed on the urgency and on the necessity of issuing the statement without delay, but the month of July was consumed with revising the draft further, obtaining the views and consent of other influential figures, and settling on the mechanics for bringing the statement out.[91] Late in the month, Morley pleaded the press of his other responsibilities and when he turned the work on the statement over to Landon, the search began anew for someone to release it.[92] Hoover and the others were, meanwhile, trying to make the statement bipartisan by obtaining some suitably distinguished Democrats to join in signing it. A natural choice was Joseph Kennedy, but he avoided committing himself until late July when he declined to sign, arguing that he preferred "to go my way alone" in opposing Roosevelt's policies.[93] Harry Woodring, Roosevelt's former secretary of war, declined to sign it if Kennedy did not participate, and no other Democrats of stature could be induced to do so, although labor leader John L. Lewis did join with the others in the statement. The decision was now made to have the statement issued by Frank O. Lowden, one of the signers.[94]

The final statement, printed in the *New York Times* on August 6, 1941, called for the American people to demand of Congress that it "put a stop to step-by-step projection of the United States into undeclared war." It called attention to the military initiatives taken by the Roosevelt administration without the sanction of Congress, which undermined the constitutional powers of the legislative branch. The European war was one of power politics and "the American people want no part of it." American participation in the war was "far more likely to destroy democracy in this country . . . than to establish it in Europe." The Axis powers were no threat to the United States or to the western hemisphere if American defenses were properly prepared. The statement emphasized some of Hoover's recurring themes, including the argument that the war was no longer between freedom and tyranny.[95] The "appeal of the fifteen" was issued over the signatures of Hoover, Landon, Lowden, Dawes, and Lewis, as well as those of academicians Ray Lyman Wilbur, Felix Morley, and Robert Hutchins, opera singer Geraldine Farrar, writers Irvin S. Cobb and Clarence B. Kelland, former diplomats Reuben Clark and Henry Fletcher, and others.

Meanwhile, Hoover had been much encouraged by the response to his June 29 speech on the German invasion of the USSR. Arch Shaw wired him that there had been an "avalanche of enthusiastic comments" and a "flood of requests for copies." W. K. Kellogg sent $5,000 to underwrite distribution costs, and suggestions were made that five million copies of the speech be distributed.[96] Hoover concluded that the speech had received a greater response than any he had delivered since leaving the White House.[97] Taft praised it as "a magnificent speech" and told Hoover that he had "heard nothing but praise for it."[98] According to Rickard, Hoover's mail indicated that he had turned many minds against intervention.[99] Hoover proposed, he told columnist Boake Carter, to "go on making nasty remarks until Congress finally declares war—even though it may only be a confirmation of a declaration of war."[100] But Hoover thought that his speeches "had better not be too frequent and must be properly timed." As he wrote one congressman:

> You will remember that when we used to boil maple syrup as young-
> sters and the syrup reached the point at which it was about to
> crystallize, it would begin to sputter. The old New England custom
> was to pour in a few drops of cold water and it would calm down. If I
> can be of that kind of service, I will have reached the only point of
> usefulness that I care about.[101]

Hoover was maintaining close contact with Republicans in Congress. In July, responding to the stationing of U.S. troops in Iceland, he wrote Senator Taft that he was "wondering if it is not time for the Republicans to take up the question of limiting all appropriations for military operations to use entirely within the Western Hemisphere."[102] He told Congressman J. William Ditter: "If Congress had the guts to limit appropriations so that they could not be used for military operations outside of the United States, it might be helpful." By this, and other devices, he thought Congress could "stop any further steps towards getting into this war."[103] Taft responded that he would "talk with some of the other Republicans to see whether we can hope to put a rider on the military appropriations bills to confine their use to the Western hemisphere."[104] From Congressman Roy Woodruff, chairman of the House Republicans, came word that the former president was held in "high esteem" by every Republican member. He told Hoover: "Always the next few days following one of your addresses, we discuss them with interest, approval and enthusiasm, and I am sure I speak the mind of all our group when I express the wish that we may see something of you in the months and years to come." Woodruff was, he said, "greatly impressed . . . by the fact that your speeches are always timely; they seem to come to us at a time when they are most effective."[105]

Despite a fair degree of solidarity among Republicans in Congress in opposition to Roosevelt's foreign policies, the Republican party, itself, was being torn apart by the division between interventionists and noninterventionists. Unfortunately for the latter, many large contributors to the party were from the Eastern interventionist wing of Republicans. While they supported the position of Willkie and his followers, they were not anxious to contribute to the fortunes of a party that would not follow his leadership. The sad condition of the party's finances was revealed by Franklyn Waltman, director of publicity for the GOP national committee, when he wrote Alf Landon late in July: "Between you and me this party of ours is in a hell of a condition" and was "floundering around without any plan or purpose." He explained:

> There is a great deal of bitterness within the party against Wendell Willkie, and, on the other hand, he has some very militant supporters within the party. The national headquarters has not been at so low an ebb as it is now since the dark days after the Hoover defeat of 1932. The greatest difficulty apparently is being experienced in obtaining funds and, were it not for the fact that we came out of the last campaign with a surplus on which we have chiefly been living this year, I do not know where we would be. As it is, the staff has been reduced to skeleton proportions.[106]

Republicans continued to be divided over what Willkie's role should be in the GOP. Some felt that Willkie, along with his supporters, should be "read out of the party," which he had so recently joined, and that the Republican party should unify as the party opposed to entry into the war.[107] Others, however, felt that the salvation of the party lay in strengthening the Willkie wing and in following his leadership.[108]

While money was becoming scarce for those who opposed war, what was even more distressing for some opponents of intervention was the smearing to which they were subjected by the Roosevelt administration, by the war-hungry elements in the news media, and even by members of their own party. Hoover had lived with smearing for over a decade and was not surprised by it, but for Landon it came as a revelation. In a speech made in late July on the subject of Roosevelt's extension of the draft, the Kansan told his radio listeners:

> The only invasion this country has suffered since the war with England in 1812 is the organized propaganda invasion by Soviet Russia. The most vicious part of this whole business is the attempted terrorization of all those who dare to say that our participation in the war is still an issue. This terrorization has all the earmarks of the methods of the Nazi, Fascist, and Communist dictators.[109]

Hoover had already addressed the issue of extremist smearing in his speech of June 29 in which he decried the fact that the extremists had so grown in intolerance that they sought "to frighten men from free speech by defamation."[110] The Hoover-Landon-initiated "appeal of the fifteen" of August had also received more than its share of smearing; but, as Hoover wrote to Landon: "While our recent statement was rubbed with mud by the war press and the war mongers, it contributed greatly to stiffen and consolidate our men in the House."[111] The two Republican leaders, so often bitterly at odds since 1936, were now close in their cooperation to spare America from the war, and their correspondence became regular and warm.

Given the smearing of opponents of intervention and the volume of propaganda to which the American people were being submitted in favor of war, Hoover was amazed that American public opinion continued to oppose American entry into the fighting. He concluded: "If we can keep from the actual shooting stage until the end of the year, I feel we may keep safely out of this mess."[112] A summer trip through the western states convinced him that "the country is getting more and more opposed, even bitter, against this war movement." But he now expressed concern that the Roosevelt administration was "doing everything they can to get us into war through the Japanese back door."[113]

On September 16 Hoover returned to the attack with a speech. Much had happened, he noted, in the preceding ten weeks. "New objectives for the American people have been advanced. The Navy has been ordered to start shooting. Our people are more bewildered and divided than before." The Roosevelt policies were leading step by step "to sending our sons into this war." American boys should not "be sent to death without the specific declaration by the Congress." Free institutions required this course, and the debate on war or peace "ought to be lifted above intolerance and accusation." The patriotism of all Americans ought to be conceded, and there should be no "smearing of men or attacks upon groups." Americans, he asserted, had no sympathy for either nazism or communism. The dangers of a victory by either of the totalitarian sides were less than they had been ten weeks earlier because "the fratricidal war between Hitler and Stalin is daily weakening both dictators." Also, England was more impregnable now than ten weeks earlier. "The actual dangers to America," Hoover concluded, "are less today than at any time since the war began." Yet Roosevelt was rapidly driving the United States closer to war through such devices as the Atlantic Charter with Churchill. The best policy, Hoover argued, was to avoid sacrificing "our sons for proved will-of-the-wisp" and to continue to aid the democracies "short of going to war."[114]

Hoover's efforts to rally the American people against intervention in the war were embarrassed in September by two incidents. The first of these was a speech by anti-interventionist and America First Committeeman Charles Lindbergh, which took an extreme anti-Semitic direction. Hoover regarded the speech as making it very difficult for him to be associated with Lindbergh thereafter and, he said, "the same is rapidly becoming true of some others, because the great body of in-between American people object to such extreme statements and extreme attitudes." Hoover recognized that he could have no influence with the American people if he became identified with those making such remarks.[115] He regarded the airman's "anti-Jewish speech" as "all wrong" and certain to "hurt all of us who are opposed to war."[116]

The other incident that embarrassed the former president was a statement issued by 176 members of the faculty at Stanford University, Hoover's alma mater and the location of the Hoover War Library, as well as the site of Hoover's home for most of the years since his leaving the White House. The faculty statement expressed opposition to "passive defense" and called for a "dynamic policy."[117] In response, Hoover quickly polled the entire Stanford faculty and released his results on October 1, 1941. The faculty-wide poll revealed that 60 percent did not agree with the statement issued by the 176 members earlier. The majority were opposed to carrying munitions to England in American-registered ships, to convoying these vessels with American warships, to naval action against Hitler, and to sending an expeditionary force to Europe. Sixty-six percent of the Stanford faculty was insistent that none of these steps should be taken without congressional approval.[118]

Late in October, Hoover was encouraged to go on the attack once again over the radio. Congressman Karl Mundt wrote him: "Your past speeches in this connection have all been highly effective, and we can always feel the impact of them here in Washington by a revival of anti-war expressions from the people back home."[119] Hoover had written three articles for the *Saturday Evening Post*, however, and he preferred to wait "until they had settled into the American consciousness" before making another speech. He told Mundt that he wanted "to do everything that can be done. Even if we can only delay the final collapse, we still have a chance for something to happen that might save us."[120] Hoover wrote Senator Vandenberg: "All of our protests may be futile but the day will come when there will be retribution in the United States. It is vital for the future that men like yourself have stood steadfast."[121] Vandenberg confessed "to a great depression as I sit in my front seat at the greatest tragedy in history."[122]

Hoover's articles in the *Saturday Evening Post* were entitled, "The First American Crusade," and dealt with the American relation to World War I as seen from Hoover's vantage point as a member of Woodrow Wilson's "war cabinet" and as an observer of the deliberations at the peace conference. His clear intention was to dissuade the American people from embarking upon another such "crusade" in 1941 by demonstrating the disparity between American ideals and European realities. As he wrote the *Post*'s editor: "The value of the article is to set out the experiences of America with just such proposals as the present Four Freedoms and the Churchill-Roosevelt declaration."[123] In the articles, Hoover pointed out that the United States was "the only nation since the crusades that had fought the battles of other peoples at her own gigantic loss." In the final installment, which appeared in the November 15 issue, he sought to demonstrate the futility of yet another "crusade." America's ideals had grown away from those of Europe during the 300 years of separation, he wrote, and Americans were unaware of the "gigantic explosive forces" that existed in Europe as a result of 400 million people, of 26 different races, living in an area two-thirds the size of the United States and burdened with "age-old hatreds" and "economic and religious conflicts." Also present were growing populations, rebellious minorities, and other fears. All of these Hoover called "the perpetual stimuli of war." America had proved during World War I that she had "the courage and genius to make war, and make it magnificently," and one system of militarism and despotism had been destroyed. But America had been unable to secure from the European leaders after the war "the adoption of concepts of justice or that far-seeing statesmanship which replaces conflict with co-operation among nations." President Wilson had tried to gain this but had failed. The United States had often been accused of "running out on Europe" after the peace treaty was signed; but on the contrary, Hoover argued, it was the Europeans who had earlier run out on America in refusing to make a peace based on Wilson's fourteen points.[124]

Congressman Mundt wrote Hoover on October 30 to congratulate him on the first of the *Post* articles. The battle in Congress was now over outright repeal of the Neutrality Act, which would be another giant step toward participation in the war. Mundt told Hoover that Republicans in Congress would "need all of the support we can get" in opposing repeal. He added:

> Willkie's indefensible attempt to inject partisanship into the issue
> has put just one more hurdle in our way. But I am glad to report that

his influence among the members of Congress is very, very insignificant. However, his repeated statements do stimulate some of the wealthy Republicans throughout the country to write in voicing support for his position. I am glad to say, though, that the great speeches which you and Mr. Landon have been giving more than offset the Willkie effort.

Mundt asked Hoover to give another radio broadcast "some time the first week in November, so that the full effect of it would be registered in the House before the fatal vote is cast on our side of the Capitol."[125]

From Alf Landon came the question of whether there might be an opportunity within the next few months for the United States to "take the leadership for a constructive negotiated peace."[126] Hoover responded that he believed "a situation will arise sometime in January or February when peace discussions between Germany and England are logical." However, he cautioned that logic was "too often submerged by emotions" in such affairs. He expected instead that the British would endeavor to get the United States to take the next step beyond naval warfare and send an expeditionary force, and he anticipated this British effort to begin within the next 90 days.[127]

When Julius Klein visited Hoover early in November, he found him pessimistic about the prospects of avoiding American participation in the war. He noted that Hoover "took a most ominous view of the world situation, pointing out that even as we talked war in the Pacific was a possibility within three days." Hoover thought that the American naval attacks on German submarines in the Atlantic might be used by Hitler to force Japan, under the terms of their alliance, "into open warfare against the United States and Russia." He had concluded: "Whether the break comes now, next week, or next month, we must face the inexorable fact that war is inevitable." When queried about his own role once war was declared, Hoover affirmed that he would support President Roosevelt. He still believed that Hitler could be beaten with the United States out of the war, but he also thought that U.S. noninvolvement now seemed to be out of the question. Hoover said that he would personally do everything he could to help, everything that he was called upon to do. However, he did not expect that Roosevelt would ask anything of him. People around Roosevelt hated Hoover personally, and perhaps they had reason to, Hoover said. According to Klein's account of the conversation:

> In his mature wisdom he has come to the regretted conclusion that war cannot be averted. He is thinking how that war can be won; how can the American standard of life be preserved; how can a peace be established that will really outlaw war in the future. He feels that immediate attention must be given now to that peace; that even now

some special groups should be considering the problems that must be faced in the final settlement that the next generation shall not face a world such as we do today.[128]

The last legislative defeat for the anti-interventionists was over the "revision" of the 1939 Neutrality Act. On October 9, 1941, Roosevelt requested that the act be revised to permit the arming of U.S. merchant ships, although he actually hoped for a good deal more. An administration bill was quickly introduced, and debate began. Further incidents involving American ships sunk by German submarines during the month led to a movement for further changes in the act, and later in the month the abolition of combat zones was added to the original change. In letters to members of the Senate in early November, Hoover sought to rally opposition to the revisions. To Senator Wallace Whyte, Jr., he wrote that he had originally opposed the passage of the Neutrality Act, as he had "felt certain it would lead to difficulties." But, he added:

> Be that as it may, the whole thing has taken an entirely new aspect today. The only practical purpose of repeal now would be to carry supplies to the British in American flag ships. The validity of this vanishes entirely under the lend lease law which authorizes the handing over of ships to the British to be operated under their flag. The British have plenty of crews or they can obtain plenty of foreign crews to supply any number of ships. The intentions of the Congress in the neutrality act, as you know, have been deliberately evaded and flouted by Panama register. Whether this was done to make sure that incidents would occur, I don't know. Obviously these Panama register ships were put to carrying contraband and they met the fate which comes to contraband ships in war. . . . Repeal now amounts to ratification of this attempt to defeat congressional will and this use of these incidents. The repeal of the act, however, moves into even higher dimensions. This act by the Congress will be claimed as a species of constitutional authority to take further steps toward war. The inevitable consequence of sending the American flag ships to Britain will be innumerable incidents of sinking of these ships with American crews. They will furnish further fuel for the fire. The clamor for an expeditionary force is the next step we have to face. . . . The actual importance of each step taken has small importance compared with the direction in which we are being taken. The ultimate of that road is an expeditionary force unless Congress puts the brakes on now. And it means all out war by a mere Congressional rubber stamp of executive action. It seems to me that it is the last chance of Congress to hold its real position.[129]

But the Democrat-controlled Congress abdicated its control over war making to Roosevelt once again. The revision was passed on November 13 and became law four days later.

The day before the vote, Hoover wrote Robert Wood of the America First Committee that he would be making another speech on November 19 over the CBS radio network. Hoover assumed that the president would have his way with the Neutrality Act and that afterwards there would be no question that the United States would become engaged in a naval war with Germany. The next issue, he repeated, would be one of sending ground troops abroad, and he intended to address that prospect in his speech since such an action would be "the final straw which will break our camel's back."[130]

When Hoover delivered his speech, it appeared that his earlier prediction of a German victory over the Soviet Union was being validated, but he argued that even this turn of events would not pose a threat for the United States. On the one hand, the German victory was proving the folly of any expectations that the United States could defeat Germany in a land war thousands of miles away, when the Soviet Union, with its "10 million men, 20 thousand tanks, 20 thousand planes, fighting on her own soil behind her own fortifications" could not defeat Hitler. On the other hand, the Germans would now add over 100 million potentially rebellious subjects to the 230 million they already controlled in Europe. Hoover did not believe Hitler would be overcome by internal revolts, but he did hold that the forces working against him from within his empire would be more successful in destroying his dreams of further conquest than would military attacks or economic blockades. Meanwhile, there was in Hoover's position not a hint of sympathy for the plight of the USSR and no identification with it as a common enemy of nazism. Rather, in Hoover's view, communism continued to be identified, along with its enemies, as an enemy of the United States. Said Hoover: "We want the end of these evil and brutal ideas of Nazism, Fascism and Communism." He asked for assurances from the administration that there would be no American expeditionary forces sent overseas without the approval of Congress. Hoover also called for planning to begin immediately for the peace conference which must follow the war.[131]

Hoover's speeches on the issue of war or peace had been devoted to the problems posed by Roosevelt's moves in the Atlantic in getting aid to Britain. But at least as early as February 1938 he began to be concerned that Roosevelt was seeking to involve the United States in a conflict with Japan.[132] The abrogation of the U.S. commercial treaty with Japan in mid-1939 left Hoover with what he described as "a foreboding that we have taken on a situation from which sooner or later we will see outrages upon American citizens and other incidents which will inflame the country and draw us into war in the east." If it was Roosevelt's desire to bring about war with Japan, Hoover was certain that the abrogation of the commercial treaty was "one step on the road."[133] Hoover expressed similar concern over the gradual application of economic sanctions against Japan.[134] By July of 1941 William Castle had concluded: "Certainly Roosevelt is doing everything he can to make Japan attack us—and the Japanese don't want to."[135] While Hoover did not sympathize with Japan's occupation of French Indochina and supported Roosevelt's actions in response to that situation, he felt that Roosevelt's "continuous sticking of vocal pins in this tiger" had contributed to Japan's action and made a solution to the problem more difficult. Still, he hoped that a modus vivendi might be reached with the Japanese.[136]

Three months before the Japanese attack on Pearl Harbor, Hoover concluded that the president was doing everything he could to "get us into war through the Japanese back door."[137] From the Japanese standpoint, he thought it more logical to wait until the inevitable disintegration of the Soviet Union at the hands of Germany and then take eastern Siberia, which "would give them [the Japanese] a vast unpopulated area into which to expand." Hoover had a "hunch" that the Japanese would give up their designs on China for such an opportunity and that this would be in the interests of the United States. But he recognized that the United States, by aligning itself with the Soviet Union, had apparently closed this off as a way out of war with Japan.[138] Three weeks before Pearl Harbor, Hoover wrote O'Laughlin: "There is no sense in having a war with Japan. But I am afraid that our people [the Roosevelt administration] are so anxious to get into the war somewhere that they will project it. They know there will be less public resistance to this [war with Japan] than to expeditionary forces to Europe." He was, Hoover told O'Laughlin, leaving for Chicago to deliver his November 19 speech: "As usual, I expect this may be my last speech on war policies, but I am going through consistently to the end."[139] It was, indeed, his last speech before the onslaught of war.

Hoover later compiled a diary of the final days before Pearl Harbor, which describes his involvement in one final attempt to avert the break between the United States and Japan. On November 23, according to the diary, Raoul Desvernine, prominent New York attorney and businessman who had been on the executive committee of the Liberty League, phoned Hoover to acquaint him with the dangerous state of the talks between the United States and Japan. Desvernine had been present at interviews that the Japanese negotiators, Ambassador Nomura and Admiral Kurusu, had with President Roosevelt and Secretary of State Hull. According to Hoover's diary:

> He [Desvernine] insisted that the Ambassador and Kurusu, the newly arrived special Ambassador were personally absolutely gen-

uine in seeking a solution; that they represented the naval and civilian elements; that these elements strenuously wished to avoid war; that they realized the future of Japan lay in cooperation with the great naval powers; that they had a most difficult corner to turn and save national face and dignity; that their thesis was that urgent action should be taken at once to ease the situation; that Hull was driving absolutely to war; that Roosevelt was apparently hanging back.

Desvernine asked if Hoover had any suggestions that might help. According to his diary, Hoover suggested:

> that he [Desvernine] find out if the Japanese would agree to a six-months' standstill agreement on all military action, they to have civilian supplies through the sanctions, a Five-Power Conference to be called at Honolulu or somewhere for the purpose of finding a formula for peace in the Pacific. The Powers to be represented being the United States, the Netherlands, Britain, Japan and Chiang-Kai-Shek's [*sic*] Government to represent China. I stated this was the test of their good faith. If they would agree to this, then the thing to do was for him or friends to see Roosevelt and suggest to Roosevelt that he propose it and take the glory. Also that this negotiation had to be gotten into Roosevelt's hands and out of the State Department.[140]

On November 26 Secretary of State Hull handed the Japanese emissaries what they regarded as his ultimatum. Desvernine felt that the ultimatum "undoubtedly meant war, as it left no way out for the Japanese to save their face." He asked for advice, and Hoover suggested that he get in touch with Roosevelt at once, "to ask him again to take the reins." The president was vacationing at Warm Springs, Georgia.[141] At Hoover's suggestion, Desvernine sought an opening to Roosevelt through Bernard Baruch, meeting with the latter on December 1, a Monday. Baruch consented to meet with Desvernine and Admiral Kurusu that afternoon. Baruch told them that "he could not go to the President without the detailed proposals reduced to a memorandum and that he could not purport to state the Japanese proposals on his own authority." Desvernine, Kurusu, and Nomura thereupon worked until 1 A.M. the next morning preparing the memorandum, which, according to Desvernine's recollection of it, proposed (1) a gradual withdrawal of Japanese troops from China under the supervision of a joint United States-Japanese commission, with the Japanese to retain three or four garrisons in China in a location and of a size to be agreed upon with the United States; (2) agreement in a memorandum with the United States on an interpretation of the Tripartite

Pact among Japan, Germany, and Italy that "would make it impossible for any war between the United States and Japan to arise from that Treaty"; (3) settlement by negotiation of the trade situation and the embargoes against Japan; (4) an international conference to be held at some neutral place, mutually agreed upon, pending which there would be "an economic and military standstill agreement"; (5) "that pending the solutions of this Conference, there should be a relaxation of the embargo in respect to non-military commodities to be imported in normal quantities."[142]

Desvernine gave Baruch the memorandum, one copy of which had been initialed by Kurusu, and that evening Baruch's secretary phoned Desvernine to tell him that an appointment would be arranged for the Japanese to see the president. On Wednesday, December 3, Baruch phoned Desvernine "and stated that the President had seen the memorandum and would like to talk to Desvernine alone." According to Hoover's diary, Desvernine met with Roosevelt the next day and was told by the president that the memorandum indicated the basis for a solution. He asked to see the Japanese directly, and that afternoon Kurusu and Nomura met with the president. The next day Roosevelt met with the two Japanese again. According to Hoover's diary:

> Desvernine talked with Nomura and Kurusu after their meeting with Roosevelt and Desvernine believed that the memorandum had solved the entire situation. Some collateral questions arose in those discussions, one of them was whether the Japanese would negotiate with Chiang-Kai-Shek [sic], Roosevelt using the expression: "Perhaps he might 'introduce them to Chiang-Kai-Shek [sic]' " to which Kurusu replied that "no one could refuse to meet and discuss matters after an introduction by the President of the United States." All seemed settled, and the next day Desvernine came to New York.

Desvernine returned to New York on December 6.[143] The next day, Japanese carrier-based aircraft attacked American naval and military installations in Hawaii and elsewhere in the Pacific. If Hoover's diary is correct, then he had suggested the basis on which conversations *might*, at least, have gone on, had the Japanese not already made the decision for their fateful strike against the United States. Emphasis must be placed on the might, since it is questionable whether at this late point Kurusu and Nomura accurately reflected the temper of their government in Tokyo. In any case, the effort was too late, and the United States was at war.

Four years after World War II had ended, William Castle wrote Hoover: "I have never forgotten [Roosevelt's] remark years ago, when he was Assistant Secretary of the Navy [during World War I], made when we were walking home one day. He said, 'It would be wonderful to be a war President of the United States.' He got his wish, which was certainly a bad thing for the country."[144] Herbert Hoover had labored mightily to prevent Roosevelt from being a war-president, but the first bomb dropped at Pearl Harbor on December 7, 1941, signified his defeat in this effort.

# 7

# A Constructive
# Opponent
# in Time of War

nti-interventionists like Hoover had a difficult time establishing their credibility after Japan's attack on Pearl Harbor. Regardless that their predictions concerning the consequences of Roosevelt's foreign policies seemed proven correct, the mood in the nation was intolerant and those who had maintained that the Axis powers were the enemies of the United States now felt they had a monopoly on patriotism. Undaunted by the smears to which he had long since grown accustomed, Hoover concentrated his attention on planning for the peace following the war, determined that the errors of Versailles should not be repeated. In this role, he exerted an influence on the mechanics of peacemaking after the war and contributed to the willingness of the Republican party to accept a role for the United States in postwar international cooperation such as he had sought, and the party had rejected, after World War I. As an experienced participant in mobilization for World War I, Hoover also found himself frequently consulted by those in the Roosevelt administration now entrusted with that responsibility and also by congressional Republicans seeking advice on legislation.

On December 7, 1941, the Hoovers motored to the John Hamilton home in Pennsylvania for a Sunday luncheon. Unaware that the Japanese had attacked Pearl Harbor, the former president was met by reporters with the news when he returned to the Waldorf-Astoria Hotel.[1] Hoover wasted no time in expressing his support for President Roosevelt under the wartime conditions now prevailing. Still, he continued to feel privately that the president's policies had provoked the attack and that if the United States had not indulged in "this constant sticking of pins in rattlesnakes," Japan "would have totally collapsed without loss of a single American life." He hoped initially that the war might be confined to Japan, but this soon proved chimerical.[2]

To the press, Hoover noted that America had been "treacherously attacked by Japan." War had been forced upon the United States, and, Hoover said, this country "must fight with everything we have." But, even then, he could not resist pointing out that he had opposed Roosevelt's foreign policies in the belief that other policies might have avoided the situation in which the nation found itself. However, it was time to put such differences in the past, he agreed, and to unite in full support of the president to ensure victory.[3] Privately, however, Hoover wrote another opponent of intervention that at some point in the future "this war will be put into the scales of judgment and when this time comes you and I will be found to have been right."[4] History, the former president was sure, would vindicate his position.

American entry into the war meant the imposition of wartime economic controls. As U.S. food administrator during World War I, Hoover's advice was now actively sought by Republicans in Congress searching for the proper response to Democratic initiatives in this area.[5] Senator Robert Taft's position on the Senate Finance Committee meant that he was ultimately involved in such questions. The former president counseled that any legislation concerning food control should be based upon two principles: (1) that a single person should be appointed to supervise all "food production, distribution, rationing, price control, government purchases and foreign relief"; (2) that the agency administering food "should be based primarily upon cooperation with the people and the trades" involved.[6]

Hoover was convinced, though, that his contribution to the war effort would be limited to fulfilling such requests for advice from Republican members of Congress. He was certain, given the animosity shown him in the past by the Roosevelt administration, that even under wartime conditions the Roosevelt administration would ignore any possible contribution that might be made by those "whom they deem as outside the New Deal aura, except for a few minor lights from the business world who can be picked up and shoved around." This disturbed Hoover, since he felt that such an attitude would "lead to stupendous mistakes and ultimate demoralization."[7] Nevertheless, this animosity was apparently not shared by Democrats in Congress. After Hoover had testified before the Senate Finance Committee on the price control bill, Taft wrote:

You would have been pleased and amused yesterday to hear yourself quoted by such leading Democrats as Barkley, Glass and Brown. They did not always understand what you had said, but they all accepted you as an authority on the subject. I think that your trip here was not only helpful to us, but it evidently left a very fine personal feeling among all the Senators, Republican and Democratic, with whom you came in contact.[8]

Hoover's articles for the *Saturday Evening Post* on the tragic results of the peacemaking after World War I had been scheduled for publication in book form. Originally titled *The Halls of Peacemaking*, the name was subsequently changed to *America's First Crusade*, as the former president believed it would be "a more effective one for the public's attention."[9] Unfortunately, the book was not ready for release until after Pearl Harbor, and what appeared to be a sound warning prior to American entry into the war no longer seemed appropriate to some as a topic of discussion when the United States was fighting for its survival. Aware of the hostility his book could expect from reviewers for the New York City newspapers, Hoover tried, too late, to keep it from being sent to them for review.[10] As he wrote the publisher: "I have no doubt as to the scolding that will come to this book in view of the event of December 7."[11] When the expected "scolding" was forthcoming in the reviews, the former president wrote that they were "a fine exhibit of how far free speech can be intimidated or destroyed by an intolerance of war psychosis." His book, Hoover pointed out, had shown the mistakes of one peacemaking attempt, which might be avoided after the present war. "These reviewers' attitudes are the attitudes of men afraid to face that problem and fearful that the American people would be corrupted by discussion of it until victory—when, God knows, it will be too late to prepare."[12] Hoover decided "to get even with them by getting as wide a distribution as possible."[13]

Having set forth in his articles and in the book the errors of peacemaking after World War I, Hoover now poured many of his energies during the war years into ensuring that the next peace would be made on a planned and rational basis. Even before Pearl Harbor, Hoover had called, in some of his 1941 speeches, for consideration of the peace to be made after the war. Chester Bowles had encouraged the former president as early as September 1941 to devote a speech "to the kind of world organization toward which we should all work after the war and perhaps, more definitely, how the war could best be brought to a close. . . ."[14] Less than ten days before Pearl Harbor, Bowles wrote Hoover:

Like yourself I am ardently opposed to our participation in the war. I am a member of the National Committee of America First. I am not, however, an Isolationist. I believe that after the war we must make every effort to contribute towards the gradual creation of a sounder and more cooperative world.[15]

Bowles' description of himself applied equally to Hoover. The simultaneous commitment of such individuals to nonintervention in the war and to international peacekeeping machinery demonstrates the bankruptcy of such simplistic terms as "isolationist" and "internationalist" to describe the noninterventionists and interventionists. The issue prior to Pearl Harbor was not "isolationism" or "internationalism"—it was war or peace.

Consideration of how future peacemaking might improve on the Versailles experience was a natural development from Hoover's articles and book on the "first crusade," and even before Pearl Harbor the former president had begun to work, together with former diplomat Hugh Gibson, on a book that would set forth the principles they believed must be followed in fashioning a durable peace. Hoover hoped that the book would "be a contribution to sanity."[16] But he wanted others to consider the problems of the postwar world as well. In January 1942, he began to press the Council on Foreign Relations to take up planning for postwar peacemaking. He refused to renew his membership in the council, he told its secretary, Allen Dulles, because there was no longer any reason for its existence unless it was "prepared to come out emphatically with a public statement that the problems and projects for the forthcoming peace must have full and frank discussion by the public now." The press, Hoover charged, was seeking to stifle discussion of such questions by insisting that all efforts should be concentrated on winning the war. This was the attitude, Hoover asserted, that had prevailed during World War I, with the result that "we went to the peace conference badly prepared for what we had to meet, and as a result so bad a peace was made that we are now in a second world war."[17] Dulles agreed, and pointed to studies that the council was already pursuing toward that end, but he refused to make such a public statement as the former president had demanded.[18] However, Hoover was sufficiently encouraged by the studies in progress that he consented to renew his membership.[19]

Hoover had no confidence in the New Deal's ability to wage a war successfully. In February 1942 he wrote Richard Lloyd Jones of the *Tulsa Tribune*: "This war belongs to the God-seekers and the New Dealers. It will be ours when they lose it. And lose it they will (in its foreign aspects) if they keep charge of it." The war might have been avoided by wiser policies, Hoover insisted, but that could not be helped now. He concluded: "We can pray that new men come to leadership quickly both here and in England or we shall fail."[20] He was sure that 1942 would see "an unending series of disasters." From these disasters he believed would come "a yearning in the American mind for more effective conduct of this war," but he did not feel that as of yet that yearning was "great enough to yield anything but curses upon those who would encourage it." He was convinced that the situation would be changed, however, by the time of the November elections.[21]

Despite the wartime conditions, which would seem to have compelled unity in America, and despite the passage of nine years since he had left the presidency, Hoover was still persona non grata at the White House, a continuing slight that led him to write O'Laughlin:

> Quite aside from everything else, this would seem to indicate that they are unaware of the old standard of courtesy from the White House. That is, former Presidents, irrespective of party should be periodically invited and welcomed to indicate the continuity of government and sportsmanship in the White House. In my time it was taken for granted that the President should take the initiative in courtesies of this sort.

The former president found it curious that Roosevelt had extended such invitations to other opposition leaders. However, he said he would continue to give "any possible support to the war efforts" and would even defend Roosevelt against unwarranted attacks by Republicans. "If I find it necessary to engage in comment on the conduct of the war," Hoover told O'Laughlin, "it will be entirely constructive, upon no petty issue and never below the belt."[22]

The closeness between Hoover and Landon, forged through their common opposition to Roosevelt's prewar foreign policies, continued into the war years. In January the former president expressed a desire to see the Kansan so that they might discuss matters that were difficult to cover in letters. Hoover feared, he said, "that we may have some major developments that will require all the thought that we are able to reassemble."[23] Both Republican leaders were exerting efforts on behalf of the GOP organization, with a view to winning control of Congress in the 1942 off-year elections. One concern on Hoover's part was that congressional Republicans who had opposed Roosevelt's foreign policies before Pearl Harbor, and who had been smeared as isolationists, should not be purged as a result of the wartime hysteria.[24] Hoover was optimistic that the inadequacies of the Roosevelt administration were now being brought into sharp relief by setbacks in the war and that these would affect the domestic political situation.[25] Late in February 1942 Congressman Joseph Martin foresaw an excellent opportunity for the GOP to carry the House of Representatives in November, a conclusion he had reached as a result of the favorable reception his speeches had received during a swing through the western states.[26]

Landon agreed that the Republican party would make sweeping gains in November, but despite urging from both Hoover and Taft, the Kansan refused to become GOP national chairman.[27] Landon believed that he could contribute more to party unity as an individual than as chairman.[28] Both Landon and Hoover were concerned that Willkie seemed intent on maintaining the division within the Republican party between interventionists and noninterventionists, to the detriment of party unity.[29] As Landon put it, Willkie desired "to keep the issue alive between isolationists and interventionists. That's his only stock in trade."[30] Hoover was concerned, as he wrote to Mrs. Ogden Reid, that "there is a small element of Republicans who believe that every Republican who was against any part of Roosevelt's foreign policies before Pearl Harbor is a leper" and that in taking that attitude such Republicans were "doing great disservice, not only to the party, but to the country, for it is an implication of lack of patriotism." The former president sought "a healing process, not the keeping of old wounds open," so that the GOP might be "welded into a real force in national service, not split by internal fights."[31]

Early in April of 1942 Hoover and Hugh Gibson traveled to the former president's home on the Stanford University campus and then northward to Oregon, where they combined fishing with work on the book dealing with the problems of lasting peace.[32] While they fished and wrote in Oregon, the GOP national committee was meeting in Chicago and seeking a compromise between the Willkie camp and the more traditional Republicans. Resolutions were proposed by both Willkie and Taft; the former put emphasis on the prosecution of the war and America's postwar role, while the latter focused on the need to preserve the two-party system during the war. Taft's resolution also called for opposition to "any effort by the Administration to use the war as an excuse for the extension to domestic affairs of unsound economic panaceas disapproved by the great majority of the people." Taft's draft tended to be combative, while the Willkie draft was more supportive of the Roosevelt administration. The final resolution adopted by the committee straddled the two drafts, incorporating language from both.[33] Hoover claimed credit for "the critical paragraph on post-war relations," which he described as "a long way from Willkie's draft."[34] That paragraph read:

> We realize that after this war the responsibility of the nation will not be circumscribed within the territorial limits of the United States; that our nation has an obligation to assist in the bringing about of understanding, comity and cooperation among the nations of the world in order that our own liberty may be preserved and that the blighting and destructive processes of war may not again be forced upon us and upon the free and peaceloving peoples of the earth.[35]

In truth, the paragraph that was adopted was not far from Willkie's own proposal and contained much of the language of Willkie's own resolution. The animosity between the two men, however, made it impossible for them to recognize their closeness in views concerning the postwar role of the United States.

On May 20, 1942, Hoover made his first major speech on the war. He warned a New York City audience that it would be necessary for the nation to suspend part of its liberties at home even while it fought for liberty abroad. In the economic sphere, the nation must likewise turn to fascist economic policies in order to defeat fascism abroad. The president must have dictatorial economic powers in order to win a total war and there must be "no hesitation in giving them to him and upholding him in them." Freedom of speech and press must be limited to deny the enemy vital information, but, Hoover argued, "criticism of the conduct of the war is necessary if we are to win the war." Blunders could not be covered up nor incompetent leaders be kept in control, lest such contribute to defeat. Not even the president should be immune from such criticism. Hoover opposed any attempts "to reform freedom and to make America over anew socially and economically during the war." All efforts should be concentrated, instead, on winning the war, and there would be "plenty of time to exercise the spirit of reform after the war is over." Taking "on the load of a new social and economic order in the middle of this dangerous stream," he warned, would "not help us to get across."[36]

Hoover also counseled against repeating the "rabid intolerance" of World War I, particularly that being shown toward those who opposed, before Pearl Harbor, American participation in the war. Such intolerance and name-calling did not contribute to national unity. He ended with four suggestions: first, that the war effort be more effectively organized than at present; second, that the nation begin planning already for the reconstruction that must follow the war; third, that preparations be made now for making the peace an enduring one; and fourth, that all "surplus food producing" countries prepare for the demands of the war and the peace, because "unless there be food there will be no foundation for peace."[37] The speech received complimentary comments from many quarters and was printed in the *Congressional Record* at Senator Taft's initiative.[38]

If some Republicans were willing to sacrifice party unity by continuing their criticism of past "isolationists," such as Willkie's group seemed intent on doing, it was natural that the Democrats should seize upon the same issue in campaigning against Republicans in the off-year elections. Concerned over this trend, and over the inactivity of the GOP national committee, Taft wrote Hoover that the Democratic strategy had to be "met head on." Taft had, however, been unable to generate any interest among GOP senators and congressmen in going on the attack.[39] Hoover's May 20 speech, delivered five days after Taft's letter, was clearly an effort to do what Taft felt was necessary. The speech, Hoover wrote Landon, had been intended to test out a number of things. Hoover wrote:

> My very proper designation of these economic measures as Fascist (a hateful word) has raised the ire of the Left Wing who foresee trouble in holding these measures after the war if this label is made to stick. Likewise the statement that the President "must have many dictatorial economic powers" went sourly with the reactionary interventionists who had assured the country that no such measures would be necessary and who don't like them anyway. It also raised the hair of the Freedom House group, who have organized to defeat all Republican Congressmen and Senators who were opposed to war before Pearl Harbor. This group is an unnatural combination of the reactionaries and the left-wingers who, for entirely different points of view, worked to get the country into war—and want a monopoly on patriotism now.[40]

A few days after the May 20 speech, Hoover suggested that Landon's Flag Day speech take up points similar to those he had raised. He suggested to the Kansan the basis of a national program to guide Republicans during the war, which consisted of: support for winning the war; ending name-calling; submitting to economic fascism during the war years, but wiping it out and restoring liberty once the war was ended; no radical experiments by the government during wartime; slashing all unnecessary government expenditures during the war; the provision of a lasting peace when the war was ended, to be "built upon sanity and cooperation which protects American ideals and American life"; and the laying of foundations "for economic recovery after the war based upon economic liberty." Without this last point, Hoover said "there will be no liberty of any kind." Hoover suggested that Landon take up these points in the Flag Day speech.[41] Landon sent Hoover a draft of his proposed speech asking for comments and Hoover responded with numerous suggested revisions.[42]

Hoover and Gibson had, meanwhile, brought their book, *The Problems of Lasting Peace*, to completion. Arrangements were made to have the Hoover War Library pay the cost of publishing the book in order to keep the price down, and *Reader's Digest* had expressed interest in carrying a condensed version.[43] The latter offered the prospect that the book would be brought into the homes of over five million Americans.[44] The authors had invited comment on early drafts of the book, and the reception had been enthusiastic. However, the publisher, Doubleday Doran, also sent advance copies of the book to some sixty leading figures interested in foreign affairs. Among those receiving an advance look at the book was Under Secretary of State Sumner Welles. Welles received the book around May 20, and on May 30 delivered a speech on foreign affairs that received wide comment and acclaim. Distressing to Hoover and Gibson was the fact that, in its constructive suggestions concerning peace-making, the Welles speech advanced many of the same proposals contained in the as-yet-undistributed Hoover-Gibson book. As Hoover remarked: "It may be just a coincidence. But if it is, it is an extraordinary one in view of Mr. Welles' previous views on this subject."[45] To prove his point, the former president drew up a memorandum entitled "An Interesting Parallel," which compared portions of Welles' speeches of May 30 and June 17 with the corresponding comments in the Hoover-Gibson book. Hoover concluded by writing:

> It is understood that these two speeches were the beginning of a series to be delivered to enlighten public opinion and clarify public thought as to our peace objectives. It is to be hoped that in future addresses he will give us his views on the remainder of the program for peacemaking formulated in the book. Since he has followed along so willingly thus far it is perhaps not unreasonable to anticipate that he will propose the rest of the program.[46]

Hoover was determined to make *The Problems of Lasting Peace* into a best-seller. Perhaps there was a certain amount of personal vanity involved, but more likely the former president recognized that the book would have a greater impact if it reached the best-seller list. In June, Hoover sent advance copies of the book to people he thought might be willing to help underwrite its promotion. As he wrote to Robert Wood, of the old America First Committee:

> It has appeared to us that it is worth some effort to secure its [the book's] widespread distribution. That can only be done by non-publishing methods. You will realize that a successful serious book (which we have reduced to $2.00 in order to get it before the public as cheaply as possible) can not be adequately promoted out of any publisher's profits. There ought to be from $5,000 to $10,000 spent in promotion. . . . We need to publish full page advertisements over the country of these views. And 20,000 to 25,000 copies should be sent out to cover all the colleges, high schools and public libraries in every town and village and every association and group engaged in this. . . . To do the whole job some $25,000 should be provided. Hugh and I have stretched our resources in costly research work and

preparation of the book. After you have read the book and satisfied yourself that it is a contribution, if you know of any quarter that might help us, I believe it would be a public service.[47]

Wood did attempt to find financial support for the promotion.[48] At a dinner with Hoover and Gibson at the Waldorf, Rickard found the conversation entirely taken up with finding ways to promote the book. The former president was seeking at least $10,000 for promotion.[49] Rickard soon had a representative contacting bookstores in midwestern cities in behalf of the book. Sales were promising, but Rickard noted in his diary that Hoover would not be satisfied until the book topped the best-seller list.[50]

*The Problems of Lasting Peace* was taken up by the Book-of-the-Month Club and quickly went into a sixth printing.[51] The efforts of the Hoover promotion were bearing results. On July 9 he wrote Taft that the book had received "an astonishingly good reception. No serious book has ever sold the way this one is. One would hardly expect it to become one of the best sellers— but that is the fact."[52] Hoover neglected to mention that the book's popularity was at least partly the result of his own well-managed and well-financed promotion campaign, as well as the purchase of books for donation to libraries and organizations.

*The Problems of Lasting Peace* began by reviewing the previous 140 years of history and then turned to a description of the dynamics of peacemaking at Versailles after World War I. In the third and final part of the book, the authors addressed the foundations of lasting peace and the methods of peace negotiations and peace preservation. "Any structure of lasting peace," they wrote, "must consist of two parts. The first is its foundation of political, territorial, military, economic and ideological settlements which restore order and recovery to the world. The second is the erection thereon of some instrumentality to preserve peace." The United Nations, as the Allies called themselves, should be clear on their aims and principles in peacemaking and should reduce them to specific and practical terms before the peacemaking began. They should also agree on the methods by which the peacemaking was to be conducted. Any peace treaties should "initiate" and "nurture" representative government in the enemy countries, and free enterprise economies should be established, "regulated to prevent abuse." Control of international trade should be restored to free enterprise. Provision should be made for international cooperation to ensure monetary stability. Tariffs should be "equal to all nations" and should "be no higher than will preserve fair competition of imports with domestic production." Reciprocal trade agreements should be abandoned as discriminatory. All nations should have access to raw materials without the interference of monopoly controls. Germany should not be dismembered.[53]

Areas of the Pacific and Africa that offered little prospect of immediate self-government should be put under "international government with equal access to all nations for immigration, trade, and development of natural resources." As an ideal, which they realized would probably be impossible to attain, Hoover and Gibson proposed the complete disarmament of the enemy countries and the establishment, instead, "of a constabulary of the police type" for the maintenance of domestic order. They also supported consultation before the end of the war on concrete steps that could be taken toward disarmament within weeks after the war ended. Experience showed that if it was not done at that time, effective disarmament was unlikely. The leaders of the Axis powers and their lieutenants must be treated no differently from "common criminals conspiring to murder."[54]

As for reparations, Hoover and Gibson argued that placing nations in economic bondage was not the way to lasting peace. They wrote: "Certainly, experience shows that no nation can be punished as a whole and at the same time leave any hope of lasting peace. This endless treadmill of punishment must be stopped in the world if there is to be real peace." The authors favored arbitration of future disputes. And there must be a provision for revising the peace treaties, they wrote:

> Certainly, experience shows that peace can best be preserved, not by preventing change and putting the future in a straitjacket, but by seeking to control change and direct it. Obviously, any attempt to maintain the *status quo* indefinitely is a direct invitation to war—for peaceful means being denied, the change can come only through force.

They would, therefore, build into international law a provision for the mechanics of treaty revision, along with arbitration, mediation, and other peacekeeping methods.[55]

The authors noted that the forces destructive to the goal of establishing a long-term basis for peace were at their high point immediately after hostilities ceased. For this reason, they argued for "the desirability of working under more favorable conditions, of giving time for destructive forces to abate and gaining time for reflection and negotiation in solving long-range problems." They suggested that peacemaking be divided into three stages: "first, immediate settlements of certain problems which will not brook delay; second, an intermediate period for rebuilding of political life and economic recovery; and third, a subsequent period, of more or less indefinite duration, for settlement of the long-view problems which require a cooling off of emotions, deliberation and careful development."

Among the problems that would require immediate settlement, Hoover and Gibson included demobilization and disarmament, the establishment of de facto governments to govern the states designated to exist within "empirically determined" temporary boundaries, the establishment of representative governments, the elimination of famine and pestilence, and the "restarting of industrial production." The long-range problems, they suggested, should be assigned to "separate international commissions, their conclusions to be brought in after political and economic life has begun to recuperate and destructive emotions given time to cool off." These long-range problems they viewed as including provision for the government of areas not yet ready for self-government, long-range economic problems, boundary disputes, the "readjustment of intergovernmental debts, settlement of private property questions, and damages from the war," and the "building of international machinery to preserve peace." Until political order had been restored, economic recovery had been attained, and the long-range problems brought to a solution, Hoover and Gibson saw no alternative but for the victorious Allies to "maintain order in the world by military force."[56]

Entirely apart from the efforts made to promote it, *The Problems of Lasting Peace* was viewed as a valuable contribution by leading Republicans. William Allen White set to work at once to press the book upon leading Republicans both in and out of Congress, since he found the views outlined synonymous with his own.[57] White found that many of the people he propagandized concerning the book agreed with him as to its merits, including some who were unlikely converts to the proposal for "international machinery."[58] Senator Capper, who had opposed the League of Nations after World War I, wrote White that he found the Hoover-Gibson work "a marvelous book," and that it would "have a far-reaching effect in this country." He said, "I thought it a good idea to bring the book to the attention of the Senate."[59] Senator Taft, who had opposed the GOP national committee taking any position on foreign policy at its April meeting, because he found "no crystallization of thought which could possibly be made the basis of party action," now found in the Hoover-Gibson book "a foundation on which all Republicans can stand."[60] Hoover amplified his own views, writing Taft that he thought "one of the most valuable contributions" the book made was the suggestion that there should be a "cooling-off" period before the actual peacemaking proceeded. Apparently that suggestion had been motivated in part by the former president's lack of confidence in the Roosevelt administration, for he wrote Taft that a "rush arrangement by the present regime would be likely to do irreparable injury."[61] So convinced had Hoover become of the value of the book that in late July he thought it "would be a good thing if the army would distribute 'The Problems of Lasting Peace.' It at least gives them something definite to fight for."[62]

Leon Stolz, chief editorial writer for Robert McCormick's *Chicago Trib-*

*une*, thought the most valuable aspect of the book was "its emphasis on the importance of the terms of peace as distinguished from any all-embracing scheme of world organization. Unless the terms are liveable, no scheme of world security will work. We mustn't be allowed to forget that."[63] Senator Harold Burton, who in 1943 would cosponsor the important Burton-Ball-Hatch-Hill resolution in the U.S. Senate in favor of American participation in postwar world organization, wrote Hoover and Gibson in mid-August 1942 that he had read the book during a trip to Alaska "with great interest and profit." He continued: "I thank you for it. I believe it will be of great value to all concerned. It is priceless to me."[64] Later in the month, Burton wrote again that he had lately had "several opportunities to consider some of the material in your book," and he said, "I am sure that I will find it valuable to me in many ways." He added that he had heard the book highly spoken of by Senator Alexander Wiley.[65] There was also encouraging evidence that the Hoover-Gibson book was finding its way into college classrooms.[66]

Throughout the first half of 1942, the former president watched the succession of Allied defeats with alarm, blaming them in large part on the mishandling of the war by the Roosevelt administration. He did not feel comfortable in alliance with the Soviet Union, regarding that regime as an untrustworthy ally that might make a separate peace with Hitler at any moment, as it had done in World War I.[67] When Singapore and the Dutch East Indies fell to the Japanese, Hoover privately blamed it on the strategic error of "too little and too late." He feared that Australia, China, and India would also fall.[68] The delays in equipping an army and constructing ships raised the possibility that by the time the United States could exert an influence on the war it would be an isolated nation.[69] Hoover found the American people confused over the purpose of the war, partly because they could not "reconcile a crusade for liberty with a Russian partner," and partly because they could not appreciate the idea "of giving millions of American lives to restore [British] mastery over the Malay races instead of [giving them] their freedom."[70] Yet he found it "very difficult for those of us who have been in opposition to criticize as we will only be discredited as being in opposition to everything. However, sooner or later the subject will have to be raised or we may have terrible consequences."[71]

As of the summer of 1942 Hoover believed that Japan would leave the Soviet Union to Germany and concentrate instead on Asian expansion, unless Hitler ran into difficulties in Russia in which case Japan might go to his aid.[72] The former president did not believe that Russia would be able to hold off the Germans, but he viewed the probable collapse of the Soviet Union as beneficial. Peacemaking would be easier with the communists eliminated, and the peace would be more enduring with that "center of revolution" eradicated. He thought that the Germans would lose an immense number of men in conquering the Soviet Union, and then would have to keep further millions there as a garrison force. The result would be that in June of 1943 the Germans were likely to be 2.5 million men weaker than they were in June 1942.[73] Hoover opposed any Allied land invasion of Europe in 1942, since it could not be sufficient in scale to ease the pressure on the USSR and would probably only result in a Japanese attack on that country. Furthermore, an unsuccessful invasion of Europe would leave Britain open to attack. And any attempt to concentrate an adequate amount of shipping for a European invasion would deprive the Soviet Union, Egypt, and Australia of supplies. Hoover preferred to see the war won by attrition and the "decomposition of enemy nations under long strain of total war," without the "slaughter uselessly" of American youth.[74]

In September 1942 Hoover grew increasingly distraught over the mobilization situation. He wrote to Arch Shaw that he walked "the floor wondering if" he did not "owe it to the country to blow off." He continued: "And then I recognize that it would not carry much weight."[75] But, the same day, he wrote Arthur Hays Sulzberger, publisher of the *New York Times*, pointing out that in December 1941 he had called the publisher's attention to the fact that the management of commodities by the Roosevelt administration "was wrong and would bring utter confusion." The "rubber folly" he pointed out as an example of just what he had warned against, and he noted that the Baruch committee had recommended reorganization along precisely the lines Hoover had recommended to the Senate Finance Committee in December. Now he urged Sulzberger that the *New York Times* push for a similar reorganization of "all other critical commodities, services, or groups of them." He did not, he told Sulzberger, want any reference to himself; but he was convinced that "unless these things are done and done promptly we will have a catastrophe."[76]

In October, Landon came to the conclusion that if the Republicans did not win control of the House of Representatives it was "going to be right close."[77] Hoover was predicting Republican victories in the gubernatorial elections in California, Colorado, Pennsylvania, Delaware, Ohio, New York, Massachusetts, and other states, as well as an increase of 6 to 8 Republican seats in the Senate and 25 to 50 seats in the House. He was pleased by the prospect that any such GOP victories, except in California, would be by "anti-Willkie men."[78] The GOP actually increased its seats in the Senate by 10 and in the House by 47. These results pleased the former president, but he quickly issued a statement to the press pointing out that the Republican victories should give no comfort to the Axis, since every candidate in the election, from whichever party, had run on a platform of "vigorous, efficient prosecution of the war. There was a strong element of protest in the vote," he declared, "but it was the protest of insistence upon more effective organization of the war and that can be of no comfort for the enemy."[79] The victory, he told Congressman Joseph

Martin, gave the Republicans two great opportunities: (1) "to insist upon a reorganization of the war agencies so as to stop this blundering delay and the loss of lives in this war," and (2) "to stop the use of war measures to permanently collectivize this country."[80] The former president was especially delighted that Senator George Norris of Nebraska had been defeated.[81]

Although there were rumors that the Roosevelt administration "hate list" had been pared down due to the necessities of the war effort and that Hoover might be called upon to assist with relief efforts in Europe, leadership of the major relief effort, the United Nations Relief and Rehabilitation Agency (UNRRA), was entrusted not to the former president, but to Herbert Lehman, former governor of New York. Hoover regarded this as "a rotten appointment from any point of view."[82] Disappointed, he first considered making his own views concerning relief known via an open letter to Lehman, but he was dissuaded by Gibson and Rickard.[83] Instead, he wrote privately to Lehman on November 24, congratulating him on the appointment and expressing his own willingness to cooperate with the new UNRRA chief in any way he could.[84] Lehman responded by inviting Hoover to lunch so that they might discuss relief problems.[85] Prior to their luncheon, the former president wrote Lehman once more, again pressing the project dear to his heart: the relief of women, unemployed men, and children in the occupied democracies and the increase of supplies to Greece. He also renewed his prewar proposal, which had been blocked by the British but had been supported by many leading Americans.[86] At the luncheon in Hoover's suite on December 3, the former president reiterated his concern for the fate of those in the occupied areas. The question, he told Lehman, was "whether the United Nations are fighting to liberate oppressed peoples or to liberate vast cemeteries."[87] When Lehman left the conference he refused to comment to reporters on the former president's proposal.[88] A similar initiative had, meanwhile, been launched in favor of food relief for the occupied areas by Socialist party leader Norman Thomas, who was the chairman of the Post-War World Council.[89]

In November, Hoover worked to ensure that the Willkie wing of the Republican party would not gain control of the GOP national committee.[90] The division between the Willkie camp and the more traditional Republicans continued to plague the party. As 1942 drew to an end, the problem was to find a chairman for the national committee who would be acceptable to both camps and who would not seek to dominate the organization of the GOP convention in 1944. William Allen White and others, including Hoover, continued to press Alf Landon to take the post, but the Kansan refused.[91] Landon viewed the party's situation in 1944 as likely to parallel that in 1920, and he considered that the GOP would probably not be able to straddle the current postwar issue as successfully as it had on the earlier occasion. But he believed it vitally important to "defeat a fourth term New Dealer."[92] To attain that goal,

Landon viewed unity as essential, and he believed that he could be of greatest service in mending party divisions and helping forge a united front in 1944 by working outside of the national chairmanship.[93]

Werner Schroeder, the Republican national committeeman from Illinois, had wide support among anti-Willkie members of the national committee and was the favorite to win in a straight pro- versus anti-Willkie confrontation. Schroeder, however, was too closely identified in some minds with Robert McCormick's supposedly isolationist *Chicago Tribune* and was unacceptable to the Willkie group, even though, according to Hoover, it was Schroeder who had written the foreign policy paragraph in the committee's platform earlier in the year, which Willkie had claimed as his own.[94] Hoover was not opposed to Schroeder and encouraged him prior to the meeting of the committee to issue a statement on postwar policies based on *The Problems of Lasting Peace*; Hoover's expectation was that the statement would silence some of the opposition to Schroeder as a *Chicago Tribune* isolationist.[95] The former president, in fact, wrote such a statement for Schroeder at the latter's request.[96]

But Hoover preferred that there not be a bitter confrontation over the chairmanship, which would be detrimental to the party. If the Willkie forces were determined to make an issue of Schroeder, then it was desirable to find a compromise candidate whose allegiance was just as strongly to the anti-Willkie camp. This would give the Willkie forces the feeling that they had accomplished something in blocking Schroeder, but put the committee in anti-Willkie hands. Thus, it was early rumored that, although Schroeder had the votes to win, he would be asked to withdraw in favor of a unanimous vote for a compromise candidate of unity.[97] At the meeting of the committee on December 7, the first two ballots were divided primarily between Schroeder and the choice of the Willkie camp, Fred Baker of Washington, with Harrison Spangler of Iowa a distant third. After a recess, Spangler was elected unanimously. Hoover claimed credit for breaking the deadlock in the committee and for the resulting election of the Iowan.[98] From the beginning, the strategy had apparently been to block Willkie's candidate with Schroeder and then offer Spangler as a compromise.[99] The former president celebrated Spangler's election as a victory over the Willkieites.[100] A week after the meeting he wrote Ray Lyman Wilbur: "Spangler's election tickles my funnybone in many places. Willkie fell into a complete trap and is just now beginning to awake to it."[101]

The balloting over, the committee reaffirmed the commitment to international postwar cooperation, which it had passed on April 20. The motion for this reaffirmation was made by Senator Robert Taft, who had opposed such a resolution at the April meeting.[102] The combination of this resolution and the defeat of Schroeder made Willkie feel that he had won a victory at the committee meeting; but the election of Spangler was no victory and, in reality, neither was the adoption of the resolution. Between the April and December meetings,

*The Problems of Lasting Peace*, which clearly accepted some role for the United States in international cooperation after the war, had been published. True isolationists, by any reasonable definition, were rare in the party, although serious differences of opinion might exist over the precise nature of the "international cooperation" that would follow the war. But neither Hoover nor Taft were recent converts to the cause of international cooperation, both having championed the cause long before Willkie.[103] If Willkie was under the ilusion, shared by his biographers and too many historians of the period, that Republican leaders like Hoover and Taft were being dragged by his leadership into reluctant acceptance of postwar international cooperation, he was badly mistaken. The sizable gulf that had separated the interventionists from the noninterventionists prior to Pearl Harbor was clearly not very wide in regards to postwar policy, nor did the pre-Pearl Harbor labels of "isolationist" and "internationalist" have any relevance to the two groups' positions on peacetime international cooperation.

On December 16, 1942, Hoover delivered a major speech, entitled "The Approaches to Peace," in Chicago. The speech reiterated the points that had been made in *The Problems of Lasting Peace*, including the transitional period and the creation of definite machinery for the preservation of peace.[104] Willkie wired Hoover that he had "read with great interest" Hoover's "very provocative address of yesterday," and he told the former president that when he returned to New York he wished to have a talk with him.[105] Hoover wrote to Willkie regarding the reception to the speech: "It is at least a novel incident when a proposal simultaneously wins high approval from the *New York Times, News, Daily Mirror, Sun, World Telegram*, the *Chicago Tribune*, and the *Emporia Gazette*! Aside from the communist press, the only critic is the *New York Tribune*." Of Willkie's desire to meet with him, the former president explained that he had "a bunch of grandchildren to shepherd over the holidays, but," he wrote, "soon thereafter I would be glad if you would have lunch with me."[106]

William Allen White was determined that the fate of international cooperation after World War II should not be the same as it had been in 1919–1920. If that were to be avoided, then it was important to get the Republican party lined up behind the Hoover-Gibson program as outlined in *The Problems of Lasting Peace*. White wrote Landon late in December 1942, encouraging him to join with a dozen Republican leaders, including Hoover and Willkie, in signing a manifesto that "would justify Republicans in feeling that the Hoover statement was our party policy so that in 1944 we need not have a convention row [as in 1920] and a probable split on the question of foreign policy, and can devote ourselves entirely in that platform largely to domestic issues."[107] This, of course, would have been completely satisfactory to Hoover. Meanwhile, Hoover was correcting the incredible impression of Walter Lippmann that he and Gibson had borrowed the ideas of Sumner Welles; he pointed out: "Despite the *New York Tribune*, our proposals were in print before his [Welles's] or Mr. [Henry A.] Wallace's speeches so we did not steal Welles's expression of a 'cooling off period.' I even used the expression 'a period to cool off' a year before."[108]

In support of White's initiative, Hoover sent White a condensation of *The Problems of Lasting Peace*, hoping that it might constitute, as White intended, "a program upon which all substantial Republicans might agree." Hoover suggested that Landon write a letter to leading Republicans asking their views of the program set forth in the condensation.[109] White, meanwhile, was attempting to bring about a rapprochement between Hoover and Willkie by offering to host a luncheon for the two men; he also passed along to the former president friendly comments that Willkie had made concerning him.[110] Landon supported, though not enthusiastically, White's proposal to make *The Problems of Lasting Peace* the basis of GOP postwar policy. He wrote Hoover that he questioned whether the timing was right, but also said that he was willing to join in the movement. He would first try out the idea on Minnesota governor Harold Stassen, and afterwards would write the former president more fully.[111] GOP national chairman Harrison Spangler also expressed hope "that leading Republicans everywhere will be able to be in circumstantial agreement on our duties and obligations after the war is over." He found many of the disagreements among Republicans concerning this issue to be "quite mythical," and likely to be "easily forgotten as time goes on." He did not, however, express a commitment to the Hoover-Gibson plan as the basis for such a Republican agreement.[112]

The former president entered 1943 with a far better frame of mind than he had entered 1942. Under attack for his "isolationist" views before Pearl Harbor, a year earlier, Hoover had now gained a prominent role in discussions concerning postwar policy as a result of his writings and speeches. During 1942 he had been called upon frequently for advice, not only in connection with postwar policy, but also in relation to relief and domestic mobilization questions. He now resolved to press once again for food relief for the occupied democracies. Early in January 1943 the executive committees of the Commission for Relief in Belgium and the American Children's Fund met and agreed to revive the National Committee on Food Relief for the Small Democracies and also to continue efforts to promote the Hoover-Gibson plan for peacemaking.[113] On January 8 Hoover lunched with the British ambassador, Lord Halifax, at the latter's request. It was apparent that GOP gains in the 1942 off-year elections had prompted the British to take a renewed interest in the Republicans. The conversation ranged over a number of topics, with Halifax expressing concern whether the United States might take an "isolationist" course after the war was ended. Hoover told the British ambassador that "he thought even in the Middle West there would be a readiness to accept a Council of the Nations. . . . something like the League of Nations without force, sanctions [,] and that there would be readiness to look after the police aspect of our problems through the maintenance of a British–American air force." He told Halifax that he did not believe the American people were ready for an international military force under such a council, which would be directed by such a mixed body, "but that this difficulty could be avoided by having us friendly to determine our own action in cooperation with Britain." According to Hoover's memorandum of the conversation, the British ambassador was so astonished "at this statement of readiness to cooperate with Britain that he went over the ground again."[114]

When Halifax probed the reasons behind such anti-British sentiment as did exist in the United States, Hoover responded that Americans wanted nothing to do with either socialism or collectivism and were appalled at evidence that Britain was moving left. The former president cast doubt upon the sincerity of the "left-wingers" in Washington, suggesting that they were more interested in close relations after the war with the Soviet Union than with Great Britain. Hoover also pressed the issue of food relief. However, contrary to intimations Hoover had earlier received about a relaxation of the British position, the ambassador refused to commit himself or his government to any relaxation of the blockade.[115] A few days later Hoover called a meeting of the executive committee of the National Committee on Food Relief for the Small Democracies. He believed that the Republican gains in the 1942 off-year elections had made the British less confident in the Roosevelt administration, and he concluded that they might now be more receptive to pressure for food relief. It was decided to expand the committee and to be ready to revive public opinion, although the former president had no specific plan of action.[116]

Hoover's conversation with Lord Halifax reveals some rather remarkable views. In suggesting Anglo–American cooperation to enforce peace in the postwar years Hoover anticipated the call Thomas Dewey would make for a postwar Anglo–American alliance eight months later. In putting his emphasis on air power as the vehicle for maintaining peace, Hoover anticipated his own position in the Great Debate over strategy and foreign policy in the early 1950s. The former statement, however, is particularly suspect, given the coolness Hoover exhibited toward Britain before, during, and after the war; and perhaps justified is the view that it was a ploy to break through the British blockade of the European continent so that food relief might reach the occupied democracies.

In January Landon met with Harold Stassen, the governor of Minnesota, and brought up the question of the joint statement on postwar policy, which White had suggested. The Kansan sent Hoover a copy of a memorandum based on their discussion. The statement endorsed the Hoover-Gibson book through its references to the necessity for recognition "of the centuries old traditions, customs, hates and fears bred into the blood and bone of minorities everywhere," by its reference to international cooperation as a sovereign action, and by its specific references to the Hoover-Gibson program for peacemaking, after which "necessary machinery" would be established for the preservation of peace. Landon told Hoover that he was sending the memorandum to Stassen and asked the former president to "treat this in the most careful confidence"; even the fact that such discussions were taking place must be confidential, because if word got out it might result in a case of "too many cooks spoiling the broth." Landon also told Hoover that he "would be most happy to have your criticisms and suggestions."[117] Hoover replied that he would "be greatly interested to know Governor Stassen's reaction." Hoover agreed that it was "important that we get out some formula upon which Republicans can agree." Then, seldom one to let well enough alone, the former president promised to send along a condensation of the memorandum in a few days.[118] He mailed the condensation to Landon on January 20, and the Kansan apparently forwarded it on to Stassen but received no reply from the Minnesota governor.[119]

Meanwhile, Hoover had been invited by Congressman Joseph Martin, the House minority leader, to meet with Republican members of the House, but had declined to do so, saying he felt that matters needed to be clarified "a little before we go into a huddle." He told Martin: "This is an era of investigation rather than policies."[120] A small group of GOP senators, however, traveled to New York for dinner with him late in January, including George Aiken, Rufus Holman, John Thomas, Hugh Butler, and Chris J. Abbot.[121] Contrary to his reply to Joseph Martin, Hoover was not averse to meeting with the new Republican members of the House, in fact he was anxious to do so. However, he sought some way to do so "outside Joe Martin."[122] William R. Castle hoped that he could soon arrange such a meeting, since he felt the Republican congressmen needed advice. "Such a large group as they are is pretty hard to manage," he wrote Hoover from Washington, "and if they could have some kind of clear directive it might help."[123]

In mid-January, Martin wrote Hoover that he had received several letters suggesting the formation of a war cabinet, which would meet daily to direct the nation's war effort at home and overseas. He asked Hoover for information on how such a cabinet would function, since Hoover had served in such a body under President Woodrow Wilson.[124] The former president promised to send something along "in a few days," but in the meantime he told the congressman it seemed to him that the "hottest iron the Republicans can strike is this whole food situation. It is a mess much greater than any press discussions would indicate. There are meat and milk famines all over the country due to mis-management." He was, he told Martin, making a speech that week "which ventilates some parts of it—with the indignation I feel left out."[125]

Hoover had for some time been receiving complaints about the entire handling of consumer needs on the domestic front by the Roosevelt administration. As one newspaper reporter wrote:

> In this war, the government is committed to rationing commodities and regimenting the people. During the First World War, there never was a ration card although there were shortages. How did you [Hoover] do it, and why can't they [Roosevelt's administration] do it now? I believe that voluntary cooperation worked for you and would work today.[126]

Hoover concluded in mid-January that he didn't "like the looks of things abroad" and didn't "like the looks of them at home." The government, he decided, was "trying to do too much too fast."[127]

A few days later, Hoover sent Martin his views on war organization, suggesting that his memorandum might furnish material for a speech by one of the Republican congressmen. He told Martin that "the American people might be appalled if the men who are really conducting the war were visualized by being collected into a war council and daily exhibited. That might in itself promote change."[128] In his memorandum, the former president called for the division of civilian activities under functional groupings, each headed by a single administrator, who would be responsible for all functions of government related to his group of activities. He also called for the creation of a war council, or war cabinet, and the basing of all mobilization activities on the maximum cooperation of the people in order to avoid the creation of a large bureaucracy. This latter aim would also be promoted through decentralization down to the state level.[129]

Hoover found it curious, he told Martin, that the organization of the army and navy had been built upon the experience and men of World War I, while in the area of civilian mobilization "the whole experience of the last war has been rejected or avoided," and the men involved in the First World War were excluded from Washington during the current war. "We have today," he told the congressman, "a confusion of boards, commissions, divided functions in organization, masses of futile coordinators and bureaucrats. There has been no War Cabinet or War Council and in consequence, lack of policies, overlap," and bickering had become rampant. Compulsion had been relied upon instead of cooperation, with the result that the people did not cooperate and the country was "rampant with snoopers and enforcers." The productive powers of industry had not been utilized and futile bureaucracy had been substituted, with a consequent growth in the number of federal employees.[130] Martin expressed pleasure at receiving the memorandum and told Hoover that it would "be very helpful to one of the boys in preparing a speech."[131]

The effort to get Republicans to agree on the Hoover-Gibson formula as the postwar policy of the party continued. After his January meeting with the small group of GOP senators in his suite at the Waldorf-Astoria Hotel, Hoover sent each of them a synopsis of the Hoover-Gibson plan and asked if each thought "it might constitute a Republican policy in this connection."[132] Senator Hugh Butler now asked the former president to travel to Washington to meet with a group of nine GOP senators who gathered together each week and whom Hoover nicknamed the "young Turks." Hoover offered to make the trip whenever a date could be arranged, and the meeting was scheduled for early February.[133] Hoover was also to appear before a Senate committee at that time to discuss mobilization.[134] In Kansas, William Allen White continued his own attempt to line Republicans up behind the Hoover-Gibson proposals. He wrote Hoover in early February that he thought "the time is right to put the foreign relations position of the Republican party on ice for the duration under your plan." He said that from talking to Willkie and Landon he had derived the impression they both supported the plan. He believed that most other leading Republicans would follow. "It would be a great service to your party," he told Hoover, "if you would get the danger averted of a major row in the Republican convention about foreign policy."[135]

Hoover was busy in Washington during his few days there in early February. His testimony before a subcommittee of the Senate Appropriations Committee was eagerly awaited. Senator Elmer Thomas of Oklahoma, a Democrat, felt that Hoover's testimony would "carry great weight throughout the country." Thomas added: "He studied the problem of supplies thoroughly in the last war and he is not involved with the government now. Most of the testimony we have received so far has been from men who are taking orders from the government."[136] In his testimony, the former president warned that the United States faced another three to five years of war, and he urged a revision of military manpower policies to free one million more workers for agriculture, mining, and oil well drilling during the next year. Hoover contended that the Roosevelt administration's goal of eleven million men in uniform by the end of the year was too high, since shipping bottlenecks would prevent their being transferred overseas or supplied. He criticized Roosevelt's farm price policy and called for incentives to be furnished for the production of urgently needed meats and fats. The importance of the home front was co-equal with that of the war front, he argued. Time was on the side of the Allies in the war, so there was no need to attempt to do everything at once and overstrain the home front.[137] Hoover's views won endorsement from two Southern Democratic senators, members of the farm bloc. Senator John Bankhead agreed "wholeheartedly" with the former president, adding that "now we have the word of the greatest living authority on wartime food problems that there is a grave shortage of manpower."[138]

In addition to meeting with the "young Turks," Hoover met with Secretary of Agriculture Claude R. Wickard concerning the food situation at the latter's request.[139] At the same time, he arranged for the introduction of a resolution in the Senate by Senators Gillette (Democrat) and Taft (Republican) supporting his attempts to arrange food relief for the small European democracies.[140] During his trip to Washington the former president found the atmosphere in the capital so congenial that he decided to move to that city if the Republican candidate won the presidency in 1944.[141]

Others, however, had in mind an earlier move for Hoover. In mid-February, Senator Arthur Capper publicly called upon Roosevelt to designate the former president as a "super efficiency expert" to eliminate waste and duplication in government and to "weed out useless bureaus and useless activities." Capper argued that it was "a crying shame that Mr. Hoover's services have not been pressed into use to accelerate a victory over the Axis. Everyone familiar with his record knows he is an extremely able administrator. Even his political foes concede that." A similar plea had been made a week earlier by Senator Davis of Pennsylvania, who had served as secretary of labor in Hoover's cabinet.[142]

Meanwhile, GOP national chairman Harrison Spangler was actively seeking to bring Republican leaders into some unified position on postwar policy. He wrote to Landon:

> . . . I had hoped that I could have you, Mr. Hoover, and Mr. Willkie as my guests at dinner in New York, at which we could have a frank discussion and at least ascertain how far apart we might be. This idea was given me by Mr. William Allen White, and Mr. Hoover thinks it would be worthwhile. I had hoped you would be here soon. . . . As soon as you can give me a somewhat definite time you will be here, I will arrange with Mr. Hoover and Mr. Willkie.[143]

However, the former president was leaving for California, and this meeting had to be postponed.[144] In the meantime, Hoover had proposed sending to a number of "representative men in the Senate" a letter seeking their cooperation in formulating a postwar policy. He sent copies of the proposed letter to Senator Butler and to Alf Landon for their views on whether it might be helpful.[145] Landon thought the former president was on the "right track" and suggested that he include with the letter a condensation of the Hoover-Gibson plan. He also suggested other names to whom the letter might be sent.[146] Butler, too, thought it a good idea and suggested that the letter be sent to all

GOP senators elected in the last three elections. He was unsure, he said, how Senators Warren Austin and Chan Gurney would react, since they were "so entirely New Dealish on most matters," but he thought that "they and all others would be honored to receive this statement and that "Hoover would hear from them."[147]

The irrepressible William Allen White fired off a new round of letters to GOP leaders in mid-March, asking that they read and make marginal comments upon the Hoover-Gibson condensation. He wrote to Senator Charles McNary: "If I could know where our open-minded Republican friends balk at the Hoover program, I believe some of us could get out a statement that all of us would sign."[148] GOP senators Joseph Ball and Harold Burton had, meanwhile, joined with two Democratic colleagues to introduce a resolution in the Senate towards the development of machinery for the settlement of peacetime disputes between nations and for the creation and maintenance of an international military force to be used against aggression by any nation. Senator Burton wrote the former president on March 19, enclosing a copy of an article he had written for *The Republican* entitled "The Roads to Lasting Peace." He had, he told Hoover, taken "my text from your book on 'The Problems of Lasting Peace.' " He had submitted the draft of the article to Hugh Gibson for his approval before publishing it. He also sent the former president a copy of the Burton-Ball-Hatch-Hill (B2H2) resolution, saying that he believed the resolution was consistent with the article he had written. Since Burton admitted that his article was based on the Hoover-Gibson book, it follows that he believed the resolution also was consistent with the Hoover-Gibson formula. He told Hoover that he was "hopeful that you believe that this Resolution or some reasonable modification of it is a helpful step in the right direction."[149]

Burton's article began with a series of quotes from the Hoover-Gibson book and pointed out that Hoover and Gibson had called "America to the important task of locating and building, now, all that we can of the roads to lasting peace." Like the former president in his talk with Lord Halifax, Burton emphasized the use of air power in America's role in maintaining peace after the war. He called for "no attempt to solve everything on a permanent basis at a single peace conference," but rather "that consideration should be given promptly to the several issues by special international boards designated for these purposes." Echoing the Hoover-Gibson book, Burton advocated immediate preparation for dealing with the "semi-military" emergencies that would arise as soon as the fighting ceased; these emergencies included demobilization, feeding the hungry, the establishment of temporary boundaries and governments, the re-establishment of homes and farms and factories, and preliminary planning. Burton called for "post-war machinery for arbitration, international litigation and continuing cooperation of an economic, social and governmental character that will improve upon the world's past experiments." But throughout the article, he preached the need for caution in making long-term commitments during the war to deal with postwar problems, since the future was unpredictable.[150]

The Burton-Ball-Hatch-Hill resolution (S. Res. 114) read:

> *Resolved,* That the Senate advises that the United States take the initiative in calling meetings of representatives of the United Nations for the purpose of forming an organization of the United Nations with specific and limited authority—
>
> (1) To assist in coordinating and fully utilizing the military and economic resources of all member nations in the prosecution of the war against the Axis.
>
> (2) To establish temporary administration for Axis-controlled areas of the world as these are occupied by United Nations forces, until such time as permanent governments can be established.
>
> (3) To administer relief and assistance in economic rehabilitation in territories of member nations needing such aid and in Axis territory occupied by United Nations forces.
>
> (4) To establish procedures and machinery for peaceful settlement of disputes and disagreements between nations.
>
> (5) To provide for the assembly and maintenance of a United Nations military force and to suppress by immediate use of such force any future attempt at military aggression by any nation.
>
> That the Senate further advises that any establishment of such United Nations organization provide machinery for its modification, for the delegation of additional specific and limited functions to such organization, and for admission of other nations to membership, and that member nations should commit themselves to seek no territorial aggrandizement.[151]

The former president apparently had no quarrel with the resolution through item (4), but his marginalia indicate that he believed revisions were needed in the remaining items. His marginalia show that he sought submission of any agreements between the United States and the other United Nations to the U.S. Senate for approval; that he believed item (5) should be modified to read: "To establish the terms and machinery for making a conditional peace to be enforced by the United Governments and for the subsequent development of machinery for settlement of disputes and controversies among nations, and for the development of economic aid and other relations which will bring a permanent peace"; and that he sought an additional item, which would call for the disarmament of the enemy and provide for temporary governments in liberated enemy territory.[152] In his reply to Burton, Hoover wrote that the purpose of the resolution was "fine." As for the contents of the resolution, he thought "it should be strengthened somewhat and the independence of the Congress and the Senate [should be] better safeguarded." He feared that the resolution, as it was written, would be interpreted by the Roosevelt administration "as a blank check to make commitments and then the Senate would be called upon to make good even though such commitments depart from the concepts which you have in mind."[153]

Hoover's actual suggestions to Burton departed somewhat from his marginalia. He suggested that to the last paragraph of the resolution be added provision for approval by the Senate of any plans or recommendations resulting from the meetings called for in the resolution; he asked for the insertion of "representative" into item (2), to make it read: . . . "until such time as permanent representative governments . . . ," since, as he wrote to Burton: "One major hope of lasting peace is to restore the people to control of governments." He also suggested an extension of item (4) to read: "And to provide the machinery and basis for an imposed conditional peace and to provide for a cooling-off period after victory during which period plans and organization for preserving peace and world economic relations can be developed in the full light of public understanding." He also suggested a change in item (5) to make it read: ". . . and to assure that the member nations seek no territorial aggrandizement and that sovereign rights be restored to those who have been forcibly deprived of them." He told Burton: "There are, of course, other questions, such as disarmament, freedom of the seas, air questions, stabilization of currencies in international trade, and private enterprise in trade, upon which I would like to see ideas developed also."[154] The former president's principal objection, it seems, was that not all of the proposals of *The Problems of Lasting Peace* were included in the short resolution.

Senator Arthur Vandenberg, along with others in the Senate, had reservations about the Burton-Ball-Hatch-Hill resolution, and it was apparent from polls of the Senate that this resolution would not pass.[155] The introduction of the resolution had, however, temporarily sidetracked Hoover's plan to distribute copies of his condensation, together with letters, to Republican senators, since he feared that such an action "might be misinterpreted by the evilminded as trying to offset or discount Senators Burton and Ball's resolution." No one, however, would consider William Allen White's actions as stemming from such base motives, and Hoover suggested that it might be better if the Kansan took the planned initiative. Hoover was willing, he said, to have the letters written for White's signature and to address and mail them for him.[156] White agreed.[157]

Hoover continued to deliver speeches and write articles. In mid-March he traveled to Des Moines to address the Iowa legislature and a meeting of the

Midwest Governors' Conference. In his speeches, Hoover warned that the United States faced a food deficit and must strengthen its food production for a long war and to help in the momentous task of feeding the world after the war. The United States must also be prepared to help police the world immediately after the war and should begin to plan now for a peace that would end economic barriers and disarm the aggressors. As in his testimony in Washington the previous month, Hoover argued that the government was diverting too much farm labor to the armed forces and to factories, as well as too much steel from farm machinery to munitions production and too much fertilizer for use in producing explosives. It was mandatory, he said, that agriculture be given the same rank as munitions manufacture in priorities of manpower and materials. He called again for the consolidation of all authority over food under the secretary of agriculture, with more authority delegated to state officials to meet local problems. Hoover also pressed the Hoover-Gibson formula for peacemaking.[158]

Less than week later, Prime Minister Churchill suggested the creation of postwar regional councils to deal with the problems of Europe and Asia. Hoover and Gibson quickly expressed approval and added Churchill's proposal to their own peace program. In addition to such councils for Europe and Asia, they added one for the western hemisphere, viewing the Pan American Union as the logical agency around which to build such a council.[159] In early April they dealt further with the new concept in an article in the *New York Times Magazine*, in which they expressed support for the regional councils possessing the primary responsibility for the resolution of disputes within their regions, with recourse to a world institution only in the event of failure on the part of the regional councils.[160]

Meanwhile, plans were under way in March for Hoover to confer with Republican members of the House of Representatives. The plan was that Hoover would meet with the congressmen in small groups; Congressman John Vorys of Ohio handled the details.[161] While in Washington for a series of meetings with the newly elected congressmen, Hoover also scheduled meetings with other prominent GOP senators and representatives, including McNary, Butler, and Martin.[162] After the meetings, William Castle reported that the congressmen had been enthusiastic about their discussions with the former president.[163] As a result of this trip, Hoover changed his mind again about the proposed letter to be distributed to the senators concerning postwar policy. As he told William Allen White: "The Burton-Ball resolution was dead so that I will not be interfering with that if I go ahead with the original line of sending out the inquiry myself. In view of discussions with many Congressmen and Senators, I am emboldened to do so."[164]

White had already written a number of GOP leaders and in early April he was encouraged to believe that "the whole thing seems to be working out about as we want it to go." His efforts to bring Willkie together with Hoover and Landon, however, had thus far failed. According to White's account, Hoover and Willkie were willing to meet, but Landon, "who has so much fox blood in him that he is skittish of his own tail," was "more or less coy." Nevertheless, White remained confident that the three leaders could be joined together "on some statement of foreign policy," and he felt sure, he wrote, "the Republican expression of our foreign policy will in the end rally under Hoover's leadership, and that the Hoover proposals, with most unimportant reservations, will finally be accepted as the party's position."[165]

Landon had, meanwhile, resolved to travel east to deliver a speech on foreign policy that he had been preparing with Hoover's help. He hoped to couple his speech-making trip with the proposed meeting with Hoover and Willkie, and he wrote the former president that he thought the meeting should be held at Hoover's suite in the Waldorf-Astoria Hotel and that "there should be no attempt at secrecy. What we discuss," he continued, "should be entirely confidential and off the record."[166] Hoover responded that both he and Spangler hoped the Kansan would come east whether the meeting with Willkie were held or not, but that such a meeting could be arranged "if it seems wise."[167] Landon, meanwhile, had been pleased to learn secondhand that Hoover regarded his speeches as "more in tune with the sentiment of the country than any others now being made."[168] For his part, Landon commented that Hoover was "much stronger in the country today than he has been at any time since 1932. I hear it on all sides."[169] In early April, the Kansan left for the East, although he had resolved to postpone his planned speech on foreign policy because of the visit of the British foreign secretary, Anthony Eden, to Washington.[170]

In early April, Hoover resumed writing to prominent Republicans in his effort to bring about agreement on the Hoover-Gibson plan as the basis for GOP postwar policies.[171] He wrote Senator Burton that he wanted his views on the proposal, explaining that his purpose "in no way conflicts with your own efforts as it proceeds upon an entirely different line and for a different purpose."[172] Willam Allen White expressed approval of the Hoover form letter and was sure that Willkie would subscribe to the principles. White wrote Hoover: "I feel that if you could talk to him [Willkie] and Mr. Landon, you can make him see it."[173] During his visit to New York, Landon conferred with Hoover, but without Willkie.[174] Hoover had found support in the Senate for the Hoover-Gibson plan from a number of senators, including Tobey, Ferguson, and Capper.[175]

A joint statement from Willkie, Hoover, and Landon was not forthcoming, perhaps because of the imminent publication of Willkie's book, *One World*. Released in April of 1943, this book contained much that Hoover could applaud, but also much that must have disturbed him. Willkie's naive acceptance of Stalin's expression of support for the territorial integrity of all nations, their right to arrange their affairs as they wished, the restoration of democratic liberties, and all of the rest must necessarily have grated on the minds of those who, like Hoover, could recall the Soviet Union's own aggression against such principles in the case of Poland, Latvia, Estonia, Lithuania, and Finland.[176] Moreover, there was disagreement between Hoover and Willkie on the timing for creating the international machinery for peacekeeping, which both advocated. While Hoover called for the creation of such machinery late in the peacemaking process, Willkie wanted it established now, while the war was being waged. "While we fight," Willkie wrote, "we must develop a mechanism of working together that will survive after the fighting is over." This mechanism, he continued, "must be created now under the cementing force of common danger." Willkie considered it "idle to talk about creating after the war is over a machinery for preventing economic warfare and promoting peace between nations, unless the parts of that machinery have been assembled under the unifying effort and common purpose of seeking to defeat the enemy."[177] The distance between the two men on this proposition meant that any basis for a common statement on postwar policy was lacking, even though both could continue to work toward the same ultimate objective—the creation of an international organization.

Willkie's book began immediately to sell at a staggering rate, apparently without any of the promotion that had supported the Hoover-Gibson book. By early May it was apparent that Willkie was beginning to angle for the 1944 nomination. Landon and Spangler were rumored to be part of a "stop Willkie" movement, and it seemed apparent that such rumors had originated with Willkie or his supporters in an effort to advance his own candidacy.[178]

In May Landon finally gave his long-planned speech on foreign policy and was lauded by William Allen White, who wrote his fellow Kansan: "Certainly we will kill the old red rooster and have chicken and dumplings now that you have publicly, unqualifiedly landed with Hoover and Willkie, or at least between them, a little to the right of Willkie and a little to the left of Hoover. I'm proud of you."[179] Hoover wired Landon that the "speech came over fine," and he asked for copies so that it could be given wider publicity.[180] For White, Landon's speech symbolized that "Hoover, Willkie and Landon, who certainly are officially leaders of the Republican party, are unanimous in their feeling against isolation." He thought it now would be possible to get their agreement on the long-desired statement and that 25 to 30 other leading Republicans could be induced to join them. White even thought Hoover might be a potential nominee of the GOP in 1944 and that he could win against Roosevelt.[181]

The cumulative effect of the efforts in behalf of the Hoover-Gibson plan, the groping by Senate Republicans for a postwar policy as evidenced by the

Burton-Ball-Hatch-Hill resolution, and Willkie's book, apparently moved
GOP national chairman Harrison Spangler to form a Republican Post-War
Advisory Council, which he had been contemplating for some time. He wrote
Landon that the council, which he had discussed with the Kansan several
times in the past, would now undertake its work and that Senator McNary
and Congressman Martin had designated committees from the Senate and
House to work with GOP governors in developing a postwar program for the
GOP in both the domestic and foreign areas.[182] Some historians have sug-
gested that Spangler's initiative resulted from the pressure of public opinion
generated by Willkie's *One World*.[183] Yet it should be clear that the movement
in behalf of a unified GOP postwar policy long predated the appearance of the
Willkie book and that, in seeking to base the foreign policy on the Hoover-
Gibson book, the movement was anything but isolationist. William Allen
White, hardly an isolationist, was at the center of that movement, determined
that the fate of international cooperation should not again be the same as it had
nearly one-quarter of a century before. In his efforts White was in close
cooperation with Spangler. On April 6, two days before the Willkie book was
released, White wrote Spangler:

> I feel reasonably certain that if Hoover, Landon, and Willkie would
> agree on a statement we could bring in with them on the statement 8
> or 10 Senators and the most important leaders in the House. The
> publication of such a statement signed by such men would do much
> to take the bitterness out of the platform fight on foreign policy. I
> can't conceive of much serious difference on domestic policy—which
> might perhaps be better said: I can't conceive that even a bitter fight
> on matters of domestic policy would leave the party badly shaken.
> The big issue is foreign policy. The split, if any, will come there and
> it seems to me most important that we who feel these matters se-
> riously should do what we can to iron out the honest differences.[184]

Meanwhile, however, Willkie and his followers continued to war against
the other Republican leaders and against the GOP organization, apparently
determined to develop the image of Willkie as the lone internationalist, bat-
tling against the "isolationism" of the "Old Guard." Willkie's smears were
increasingly alienating his fellow Republicans. One such smear against
Landon, in June, disturbed the Kansan; but he said he did not believe it was
"time for an open break with Mr. Willkie as much as I resent this smearing
attempt." Landon still believed it necessary to "preserve a reasonable unity in
the Republican Party." He observed that Willkie had "broken with all those
who had most to do with his nomination" and had demonstrated during the
1940 campaign, and ever since, that he lacked the understanding of the princi-

ples of political leadership, which were requisite in a president of the United States.[185]

The Willkie wing of the party was involved in the creation of a Republican Postwar Policies Association, which, though it adopted the Willkie line, claimed that it had no candidate for 1944 and that it received no Willkie money. Republican party national chairman Spangler sought to prevent the group from having a divisive effect within the party and sent a letter to Senator Warren Austin, a staunch Willkie supporter, in an effort to dissuade him from addressing the group, since the speech might affect Austin's influence in the Republican Advisory Council. Austin revealed the self-righteous attitude of the Willkieites and the weakness of their understanding of fellow Republicans when he scribbled across Spangler's letter: "Palaver of an America firster."[186]

The smear tactics of the Willkie camp and their unwillingness to cooperate with the Republican organization led both Hoover and Landon to begin casting about for a candidate for 1944 who could derail Willkie's drive for the nomination. Late in May Hoover began to connive with other Republicans in an effort to undermine Willkie's popularity.[187] He made efforts to build up Earl Warren, governor of California, as a potential candidate, though Warren was widely identified as a Willkie supporter. It was patently an effort to divide the Willkie camp.[188] Landon expressed a high regard for Warren and viewed the 1944 convention as one in which "anything can happen—except the nomination of Willkie." He could not see where Willkie could get any delegates to speak of, despite his intense publicity effort.[189]

Former GOP national chairman John Hamilton reported to Hoover on a meeting he had held with ten Republican congressmen, which led him to think that the opposition to Willkie might ultimately center on Senator Robert Taft.[190] This, however, was unlikely, since Taft and Governor John Bricker of the same state had agreed that the senator would forgo a candidacy in 1944 so that Bricker might make his try, with Taft's opportunity to come in 1948.[191] As a result, Hoover had been giving Bricker's candidacy his covert support.[192] He was also working once again for an uninstructed delegation from California to the GOP convention.[193]

The Burton-Ball-Hatch-Hill resolution having failed to make any headway, Senator Arthur Vandenberg joined with Senator Wallace White to draft an alternative, which was introduced in the Senate on July 2, 1943. Vandenberg's resolution differed from that of the four senators in a number of respects, but of particular note is the fact that it met one of Hoover's primary objections to the Burton-Ball-Hatch-Hill resolution by stating that all American peace actions should be by "due Constitutional processes," which, as the Michigan senator put it, eliminated "the Roosevelt habit and desire to bypass Congress in these respects." It also pledged "faithful recognition of *American* interests" and called for cooperation among sovereign states, thus precluding the possibility of a world state such as some of the more idealistic and utopian were demanding.[194]

In late July a committee of the Willkieite Republican Postwar Policy Association met with Spangler, who assured them that he would pass along to the Republican Advisory Council any recommendations they might have. He suggested, however, that the resolutions of the association were "quite general and do not disagree with the view of all thoughtful Americans who are of the opinion that when the war is over we must cooperate with other nations of the world," nor did the resolutions "disagree with the position the Republican National Committee has taken on two different occasions during 1942," nor did they disagree with "the resolution adopted by all Republican members of the lower house of Congress on September 22, 1942." So much for the supposed differences that the Willkieites were seeking to exploit. However, Spangler did say he was distressed that the "New Deal political machines" were using the existence of the association "to make it appear that our party is divided." On the contrary, Spangler noted, he had not been able to find any fundamental conflict among Republicans on the issue.[195]

Hoover had remained constructively critical of the New Deal's handling of the home front in newspaper and magazine articles, in testimony before congressional committees, and in speeches. When, early in June, Bernard Baruch was appointed by the Roosevelt administration to be an advisor to the Office of War Mobilization, the *New York Times* pointed to Baruch's lifelong association with the Democratic party and concluded: "Therefore, his formal association with government for the first time since 1920 offers no special basis for hope that many more members of the country's 'first team' will be taken into the war administration." But, the *Times* went on:

> As has been demonstrated, positively, in the last few months, some of these [first-team members] can be very effective on the sidelines. The most recent contributions of former President Hoover to a solution of the problems of food and—in collaboration with Hugh Gibson— of post-war planning have been valuable. The comment could fairly be made that clearer and more constructive ideas are to be found in these utterances than in any that have come on the same topics from members of the administration.

The newspaper went on to add that the difference between Hoover's and Roosevelt's speeches on the food problem represented the "difference between facts and good intentions," while the Hoover-Gibson peace plan was "more soundly imaginative and promising than any that has come from an official source." The *New York Times* concluded: "Thus from the sidelines men like Mr. Hoover, whose talents are not wanted officially, can serve the nation and the world in abundant measure."[196] But how much more effective might the war effort have been, had this member of the "first team" been called to service?

The recognition of Hoover's ability was increasing, however. The day after the *New York Times* made its observations, Chester C. Davis, administrator of the War Food Administration, wrote him: "If and when conditions here become stabilized so that I can discuss policy with some assurance, I hope very much to have the opportunity to counsel with you." In the meantime, he had directed his assistant to call on Hoover in California for advice.[197] Hoover responded that he "would be glad to be of any service at any time, in any way that I can." He could not believe, Hoover told Davis, "that the seriousness of the situation is being realized by the people with whom you have to work."[198] Viewing the situation on the home front, Hoover wrote one correspondent that the slogan of the First World War had been: "Win the war by cooperation," while in the present war it seemed to be: "Win the war by suffering."[199]

Late in July Hoover wrote GOP chairman Spangler to suggest that the Republican Advisory Council adopt something like the Hoover-Gibson program for peacemaking. The party must take new and constructive action, he urged, in order to dispel once and for all the charge that it was isolationist."[200] He wrote Clarence Kelland: "The way to kill off phrase-makers is to produce something new and worthwhile out of the Advisory Committee. This program is not only sound, but new and prevents a thousand frictions."[201] Former GOP chairman John Hamilton agreed, saying: "We should do all we can, and the Republican [Advisory] committee seems the proper place to do it to dispel any thought that the Republican Party is isolationist in any respect."[202] Hoover had also lobbied others on behalf of his plan, including New Jersey Senator Albert Hawkes. Hawkes promised that he would "follow through on the plan suggested by you [Hoover] . . . because I think it is very sound and practical."[203]

On August 5 Senator H. Alexander Smith wrote Senator Warren Austin that he had been asked by Spangler to draft some formal resolutions that the Republican Advisory Council might adopt. Smith told Austin that in his draft he had sought to incorporate sufficient language of the various GOP expressions on postwar policy, including the Vandenberg-White resolution in the Senate, that the resolutions might draw support from the various elements of the party whose views were represented in the expressions. The recommendations of his draft resolution were general, Smith admitted, because he felt that at the forthcoming meeting of the advisory council on Mackinac Island in Michigan, it would be "unwise to go into specific topics which our report will ultimately cover." He believed that his draft should only "indicate the general framework in which we propose to present our report."[204]

Smith's draft called for "the participation of the United States in postwar cooperation between sovereign nations to prevent by any necessary means the recurrence of military aggression and to establish permanent peace with justice in a free world." There was no mention of participation in an international organization, and Austin was quick to pencil this addition into the Smith draft.[205] By now, however, even Austin realized that the Republican party had moved away from any interest it might have had in isolation and that the question before the GOP advisory council would be how the United States would cooperate with the rest of the world rather than whether it would cooperate.[206] Austin noted that the resolutions Smith proposed for the conference indicated a "broader vision," which Austin concluded "the country at large is rapidly embracing, however reluctantly, in all but a notably and admittedly very important group of fine midwestern states."[207]

As the date for the Mackinac conference approached, Hoover continued to work to ensure that the postwar program adopted would embrace the Hoover-Gibson proposals.[208] Writing to Governor Bricker, who was a member of the GOP advisory council but would not be on the foreign policy committee, he expressed his concern over the foreign relations plank that would be adopted at the conference. Hoover told Bricker:

> Your Conference will probably be presented with something like the resolutions before the House and Senate which are about as follows: "Resolved, that the Republican Post-War Advisory Council unanimously approves: 1. Prosecution of the war by a united nation to the absolute and unconditional surrender of all our enemies. 2. Responsible participation by the United States in post-war cooperation among sovereign nations to prevent military aggression and to establish permanent peace with justice in a free world.

Hoover had no objection to such a statement, but he considered it insufficient. He sought from the party "some bold, constructive, specific proposals that will get outside of words and their traps and will give the Party some distinction of determination." He suggested, therefore, that the essence of the Hoover-Gibson program should be included in any resolution of the council, including the specification for a provisional peace, or "cooling-off period," and "the development of a world institution to preserve peace."[209] Of note is Hoover's insistence that the council go beyond a statement favoring American participation "in post-war cooperation" to one that included "the development of a world institution."

If these additional items were added to the council's resolution, Hoover asserted, they would accomplish six things: (a) Prevent commitment of the Party to New Deal peace plans until we have had a chance to consider them. (b) Give a distinctive and new approach to the whole problem of peace. (c) It will be in effect an assertion that we must get away from the futile methods of the past. (d) It avoids throwing the Republican Party into a debate as to how much national sovereignty will be parted with by "policing the world" because that question cannot arise until the world has had a chance to cool off and do its job constructively. (e) It is a program upon which we could get much unity. It would not conflict with any known proposals of the New Deal and, therefore, could not be charged with dividing the country's unity. (f) It would demonstrate that the Conference had not been dominated by certain destructive persons.

He was making a speech over the radio on September 3, Hoover told Bricker, which would go further into the reasons for his proposal, and he was also writing to other members of the council to urge that his plan be taken up at Mackinac.[210] A day later, Hoover sent Bricker a shorter paragraph, since it had been suggested that his earlier version was too lengthy. In the shortened version, he urged the adoption of the following statement by the council:

> We approve the principle of establishing the leading nations as the provisional Trustees (or Custodians) of Peace and a Transition Period of some years for the constructive solution of the world problems, including the creation of a world institution to preserve peace which shall replace the Trustees. Thereby the American people may have time for understanding and deliberation, and thereby the mistakes of hasty action which may again lay tinder for another world war may be avoided.[211]

It is noteworthy that Hoover did not feel it necessary to qualify his reference to a world institution with any mention of "sovereign nations."

Hoover's speech in Minneapolis on September 3 was, by timing and by topic, clearly designed to influence the debate about to begin on Mackinac Island, and he had mailed off advance copies of the speech to members of the Council, including Senators Austin and Vandenberg.[212] The American people, Hoover told his listeners, were "alive to the need and determined that we must have a lasting peace this time." The discussion on postwar policies was dominated by two kinds of people—those who had looked to the past and who were attempting to propose "something definite and positive" and those who "live in the indefinite or the infinite" and whose ideas were mostly "nebulous words" on the need to preserve peace and restore prosperity. Nations that were successful in making war were all too often failures in making peace. It was time for a new approach to peacemaking, and one that "must leave the century-old bright lights of eloquence and nebular words and explore the hard road of experience." Hoover then discussed the Hoover-Gibson program for his listeners, including, the program's fourth step: the creation of a world institution to preserve peace.[213]

A few days later, Hoover wired Arch Shaw that his speech had aroused a good deal of favorable editorial comment in the nation's newspapers. Hoover also said in the telegram: "At yesterday's press conference the President practically adopted the line himself. The newspapers here comment on the fact that it is my proposal." Under the circumstances, Hoover wondered if Kellogg might be interested in underwriting the printing and distribution of one-half million copies since, he said, it seemed possible that the speech was something on "which we might get common agreement throughout the country."[214] Hoover apparently did not feel that the nation was yet saturated with the Hoover-Gibson proposal, despite its distribution in book and article form as well as in speeches and in the numerous condensations he had circulated throughout the country.

The Mackinac conference, however, ignored the Hoover-Gibson four-step peacemaking process. The declaration of the conference was largely lacking in content and certainly devoid of anything new. The product of a committee that consisted of Senators Vandenberg and Austin, Governors Dwight Green and Edward Marvin, Congressman Charles Eaton, and Congresswoman Frances Bolton, the resolution disclaimed any attempt "at this time" to put forth "a detailed program for the accomplishment" of the great aims it envisioned. Instead, the council declared its approval of "prosecution of the war by a United Nation to conclusive victory over all our enemies" and of "responsible participation by the United States in post-war cooperative organization among sovereign nations to prevent military aggression and to attain permanent peace with organized justice in a free world." Participation in the "post-war cooperative organization among sovereign nations" was, however, hedged with numerous qualifiers relating to the national interest and the Constitution.[215] Historian Robert Divine has described the statement as "the most important step yet taken toward American involvement in a future international organization."[216]

The attempts of Willkie and his supporters in politics and journalism to make internationalism a divisive issue in the Republican party that Willkie could exploit for his own political benefit have obscured for many historians the consensus among Republicans regarding the postwar role the United States should play in an international organization and also obscured the more important role played by Herbert Hoover and the supporters of the Hoover-Gibson program in bringing about that consensus and the declaration at the Mackinac conference. While Willkie's influence with GOP leaders was waning, these same leaders were bombarded with the Hoover-Gibson postwar program and with appeals from those like William Allen White that the program be made the basis for Republican postwar policy. As for the Mackinac conference itself, Hoover later claimed to have been the one "probably responsible for the committee which resulted in the Mackinac conference," and the claim cannot be easily dismissed when it is recalled that it was longtime Hoover ally Harrison Spangler, who spearheaded the call for the Republican advisory committee, which led to the conference.[217]

Through *The Problems of Lasting Peace* and numerous magazine articles and speeches, and through widespread distribution of condensed and revised versions of the Hoover-Gibson program to influential Republicans in and out of Congress, Hoover and the program's supporters had done more, certainly, than Willkie or any other individual to prepare the Republican party to accept American participation in a postwar international organization. The Mackinac declaration, in fact, fell short of the position Hoover had taken. While "internationalist" Senator Warren Austin was encouraged that the declaration had abandoned "cooperation" for "cooperative organization," Hoover's draft statement and his speech of September 3 had called for "a world institution."[218] William Allen White agreed that Hoover's draft and speech were preferable to the declaration issued by the conference, which he described as an "innocuous straddle," necessary to reconcile the extreme internationalists with the extreme nationalists. "But," White wrote, "because I felt the straddle was going in the right direction, I didn't complain much."[219]

Indeed, White had little to complain about. With the help of another Hoover ally, Harrison Spangler, his efforts on behalf of the Hoover-Gibson approach to postwar policy had been rewarded in what he regarded as their most important aspect, the commitment of the GOP to international cooperation. The United Nations organization would not meet the fate that had crippled the League of Nations at its birth.

# 8

# Preparing for Peace

ll but a minority of Republicans were pleased with the Mackinac conference statement, with approval registered in GOP newspapers ranging from the *Chicago Tribune*, widely regarded as isolationist, to the "internationalist" *New York Herald Tribune*.[1] Hoover's friends on the council were apologetic at the failure to adopt his paragraph as part of their declaration. Robert Taft explained that the committee on foreign affairs had been "faced by a very difficult problem which superseded every other consideration"—the desire on Vandenberg's part to obtain unity on a statement that would assert "the continued sovereignty of the United States." Taft felt that Vandenberg's efforts to bring Austin and his group to agreement on this had used up all of his energy, otherwise he would have been happy to include Hoover's paragraph. Still, Taft was pleased that the declaration excluded "extreme isolation on one side and the Stassen international state on the other." There had been, he told Hoover, no discussion of a transition, or "cooling-off" period, but he had found no opposition to the idea, only an "unwillingness to go any further than the resolution adopted."[2]

In any case, the Mackinac statement was only a preliminary declaration. The committees would now work out a more detailed program for the Republican convention in 1944. Hoover was encouraged that his other proposals might be adopted by the GOP when Senator Warren Austin wrote him a few days after the Mackinac conference to ask for a copy of the Hoover-Gibson program "for my use in future meetings of the permanent committee on Foreign Policy."[3] The former president responded with a copy of *The Problems of Lasting Peace*, a condensation which had appeared in *Collier's*, a copy of his September 3 speech, and the paragraph he had suggested for the Mackinac declaration.[4]

Hoover also derived some satisfaction from the fact that his clipping service found more newspaper editorial support for his Minneapolis speech than for the Mackinac declaration.[5] Even the *Chicago Tribune* had reproduced the Minneapolis speech.[6] Another source of satisfaction, but also of some chagrin, was the increasing evidence that the Roosevelt administration was committing itself to the Hoover-Gibson program. The day after the Mackinac conference had failed to incorporate his "short formula" in its declaration, President Roosevelt had, in Hoover's view, "snapped it up" at his press conference.[7] It seemed that Hoover's ideas on postwar peacemaking were fast becoming policy for the Democratic administration in Washington, even while many of them were being ignored by his fellow Republicans.

Neither Roosevelt nor Welles would, of course, credit Hoover and Gibson with paternity of the idea of a transitional period before the peacemaking, although they apparently appreciated that Hoover was contributing to the acceptance of the idea by public opinion.[8] And shortly after the Mackinac conference, Hoover received, via John Callan O'Laughlin, evidence that his stance on postwar policy was receiving a sympathetic ear within the State Department when O'Laughlin transmitted to him a message from Secretary of State Hull, which he said was "substantially as follows":

> Please say to President Hoover that I deeply appreciate his approval of what I am attempting to do, and that I am grateful for his kind offer to help me. I think his proposal for a transitional period in connection with the peace is one of very great importance, and he may be sure that I will give it my most earnest consideration. . . . I think the contributions Mr. Hoover and Mr. Gibson made in their book were admirable. Unfortunately, in these times the crackpots rise to the surface, and it is gratifying that sane men are giving their thought to the important subject of the peace terms.[9]

On the eve of the Mackinac conference, Thomas Dewey had called for a postwar alliance between the United States and Great Britain. Despite Hoover's suggestion of something very similar to the British ambassador the previous year, he was now opposed to any such alliance. He was sorry, Hoover told Landon, that "Dewey got off wrong on this line" and did not consider it "helpful either to him or the country."[10] Similarly, he thought that Walter Lippmann's book, *U.S. Foreign Policy: Shield of the Republic*, was having "a great influence for evil," and he asked J. Reuben Clark if he would not write a response to it. He wrote Clark: "The whole book is built upon the premise that the British have been our friends and guardians over 120 years and consequently we ought to do various things with Great Britain. Lippmann belongs to a great clan developing in the United States who would like to see our re-entry into the British Empire."[11]

Throughout 1943 Hoover and other Republicans became increasingly concerned that the Roosevelt administration was deserting the noble ideals of the Atlantic Charter for a reliance on alliances and the balance of power in postwar international relations. They were especially alarmed at what this might mean for Soviet dominance of eastern Europe. For Hoover this feeling had begun at least as early as June of 1942, when it became clear to him that the Soviet Union aspired after the war to extend its boundaries to "include half of Poland, half of Finland, Estonia, Latvia, Lithuania and Bessarabia." The negotiations that month between Britain and the USSR had indicated a "return to the old ways of military alliances and balances of power. Those American wishful thinkers who believe that this is an abolished practice in the world should have a rude jolt."[12] One peace organization, the National Council for the Prevention of War, which had supported Hoover's efforts to get food relief into the occupied democracies, began to agitate in February 1943 for a negotiated peace, since it argued that "a war in Europe fought to the bitter end can result only in the triumph of communism" and the conquest of Japan "would merely extend communism throughout China and neighboring countries." The organization argued that five more years of war would also "leave our country denuded of much of its youth, impoverished and thoroughly regimented under either a Nazi or a communist type of dictatorship."[13] Hoover was certain that Stalin had no intention of giving up any of the territories he had acquired by force in 1939 and that Poland was doomed, while "all the New Deal and British columnists and radio commentators are now busy conditioning the American and British mind to the notion that this rape is no violation of the Atlantic Charter or the purpose for which Britain declared war."[14]

Landon, too, by mid–1943 had found evidence that Roosevelt was "shifting to a balance of power policy and is himself abandoning the Four Freedoms and the Atlantic Charter to that effect."[15] Even Walter Lippmann was predicting a postwar world that would be a continuous armed camp with the only peace based on power politics.[16] The realities of the emerging world situation were clearly at variance with the Atlantic Charter, which Americans had been led to believe embodied the ideals for which they were fighting. As one congressman wrote Landon late in August 1943, it seemed that the Soviet Union, with the largest army in Europe, would dictate the terms of the peace and had already indicated a policy "in relation to eastern Europe and Germany or central Europe, the antithesis of that announced by Great Britain and Roosevelt. This means either that eastern and central Europe are to be Bolshevized or a war."[17] Others, too, were quick to note "the new line—balance of power and alliances."[18] In late October Landon attacked the new direction he perceived in international relations in a speech and received warm approval from Hoover, who wrote: "I thought it was a good thing that you challenged Roosevelt on the question of military alliances. It brought that subject out where it ought to be."[19]

Hoover was somewhat encouraged, however, by the results of the foreign ministers' meeting in Moscow in November 1943. The declaration at the end of that conference indicated that Secretary of State Hull had adopted the Hoover-Gibson formula for peacemaking and had succeeded in obtaining the approval of the Soviet Union, as well.[20] O'Laughlin recalled the message that Hull had earlier sent to Hoover via him and added: "Obviously the proposal which you and Hugh made guided Mr. Hull in the highly successful negotiations he concluded at Moscow."[21] Taft agreed that there was "no doubt that Secretary Hull had followed your pioneering thought in the Moscow provisions dealing with the method of peace."[22] Landon said he was glad to see Hoover "getting the credit you deserve out of the Moscow Declaration."[23] Hoover agreed that the only significant difference between the Hoover-Gibson plan and that enunciated at Moscow was that "Mr. Hull himself elected the four powers to guide the world over the Transition Period instead of waiting to go through the form we suggested of having the United Nations elect them!"[24] To publisher Roy Howard he wrote that the Moscow declaration had followed the approach to peacemaking

> in exactly the methods that Hugh and I have been agitating during the last 18 months. You will find it in the following approach:
>
> In its peace phases the Declaration is notable by the absence of any reference to a general peace conference or any armistice or any long-term military alliances. Instead it envisages:
>
> a. The leadership in restoring order in the world by the *four leading powers*—their action to proceed by consultation and collaboration;
>
> b. A *transition* period after surrender and pending the establishment of some sort of world institution to preserve peace during which *the leading nations* will establish law and order.
>
> c. The creation of such a world institution "based on the principle of the *sovereign equality* . . . and open to membership by all nations."[25]

The *New York Times* agreed that while the State Department committee that drafted the Moscow Declaration "did not include Herbert Hoover or Wendell Willkie," the text did reveal "how directly both contributed to the great achievement, giving the Republican party the right to claim a large and important share." Willkie's advocacy of an international organization was well known, the *Times* observed, and it erroneously credited Willkie with being chiefly responsible for the GOP's support of American participation in postwar international cooperation. The *Times* added:

> The part played by Mr. Hoover, however, in association with Hugh Gibson is not so well realized, but the blueprint of Moscow bears, among others, the Hoover-Gibson signature, and in very large letters. . . . A comparison of their proposals with the Declaration of Moscow reveals a striking parallel. Except for the fact that the Four Powers assigned the transitional world leadership to themselves instead of having themselves elected by the United Nations, no important disparity is visible.[26]

From Secretary of State Hull, via O'Laughlin, came "keen satisfaction" at Hoover's approval of the Moscow Declaration. Hull did not think that there was any substantial difference between the declaration and the Hoover-Gibson plan even in the selection of the nations assigned to "guide the world over the transition period," since it was still possible that the United Nations might be called upon to select the four trustee powers. Hull told O'Laughlin that he had drawn on advice from all quarters before going to Moscow and had found Hoover's "proposal especially acceptable, and it guided him in the formulation of the paragraph of the agreement cited above." O'Laughlin concluded that Hull was obviously "grateful for the transition period idea."[27]

Early in December, Landon visited with Hull and subsequently issued a statement critical of the Moscow agreements. Concerned that Landon's statement had given "Willkie another chance to start a cry of isolation in the Republican Party, all of which the [*New York Herald*] *Tribune* and [*New York*] *Times* took up to further Willkie," Hoover quickly got "Alf on the carpet" and afterwards issued a statement that he thought stopped "them from getting anywhere." Landon, he argued, was not opposed to the Moscow declaration, but had "rightly objected to advance pledges of Republicans to commitments on peace settlements until these proposals are made known." This, Hoover maintained, was a position that "every sensible citizen, irrespective of party," should hold.[28] Hoover was especially upset with an inference by columnist Arthur Krock that he had encouraged Landon in his objections. On the contrary, Hoover told O'Laughlin, he had not talked with Landon beforehand, and he had moved quickly to correct the impression that the Kansan was opposed to the Moscow agreement. His own statement, Hoover claimed, had:

> served to stop division that would only have added confusion in the public mind on the whole foreign situation. The Governor went a considerable distance. He feels deeply that the New York press is trying to stop free discussion. The important thing is to keep the forty or fifty prominent Republican leaders on the constructive side. It is not so easy when criticism is so easy and most men so suspicious of the Administration.[29]

Hoover had found it necessary, he told O'Laughlin, "to stop outbreaks from eight different Republic Governors during the last four days. I have felt that some semblance of solidarity on the foreign relations must be maintained."[30] O'Laughlin expressed approval of Hoover's actions and promised to bring them to the attention of Secretary of State Hull.[31] The former president was clearly seeking to still GOP criticism of a foreign policy that he considered to be essentially of his own design.

Food questions, both foreign and domestic, also occupied a good deal of Hoover's attention during 1943. On the domestic front, he urged Congressman Joseph Martin to establish a Republican food committee of House members in order to monitor management by the Roosevelt administration of the nation's food supply. He suggested that the committee be given "a consumers' complexion" through the appointment of half its members from consumer areas and the other half from agricultural areas.[32] Martin appointed Congressman Thomas A. Jenkins as chairman of the committee, since his New York district was both urban and rural.[33] On April 7, Hoover wrote Senator Taft that the "food situation is getting worse and worse for having started down the line of their [the Roosevelt administration's] particular idea of ceiling prices at retail outlets," and the Roosevelt administration was now "plunging deeper and deeper into the mire." All such methods by other countries during World War I had failed, Hoover argued, and the U.S. Food Administration, under his leadership, had concentrated instead on "stimulating production, in smooth distribution, in preventing black markets and local famines, and in protecting both the farmer and consumer." Hoover enclosed a memorandum on the methods of the food administration during World War I in handling meats and wondered if it were not time for Taft to "make an effective speech on this subject and at an early date."[34]

In early June, Hoover attacked the administration's food policies in a speech to the Federated Farm Bureaus. He advised Jenkins that his speech would point out some aspects of the food situation that needed congressional investigation, and he was assured that all members of the committee would be listening.[35] In the speech, Hoover demanded reorganization of the administration's food program to clear up "this muddle of uncontrolled food prices, local famines, profiteering, black markets and stifled farm production." His suggestions included: (1) consolidation of all authority over food production and distribution under one responsible administrator, in the person of food administrator Chester Davis, who should also be Secretary of Agriculture and a member of the Office of Manpower Mobilization; (2) decentralization of the work under state, municipal, and county administrators; (3) increase in farm manpower over the prewar level and the planting of 40 to 50 million more acres in 1944 than in 1943; (4) shift of industrial production to provide large additions of farm machinery; (5) abolition of the present system of retail and wholesale price ceilings; (6) encouragement of farmers to appoint war committees to engage in collective bargaining on prices, with parities abandoned for the duration of the war; (7) fixed rationing to balance consumption with production; (8) establishment of war committees in the processing and distributing trades to keep the flow of food moving to the right places and enforcement of the dealer licensing system to stop black markets; (9) abandonment of subsidies to either farmers, traders, or consumers.[36]

The speech was interrupted by applause several times, and Edward A. O'Neal, president of the American Farm Bureau, told Hoover at the end of the speech: "Most of the farmers of the nation are for you and the program you have announced."[37] The speech received favorable comments from Republicans, but Roosevelt a few days later labeled Hoover's criticism of his administration's food management as absurd. Hoover wrote to his former secretary of agriculture, Arthur Hyde:

> The speech apparently got under the President's hide and he made an extraordinary statement about it just the other day. I can quite well believe that it all sounds "absurd" to him and especially when we in the last war had no black markets, no local famines, we were shipping more supplies to our allies than we are now, when prices rose less, and when even after the armistice we were able to ship 30 billion pounds to Europe, and now just the reverse of these things is happening under the machinery in motion in Washington.[38]

But Roosevelt had insisted on ignoring the tested methods and the experienced men of World War I. The food situation would remain in chaos through the war years, with serious consequences when a world famine loomed in the postwar years.

In September 1943 the Roosevelt administration retreated on one front where it had been under attack by Hoover and others. Arthur Krock reported in the *New York Times* that the U.S. army was planning to cut its projected strength from 8.2 million troops down to 7.7 million. The decision had come only after much insistence that such a cut was necessary to prevent disruption of the home front. Krock wrote: "Nevertheless, as in previous instances, those who pointed out obvious flaws in the domestic program met with stubborn opposition and were called hard names. Former President Hoover was one of these." The columnist recalled Hoover's testimony of February 8, 1943, before a Senate subcommittee, in which he had criticized the mobilization plan as taking needed workers away from the farms, mines, and petroleum fields. His testimony had been quickly challenged by Under Secretary of War Patterson, who claimed that due account had been taken of domestic needs. "Yet," Krock wrote, "in that very period this correspondent, who for two months had been making diligent inquiry among informed persons, reported that many of those 'charged with the heavy responsibility of winning the war' agreed with Mr. Hoover." The administration and its allies in Congress had, however, been "totally uncompromising." Vice-President Wallace and Senator Green of Rhode Island had then made a clumsy attempt to smear Hoover by seeking to prove, through a doctored document, that he had opposed a large American expeditionary force in 1917. And the "character and patriotism" of Hoover and other critics of the mobilization plan had then been attacked by Secretary of War Stimson. But now, Krock noted, the cut in the projected army size was proof that Hoover and the other critics had been correct.[39]

Late in September, Jenkins solicited Hoover's views on the situation and suggested that a member of the committee consult with him in New York.[40] Hoover welcomed such a visit. The problems, he wrote Jenkins, had not changed except that they were worse. He added:

> The folly of divided administrative responsibilities is more evident every day. The folly of subsidies of the farmers from the public's point of view is the same. Their political purpose just as evident. The driving of cattle away from feed lots, the use of a vastly unnecessary amount of skim milk for hogs, the famines in beef and dairy products are all samples of mismanagement.[41]

In agreement with Hoover's views, Jenkins told him that the committee planned to introduce legislation that would centralize food activities under one head and would seek immediate steps to increase food production in 1944. The committee also sought "that all price control and rationing be lifted on beef for a period, at least, by reason of the fact that western stockyards are crowded with beef cattle." The committee also planned to give ample publicity to the fallacious nature of the administration's food policies and their effects on consumers.[42] Jenkins was sure that the activities of the GOP food committee in publicizing the mismanagement of food production by the Roosevelt administration would at least have an effect on the 1944 election, even if it were unsuccessful in bringing about any changes.[43]

On the foreign front, there was little lessening of Hoover's desire to get food relief to the women, children, and unemployed men in the occupied areas of Europe. Late in March 1943 his hopes were momentarily raised by rumors that the Roosevelt administration had "at last made proposals to the British on our lines."[44] Nothing, however, came of the rumored initiative. The Gillette-Taft resolution, favoring food relief to the occupied democracies, was still pending in the Senate Foreign Relations Committee. Late in April, in response to an expression of support for the resolution by the Women's International League for Peace and Freedom, Senator Gillette asked Taft if the time had not come to push for passage of the resolution by scheduling hearings before a subcommittee and hearing testimony.[45] Taft wrote Hugh Gibson that he and Gillette had been trying to discover whether there was any prospect of getting the resolution through the Foreign Relations Committee. Much would depend on the testimony of the witnesses, and Taft asked Gibson if he could supply two or three who could substantiate the statements and the memoranda that had been furnished by the National Committee on Food for the Small Democracies in support of the resolution.[46] Gibson suggested several potential witnesses, particularly Hoover.[47] Early in May, Gillette agreed to ask Senator Connally, chairman of the Foreign Relations Committee, to appoint a subcommittee to hold hearings on Senate Resolution 100, the Gillette-Taft bill, which called for the immediate extension of food relief to the occupied countries in Europe where such need existed.[48] Expressions of support for the resolution were coming from a number of directions, including organizations, congressmen, and state legislatures.[49]

Hoover also continued to be interested in the United Nations Relief and Rehabilitation Agency and postwar relief plans. Late in June he wrote Herbert Lehman suggesting that it would "be desirable in the United Nations agreement for relief that provision should be made which will prevent the consumer nations (which are a majority) from determining the prices of food to the American farmers in supplying nations. The experience after the last war indicates the urgent need for such protection."[50] Hoover also argued in favor of selling food on credit, as opposed to making it an outright gift, since the use of loans stimulated efforts at productivity and conservation in the recipient countries and encouraged an early return "to a commercial basis of living" there.[51]

Hearings began on the Gillette-Taft resolution in November.[52] Hoover had received intimations that President Roosevelt was, himself, interested in getting food relief to the occupied democracies and hoped sufficient sentiment might be developed in the United States to force his hand in taking up the issue with Churchill, who remained adamantly opposed.[53] But the hearings them-

selves were a disappointment and brought protests from many who supported
the food relief proposal. From Nevin Sayre, secretary of the Fellowship of
Reconciliation, came the demand that the hearings last more than the mere
two days that had been scheduled, for Sayre argued:

> They must give opportunity for public expression to others besides
> Mr. Hoover and the Quakers. Everyone knows of their valiant fight
> since 1940 to get permission to send milk, vitamins etc. through the
> American–Anglo blockade. What Congress and the country need to
> hear is the expression in favor of feeding by leading Democrats,
> labor and farm groups, non-Quaker churches, peace organizations,
> etc.[54]

Socialist Norman Thomas, chairman of the executive committee of the Post-
War World Council, similarly wrote the chairman of the subcommittee that he
considered it "unfortunate that your subcommittee is so greatly curtailing
hearings on the Gillette-Taft resolution." Such a curtailment, he argued, made
the resolution look "too much like an exclusive Hoover" proposal and greatly
reduced "the give and take of opinion between the country and your subcommittee."[55] It was obvious that Hoover was not alone in the fight and that a
profound spirit of humanity still existed in many Americans even in the midst
of the barbarism of war. The resolution was finally adopted by the Senate on
February 15, 1944, but had no apparent effect on either the Churchill government or the Roosevelt administration. Still, as Hoover remarked in his account
of the relief effort, "devoted men were demonstrating that compassion was not
dead in America."[56] But that compassion counted for little since it was not
shared by Roosevelt.

Meanwhile, Hoover continued to monitor the political situation. At the
time of the Mackinac conference, the GOP national committeeman from
Minnesota told him that after a two and a half hour session with Willkie he
had concluded that the 1940 nominee was finally becoming more orthodox in
his Republicanism and more willing to listen to those in the party with greater
experience.[57] This was certainly a change, if true, from Willkie's earlier
attitude, but Hoover responded: "The gentleman you mention could never be
elected despite his sudden getting of religion."[58] Hoover was sure that the
Mackinac conference had strengthened the party by demonstrating to the
country that it possessed "leadership and cohesion." He counseled Bricker that
the Republicans in 1944 should strive for the support of the Jeffersonian wing
of the Democratic party, but should "not try for the New Dealers whom we
can never get."[59]

Hoover was also working closely with Dewey, writing to the New York
governor in mid-October, 1943, to ask that he telephone Governor Earl War-

ren to suggest to him the importance of choosing and leading the GOP delegation from California to the 1944 convention. He did not, Hoover told Dewey, "know anyone who could put this to him as effectively as you could."[60] Dewey agreed to do so.[61] Hoover's intention clearly was to separate Warren from Willkie. Later in the month Hoover phoned Dewey urging him to waste no time in taking the matter up with Warren. In a letter, which Hoover dictated to Dewey before deciding to phone him instead, Hoover expressed his concern that Willkie's claim of having the support of the California delegation must be quickly countered since such claims were "making an impression in other areas."[62]

The new year of 1944 began on a tragic note for Herbert Hoover. On the evening of January 7, as he prepared to depart for a dinner with Edgar Rickard and Hugh Gibson, the former president found his beloved wife Lou Henry collapsed on the floor of her dressing room. The Waldorf-Astoria Hotel house doctor pronounced her dead.[63] Friends hurried to Hoover's side to help him through the difficult days that followed. A few days later he left for California to recover from the tragedy. But for a man so deeply involved in so many issues of importance, there was little time to be spared away from public life, no matter how deep the sorrow.

One issue that arose early in 1944 was a growing feeling among Republicans that the formation of the contemplated international organization should not be delayed after the end of the war.[64] Hoover's position continued to be that the timing for its formation should depend on world conditions and could not be specified in advance. As he wrote to David Lawrence in November 1943, Hoover believed "we must this time establish fundamental order before we load such an institution with an impossible task . . . for I believe that is what destroyed the ultimate effectiveness of the League—not because it was incorporated in the Treaty of Versailles, but because the world did not first establish order before giving it that job."[65] But growing suspicion of Soviet intentions led others to advocate an early establishment of the postwar peacekeeping organization. Hoover's former under secretary of state, William R. Castle, favored a six-month limit on the transition period since he had concluded that Secretary of State Hull was being duped by the Soviets, while Stalin had "done nothing to show that he intended to live up to whatever promises he may have made in Moscow."[66] Under such circumstances, the prospect of offering the Soviet Union a role as one of the peacekeeping "trustees" under a prolonged transition period was singularly unappealing. There was, however, no apparent opposition to maintaining a "transition period" before concluding the actual treaties of peace with the defeated enemies, such as Hoover and Gibson had suggested.

Hoover's own suspicions of the Soviet Union were of long standing, but they did not distract him from pursuing the Hoover-Gibson formula for peacemaking. The revelations of Soviet expansionist designs were only serving to bring home to other Americans what he had warned them of all along. When the Supreme Soviet announced that it was considering the grant of greater autonomy to the Soviet Union's member republics, Hoover noted that the Baltic states of Latvia, Lithuania, and Estonia were included on the list. The American people, he told O'Laughlin, had not yet "grasped the import of Stalin's sixteen republic declaration," but it meant the "Communistic enslavement of five—and possibly nine—formerly independent nations." The United States could not challenge the Soviet action because the USSR was needed as an ally, yet the "declaration has changed the whole course of international relations; it has destroyed the Atlantic Charter completely; it has abolished the whole idealistic concept of the American purpose in this war." The world was now left with "three great centers of power committed to sheer Imperialism under new names and methods."[67] James Reston, in Moscow, agreed. He wrote in the *New York Times*:

> Soviet Russia . . . has not accepted the principles that spheres of influence should be abandoned and that a general European settlement is to be arranged with each power having an equal say in the settlement of every area on the Continent. There is, in fact, a growing feeling that Russia, while willing to cooperate with the United States and Britain in other parts of the world, is demanding the right to establish a Russian sphere of influence to the east of the line running from Trieste to Prague and Stettin and that east of that line she is going to insist upon the creation of "friendly" governments that would form a sort of cordon sanitaire in reverse, a chain of states, not to protect western Europe from Russia but to protect Russia from the possibility of any coalition that might be formed in western Europe.

In summary, Reston wrote, the consensus among Western diplomats in Moscow was that the Soviet Union was "laying the groundwork for an even greater empire than she now has and is pointing the way, not to a system of the present collective security but toward a world divided" into four great spheres of influence.[68] Stalin had apparently not read Willkie's *One World*.

Even this exhibition of the Soviet Union's long-term intentions did not, however, lead Hoover to abandon hope that a lasting peace could be attained in the postwar world. He wrote Gibson in mid-February 1944:

> Peace can be made only by collaboration and cooperation of these great centers of power. It will take time and will require a period of transition during which the world can be organized for a more

universal participation in the maintenance of peace. We have been cooperating and collaborating in the conduct of war, there is no reason why we should not cooperate and collaborate from war to peace—the ultimate aim of which must be to establish some world institution for the maintenance of peace.[69]

As 1944 began, Republicans looked ahead with some optimism to the presidential election and to the convention at which they would pick their nominee. Of the three men regarded as leaders of the party, only one was actively pursuing the nomination—Wendell Willkie, the 1940 standard-bearer. Neither Hoover nor Landon were candidates, but both were determined that Willkie should not again receive the nomination. Landon strongly supported New York governor Thomas Dewey for the nomination, while Hoover's choice seems to have been Governor John Bricker of Ohio, although he also maintained close relations with Dewey. Both Landon and Hoover, however, seemed less committed to particular candidates than to denying the nomination to Willkie. In mid-March Hoover viewed the political situation as "developing in the way Republicans generally anticipated." He found grounds for optimism in the fact that Willkie had won only six of New Hampshire's eleven convention delegates, although he "had twice stumped that state, had a large organization there and had no opposition." He believed that if the convention "took place tomorrow . . . Dewey would be elected," but he recognized that much could happen in the next few months and concluded that "Bricker ought to be in a substantial position. In any event, Bricker ought to take a large part in national public affairs as he is a very useful man even if he were not nominated for the Presidency at this time."[70]

Later in the month Dewey dined with Hoover, and the two men discussed the political situation. Hoover gathered from their conversation that Dewey preferred to be drafted by the Republican convention, but, he said, "I got the impression that he was going to see that the draft machinery was in high gear." Dewey sought advice on what his tactics should be before the convention and afterward. He obviously took it for granted that he would be the nominee, probably on the first ballot, and he wanted Earl Warren for his running mate. Hoover found that John Foster Dulles had drafted a speech for Dewey on the subject of foreign relations to be given the next month. He recorded in his memorandum of the conversation:

> I told him that John Foster Dulles was filled with a lot of fuzzy ideas; that he was living in a dream-land which had been completely knocked into a cocked hat by Joe Stalin; that the outlook for the world had been changed; that there would be nothing in the nature of a "world government" and that there would be no surrendering of

sovereignty; that irrespective of what might be the attitude of the United States, neither Russia nor Britain would accept any such fuzzy ideas.

Hoover told the governor that if he were elected president "he would have to create a special bureau of 600 lawyers and 2000 detectives to expose at least one case per day of the corruption of the present regime; that this would be the only method of preventing the New Dealers from undermining him during the next four years and thus defeat him for a second term." Dewey responded that Hoover was wrong, that it would take "6,000 lawyers and 20,000 detectives and some new jails." Hoover suggested General Douglas MacArthur as a possible vice-presidential nominee, but found that Dewey did not take to the idea.[71] In his memorandum of their discussion, Hoover wrote:

> I came out of the long discussion with confirmation of my high esteem for Dewey's intellectual capacities, his energy, and his political ability, but in some way I have a reservation as to his character. Nevertheless, at the moment, he seems to be the inevitable candidate, and the spiritual winds that blow through the White House may strengthen any of the deficiencies on the character side. He has fewer of the human qualities than Bricker has. Whatever humanitarism [sic] he has is coldly calculated in the terms of votes.

But Hoover found that some of Dewey's negative qualities seemed to have softened since 1940, and he believed the New Yorker to be a better candidate now than he would have been four years earlier. "The great contrast between Bricker and Dewey as candidates," Hoover wrote, "can be seen in the political management Dewey has already set up around himself whereas Bricker has none of importance."[72]

Through March and April of 1944 Hoover continued to supply Bricker with ideas to incorporate into his speeches.[73] He found it a curious situation that the dominant mood of the GOP convention would be against a candidate, rather than for a candidate or candidates, since he felt, he told Landon, that "probably 600 delegates or more are going there pledged to anti-Willkie."[74] Most observers agreed with the Hoover-Landon assessment that Dewey would definitely be the party's nominee, and many felt that he would stand a good chance of election in November. The New Yorker's prospects seemed enhanced all the more when Willkie withdrew from the race in early April after a disappointing primary showing.[75] Hoover wrote Richard Lloyd Jones that he would now have more time to devote to nonpolitical matters since "Mr. Willkie has been retired as a national danger."[76]

If Dewey was to be the GOP nominee, Hoover considered it all the more important to checkmate some of Dulles' influence on the New Yorker's foreign policy. He was concerned that what he regarded as excessive idealism in Dulles should not shape Dewey's thinking. Dewey had scheduled a speech on foreign affairs for April 27, and on April 5 Hoover wrote him: "Certain things have come up which I think are of importance." He asked for fifteen minutes of Dewey's time.[77] On April 10 Hoover wrote Dewey again, this time in regards to Dewey's proposed speech. Perhaps recalling Dewey's advocacy seven months earlier of a U.S.–British alliance after the war, Hoover cautioned against a speech on foreign policy, noting that Dewey was already a signatory to the Mackinac declaration in favor of American participation in an international organization, that the international situation was confused, and that the Roosevelt administration still had not produced a definite postwar program of its own to criticize. He told Dewey that it was "desirable that you should come to the American people in the campaign with new and not worn garments."[78]

However, on April 25, Governor Bricker spoke before the Ohio Society of New York City and called for American participation "in a cooperative organization of sovereign nations." Hoover's influence on the Ohioan was obvious.[79] If Bricker was to speak on foreign policy, there was certainly nothing to bar Dewey from doing so too, and despite Hoover's advice to the contrary he delivered his speech on April 27. Hoover concluded that his doubts had been unfounded. He wrote Dewey that his "judgment was better as to the timing of that speech than mine." Had he seen it in advance, Hoover said, he "certainly would have been enthusiastic over it as it steered between the rocks about which I have been particularly fearful at this time. I do not pretend that you are adopting my ideas, but the central theme of it has been my steady agitation for the last two years and therefore I could not help but approve."[80]

Whether or not Hoover was being completely honest in his praise is not entirely clear. Others certainly did not think highly of the speech. Taft had no enthusiasm for the speech and was concerned that Dewey, if elected, would appoint Dulles as secretary of state.[81] Robert E. Wood wrote Vandenberg:

> If Dewey in his New York speech had had the sense to adhere strictly to the Mackinac declaration, which any sensible nationalist or, for that matter, any sensible internationalist can subscribe to, he would be on safe ground, but when he made the speech he did on foreign policy, which was primarily intended for New York City listeners, it looks to me as if he is in the hands of the very same group that supported Willkie, and it indicates that he will lose out in the middle west. Without the middle west he cannot be elected.[82]

Unless Dewey stood on the Mackinac declaration, Wood added, "I will not trust his foreign policy any more than I do F.D.R.'s."[83] Some Republicans called upon Hoover to attempt to influence Dewey away from the Willkieite variety of "internationalism," which Dewey had begun to expound.[84] Hoover refused to do so.[85]

On May 25, 1944, Hoover took himself out of the candidate selection process by issuing a statement to the press:

> Until now I have ignored the continuous efforts by ill-informed people to link my name with various possible nominees for President, including Governor Bricker, Governor Dewey, and General MacArthur. I am taking and expect to take no part in the selection of the Republican nominee. The people and their duly elected delegates will take care of that themselves.[86]

According to the diary of Edgar Rickard, Hoover issued the statement at the request of Governor Dewey, lest the Democrats attempt to smear the New Yorker in the campaign by linking him with Hoover. From the statement, Rickard concluded that the 1944 campaign would follow the trend of those in 1936 and 1940, when the GOP candidates had sought to avoid, as much as possible, any association with the former president.[87] Yet, while he sought no public identification with Hoover, Dewey continued to seek Hoover's advice, and especially Hoover's assistance in getting California governor Earl Warren to join the ticket as vice-presidential nominee.[88] Meanwhile, wearied by this general attitude, Hoover decided to write into his convention speech a farewell to public life, only to change his mind a few weeks later.[89]

The former president addressed the Republican convention on June 27 and did not include any statement about withdrawing from political life. In his speech, Hoover pointed out:

> At each of the great rallies of our party in 1936, in 1940 and today in 1944 I have been called to speak upon the encroachments and dangers to freedom in our country. Each time I knew before I spoke that our people would not believe that the impairment of freedom could happen here. Yet each subsequent four years has shown those warnings to have been too reserved, too cautious. The reason why these warnings have been accurate is simple. From the beginning the New Deal in a milder form has followed the tactics of European revolutions which have gone before. The direction being set, the destination is not difficult to foresee.

He reviewed the encroachment upon American liberties under the New Deal and added: "With the blessings of the Attorney General, the Communists and the fellow travelers are spending vast sums to re-elect this [Roosevelt's] regime. Would they spend their money to support the freedom of men?" He questioned the likelihood that the New Dealers would restore the liberties usurped under the excuse of the wartime emergency. "Can a regime which forged 'shackles on the liberties of the people' in peacetime be trusted to return freedom to the people from the shackles of war?" Hoover thought not. On the contrary, he asserted:

> Already the New Dealers have planned a large number of Trojan horses labeled "liberalism" and "freedom" stuffed with a mixture of totalitarian economics and doubtful statistics. The easiest task of government is to suppress individuals, subject them to bureaucracy and subsidize them to lean on governments—or a political party. If a government has enough power, it can always do that. The hard task of government and the really liberal task, is to build self-reliance, stimulate initiative, and thereby create men and women of energy, of dignity and of independence. That is the motive power of America.

The decision between these two philosophies of government must be made now, Hoover declared, for the postwar peace plans had to be made now. "We cannot be without a peace program as we were without a preparedness program. We owe it to our fighting men that they find no delays in productive jobs."[90]

Turning to foreign policy, Hoover told the Republicans: "It is obvious from the rise of nationalism that ideas of world super-government, no matter how idealistic, are already dead from these cold blasts of realism. Peace must be based upon cooperation between independent sovereign nations." He reiterated his thesis of three great centers of power after the war, with possibly China constituting a fourth, and eventually France becoming yet another center. He advocated a world organization, but one split into three divisions— Europe, Asia, and the western hemisphere—with each division possessing primary responsibility for peace in its area. This was especially important for Europe, "where the dangers of world wars come from." He argued again for a long transition period in which to lay the foundations for a stable peace. "Unless these foundations are surely laid, any temple dedicated to preserving peace will be built upon sand. That was the disaster of the League of Nations. A good league has never cured a bad peace."[91]

Hoover lashed out at the direction of Roosevelt's foreign policies as it had developed, most notably at Tehran. "So far as these published descriptions go of this method [of Roosevelt's diplomacy] it is power politics and balance-of-power diplomacy. That is not the diplomacy of freedom and worse still, apparently the United States is to furnish the balance between Britain and Russia." In that case, the United States must certainly end up by gaining the enmity of both. "The basis of lasting peace for America must be friendship of nations not brokerage of power politics." Hoover suggested that, in the future, Roosevelt remain at home, rather than diminish his influence and prestige by participation in summit conferences. He ended his speech by pointing out: "The convention is handing the leadership of the Republican party to a new generation," which would soon be swelled in numbers by millions of returned servicemen.[92] This was as close as Hoover came to a farewell.

The foreign policy platform adopted at the convention called for the attainment of postwar peace and security "through organized international cooperation and not by joining a world state." It favored "responsible participation by the United States in postwar cooperative organization among sovereign nations to prevent military aggession and to attain permanent peace with organized justice in a free world," but it gave no timetable for the creation of such an organization. The policy did give a hint of support for the Hoover-Gibson advocacy of a transition period and enforcement of the peace by "trustees," by pledging that until the international organization was formed "to prevent or repel military aggression" the United States would collaborate "with the United Nations to assure those ultimate objectives."[93] Wendell Willkie expressed disappointment with the foreign policy plank adopted by the convention.[94] As the Republican delegates met in the convention, President Roosevelt had at last enunciated his own general proposals concerning postwar policy, and these proposals were similar to those adopted by the GOP convention. Journalist Anne O'Hare McCormick examined Hoover's influence on both the Republican platform and Roosevelt's proposals and concluded: "In a way it may be said to be his program, for he [Hoover] was the first to outline the procedure and set the limits of American participation that are now embodied in both proposals."[95]

Hoover's speech was well received by the convention, and the former president was pleased. As expected, the convention nominated Dewey to head the Republican ticket. Earl Warren refused to accept the vice-presidential spot, and Hoover claimed credit for obtaining Bricker's consent to take this nomination, although his actual contribution may have been less than he claimed.[96] In sum, Hoover, the elder statesman of the party, expressed satisfaction with the results of the convention. He told the press that he approved of the ticket but did not expect to take an active part in the campaign. He would, however, do whatever was asked of him. He was, he told reporters, busy writing a book.[97] He was also approaching his seventieth birthday. To one correspondent he wrote: "It has been a long road to get the party back on the track again; —the futility of Landon; the extraordinary machinations of Willkie; the sudden dropping out of Warren and the quick action necessary to complete the ticket; but finally we have at last a fighting team and I think we can win."[98] To Bricker he wrote: "Now that the smoke has cleared away, the nobility and sportsmanship of your decision stand out even more vividly everywhere in the country. You have immeasurably strengthened the ticket and confidence in winning."[99]

In his letter to Bricker and in one to Dewey, Hoover included a memorandum that repeated a recommendation he had earlier discussed with both men. That recommendation related to a coalition between conservative Democrats and Republicans in the 1944 election. Hoover suggested that ten to twenty "Democratic leaders of first rank" and a similar number of leading Republicans should announce that "the thirty principal offices of Cabinet and War Agencies would be appointed equally from the two sides but no specific position or appointments" would be announced. He felt that such a proposal for a coalition government would attract the votes of numerous anti–New Deal Democrats, but he cautioned against doing it unless the Democratic leaders who joined in the manifesto were truly "first rank" (including senators, former cabinet members, ambassadors, and governors).[100] Dewey responded that Hoover's proposal contained "fascinating possibilities." He noted, however, that Roosevelt was creating some drama over his choice of a vice-presidential nominee, "which is a masterful political move," and he thought that "if it should result in a good Democrat it would greatly temper the enthusiasm of the rebels of the South." He thought it best, therefore, to await the outcome of the Democratic convention.[101] At the convention, Roosevelt dropped Henry A. Wallace for Harry S. Truman of Missouri, thus placating many of those who might have deserted the Democratic ticket for such a coalition proposal.

Hoover did not expect to have any role in the 1944 campaign. Anticipating neglect, he wrote John Hamilton that he believed he had, in his convention speech, "laid the foundation for proper absence from the campaign unless pressed by the powers that be to help—which I do not anticipate."[102] When the new chairman of the GOP national committee, Herbert Brownell, wrote to him to outline the plans for the campaign, there was no mention of a role for Hoover.[103] When the press raised the question of Hoover's support for Dewey's election at an interview in Spokane, Washington, Dewey responded that he had not seen the former president since the convention and had no plans to see him again.[104] It was apparent that Hoover was to be ignored by the candidates in the campaign. Early in September he wrote to Ruth Hanna McCormick Simms:

> It having been plainly indicated that I was a liability, I naturally (like you) took to the mountains. I have no such serious duties as

> looking after cows, but have given great attention to the fish. Of
> course, every new candidate has to make his own campaign and the
> problems, of course, are new and the experience of other campaigns
> never seems very real. I have great confidence in the political abili-
> ties of both Dewey and Brownell.[105]

Privately, however, Hoover was annoyed with Dewey's neglect of him.[106]
And he was growing increasingly disenchanted by Dewey's willingness to
commend some aspects of the New Deal as Willkie had done.[107]

But Hoover's view of the New Yorker waxed and waned depending upon
the particular speech Dewey made.[108] Overall, he still viewed Dewey's election as vital so that "the country will stop this stampede to the left and turn in
some degree toward the right."[109] And if the United States became more
conservative, it could lead the rest of the world in a conservative direction.[110]
Hoover was convinced that a Republican administration in the White House
offered the only hope for checking the spread of Soviet influence throughout
continental Europe.[111] As he wrote one correspondent:

> ... the Stalin form of Communism seems certain for Poland, Es-
> tonia, Latvia, Lithuania, Jugo-Slavia, Bulgaria and Roumania. De
> Gaulle looks like the introducer of it to France, and if the "Free
> Germany Committee" in Moscow is installed in Berlin, it probably
> will pervade there also. The Communist sections of China seem to
> be a base for its extension there. Altogether these left-wing ideas are
> sweeping the world. The only stop I see is to win this election in the
> United States.[112]

Early in October 1944, Wendell Willkie died. Hoover's statement to the
press concealed the antagonism he had felt toward the man:

> The death of Mr. Willkie deprives the nation of a great and deeply
> patriotic citizen. His colorful personality, his indomitable energy,
> and his active mind have stirred national consideration and under-
> standing of the difficult problems of our time. His passing will be a
> great loss in finding their solution.[113]

Willkie's funeral brought together the leading figures of both political parties
in a rare gathering. Dewey, who shared the same pew with Hoover, avoided
speaking to the former president, while, by contrast, Eleanor Roosevelt was
very friendly toward him.[114] Despite his persistent snub of Hoover, however,
Dewey was defeated in the presidential election the following month, although
Roosevelt's vote was below that of 1940. For Hoover, Dewey's defeat was only

further proof of the folly of attempting to straddle on the New Deal and of refusing to tackle the Democrats head-on in defense of pre–New Deal Republicanism. The only consolation for Republicans from the election, in Hoover's view, was that the reduction in Roosevelt's vote might restrain him in his policies.[115]

With the Democrats entrenched in the White House for four more years, it would be necessary, Hoover told William Castle, "to start pushing the stone uphill again."[116] To another friend Hoover confided that he was "considerably in the dumps; there is no island of safety in the world; we shall edge further into a collectivist system in this next four years. Perhaps there is some consolation in the fact that the New Deal will have to take the bumps." He was now, more than ever, convinced that the salvation of the nation would require "a coalition of the conservative forces."[117]

While John Callan O'Laughlin furnished Hoover with information concerning the administration's foreign policies and war strategy, which the publisher gained from his many contacts in Washington, the former president was also receiving unofficial briefings from the War Department.[118] He knew, at least as early as December 1944, of the race between the United States and Germany to develop a uranium bomb. When the State Department rebuked the British for interfering in the governments of Italy and Greece, Hoover praised the British for seeking to check the growth of communist influence in Europe.[119] He continued to decry Roosevelt's willingness to meddle in "European power politics," since it meant only "disaster for Europe."[120] Late in January, as Roosevelt left for the historic Yalta Conference with Stalin and Churchill, Hoover wrote Ray Lyman Wilbur that Roosevelt "will come back with a lot of Uncle Joe's [Stalin's] promises which will fade out as fast as the so-called Moscow Declaration faded. At the moment it is useless to say anything without being justifiably accused of creating difficulties, so I am keeping still."[121]

When the first public details of the Yalta agreement were released, Hoover issued a press statement in which he expressed the belief that "it comprises a strong foundation on which to rebuild the world. If the agreements, promises, and ideals which are expressed shall be carried out, it will open a great hope to the world."[122] Privately, however, Hoover had little expectation that they would be carried out, but he had worded his press statement in order to be, he explained, in a "more strategic position when I have to challenge their failure."[123] Still, his statement aroused negative comment from his friends. William Castle wrote: "I have had any number of people ask me how you happened to make the statement about the Crimea Conference which the papers here quoted, something along the line of preparing the way for a better world." Among those who had expressed surprise was the Polish ambassador. "People come and ask me every day about it," Castle wrote, "and I don't want to try to interpret what you intended to say, especially as I have nothing to go on except the one or two sentences published here." He asked Hoover for guidance on what line he should take when questioned. Castle's own view was that if "there ever was a time when Roosevelt simply ate out of the hands of Stalin it was this last conference." He found the terms for the distribution of territory "just about as contrary to the principles of the so-called Atlantic Charter as anything could be."[124]

Alf Landon also wrote Hoover to ask him his opinion of the Yalta declaration, and the former president replied on February 18. He also sent a copy of his letter to Landon on to William Castle. Hoover explained that the American people yearned for peace. The Roosevelt administration was attempting to put together the machinery for peace in the postwar world. That machinery, he admitted, had "many faults and weaknesses that are dangerous both as to peace and to our country," but to correct them required that they be amended, and "blind and futile opposition" was not the answer. He told Landon:

> The Atlantic Charter, the Moscow pact, Dumbarton Oaks, the Yalta declaration, etc. all reiterate certain ideals and principles which, if carried out in good faith, comprise a foundation for such an organization. The odds are that they will not be carried out in good faith. And in that case these promises come to nothing. But at least we can hold up the ideals and promises as a basis of real peace and hold them to carrying them out. . . . To take the attitude of withdrawing from the whole mess at this time would not get support from the American people and it would be only a futile gesture to urge it. . . . Put another way, I am for helping design an experiment. If it has the elements of success, to support it; if it is hopeless, then to damn it. And I want to see it succeed.[125]

In his letter to Castle, Hoover also wrote that it was important for the three centers of power to cooperate until Germany was defeated. As for Poland, "is there any hope," he asked, "that voices of protest *now* will alter the result? Is not the only hope to insist that Dumbarton Oaks be made a workable place where the nations still held in subjection may have a court of appeal?"[126] Castle replied that he could not quarrel with anything Hoover had said in the letter to Landon because "it is all true." His only reservation had to do with Hoover's press statement, which Castle wished had included a statement saying: "Although much which has been done seems to be contrary to the terms of the Atlantic Charter, and even to the plan of Dumbarton Oaks, I nevertheless feel that if we can have the organization envisaged by the conferees in the Crimea, such unfairness as may have crept into their immediate decisions may be corrected, eventually, by the organization itself."[127] From

Hoover's explanation for his statement, and Castle's interpretation of it, it is clear that the former president had abandoned one of the principles he had advocated so strongly in his speeches and writings since before Pearl Harbor—the insistence that no international organization could correct, or should be based upon, a bad peace. Increasingly, as the wartime agreements proceeded at variance with the principles of the Atlantic Charter and with what Hoover regarded as right, he was forced to fall back upon the international organization for their correction, even as Wilson had been forced to do at Versailles. America's "second crusade" was following the course of the first.

On April 12, 1945, President Franklin Delano Roosevelt died. Hoover issued a statement to the press that read:

> The nation sorrows at the passing of its President. Whatever differences there may have been, they end in the regrets of death. It is fortunate that in this great crisis of war our Armies and Navies are under such magnificent leadership that we shall not hesitate. The new President will have the backing of the country. While we mourn Mr. Roosevelt's death, we shall march forward.[128]

The man who had sought constantly to discredit Hoover, who had denied to him even the minimum of courtesies expected of a president to a former occupant of the White House, and who had ignored his abilities in peace and in war, was gone from the scene, replaced by Harry S. Truman.

Perhaps as an indication of the new atmosphere in Washington after Roosevelt's death, Hoover was now extended an invitation from Secretary of State Edward Stettinius, Jr., to accept a box in the San Francisco opera house for the opening session of the conference on international organization, set for April 25.[129] Such an invitation would have been highly unlikely had Roosevelt continued to occupy the White House, despite Hoover's contribution to American foreign policy during the war years. Cautioned by years of deceit and neglect and abuse from Washington, however, Hoover suspected that the invitation was either "evidence of offensive ineptitude—or a foundation for smearing."[130] He declined the invitation, noting in his reply that he was not in Palo Alto (where the telegram was sent), but in New York City.[131]

Only a few hours before Roosevelt died, Hoover had told Felix Morley that he hoped the president "would live long enough to reap where he had sown."[132] Now he thought that Truman would be a change for the better.[133] He approved of the new president's initial speech to Congress.[134] Intrigued by the man from Missouri, Hoover wrote Truman's fellow Missourian, Arthur Hyde, to ask: "What do you know about Truman?"[135] Hyde responded that where firsthand knowledge was concerned, "the honest answer is nothing." However, Hyde entertained "a considerable hope for his administration" and believed that Truman's background would tend to a more conservative regime than that of Roosevelt.[136] Hopeful, Hoover wrote to his sister: "Now that there has been a change in Washington, I may be on the move often." But he added: "Time moves on and I can feel 71 in my bones, especially when I go fishing."[137] Little could the former president anticipate how much "on the move" he would be under the new president.

Certainly in April of 1945, however, Hoover could feel that a corner had been turned in his life. The war seemed fast approaching an end. He had outlived his longtime antagonist in the White House and there was the prospect that despite the Republican loss in 1944, the new president might turn the nation away from the leftward drift it had taken under Roosevelt and rally the free world against Soviet expansionist aims. And Hoover could sense, in other ways, a conservative revival in the United States. Since 1944 Hoover and Landon had supported Frank G. Hanighen's new conservative journal, *Human Events*.[138] Hoover also interested himself in an attempt to bring out another conservative journal to compete with such liberal and left-of-liberal journals as the *New Republic*, *Nation*, and *New Masses* in the universities and other intellectual centers.[139]

On April 17, 1945, Hoover delivered a speech in Philadelphia that was timed to present his views on the planned international organization before the San Francisco conference took up its work.[140] Three weeks earlier, between March 25 and 28, he had published four articles outlining his suggested additions to the Dumbarton Oaks plan for a United Nations organization. In those articles, he made seven suggestions that he believed would "greatly strengthen this chart of peace." These suggestions were:

> First: Positive standards of the political rights of men and nations and the establishment of a World Committee to promote these political rights. This Committee to rank with the Economic and Social Committees already proposed in the Dumbarton Oaks plan.
> Second: Provision for revision of onerous treaties between nations at, say, ten year intervals, in order to assure that the peace settlements are dynamic and not static.
> Third: Regional organization of the organization to preserve peace into [sic] three areas, Asia, Europe and the Western Hemisphere; the regional organizations to be subject of course to the Security Council.
> Fourth: Absolute disarmament of the enemy powers.
> Fifth: Immediate relative disarmament of the United Nations and the establishment of maximum limit of armies, navies and air power among them.
> Sixth: While it is probably not a part of the charter itself, when it is adopted by the Congress the authority to use force should not be

given the American delegate on the Security Council, but that power should be delegated to the President of the United States with the provision that he be bound by the majority of the joint Foreign Relations Committees of the Senate and the House as to whether a vote to employ American force shall be submitted to the Congress as a whole.

Seventh: Take enough time in formulating the Charter of Peace to do it right.[141]

In his Philadelphia speech, Hoover told his listeners that these suggestions had also been "put forward by the representatives of the peace committees of the three great religious groups, the Protestants, the Catholics and the Jews." Now he had two more suggestions to add to his original seven: "There should be a control of military alliances. There should be a definition of aggression." He also felt that Senator Arthur Vandenberg's suggestion that the General Assembly be given "freedom of initiative" should be adopted. Hoover told his listeners:

> The purpose of these additions is: First, to surround the mechanistic bones of the Charter with moral and spiritual forces. Second, to create those standards of conduct which should be the base of decision by the Security Council. Third, to reach into the causes of war much more deeply than just the settling of quarrels and the curbing of gangsters. And fourth, to simplify the work of the organization.

He regarded the "primary weakness of the Holy Alliance, the League of Nations and Dumbarton Oaks proposals" to be "the failure to face the facts as to the real causes of war." He reiterated for his listeners the points, in brief, that he and Gibson had made in *The Problems of Lasting Peace* and in subsequent changes and additions to their original book. Another weakness of the League of Nations had been "its failure to incorporate a bill of rights and standards of conduct of nations and men." Such a bill of rights should be incorporated in the new charter. The league had also made no "adequate provision to ease strains by orderly change in agreements between nations when they became onerous or inapplicable," and such a provision should be included in the new charter. The council of the League of Nations had been "overburdened with all the minor troubles and confused voices of the world at every session." That could be avoided in the new organization by regional suborganizations, which would have the first responsibility to keep the peace and devise policies for peace, thus freeing the council "to deal only with questions that contain dangers of world war." It would give the smaller nations a greater voice and "relieve America and other nations from the strains of many a minor foreign dispute." He noted that Churchill had endorsed such a principle.[142]

The League of Nations had also failed to include adequate provision for disarmament or to control alliances. Said Hoover: "The multitude of these alliances after the last war inspired fear, counter-alliances, increase of armament. They made for balances of power, and they created voting blocs in the League. They not only weakened the League but they contributed to World War II." The new organization's charter should include such provisions. The changed nature of aggression required that it be defined in the charter in all of its forms, including "direct or indirect subsidized governmental propaganda in other nations." Finally, Hoover cautioned that the framers of the charter of the new organization should not hurry. He said: "If we take six years to make war it might be a good idea to take a few more months to build a sound organization to keep the peace. It was seven years from Yorktown to the Constitution." The United States had made many sacrifices in the war, and it must not fail in providing for the peace.[143]

A few days later, on April 21, 1945, Secretary of War Henry Stimson phoned Hoover, but the former president was out. Stimson phoned again the next day to invite Hoover to spend the day at his Long Island home. Hoover declined the invitation. A few days later Stimson phoned again to ask Hoover to travel to Washington to "discuss with him the postwar situation of Europe, which he said had degenerated into a dreadful state." Stimson had, he told Hoover, discussed his invitation with President Truman, and the president believed that Hoover's advice would be very valuable. However, Hoover refused to go to Washington to give the desired advice unless the invitation came directly from the president and was specifically to see Truman himself. Hoover insisted that such an invitation would at least "be a sign to the country that I am not a seeker of interviews" and that if the president then directed him "to talk to the Secretary of War that I would be delighted to do so." Hoover recounted for Stimson an incident O'Laughlin had related to him, which explained his imposition of these conditions for any such visit. O'Laughlin had urged Steve Early, Truman's holdover press secretary from Roosevelt's presidency, that Hoover's advice should be obtained by the administration. According to O'Laughlin, Early had responded: "That if Hoover wanted anything he would have to come down on his knees to get it." That this reflected the attitude of a Roosevelt New Dealer did not surprise Hoover, but that such advisers remained around Truman convinced him that "whatever good intentions the President may have had about this, he has been coaxed by the men around him into the old vindictiveness." Hoover told Stimson that his "only protection from the left-wingers and people like Early would be to have an invitation from the President and that if Truman did not think it worth while to pay this small courtesy to me for the benefit of my advice, they had better not continue to attempt to get it."[144]

Others, like O'Laughlin, were urging that Hoover's counsel be sought by the new president as one method of creating "an era of good feeling."[145] Senator Ralph Brewster took the subject up with President Truman and found him interested but insistent that it was Hoover who must take the initiative in calling on him, in which event, Truman assured him, Hoover would have an "A-priority" on the president's time. However, the Republican elder statesman continued to hold out for an invitation from the White House.[146] In the meantime, however, Hoover addressed the deteriorating food conditions in Europe in a speech before a war relief meeting in New York City's Carnegie Hall and called upon the War Department to handle the problem. Eight days later, on May 16, Hoover repeated the message in a nationally broadcast talk. Between these two addresses he had finally met with Stimson at the latter's request.[147]

On May 13 Hoover motored to Stimson's home on Long Island. The secretary of war was still insistent that Hoover should call on Truman; Stimson assured Hoover that the president was anxious to see him and to discuss the food situation. But Hoover was equally insistent that Truman himself must request the visit. Stimson told Hoover that Truman agreed with his public suggestion that the army should take over the European relief effort.[148] The secretary of war was apparently very complimentary in his description of the new president, for though Hoover refused to yield in the matter of a visit to the White House, he came away from the meeting with the feeling that Truman, although a Democrat, might well be a better president than Dewey would have been.[149]

In that same month, Hoover began to consider the terms under which peace might advantageously be made with Japan. Joseph Kennedy called on him the morning of May 15, and they discussed the world situation. In a memorandum of their meeting, Hoover recorded: "Kennedy agreed with me entirely that it is urgent that we make peace with Japan and thinks it should be done as soon as possible if it can be done upon terms of the restoration of China and disarmament of Japan for at least 30 to 40 years. We ought to allow Japan to keep Formosa and Korea to save her face and recover her economic life."[150] One memorandum in the Hoover papers, on which is written in Hoover's hand, "A memorandum furnished Secretary of War Stimson on May 15, 1945," indicates Hoover's position on the issue, perhaps influenced by his conversation with Joseph Kennedy. In the memorandum, Hoover argued that as a result of the war the "British, French, Belgian and Dutch Empires are safe for a while," while the Soviet Union had, by annexations and the creation of puppet governments, extended its political domination over Latvia, Estonia,

Lithuania, eastern Poland and Bessarabia, Rumania, Bulgaria, Yugoslavia, Finland, Czechoslovakia, and Austria. This meant that there would "no longer be an opportunity for American or British enterprise therein." There remained, then, "only three great areas in the world where the Americans and British might have freedom and opportunity in economic life." These were the European colonial empires, the western hemisphere, and "Asia outside of Russia." The probable outcome of a total defeat for Japan would be Russia's seizure of Manchuria, North China, and Korea, and from these she would likely "expand over the balance of China and over all Japan by ideological penetration." The likelihood of this scenario "increases every day the war with Japan continues." The Soviet Union, however, probably would not enter the war against Japan until the major fighting was over. To prolong the war with Japan would require millions of Americans for an attack on Japan and the Asian mainland, and "we are likely to have won the war for Russia's benefit just as we have done in Europe."[151]

In his memorandum, Hoover suggested that Chiang Kai-shek and his Anglo-American allies should make peace with Japan on terms that would require Japan to withdraw from China, including Manchuria, but retain Korea and Formosa. Japan would be required to totally disarm and would be supervised by a disarmament commission, but no reparations would be required of her other than the transfer of all of her economic concessions in Manchuria to the Chinese. The results for the United States would be the saving of lives and resources that would otherwise be spent in continued war with Japan; the United States would be spared the prostration that might make it impossible for her to aid the recovery of other nations. Everything would be gained that could be obtained by fighting the war to a finish: Russian expansion would be checked in the Asian and Pacific areas, and the area would remain open to free enterprise; Japan could recover economically; the Japanese would be in a position to govern themselves without the intervention of a joint Allied military government; and "under such terms there would be the hope that Japan would return to cooperation with Western Civilization and not agitate for revenge for another century as is likely to be the case otherwise."[152]

As indicated by Stimson's earlier attempts to draw Hoover into the food relief problem in Europe, considerable alarm was felt in Washington over the food situation there. Hoover had frequently expressed his disgust with the entire handling of relief by the United Nations Relief and Rehabilitation Agency (UNRRA), most recently in a letter and memorandum to Congressman John Taber on May 15. On May 23 Hoover was called upon by a delegation from the War Department sent by Stimson. The delegation included Assistant Secretary of War John J. McCloy and other individuals close to the situation. Despite Stimson's comment to Hoover earlier in the month that Truman had accepted his suggestion that the army take over European relief, Hoover now concluded that "the whole conference was staged to convince me that the Army would not take over the relief of the liberated countries during the next 90 day emergency." The War Department representatives "explained the measures taken by the Army and blamed UNRRA for not having performed its original functions." They then discussed with Hoover the various problems faced concerning relief in Europe during the next 90 days; and the former president adhered to his position that the army "would have to furnish the Staff" for the relief effort and insisted that one man should be assigned "dictatorial" powers over the economic life of "the liberated countries from Italy to Norway, with Shipping, Transportation, Food, Coal and other divisions under strong men," with a man in Washington "to coordinate and direct the American agencies." He also recommended that an American railway president be put in charge of the shipment of food and other necessities to American ports. Unless his recommendations were followed, Hoover warned, "the liberated countries are likely to go communist."[153]

On May 24 Rickard recorded in his diary that he found Hoover very disappointed at the War Department's opposition to undertaking the relief, particularly since they were on the ground in Europe and possessed the men and facilities to do the job.[154] However, on the following day, President Harry Truman penned the sought-after invitation to the former president, saying: "If you should be in Washington, I would be most happy to talk over the European food situation with you. Also, it would be a pleasure to me to become acquainted with you."[155] After a dozen years, the stage was now set for Hoover's re-emergence into official service, and the basis for a warm friendship was being laid. Hoover accepted the invitation and was pleased by the prominence given to the forthcoming meeting by the media.[156] The next day, Hoover busied himself with gathering material to take to Washington in case Truman needed real help. He lunched with Bernard Baruch, confiding the recommendations he planned to make to Truman and seeking Baruch's backing if it became necessary. Rickard found Hoover elated at the opportunity to give advice and at the public recognition of his experience.[157]

On May 28, 1945, Herbert Hoover entered the White House for the first time since he had left the presidency in March 1933. Truman, according to Hoover's memorandum of the conversation, wanted his views on "the whole situation." Hoover responded that the "situation was degenerating all over the world, partly, of course, due to the war and partly due to mismanagement; but that [Truman] had to take it as it is and that there was no time to be bothered with recriminations as to what might have been." Hoover advocated that the parts of Europe that were under Soviet domination should be left to the USSR to feed, and Truman agreed. As for the Mediterranean area and northwestern Europe, including U.S.-occupied Germany, there was an emergency to meet during the next 90 days, until the harvest was in, and a long-term approach would be necessary after that. It was impossible to deal with the present emergency as Hoover had during the armistice after World War I, he observed, because there was not now a peace conference in session to grant the kind of authority he had possessed then. Therefore, Hoover argued, the army must take over during the emergency, since it was already handling part of the problem and was the only agency capable of cutting through red tape. He then repeated his earlier recommendations to McCloy and the others. Truman responded that Stimson was against army involvement in relief, but said that after listening to Hoover's argument he agreed that there was no choice, and asked Hoover to talk to Stimson.[158]

Hoover was also queried by the president regarding the domestic food situation which he described as "terrible." While fats were the first priority of wartime food production, the number of hogs in the United States had decreased from 82 million to 60 million in twelve months. There was also considerable discussion of the method of price fixing. Hoover again suggested, as he had so many times since the war began, the creation of an economic war council to determine broad economic and other related policies. Truman then asked for his views on the foreign situation, and the former president expressed his distrust of the Russians. They were "Asiatics," Hoover told the president, and therefore did not "have the reverence for agreements" that Western nations entertained, but he argued that the Russians must be taken as they were and the United States ought not to go to war with them. Nor should the United States try to bluff them or follow policies just "short of war," but ought always, instead, "to persuade, to hold up our banner of what we thought was right and let it go at that." A war with the USSR was unthinkable, Hoover said, since it would "mean the extinction of Western civilization or what there was left of it." He also advocated to Truman a joint U.S.-British-Chinese declaration of objectives in the war with Japan and argued for the kind of negotiated peace which he had suggested to Stimson earlier in the month. Japan should be allowed to keep Formosa and Korea, he told Truman, because "Korea had a much worse government before the Japanese had taken it over" and because "the United States had made a treaty with Japan acknowledging the Japanese sovereignty over Korea and . . . legalistically we had no claim for its separation now." Hoover repeated his view that the Soviet Union would not "come into the war with Japan except perhaps in the last five minutes."[159]

Hoover's interview with the president lasted for nearly an hour, but Hoover concluded that Truman had been "simply endeavoring to establish a feeling of good will in the country, that nothing more would come of it so far as I or my views were concerned."[160] To Rickard, Hoover opined that the invitation had been entirely political. Any expectation he had that Truman meant to appoint him to an administration post was swept away by the meeting. But

Hoover felt that both he and Truman had gained from the meeting—the president had given the public an impression that he was broad-minded and above partisan politics, while in Hoover's case those who had continually smeared him with the support (or at least without the objections) of Roosevelt, would no longer feel encouraged by the attitude of the man in the White House.[161]

While in Washington for his meeting with the president, Hoover also conferred at William Castle's residence with nine Republican senators, including Taft, H. Alexander Smith, Bourke Hickenlooper, and Alexander Wiley. At that meeting he again advocated a negotiated settlement with Japan. Castle wrote a few days later:

> I am . . . sure that what you have to say about Japan will sink into the minds of the Senators who were here and will do good. Yesterday afternoon I was discussing the matter at some length with Hugh Wilson who, as you know, is the advisor on foreign matters for the Republican National Committee. He is very enthusiastic over your plan and says that it would seem to him to give an opportunity for the minority in Congress really to take the lead, that probably Vandenberg would be the man to introduce the matter. The speech would have to be written with the greatest care so that the general public would not feel that we were backing down in our demands on Japan; that we were asking what we must have as a result of the war, but not in a way which will prolong the war.

Castle found a great deal of favorable comment in Washington regarding Hoover's meeting with Truman.[162] The conference, after Hoover had been isolated from the administration for twelve years, stirred a good deal of comment in the media.[163]

At Truman's request, Hoover also met with Stimson and McCloy concerning the European food problem. Hoover told Stimson that he realized the army did not wish to get involved in relief activities, but he reiterated that the only way it could extricate itself from relief and transportation and other economic functions "was to go deeper in; that they should take over very much larger responsibilities than they now had. . . . I said I could see no one else who could bring this food to the seaboards and no one else who could have at its command the necessary authorities." He repeated the suggestions he had made to McCloy and the others during their visit to New York and in his talk with Truman. Hoover now found these people in agreement with him, perhaps because of the president's support for his position.[164]

Hoover also sent Truman a memorandum (at Truman's request) dealing with the subjects they had discussed. The memorandum summarized their discussion on the European and domestic food situations, Hoover's recommendation of a war economic council, and his argument for a negotiated peace with Japan. This memorandum, dated May 30, was slightly modified from the one Hoover had earlier submitted to Stimson in its discussion of the Japanese question. The May 30 memorandum did not argue for a negotiated peace from the standpoint of preserving an "open door" for British and American enterprise in East Asia, but solely on the basis of saving American lives and resources. There was no mention of the Soviet Union or of the probable spread of communism to China, Korea, and Japan in the event of a prolonged war. There was now provision for the trial of war criminals and for the ceding of "certain islands held by Japan" which were considered to be "necessary protection against the future and to enforce disarmament." Japan's retention of Korea and Formosa would now be under a trusteeship, presumably under the new international organization. The Japanese government would also be warned that if it did not accept the terms proposed, "that they are unfit to remain in control of the Japanese people and we must need proceed to their ultimate destruction."[165] The president responded to the memorandum with appreciation and added that it "will be very useful to me." Across the bottom of his letter to Hoover, Truman scribbled: "I appreciate it very much your coming to see me. It gave me a lift."[166] Certainly the atmosphere in Washington was much improved for the former president over what it had been barely two months earlier.

Hoover had contributed ideas to the postwar policies of the Roosevelt administration, and he had supported Roosevelt's postwar policies as long as they seemed to echo his own position, as at the Moscow conference, while at the same time he sought to mute opposition on the part of other Republicans to those policies. Though neglected by all but a handful of historians, Hoover's contribution to the forging of a bipartisan approach to postwar policy was already obvious even before Roosevelt's death. His influence as a potential leader of opposition to the wartime agreements forged under Roosevelt had not only been stilled, but such influence as he had was supportive. Now, with Truman in the White House, it was even easier to support bipartisanship in foreign policy, and the administration openly sought his assistance. Early in June 1945 Dean Acheson and William Clayton of the State Department lunched wih Hoover and asked him to use his influence with Republicans in Congress to help the administration get approval of a renewal of the Reciprocal Trade Act and support for the Bretton Woods financial legislation. The Reciprocal Trade Act was due to expire on June 12, while the Bretton Woods agreement provided for the creation of the International Monetary Fund and the International Bank for Reconstruction and Development. Hoover sent O'Laughlin an account of the meeting and reported:

I told them that I was on the other side of the fence as far as the reciprocal tariff was concerned, but had taken no active part in the discussion, and that I could not, therefore, be of much help in that particular. I said that I would intervene with my friends on the Hill in the matter of Bretton Woods. I subsequently telephoned several of our friends on both sides and urged them to put up no organized opposition but to let it go as a non-partisan measure. I noticed that [Congressman Joseph] Martin announced this policy the next day.

He then suggested that O'Laughlin might want to get news of what he had done "back to the proper quarters," by which he meant the State Department.[167]

Much encouraged by the more conservative and cooperative atmosphere in the White House, Hoover had kind words for Truman in an interview with reporters. Hoover's statement, combined with Dewey's and Landon's expressions of support for Truman's foreign policies, had, O'Laughlin wrote Hoover, "caused the Capitol Republicans to wonder what has happened to the GOP."[168] Hoover wrote to California Republican publisher William F. Knowland: "Never has this country ever felt so relieved as during the last 90 days. The new President is rapidly altering the 'party line' and there is a much more hopeful feeling that we will pull through the postwar troubles. It is not going to be easy."[169]

There had, however, been no improvement in the domestic food situation, and late in June Congressman Jenkins again solicited Hoover's counsel. As the chairman of the GOP Congressional Food Study Committee wrote, some of its recommendations had "been accepted in principle by the Administration and with very good results. But the Administration still stubbornly clings to most of its policies and practices in spite of the fact that the situation is getting worse and worse." Jenkins again asked Hoover to "outline for us how best to organize the Animal Products Industry of the Nation so as to relieve the terrible meat situation." The shortage of fats and oils from animal production, he noted, was "fast becoming distressing since it involves the production of baked products, such as bread, and sanitary products, such as soap."[170]

Hoover responded with an eight page letter on June 20, 1945. The food problem, he observed, was not a partisan matter, but one involving both the well-being of the American people and the ability of the United States to handle the problems of relief in the liberated areas of Europe. Many of the difficulties had been created by the mismanagement of the Roosevelt administration. The problems were many—the decline in hog, sheep, chicken, and beef production; difficulties with distribution, which were creating shortages across the nation; the existence of black markets in meat and fats "in every city of the country" as a result of the "breakdown in control of both distribution and price"; and continuance of the policy of subsidies to producers, which came out of the taxpayers' pockets and helped nothing. The fault, Hoover reiterated, lay in the "method of organization where the control of food has been divided over six or seven agencies, and where the whole price control machinery is based upon ill-advised concepts and where the organization has considered coercion more useful than cooperation with producers, distributors and consumers." The Roosevelt administration had tried to fix prices at the retail level and then work backward to the farmers, while using "subsidies and constantly changing prices to open the multitude of bottlenecks." Hoover's method in World War I had been "to fix prices as near the farmer as possible and to work forward to the consumer by additions of normal trade differentials and without subsidies." World War I had produced no black markets, he claimed, nor famines, card-rationing systems, or rapid inflation, while it had led to less consumption per capita than was the case in 1944 and to constantly increasing production of all animal products to the point where it had been possible to supply not only the American people but also to save the children of Europe.[171]

In his letter to Jenkins, Hoover suggested the desirability of reconstructing the World War I method and administration even at this late date. He recommended again that the secretary of agriculture be granted, in addition to his existing authority as food administrator, all of the powers and staff of the Office of Price Administrator, as well as control of all "allocation and buying of major animal products for the Armed forces, Lend-Lease and relief." He called for an administrator of animal products, as well as an advisory committee representing the military services, lend-lease and relief allocations, as well as committees of the major agricultural units (livestock growers, packers, commission men, and retailers). Prices to be paid to the farmers for the various grades of animal products should be set; the packers and commission men should be directed to pay no more than these agreed ceilings and no less than the agreed minimums, with the packers allowed an agreed mark-up to cover their costs and a proper profit. The retailers, too, should be given their usual markup. The advantages of his plan, which he had been advocating since the outbreak of war, would be, Hoover maintained, lower prices, a normal flow of trade, no local famines, no need for subsidies, increased production, and a minimum of policing by the government. "That this plan of organization and administration works was shown by the experience of the last war," he wrote Jenkins. "That the plan now in use has failed requires no demonstration." If his plan were not followed, Hoover warned, the difficulties would only multiply, "and the hope of aid in meats and fats to women and children abroad becomes hopeless."[172]

As President Truman prepared to leave for the Potsdam summit conference, Hoover joined with other prominent Americans, including Hugh Gibson, Alf Landon, John Dewey, A. Philip Randolph (president of the porters' union), and Matthew Woll (vice-president of the AFL), in signing a memorial to the president. This memorial asked the three heads of state to agree on the terms that would permit free elections in the areas liberated by the Soviet Union; ensure the right for members of all democratic parties to participate; provide for freedom of speech and press, international supervision of the first election, the withdrawal of Soviet troops before the election (or provide for the joint occupation by U.S. and British troops during the electoral period); and establish the right of news correspondents and representatives of the Red Cross and other charitable organizations to circulate in Poland and other Soviet-occupied territories, and other provisions.[173] Here was a clear expression of America's mistrust of the objectives of the Soviet Union, but given Hoover's realism concerning that country, it is doubtful that he held much faith that such provisions would be honored by the Russians even if accepted at Potsdam.

On July 18 Hoover spoke in San Francisco in behalf of the United Nations Charter, which had been framed in that city. Continuing his support for the administration's efforts to take the United States into that international organization, Hoover described the charter as "probably as good as could be obtained under the existing emotions, the present governments, the conflicting ideals and ambitions in the world." He called for it to be "ratified by the Senate promptly." But he warned that the American people "should be under no illusions that the Charter assures lasting peace." At best it was only "an expression of desire and machinery to advance peace." Peace would depend also upon "the economic and political settlements among nations by which this war is liquidated." These would have much more effect on questions of peace or war than the charter, he argued, since "the Charter could not preserve a bad peace." There remained many weaknesses and omissions in the charter, in his view. There was still no "bill of rights" for nations and peoples, such as he had advocated. The veto power in the Security Council was likely to hamstring the United Nations' attempts to respond to military aggression. The charter had still failed to even define aggression, and there was no mention of "the new disintegrating forms of aggression of one nation upon another through propaganda and fifth columns."[174]

These were "positive defects" in the charter, but Hoover found other aspects of the charter that also left much to be desired, including the absence of a commitment to disarmament. In ratifying the charter, the Senate must, Hoover reiterated, ensure that the U.S. delegate to the Security Council did not have the power to commit U.S. military forces without recourse to the congressional responsibility for declarations of war. "The plain fact," Hoover pointed out, was that the success of the United Nations and of peacemaking and peacekeeping would depend on "the successful collaboration of the three centers of power—that is, Russia, Britain and the United States"—and it would continue to rest there for "many years to come." Hoover added:

> But lasting peace cannot be based upon the dominance of three or four or even five powers forever. The Charter will offer a forum for world opinion and advice to these responsible powers. The retreat from the Atlantic Charter, the ambitions and emotions of war, the omissions from the San Francisco Charter emphasize that these three great powers are really the trustees of world peace rather than the Charter itself. There must be a transition period where this collaboration will require much patience, it will require great firmness. It will take time and much good will to find lasting settlements after the high emotions of war, of national ambitions, of differing national purposes.[175]

Hoover had advocated since early 1942 that there be a transition period during which world problems could be solved, before any international organization was formed. However, the international organization had been formed even before the end of the war. But Hoover pointed out, rightly, that with or without the international organization the transition would be a reality, with the three "trustees" responsible for peace rather than the international organization.

In August of 1945 there briefly seemed a prospect that Hoover might, himself, have an opportunity to deal with postwar problems from the vantage point of a seat in the United States Senate. At least as early as January 1945, the former president expressed interest in being appointed to the Senate from California if Hiram Johnson died.[176] When Johnson did die, in August, John Callan O'Laughlin was pressed into service to ascertain if the senator's widow and son might intervene with Governor Earl Warren in behalf of Hoover's appointment to fill out the unexpired portion of Johnson's term.[177] Many letters were sent to Warren in Hoover's behalf, and the *New York Times* supported his appointment in an editorial.[178] When Governor Warren appointed William Knowland instead, Hoover expressed an insincere sense of relief to disguise his disappointment at not being chosen.[179] However, political considerations aside, Hoover's long absence from California during his residence in New York City made him an unlikely prospect to represent the people of that state.

On the eve of Japan's surrender, Hoover wrote down his views on the agreements reached at Potsdam and on the use of the atomic bomb against Japan. The Potsdam agreements he found to be further confirmation of his earlier suspicions that the Soviet Union intended to annex east Finland, east Poland, Latvia, Estonia, Lithuania, and Bessarabia, as well as proof that the governments of Rumania, Bulgaria, Finland, Yugoslavia, and Hungary would be communist-controlled, while the election to be held in Poland would probably be manipulated to take that country, too, into the Soviet orbit. Germany, in Hoover's view, was left with little hope from the economic standpoint, with the result that the rest of Europe would probably be impoverished and rendered unstable as a result. Of the dropping of the atomic bomb on Japan, Hoover wrote: "The use of the Atomic bomb, with its indiscriminate killing of women and children, revolts my soul." He found the only difference between the use of the bomb and the use of poison gas in the fact that the United States alone had the bomb and therefore had no need to fear retaliation. He suspected that the bomb was "being exploited beyond its real possibilities to frighten the Japs."[180]

But the war would soon be over, and peace would bring new problems and responsibilities to the former president.